GENERAL METAPHYSICS

GOTTFRIED MARTIN

GENERAL METAPHYSICS

ITS PROBLEMS AND ITS METHOD

———◦———

Translated by Daniel O'Connor

London

GEORGE ALLEN & UNWIN LTD

RUSKIN HOUSE   MUSEUM STREET

PRINTED IN GREAT BRITAIN
in 12 on 13 point Fournier type
BY UNWIN BROTHERS LTD
WOKING AND LONDON

CONTENTS

7

12146

General Metaphysics

PART II: THE GENERAL

SECTION I: LOGICAL PROBLEMS ABOUT THE GENERAL

IV: THE UNITY OF THE GENERAL

V: THE EXACT DEFINABILITY OF THE GENERAL

SECTION II: THE ONTOLOGICAL DETERMINATION OF THE GENERAL

VI: THE GENERAL AS IDEA: PLATO

VII: THE GENERAL AS LAW OF NATURE: ARISTOTLE

8

Contents

A*   9

General Metaphysics

INTRODUCTION

I. OBJECTIONS TO THE POSSIBILITY OF METAPHYSICS

Is metaphysics possible? The question has always been asked, and it always will be asked. In our time objections to the possibility of metaphysics have been pressed with particular emphasis. The objections can be divided into three groups, those maintained by empiricism, and those maintained from the standpoints of linguistic philosophy or the history of being.

In order to test the objections of empiricism, and here it will always be radical empiricism, one thinks in the first place of Comte[1] and Mill.[2] Their basic thesis is that there are only empirical propositions; on this interpretation metaphysics is ruled out from the start as impossible. But even when the basic thesis is granted, the refutation of metaphysics derived from it is not so conclusive as it at first appears. One soon sees that from this point of view the concept of an empirical proposition must be taken much more broadly than is usual. Obviously, radical empiricism must take the concept of an empirical proposition so broadly that it also includes logical and mathematical propositions. And in fact logical and mathematical propositions do contain an empirical element, if one will only construe the concept of the empirical carefully enough. But then a problem occurs which has never been faced by radical empiricism. One must inquire whether the argument against the possibility of metaphysics is still valid after this necessary expansion of the meaning of 'empirical'. It seems very unlikely that it would be; it is much more likely that the expanded meaning of an empirical proposition leaves enough room for metaphysical propositions too, however it stands with them otherwise. The objection of radical empiricism thus cannot be sustained.

The second group of objections against the possibility of

metaphysics comes from linguistic philosophy. We will consider Ludwig Wittgenstein as typical of this point of view. In the *Tractatus* Wittgenstein divides meaningful propositions into two groups, elementary propositions and logical propositions. The elementary propositions are assertions about the world,[3] the logical propositions are tautologies.[4] If this classification is accepted as correct and exhaustive, then mathematical propositions must be grouped with the logical, and they must therefore be tautologies. But Wittgenstein has not succeeded in finding general recognition for this interpretation of mathematical propositions. What is the status of metaphysical propositions? There is no place at all for them in the *Tractatus*. They can be characterized negatively: they are not meaningful propositions for they are neither elementary propositions nor tautologies. They can also be characterized positively as false uses of language. According to the doctrine of the *Tractatus* metaphysical propositions contain signs (usually words) to which no meaning is assigned; and in Wittgenstein's conviction, no meaning can be assigned to them.[5] This allows Wittgenstein to say: 'All philosophy is "Critique of language" '[6]—and not metaphysics, as one would have to finish the sentence.

One could of course take issue with the *Tractatus*. One could show that the concept of an elementary proposition introduced there is questionable, perhaps more questionable than many claims of metaphysics. But in the development of his thought Wittgenstein has removed himself so far from the *Tractatus* that one would much sooner have to defend this work against its author. Support for a positive interpretation of the *Tractatus* emerges from Wittgenstein's later trains of thought in which it becomes clear that his reflections rest on a very broad notion of language. For example, constructing an object from a description (a drawing) belongs to language even when the hand-worker does not explicitly speak.[7] Now this is a much wider meaning for language than the usual, in particular wider than the purely philological. This broad meaning for language is clearly close to the meaning of *logos*, in the sense that man is characterized by the Greeks as a being who can speak. But with such a broad meaning for language linguistic philosophy and criticism of language pass over in practice into an analysis of man, who can speak. In linguistic philosophy thus understood there is room enough for metaphysics, in any case for metaphysics as Plato and Aristotle wished it to be.

The rejection of metaphysics from the standpoint of the history of being, now vigorously represented by Heidegger, was begun by Nietzsche. It can be formulated in the thesis: metaphysics is no longer possible.[8] Turning first to Nietzsche we may understand his point to be that metaphysics was possible for Plato and Aristotle, and also perhaps for the Middle Ages, but no longer for today. As persuasive as this thesis may seem at first glance and in spite of the enthusiasm with which it has been received, it contains two fundamental and, in my opinion, irremediable defects. It has not been explained how metaphysics is here understood, nor what it means to say that metaphysics was possible formerly, but today not possible. With Nietzsche at least, we are somewhat clearer about the meaning attached to the word 'metaphysics'. By metaphysics Nietzsche understands a naïve two-worlds theory, a theory which sets up a second world behind this one and then takes this second world for the real world. But one can doubt with good reason that such a naïve two-worlds theory was Plato's final opinion, and we will later enter into a thoroughgoing discussion of that question. That such a naïve two-worlds theory was Aristotle's opinion no-one will claim, including Nietzsche if he had specifically raised the question. But how can one oppose metaphysics if one understands thereby a theory in which the metaphysics of Aristotle cannot be included? The meaning of metaphysics which underlies Nietzsche's opposition must be regarded as not satisfactory. And wholly unsatisfactory is Nietzsche's treatment of the second point. What is it supposed to mean that metaphysics was possible for Plato but today no longer possible? The claim is so sweeping that one must require an exact account of the concepts of possibility and impossibility employed therein. The thesis: today metaphysics is no longer possible presupposes that it was possible earlier and in fact Nietzsche says that. He says explicitly that one must grasp the 'historical justification'[9] for metaphysics. But this is easier required than achieved. How was it that for Plato metaphysics was possible? If one tries to imagine such an historical proof concretely one sees the difficulty at once. Initially we can leave undecided the question whether we should understand Plato's metaphysics as the theory of Ideas itself or the interpretation of the theory of Ideas as a two-worlds theory. In any case one will have to consider the *Phaedo*. We don't know exactly when the *Phaedo* was written, the year 380 may be taken as a reference point. What does it mean then to say that in the year 380 a theory of Ideas or a two-worlds theory was possible, and how would that be demonstrated? Until now no-one, including Nietzsche, has even made the attempt to demonstrate it. What we are dealing with is a general thesis which cannot be realized concretely.

Heidegger has taken up the rejection of metaphysics and carried it further. He speaks explicitly of the 'process including the beginning, the development and the end of metaphysics'.[10] Here the simplified view of metaphysics as a two-worlds theory is avoided. Aristotle's metaphysics is carefully considered. But the question why metaphysics should have been possible for Plato and Aristotle and why it should no longer be possible for us is also not answered by Heidegger. In particular, it remains obscure what meaning the concept of metaphysics is supposed to have. Against this thesis from the history of being one must, in the spirit of Plato and Aristotle, pose the counter-thesis: metaphysics was always equally possible and impossible.

2. THE GREAT PHILOSOPHERS AND THE POSSIBILITY OF METAPHYSICS

It has been the great philosophers themselves who have repeatedly questioned the possibility of metaphysics. Plato is the first to raise explicitly the question about being and he immediately emphasizes its difficulties. In the *Sophist* he says: 'We are completely puzzled, then, and you must clear up the question for us, what you do intend to signify when you use the word "real".

Obviously you must be quite familiar with what you mean, whereas we, who formerly imagined we knew, are now at a loss.'[1] Plato here speaks as much about the perennial situation of metaphysics as about his own momentary situation. Metaphysics is the theory of being, we will show this in detail. Such a theory of being begins unproblematically. To speak of being, as one speaks of animals, stars, or numbers, seems at first to present no difficulties. A mental effort is necessary to overcome the initial obviousness, to discover the aporematic character of the theory of being. We will have to show that Plato has himself in mind in this formulation from the *Sophist*, and in particular that he refers to his doctrine in the *Phaedo* when he writes 'formerly we knew it'. That the theory of Ideas contains an assertion about the being of Ideas caused Plato no difficulties when he was writing the *Phaedo*. In this dialogue the assertions about being are repeatedly expressed in lapidary sentences: the Idea is *ousia*, the Idea is real being. How problematic these assertions are Plato did not then see. Only much later did he recognize that it is necessary to ask: what am I really claiming when I say: the Idea is real being? This problematic is the theme of the *Sophist* and the *Parmenides* and Plato can then say in fact: earlier I knew that, now I don't know it any more.

But this is not just Plato's situation, it is the situation of metaphysics in general. It is thus understandable that Aristotle says the same thing: 'And indeed the question which was raised of old and is raised now and always, and is always the subject of doubt, viz. what being is, is just the question, what is substance?'[2]

The Platonic-Aristotelian question: What is being? grew out of the Socratic question: What is . . .? It becomes understandable then that the aporetic of the Socratic question is maintained in the general question of being. Aristotle is little inclined towards aporetic but he holds fast to the aporetic of the question about being. We must not therefore consider Book III of the *Metaphysics* merely as a pedagogically well-conceived introduction. Instead we are dealing with a genuine, systematized aporetic. 'Metaphysics is strangely bitter,' Kant once remarked in a reflection.[3] The usual interpretation of Kant, that he completely rejects metaphysics, cannot therefore be correct. This interpretation goes back to Mendelssohn who thought that the writings of 'the all-destroying Kant'[4] had abolished metaphysics. This is also the way the Neo-Kantians understand him. But our suspicions about this interpretation should be raised by the fact that Hegel does not see him this way at all. How could Kant write the *Metaphysical Foundations of the Natural Sciences* or a *Metaphysics of Morals*, had he totally rejected metaphysics in every form? So also the *Prolegomena*, which one usually refers to in this shortened form, bears the exact title: *Prolegomena to any Future Metaphysics which will appear as a Science*. It is of course true that Kant, in the preface to the *Critique of Pure Reason* compares metaphysics to Hecuba who bemoans the tragic end of her happiness.[5] And there certainly are numerous citations which on first inspection seem to suggest that Kant wanted to put an end to metaphysics as such. On a more careful reading, however, one soon sees that Kant is only adverse to certain points of view and certain methods of metaphysics. For example, he rejects proofs for the existence of God oriented on mathematical methods. Hardly anyone would disagree with that. With his questions about the being of space, time, and nature Kant stands squarely in the metaphysical tradition. The basic question of the Transcendental Aesthetic does not run: How can I know space and time? Rather it runs: 'What then are space and time?'[6] To be sure, Kant rejects the notion that space and time are things, for he is convinced this is an absurdity. As against a transcendental realism Kant posits a transcendental idealism. Now this may be correct or false, but it does show that Kant doesn't reject metaphysics as such, he only rejects a particular metaphysical point of view. In this vein he closes the Transcendental Analytic with the important third section: 'On the Basis of the Distinction of all Objects in General into Phenomena and Noumena.'[7] In this section he is concerned with noumena only in the negative sense, but already in the *Critique of Pure Reason*, particularly in the Transcendental Analytic, he holds the positive sense before him. Noumena in the positive sense acquire a steadily increasing importance and in the *Critique of Practical Reason* Kant inserts a special inquiry into the problems that arise therein.[8] Kant's metaphysics culminates in the question about the reality of the 'I think'. Here Kant is fully aware of the necessity but also of the problematic of metaphysics and the text cited above must be understood in that way, 'metaphysics is strangely bitter'.

If Plato, Aristotle and Kant emphasized in this way the difficulties of metaphysics, it becomes understandable that not a few have rejected metaphysics entirely. But metaphysics is not impossible, even though it is a difficult task, perhaps the most difficult task for human reason.

3. BEING AS THE THEME OF METAPHYSICS

We define metaphysics as the theory of being and thereby hold on to the old definition. Plato was the first to use it and Aristotle formalized it when he raised metaphysics to a separate discipline.

In the *Sophist* Plato requires an ascent to the first and highest question. Theatetus responds to the requirement by saying: 'Of course you mean we ought to begin by studying "reality" and finding out what those who use the word think it stands for'.[1] Plato is alluding to the early thinkers and their doctrine of the elements. If it is claimed, for example, that warmth is the element of all things, or cold, or both together,[2] then we have an assertion about being. To claim that warmth is the element of all things is to claim that warmth is real being. But if one says this, one must be able to say what the expression 'real being' is supposed to mean. Therefore Plato can now raise the question: 'How are we to understand this "reality" you speak of'.[3] He has himself come up against this question in his own theory of Ideas, as we will see, so he can put the question also to these others. Thus Plato poses the question explicitly: What is being? He characterizes it at once as the highest question.[4]

Aristotle then used this question: What is being? as the foundation of his definition of metaphysics. Of course we find in his writings different characterizations of the task of metaphysics. For him metaphysics is the theory of principles as well as ontology, and as ontology it is for him the theory of the highest being as well as the theory of being as such. In our opinion the most fruitful definition of metaphysics is that it is the theory of being as such, and we will therefore neglect the theory of the highest being as well as the theory of principles. We shall have to justify this procedure later. In this Introduction let us content ourselves with observing that Aristotle too regards the question: What is being? as the highest and most important,[5] and that in fundamental places of his analysis he treats metaphysics in this sense.[6]

We find the question: What is being? formulated in various ways by both Plato and Aristotle. In some places we find the substantive infinitive, in others the participle.[7] This linguistic nuance is not possible in all languages. German can distinguish between the two forms 'das Sein' and 'das Seiende', though the participle 'das Seiende' is not good German. French has only the substantive infinitive, while English has only the participle. Heidegger has based his theory of the ontological difference on the distinction between 'das Sein' and 'das Seiende'.[8] There is a genuine and fundamental ontological problem here but it may be doubted whether it is advisable to couple the systematic problem directly with the linguistic difference between participle and substantive infinitive. The Greeks don't seem to have done this and in the above citation from the *Sophist* Plato uses both forms without distinguishing them. In these investigations I will not distinguish 'das Sein' and 'das Seiende' in the sense of the ontological difference, I will use them in Plato's sense as equivalent. The systematic problem is not decided through linguistic usage.

It seems appropriate to reflect provisionally here on the relationship of metaphysics to language. We have already mentioned Wittgenstein's thesis: 'All philosophy is the critique of language.'[9] We found difficulties in the extreme character of this thesis and, in fact, extreme theses in philosophy are suspicious from the outset. It is certainly correct that Descartes, Leibniz and Kant regarded language almost exclusively as an instrument and Kant was even less interested in it. Against this background it was necessary to make a new emphatic study of the relation between thought and language. This had always been done by the Greeks. Socrates, who discovered the general, locates it essentially in the generality present in language. And the above citation from the *Sophist* gives an instructive example of Plato's continual recourse to language.[10] Aristotle raises language to a philosophical investigation with an investigation of linguistic usage. The fifth book of the *Metaphysics* is preoccupied with such questions. Those who are once again stressing the importance of language for philosophy pay surprisingly little attention to the Greek attitude. We intend to reappropriate the Greek attitude. But from this to the extreme thesis: all philosophy as critique of language, is still a long way. The extreme thesis is unproven and, we believe, unprovable.

Two further considerations may be recorded here. I will use the two terms 'metaphysics' and 'ontology' as synonyms in the strong sense. Currently the term 'metaphysics' designates a work in Aristotle's writings and at the same time a philosophical discipline. The Greek term does not itself occur in Aristotle's book. When it came into use and whether it was supposed to designate a reality or only the position of that book among Aristotle's works is still disputed.[11] The usual interpretation of the term 'metaphysics' retains the meaning underlying the Greek expressions, that is, that metaphysics is the theory of what lies beyond nature. I do not myself use the term 'metaphysics' in this traditional sense. Instead I determine its meaning, in a way that requires further clarification, exclusively through the question: What is being? The term 'ontology', so far as I know, was introduced in the seventeenth century. Christian Wolff[12] and in our time Nicolai Hartmann[13] have preferred to use this term. In German usage a certain difference may be felt between the two words. The word 'ontology' does not convey as strongly the idea of something lying beyond nature as does the word 'metaphysics'. Hartmann had this difference in mind when he preferred the term 'ontology'. I will ignore this difference and use the two terms in the same sense.

With the designation 'General Metaphysics' I employ a distinction which Christian Wolff introduced between *ontologia generalis* and *ontologia specialis*. Following this, metaphysics is sometimes used to mean a theory which from the outset is developed from a definite standpoint. It is understood, for example, as conceptual realism or as natural theology. Nietzsche had such a meaning in mind in his fight against metaphysics. In this sense metaphysics is practically identical with a naïve Platonism. If I may repeat, I myself define metaphysics through the question: What is being? If metaphysics is defined through this question, then it follows that every answer to this question is metaphysics. The only issue is whether the answers given are good or bad. I will atempt to show that a naïve Platonism is one of the worst answers one can give. If one defines metaphysics by that question then, to bring in an opposite standpoint, extreme nominalism is also metaphysics. One can debate whether extreme nominalism is good or bad metaphysics, it is perhaps no worse than extreme realism. But it is not a primary goal of our investigation to take sides with one or the other standpoint. Our first goal is rather to understand metaphysical standpoints.

4. BEING HAS SEVERAL MEANINGS

Once the possibility of metaphysics as a theory of being is admitted, one finds that the word 'being' has a property which it shares with nearly all words in the German language. As a rule a word has several meanings. In the sentences: 'the child runs', 'the tap runs', 'time runs'—the word 'runs' is used in different meanings. Dictionaries therefore regularly assign several meanings to every word.

According to the traditional theory developed by Aristotle three possibilities are distinguished. A word can have a single meaning, in which case it is univocal. A word can have several meanings standing in a relationship, which must be described further; then it is called analogous. Or finally a word can have several meanings, between which there is no relation, and then it is called equivocal.[1]

It is ordinarily the case for equivocations that there was once a relation which has now ceased to be conscious. It is perhaps also possible that a word acquires strange meanings through phonetic similarities. A genuine equivocation occurring as an original phenomenon is hard to imagine. And as there are no equivocations in the strict sense, so it seems also that there are no strict univocations in ordinary speech. The living stream of language changes, expands, constantly unfolds new meanings. For that reason we find strict univocations only in artificially fused meanings, for example, in mathematics, the natural sciences and law. Thus also it is understandable that in everyday speech a word regularly has several meanings. One can guess from the outset then that this will also be the case for the word 'being'.

When a word has several meanings one of them is as a rule pre-eminent. The dictionaries distinguish this pre-eminent meaning as the original and the others as derivative. It is not always easy, however, to decide which meaning is original. The word 'in' may serve as an example. Grimm's dictionary gives a series of meanings for 'in'; the purely spatial one is regarded as the original meaning, the other meanings are derived from that one.[2]

It is, however, debatable whether the purely spatial meaning is the original. In any event, Heidegger considers the existential meaning as original and the purely spatial as derivative.[3] This kind of difficulty has often been noticed; it has led to the ironical remark that dictionary entries should be read in reverse order. But the difficulty of distinguishing the original meaning in a given case does not, in my view, negate the reliability of the Aristotelian distinction between the original and the derived meaning. In the case of 'being' we will doubtless have to decide between an original meaning and one of several derived meanings. Aristotle's example is the word 'health', the original meaning of 'health' is a condition of man. If one characterizes medicine or a bath as healthy, as we do in everyday speech, then the word is used in derived meanings. The meaning is that medicine makes man healthy and the bath preserves health.[4]

Aristotle analyses the meanings of 'being' in the fifth book of the *Metaphysics*.[5] Indications of the plurality of meanings for 'being' are also found in other places.[6] Particularly instructive are the parallel analyses of 'unity'.[7] According to Aristotle 'being' has several meanings. Among these the being of an individual is the original meaning, the other meanings, especially the being of the general, are derived. We will have to discuss these problems in detail later.

Thomas Aquinas formally adopted this theory of Aristotle's. Not surprisingly, he carries it forward in considerable detail in his *Commentary on the Metaphysics,* but he develops it also in the theological works.[8] Still the Aristotelian-Thomistic theory on the analogical character of the concept of being was by no means the common doctrine of scholasticism, as people frequently suppose. In contrast to Thomas, Duns Scotus and Ockham defend a univocal concept of being.[9] Nevertheless, the theory of different meanings for the concept of being remained in fact fundamental, in Descartes, in Leibniz, and in Kant. But in form, as an explicit piece of theory, it has continually faded. For that reason it seems to me necessary to return to the standpoint of Aristotle. It seems probable from the outset that in the expressions 'the being of the individual', 'the being of peoples', 'the being of numbers', 'the being of natural laws', the word 'being' is used in different meanings.

5. THE MODES OF BEING

If this multiplicity of meanings of being is to make sense, there must be a multiplicity of modes of being corresponding to it. One of the most fundamental problems in the history of philosophy is the determination of modes of being. Plato begins with his great distinction between the Ideas and sensible things. Already in the *Phaedo* he speaks of two modes of being.[1] Aristotle generalizes the Platonic distinction to a distinction between the individual and the general and adds further distinctions, in particular the distinction between substance and accident. Descartes gives two fundamental distinctions of being. The first is between *res cogitans* and *res extensa*; the second is between the *esse reale* of the *res cogitans,* on the one hand, and the *esse in mente tantum* of *veritates aeternae,* on the other. Leibniz distinguishes between the real being of the monads and the phenomenal being of the determinations founded in them, in particular, of space, time, and the laws of nature. Kant develops the distinctions of Plato and Leibniz further and distinguishes between phenomena and noumena, between the appearance and the thing-in-itself. These distinctions constitute the heart of the Kantian philosophy but they also constitute its distinctive difficulties. In our time, distinctions of being have an important meaning for Whitehead and Nicolai Hartmann. Whitehead distinguishes between the actual entity and the eternal object. The actual entity develops Aristotle's individual and the monads of Leibniz, the eternal object develops the Ideas of Plato. Hartmann distinguishes between the different spheres of being, in particular between real and ideal being.

The necessity and the possibility of distinctions of being will be the central theme of our investigations. In this Introduction we confine ourselves to asking whether it is at all necessary to distinguish modes of being. Is it not possible, on the contrary, to assume only one mode of being? Is it not even necessary to start from the assumption that being can be given only in one mode? How this problem should be attacked is not immediately clear. One can only attempt to get some orientation from the history of thinking. As far as I can see, there is only one philosophical school, that of Pythagoras and his followers, which has seriously pursued the theory that there is only one mode of being.

The philosophy of the Pythagoreans is not well known, but the thesis: all is number[2] may be regarded as a summary statement. Aristotle understood this as a determination of being. He assumed that the usual distinction between numbers and numbered things was also fundamental for the Pythagoreans.[3] But self-evident as this distinction may be, it is perhaps not self-evident to presuppose it here also. Perhaps one must take the axiom of the Pythagoreans literally. Then we would be assuming that, according to the Pythagorean conviction, everything really is number, and that there are no numerable things in addition to number. If one considers the thesis in this interpretation, it seems, strange to say, irrefutable. A refutation would require the proof of a contradiction in the basic thesis. Till now no attempt at such a proof has been made. Great difficulties are created by the attempt to imagine the thesis. A true imagination of the Pythagorean thesis in its extreme interpretation is perhaps not even possible. That would mean that the rejection of any differentiation of being in its Pythagorean form cannot be refuted, but also that the thesis cannot be imagined in the pictorial sense.

For our problem, a second consideration suggests itself. One can study conceptions of being which are very simple. One of the simplest is presented by mechanistic materialism. In its simplest form it occurs as atomism. The Greek version of atomism recognizes as being only atoms and the void.[4] It took on a new form when Newton discovered the laws of motion, and when materialism subsequently regarded the Newtonian laws as the sole and absolute laws of nature. With that decision the radical materialism of modern times is driven to a differentiation of being, which it does not of course explicitly formulate, but which remains nevertheless an inescapable presupposition of its standpoint. Materialism must distinguish between atoms and the natural laws which govern the movements of atoms. The natural laws are obviously not themselves atoms. The materialist could avoid the necessity of a differentiation of being if he would regard the laws of nature as mere imaginings, but that is just what he will not do. He insists on the absolute reality of the laws of nature and, in addition, reduces the laws of nature to the Newtonian laws, which clearly take on for him a mythical sacredness. But with this interpretation of the laws of nature a differentiation of being has become unavoidable. One therefore concludes that the simplest conception of being according to the Pythagoreans, radical materialism, necessarily implies a differentiation of being.

In sum, it appears that the Pythagorean conception of being, if understood in a literal sense, is not refutable, but also probably not imaginable in the true sense. It also appears that the simplest conception of being meeting the Pythagorean condition, radical materialism, already implies a differentiation of being. The inference must therefore be drawn that differentiations of being are unavoidable. Thus it becomes understandable that there are many meanings of 'being'. I draw the conclusion that we must follow Aristotle in this matter. And our investigations must establish two things: firstly, there are many meanings of 'being' and among them a pre-eminent meaning and secondly, there are several modes of being and among them a pre-eminent mode.

PART I

INDIVIDUAL BEING
AND ITS DETERMINATIONS

CHAPTER I

THE GREEK GIGANTOMACHY
ABOUT BEING

―――――――

6. PLATO'S THEORY OF IDEAS IN THE *PHAEDO*

In the *Sophist* Plato characterizes the confrontation between the materialists and the advocates of Ideas as a gigantomachy about being. This expression, which reflects the vividness of Greek thinking, becomes still more appropriate when one adds to it Aristotle's struggle with the ontological problem and his confrontation with Plato's theory of Ideas.

We begin with the *Phaedo* and ask about the ontology which lies at the basis of the dialogue. It presents itself above all as the distinction between Ideas and sensible things. Plato gives many examples of the distinction: the Idea of beauty on the one side and beautiful human beings, beautiful horses, beautiful garments on the other.[1] The Idea of equal on the one side, and equal timbers on the other.[2] German has many linguistic difficulties on this point. In Greek the plural of the neuter gender is readily available and Plato can therefore say without further ado τὰ καλά.[3] In German the plural of the neuter can of course be formed, but it is not distinct in form from the plural of the masculine and the plural of the feminine. One therefore encounters difficulties in translation. If one doesn't want to paraphrase, then τὰ καλά can hardly be rendered otherwise than by 'the beautiful things'. But the addition of the word 'things', hard to avoid, adds a nuance in the German translation which is not present in the Greek text.

Ideas and sensible things are distinguished in various ways.

Ideas are accessible through pure thought,[4] sensible things are grasped through the senses and predominantly through seeing.[5] While the Ideas are eternal and unchangeable, sensible things endure only a short time; they are subject to continual change.[6]

As has always been noticed, two basic functions of the Ideas can be distinguished: an epistemological and an ontological. Beautiful things are beautiful through the Idea of beauty, this is the ontological meaning of the Idea. Beautiful things are recognized as beautiful through the Idea of beauty, that is the epistemological meaning of the Idea.

In the *Republic*, the theory of Ideas appears in the same form, although further developed in many respects. Thus in the *Republic* the difficult but unavoidable question of the highest Idea has become an important problem, and it is the Idea of the Good that Plato considers the highest Idea in this dialogue.[7]

In these two dialogues the theory of Ideas presents a reasonably unified picture and so the interpreters have also been largely in agreement. Though there is no lack of problems requiring interpretation, even in the *Phaedo*.

There is first the question why Plato has Socrates expound the theory of Ideas in this decisive form. Why Socrates, particularly in the *Phaedo*, where the dialogue is in large part undoubtedly a historical account? From this, recognized experts—I mention, for example, Burnet[8] and Taylor[9]—have concluded that it was Socrates who developed the theory of Ideas. One should not forget that there are good grounds for this interpretation. But there are also good grounds for the opposite view. Aristotle's testimony, that the theory of Ideas must be attributed to Plato rather than to Socrates, carries great weight.[10] Supporting this is the fact that the early dialogues of Plato, which are rightly called Socratic since they give the liveliest picture of Socrates, do not explicitly mention the theory of Ideas. Although such historical questions are of secondary importance for our systematic investigations, I will take sides here for the traditional interpretation, attested to by Aristotle, that the theory of Ideas stems not from Socrates, but rather has Plato for its originator.

At least two places in the *Phaedo* reveal that a certain discussion about the theory of Ideas was already in process as Plato wrote this dialogue. From the brief remarks one cannot be sure whether Plato weighed these questions in solitude or whether a discussion had already begun among Plato's students and friends about the meaning of the theory of Ideas.

The first place occurs when the question is thrown up, how sensible things are related to the Ideas. Is it by a *parousia*?[11] Or a *methexis*?[12] Or is there some other way to think the relation? Socrates, as Plato has him speak in this dialogue, will not enter into this question. He simply rests content with the statement that beautiful things are beautiful through the Idea of beauty, however it may be necessary to think their relation.[13] This exchange makes sense only if we assume that the later discussion about the problem of *methexis* has already begun.

The frequently discussed section on hypothesis presents even greater difficulties. One must hold on to the secure bulwark of one's hypothesis, says Plato. If the hypothesis is attacked, then one should disregard the attack, and instead investigate the consequences which follow from the hypothesis to see whether they are mutually consistent or mutually contradictory. If a hypothesis leads to contradictions it is thereby refuted. If it appears free of contradictions, a proof can be attempted by ascending to a more ultimate hypothesis. One must take care to reach the best of the more ultimate hypotheses—there are obviously several—and thus arrive at a satisfactory one.[14] The test seems at first quite clear and yet it is difficult to say in detail what Plato meant. The difficulty consists in the fact that one cannot say exactly what Plato understands here by hypotheses. If one relates the discussion generally to scientific hypotheses, it is already bold enough. It would then mean that the fundamental assumptions of science must be understood as hypotheses which require testing. There are various fundamental assumptions, some better than others. There must therefore be a best one among them. This is rather close to certain interpretations of modern theoretical science, which could therefore provide good examples. But what could Plato have had in mind when he construed the theory of hypothesis so generally? Where did he learn about the replacement of contradictory or unfruitful hypotheses through better ones. Perhaps he was thinking of certain notions in the astronomy of his time.[15] But it may be better to relate the theory to geometry, as Taylor does.[16]

The difficulty becomes greater when one assumes that Plato understands the theory of Ideas itself as such a hypothesis. The beginning of the excerpt suggests this, for Plato there speaks explicitly of the Idea of duality.[17] But how shall we understand the quotation? Does Plato entertain the possibility, here in the *Phaedo*, that mutually contradictory consequences can be inferred from the theory of Ideas? Does he consider it possible that the theory of Ideas can be based on a higher and better hypothesis or that it can be replaced through another hypothesis? Plato gives no clue as to how such an alternative and higher hypothesis might look. In the other occurrence in the *Phaedo* the theory of Ideas is asserted with definite certitude. Natorp takes the hypothesis as the basis for his interpretation,[18] but his presentation of this point is not satisfying.

The real difficulty of the *Phaedo* is, however, systematic. It consists in what has sometimes been called the Eleaticism of the theory of Ideas. In our time this trait has been heavily emphasized by Bruno Liebrucks.[19]

The theory of Ideas as presented in the *Phaedo* contains an ontological thesis in the strict Eleatic sense. The Idea is, sensible things are not. This fundamental assertion is constructed along the lines of the Eleatic thesis: being is, non-being is not, there is no middle ground between them.[20] In the *Phaedo* this Eleatic disjunction defines the relation between the Idea and sensible things. In the *Sophist* Plato himself formulates this interpretation which underlies the *Phaedo*. He says there, referring to the advocates of Ideas:

(They) 'are very wary in defending their position somewhere in the heights of the unseen, maintaining with all their force that true reality consists in certain intelligible and bodiless forms. In the clash of argument they shatter and pulverize those bodies which their opponents wield, and what those others allege to be

32

true reality they call, not real being, but a sort of moving process of becoming.'[21]

The line of thought must be so developed that becoming is defined in Parmenides' sense, as non-being. Hegel in his *History of Philosophy* appropriately characterizes this Eleaticism of the *Phaedo*, when he says summarily of Plato's Ideas: 'They are, and they alone are being.'[22] This is in fact what Plato wants to say in the *Phaedo*: The Ideas have true being, and Ideas alone have true being. In this fundamental assertion of the theory of Ideas lies the true meaning, but also the true difficulty, of the theory of Ideas. We must continually return to the consideration of these difficulties in the course of our investigations. Here we attempt only a first outline. According to this fundamental assertion the Idea of beauty alone has true being, beautiful things in their transitoriness and imperfection do not have true being, for in the sense of the Eleatic disjunction there is either true being or non-being, but no middle ground between them.

But is this Eleatic disjunction itself possible? Plato will himself pose the question in the *Sophist*. For the moment we ask only: Is the Eleatic disjunction possible in the theory of Ideas? When applied to the relation between Ideas and sensible things, doesn't the Eleatic disjunction simply cancel out the theory of Ideas as such? If beautiful things are nothing, doesn't the Idea of beauty itself lose its meaning? What could be the meaning of the Idea of beauty if it did not appear in beautiful things, if beauty itself did not shine forth in beautiful things?

If one admits the legitimacy of this line of thought, then one cannot avoid the consequences. If the Idea of beauty is supposed to have a meaning, then beautiful things must have reality and being in some fashion. It is therefore no longer possible that the Idea alone should have being. But how is the being of the Ideas related to the being of sensible things? This question must necessarily reach out beyond the *Phaedo*, although it is to some extent included therein. This is the question Plato poses in the later dialogues, the question that brings forth metaphysics, and it is this same question that will define metaphysics for all times.

7. PLATO'S ONTOLOGY IN THE *SOPHIST*

Testing the Eleatic disjunction now becomes a task. The thesis formulated so clearly by Hegel: The Ideas alone have being, cannot be allowed to stand in this exclusiveness, it must be modified in some way. Somehow sensible things must also be accorded being. This task can be considered from a purely systematic standpoint, but it can also be regarded as a task which Plato is forced to set himself by the course of his thinking. From a systematic viewpoint the question would be phrased: How is it possible to assign being not merely to the Ideas, but also in some fashion to sensible things? Looked at historically, or rather personally, Plato's problem was that he felt compelled to reflect on the presuppositions contained in the *Phaedo* and the *Republic* It is understandable that Plato should put aside all doubts when the theory of Ideas first occurred to him and that he should represent it as a perfect whole.

But the fascinating form in which the theory of Ideas is presented in the *Phaedo* cannot, in the long run, conceal its difficulties. One day Plato would have to reflect: What have I really claimed with this theory of Ideas? One day he would have to ask: What are the presuppositions underlying this theory of Ideas? This reflection and these questions come to light essentially in two dialogues, the *Parmenides* and the *Sophist*. For our systematic considerations we can turn immediately to the *Sophist*, the *Parmenides* will be considered later.

In the part that interests us now, the *Sophist* appears as a confrontation between Parmenides and Heraclitus. Parmenides is the champion of those who would bring being to a standstill. For him being is unchangeable, always one.[1] In decisive contrast to Parmenides, Heraclitus sees being as continual movement. For him all permanence is paralysis, a loss of being.[2]

Plato knows that each of these standpoints in its extreme form is impossible, since each negates itself. Heraclitus sees everything in flux. He lacks anything abiding, a necessary condition for any abiding knowledge and therefore a necessary condition for the knowledge of Heraclitus.[3] Parmenides denies any plurality. But a proposition is already in itself a plurality. Without plurality, all propositions and therefore all knowledge would be impossible. Then the knowledge of Parmenides also becomes impossible.[4] Plato tries to remedy this in a synthesis of the two great standpoints.[5]

Plato relates the task of synthesis directly to the theory of Ideas. As a device he presents a discussion with the advocates of Ideas.[6] Whom does he have in mind as advocates of Ideas? Many interpreters, especially in the nineteenth century, could not imagine that Plato meant himself and his own teaching in this criticism of the theory of Ideas. But two of the best Plato scholars of the present day, Ross[7] and Cornford[8], have concluded that in this text Plato is referring to his own early and original form of the theory of Ideas, and they can gain support for this interpretation from earlier interpreters.[9] From our systematic standpoint this interpretation appears correct. We suppose that Plato would reflect about the meaning of his theory of Ideas and that in fact he has done just that. This leads to the interpretation that Plato meant himself, his friends and students by the phrase 'advocates of Ideas'.

This discussion with the advocates of Ideas aims at disengaging the Ideas from their Eleatic rigidity. The first argument says: Life is a fundamental characteristic of being. Being necessarily means being-alive. If then the Ideas are supposed to have reality and being, they must not lack the fundamental characteristic of being, to be living. Therefore the Ideas have life and therewith change and movement.[10]

The same result follows from the second argument, which takes its departure from knowledge. But here Plato makes an assumption that seems strange at first sight. All agree, he says, that knowing is an activity and thus a movement and an alteration. But, and here Plato makes his assumption felt, becoming-known or more exactly, becoming-done, is also an acting and hence a movement and an alteration. One will at first hesitate to grant this assumption. But it can be made evident in the relations of men with one another. To be known, to be known in his true being, is an important event for every man, perhaps also an ultimate condition of his existence. How far such an analysis can be made fully clear we need not presently inquire. What Plato wants to say is clear. The Ideas must be knowable. If they were not then, on this basis too, the theory of Ideas would lose its meaning. But if the Ideas are knowable then they are drawn into the living stream of knowing and thereby also into movement and change. This is another argument Plato uses to remove the Ideas from their Eleatic rigidity.[11]

All these questions run together when Plato in the *Sophist* asks for the first time the basic question of metaphysics, when he first asks, what is being?[12] This question constitutes the Platonic-Aristotelian ontology and it will constitute every other ontology. Considering the meaning this question has for Aristotle's ontology, one is inclined to take it as a specifically Aristotelian question, and I have myself for a long time done so. But it is in fact Plato who poses this question in the *Sophist*, thereby founding ontology.

In order to understand this question of the *Sophist*, it is important to realize that the Platonic question, what is being?, grows out of the Socratic question, what is . . .?.[13] But, in contrast to this general and abstract question of Plato's, Socrates' questions are always in some respects concrete. He asks, what is courage?,[14] what is piety?,[15] what is justice?.[16] But Plato ascends to questions of ever increasing abstractness. It is already likely that the question posed by the *Theatetus*, what is knowledge?,[17] is more abstract than any posed by Socrates himself. But it seems to me certain that the most general and highest questions: what is being?, what is unity?,[18] were first achieved by Plato. The widespread conviction that these are actually Aristotelian questions contains one valid point: Aristotle was the first to make the investigation of these questions a special discipline. With respect to the method of the Socratic question and the possible answers it can receive, Aristotle's formulation remains the best: Socrates gives no answers, he only asks.[19] In fact, Socrates contents himself with an aporematic and dialectical treatment of questions and their possible answers. Whether this Socratic treatment of questions will remain valid also for the highest questions achieved by Plato—this is one of the central themes of our investigations.

First one must recognize that this general question, what is being?, is only possible in a late Platonic dialogue, and also that it is a necessary question therein. The question receives its possibility and its necessity from a reflection on the meaning of the theory of Ideas. It grows out of Plato's insight that an ontological assertion about the being of Ideas underlies the theory of Ideas.

We have seen that the theory of Ideas begins with an Eleatic disjunction: the Ideas are, they alone are, all else is not. But this extreme Eleaticism cannot be maintained for long. One day Plato sees clearly that the Ideas are and remain true being, but that sensible things have being in some sense. Now for the first time the general question can be asked, what is being?, now for the first time, the ontology defined by this question becomes possible.

It is already remarkable to notice, when considering the Socratic questions, that no-one up to that time had asked questions of that form. To us, the question, what is that?, has become so natural that we can only imagine with difficulty that there was once a time in which this question had not yet been asked.[20] The same holds true for the general question about being. Only with difficulty can we imagine that Plato was the first to raise it and then only in the late dialogues. But it is understandable that the question was not possible earlier.

Thales did not ask, what is water?, and he could not ask it. Now we don't know exactly what he said, or rather, we don't know exactly how he said it. Basically we know the Pre-Socratics only through the reports of Plato and Aristotle and the elucidations of those reports offered by commentators. Yet there is no doubt about Thales' basic thesis: all is water.[21] The true content of his thought is contained in this basic thesis. But how could he come to ask, what is water? All is water, that is the only answer he gave and the only answer he could give. Beyond that there is nothing to ask and nothing to answer. Thales was not able to frame the still relatively concrete question, what is water? The general question, what is being?, was wholly impossible for him.

It is no different with Pythagoras and his students. Here too the form of this basic thesis is as hard to grasp as its meaning. It can be summarized as follows, all is number.[22] This thesis is as strange as it is momentous. Hegel expressly alluded to its great significance.[23] For our purposes it should be noted that only the apodictic thesis is uttered, all is number, and that the question, what is number?, is not and could not have been raised. The Pythagoreans say, all is number, and there is nothing but number. They can then ask which number is involved in particular cases. But when it has been shown, for example, that the octave is the relation 1:2, then everything has been said which can be said. Beyond that there is nothing to ask. The question, what is number?, can therefore neither be raised nor answered. Still less is the general ontological question about being possible for them.

In a certain sense this is also true for Parmenides. He is the first who speaks explicitly of being. Being is, that is his fundamental assertion,[24] which he unfolds through a whole series of further assertions about being. Among them the definition, being is one,[25] is the most important. Being and thinking are the same,[26] —for this great principle of Parmenides no satisfactory interpretation has yet been found. Being is, non-being is not; this is the Eleatic disjunction which became so important for the construction of the theory of Ideas, the disjunction which Plato discusses in a fundamental way in the *Sophist*. As fundamental and far-reaching as Parmenides' thoughts and expressions about being, the question, what is being?, is not included among them and it could not be included among them. Being itself is the ultimate behind which nothing further can be asked. How could one ask what is behind the ultimate? What could be answered to such a question? There is nothing else to which the ultimate could be traced back.

In a certain sense Plato is still in the situation of the earlier thinkers in his *Phaedo* and *Republic*. Ideas alone are being and there is nothing else to which the being of Ideas could be traced back. Here the being of the Ideas is a matter of course. Whoever hears the theory of Ideas either understands it or not. Thus it becomes understandable that Plato in the *Sophist* can say, 'we who formerly imagined we knew.'[27]

In the *Phaedo* Plato has in fact repeatedly ascribed being to the Idea. It is being, it is the real being. In these assertions he saw no problem, he thought he knew what the assertions claimed. But now, in the *Sophist*, he has become aware of the problematic and he must say, 'we who formerly imagined we knew, are now at a loss.'

The general question, what is being?, first becomes possible when different modes of being have been distinguished. It was first possible when Plato distinguished between Ideas and sensible things. It was first possible when he assigned true being, just as before, to the Ideas, but now allowed being in some sense to sensible things as well. For then the question is necessary, what strange being it is which belongs in the true sense to Ideas, but nevertheless also belongs, even though in another, different sense, to sensible things. In what sense does being belong to Ideas, in what sense does being belong to sensible things?

When Plato earlier thought he knew and now knows no longer, this is not just Plato's situation at one definite moment, it is the perennial systematic situation of metaphysics as such. Heidegger has shown anew[28] that being is first taken to be self-evident and that it requires a constant effort of thought to overcome again this seeming self-evidence, in order to bring oneself once again into the situation: before I knew it, now I don't know it any longer.

We have now the possibility of making clear once more what we understand by metaphysics. According to the prevailing interpretation, the *Phaedo* is metaphysics in the true sense. According to this interpretation, metaphysics is the doctrine of that which lies behind nature, behind sensible things, and the *Phaedo* in fact teaches the being of the Ideas behind and beyond sensible things. According to the interpretation attempted here, however, metaphysics should be defined by the question about being. It begins therefore only when the question about being is explicitly and formally raised. For the relation between the *Phaedo* and the *Sophist*, this means that metaphysics does not yet exist when the being of Ideas is simply asserted. Metaphysics exists only when we reflect on the being of Ideas and expressly ask what being signifies. Only when Plato asked himself what he had meant and now means when he says, the Ideas are being, only in the *Sophist*, does metaphysics begin. Not therefore the thesis, the Ideas are and they alone are being, but rather the reflection about the meaning of this thesis constitutes metaphysics on my interpretation. So, not the *Phaedo* but first the *Sophist* is both the beginning and a high point of metaphysics.

8. THE CONCEPT OF *OUSIA* IN PLATO

The development of Plato's thought would have to be manifest in the development of his fundamental philosophical terms, and in fact it is manifest in the development of the term '*ousia*'. When Plato in the construction of the theory of Ideas needs a particular philosophical term to characterize the true reality of the Ideas, he makes use of the expression '*ousia*'. Burnet has speculated that the Pythagoreans had already used this word, a common one in everyday Greek usage, in a new philosophical meaning.[1] But the new usage first takes firm hold in Plato's writings. In ordinary usage the word '*ousia*' means 'possession', 'property', and Plato continues to use the word with these everyday meanings alongside his new philosophical meaning.[2] The word '*ousia*' lent itself very well to Plato's intended usage, for it has the particular connotation of firm possession, and above all, basic possession.[3]

Plato applies the old word in its new meaning first to the ontological definition of the Idea. The Idea is *ousia*, says the *Phaedo*,[4] and in this dialogue only the Idea is *ousia*. To that extent the term has entered into the Eleatic disjunction of the theory of Ideas of the *Phaedo*. But we found that the Eleatic disjunction negated the meaning of the theory of Ideas. If there is only the Idea of beauty, and beautiful things do not possess being in any sense, then the Idea of beauty also loses its meaning. The Idea can retain its meaning only if beautiful things have being in some way. The later dialogues turn on this question.

With respect to *ousia* this development in Plato's thought must lead to the conclusion that not only is the Idea an *ousia*, but in some sense still to be determined the sensible thing must also be an *ousia*. The term must therefore undergo a change of meaning or, more exactly, a development of meaning in the later dialogues. This is in fact the case, even though an exact investigation of this development of meaning is still awaited. In the later dialogues, Plato applies the term '*ousia*' to Ideas but he also lets it apply to sensible things, he even speaks of an *ousia* coming-into-being.[5] So far as I know, the first to call attention to this development of meaning for *ousia* was Peipers,[6] later Natorp also mentioned it.[7]

This presentation of Plato's philosophical thought is, of course, idealized. A theory of Ideas constructed on the radical Eleatic disjunction is not possible, because the radical Eleatic disjunction is itself impossible. Plato demonstrates this formally in the *Sophist*. So it becomes understandable that these two levels: the theory of Ideas in its Eleatic form in the *Phaedo*, and the theory of Ideas in the stage of ontological reflection about its own presuppositions as presented in the *Sophist*, cannot be so radically separated in the actual dialogues as we have just done from a systematic point of view. For Plato, obviously, the theory of Ideas itself and the reflection on its ontological presuppositions directly affect one another. We have seen that already in the *Phaedo* the first signs of a reflection on the theory of Ideas can be found. Nevertheless it seems to me that the radical, systematic separation is what allows a deeper insight into the development of Plato's thought.

9. ARISTOTLE'S CONCEPTION OF BEING

Plato founded ontology, Aristotle raised it to an independent discipline. Every ontology therefore needs a continual confrontation of Plato and Aristotle. For Aristotle, metaphysics as a discipline is not yet fixed terminologically, at least not in the same degree as logic, ethics and physics. His *Metaphysics* in its present form as a book of fourteen chapters does not constitute a real unity. One can say with great security that several of these essays were originally independent and that it was not Aristotle, but some later editor, who put the fourteen chapters into one book.[1] The problem of inner unity is more difficult. Aristotle pursues different ends in his investigations. And thus his metaphysics is at once *ontologia generalis*, *theologia naturalis* and *scientia universalis*. It is *ontologia generalis* in so far as it is the theory of being as being.[2] It is *theologia naturalis* in so far as it is the theory of the highest being.[3] It is *scientia universalis* in so far as it is the theory of principles.[4] Between these three tasks there is an inner connection, which can still be made clear in its essential determinations. I do not believe, however, that metaphysics today can still be held to this threefold task, in the way that Aristotle has actually done. I believe that today one must choose one of the three possibilities. I myself choose to regard the task of metaphysics as *ontologia generalis*. Whether this decision is well founded and fruitful can only be shown by following it out.

Aristotle's presentation of metaphysics as *ontologia generalis* is first shown in the third book of the *Metaphysics*. In this book the tasks of metaphysics are developed as aporias. In the first chapter Aristotle enumerates the aporias, and in the following he discusses each one in detail. Already in the first inventory the question about the ontological determination of being and unity is characterized as the most difficult and most aporematic of the aporias.[5] In the treatment of this aporia in the fourth chapter Aristotle characterizes it as the most difficult of the aporias to discuss and yet the most necessary for the knowledge of truth.[6] Here Aristotle expressly asks the question: what is being? Here also he treats the parallel question, what is unity?[7]

In preparing to answer the question, Aristotle first explains that the terms of philosophy are words which regularly have several meanings. In particular, the word 'being' has several meanings. This insight is fundamental for Aristotle and it is certainly no accident that the great discussion with Plato in the first book of the *Metaphysics* closes with the hint that every philosophical insight is impossible when the plurality of meanings for the concept of being has not been recognized.[8]

Aristotle gives the systematic treatment of this interpretation in Book V of the *Metaphysics*. In thirty chapters this book

analyses respectively the plurality of meaning for thirty fundamental concepts of philosophy. These investigations were so
important for Aristotle that he collected them in one special book,
although parallel investigations of plurality of meaning occur in
numerous other places. For example, the plurality of meaning
for unity is investigated in Chapter 6 of Book V, and the parallel
analysis can be found in Chapter 1 of Book X. The plurality of
meaning for being is analysed in the seventh chapter, and the
parallel analysis is found in Chapter 1 of Book VII. Since Aristotle
cites Book V in other places as a separate work,[9] it must have
been independent before being added at some later date to the
fourteen books of the present *Metaphysics*.[10]

Aristotle analyses the plurality of meanings for being in the
seventh chapter. He distinguishes there four main meanings
which are themselves further sub-divided into several meanings.
The four main meanings of being are: 1. accidental or incidental
being, 2. the being of the categories, 3. being true or being false,
4. being possible or being actual.

As examples for purely accidental or incidental being, Aristotle
gives the merely accidental coincidence of attributes such as the
coincidence of being just and being educated.[11] The second main
meaning is represented by the categories. In this text Aristotle
names eight categories. This second main meaning is subdivided
into several meanings in such a way that, though there is one
meaning for each category, various meanings of being are in
play over the whole series of the categories.[12] For example, in
the being of substances and the being of numbers, different
meanings of being are present. If I speak of the being of Socrates
and the being of seven, I am using 'being' in different meanings.
It can be said that the plurality of meaning for being, which
unfolds over the series of the categories, was the most important
for Aristotle.[13] Finally, there is the third meaning of being true
or being false[14] and, as fourth main meaning, being possible and
being actual.[15]

This concludes the analysis of the concept of being in Book V.
In the first chapter of Book VII Aristotle extends this analysis
one step further by introducing the notion of a pre-eminent

meaning. The second meaning mentioned above, categorial being, emerges as the pre-eminent meaning, and from the meanings of categorial being the being of substance in particular emerges as the pre-eminent mode.[16]

This entails an important difference in contrast to the analogical character of the concept of being as it was further developed in Scholasticism. To the extent that the Scholastics, in dependence on Aristotle, maintain this theory, the most important meaning of being for them is the analogy between the being of God and the being of created things, in particular, the being of men.[17] Aristotle, by contrast, regards the series of the categories as giving the most important meaning of being. The Greek conception of God does not contain the same transcendence as the Christian. The gods of Greek polytheism are certainly separated from men by a great distance, and yet at bottom they share the same being with men. They dwell on the heights of Olympus, therefore in a place which men avoid from pious awe, but nevertheless a place which is basically like the place of men. Thus the gods could readily appear among men in animal or human form. This nearly complete absence of transcendence endures even after the Greek philosophers have risen to monotheism. The Christian concept of God is, by contrast, pervaded by the idea of transcendence. Thomas Aquinas finds in Aristotle's concept of analogy a philosophical means by which to express this transcendence. But he thereby shifts the centre of that theory.

The theory of the plurality of the conceptions of being reaches deeply into the Aristotelian determination of metaphysics as the theory of being as such.

In the sense of this determination Aristotle requires the existence of a science which investigates being as being. 'There is a science which investigates being as being and the attributes which belong to this in virtue of its own nature.'[18] For the construction of this science Aristotle in Book VII begins immediately with the analogical character of the concept of being and the existence of a pre-eminent meaning. He develops this theory on the example of being healthy. 'Being', he says, is used in a variety of ways, but these meanings hang together by relation to a pre-eminent meaning, there is no question here of mere equivocations. The usual example is the plurality of meanings of 'healthy'. All meanings of health refer to one pre-eminent meaning, the sense in which a man is healthy. Other meanings are derived from this one. That is healthy which preserves health, or produces it, or is a symptom of it.[19]

Aristotle begins Book VII also with an investigation of the plurality of meaning.

'There are several senses in which a thing may be said to "be", as we pointed out previously in our book on the various senses of words; for in one sense the "being" meant is "what a thing is" or a "this", and in another sense it means a quality or quantity or one of the things that are predicated as these are. While "being" has all these senses, obviously that which "is" primarily is the "what", which indicates the substance of the thing ... And all other things are said to be because they are, some of them, quantities of that which *is* in this primary sense, others qualities of it, others affections of it, and others some other determination of it.'[20]

From this analysis, which we have partly translated, partly paraphrased, as we will often do in rendering key passages, Aristotle rises to a definition of metaphysics which is decisive for our investigations: 'And indeed the question which was raised of old and is raised now and always, and is always the subject of doubt, viz. what being is, is just the question, what is substance' (*ousia*).[21]

Here we have together all the moments which are constitutive for the metaphysics of Aristotle, as it is interpreted in these investigations: the doctrine of the plurality of meanings for the concept of being, the idea that one of these meanings is pre-eminent, the definition of metaphysics through a question, namely the question, what is being?, and finally the determination of the method of metaphysics as an aporetic.

For the methodological considerations of our investigations the aporetic has a special importance. There is no doubt that Aristotle had little sympathy for dialectic and aporetic. It is all the more significant then that he attributes great importance to aporetic in the *Metaphysics*. We must be quite clear that the great aporetic of Book III does not have a merely pedagogical task. The Book is certainly written from a pedagogical standpoint. Its purpose is to introduce metaphysics, and this it does in an excellent way. But ultimately the aporetic of this Book has systematic rather than pedagogical grounds. The aporetic is directly connected with the definition of metaphysics by a question. In such a definition of metaphysics and in the recognition of the aporetic that develops from it, Aristotle is the true heir of the Socratic and Platonic question and the Socratic and Platonic aporetic.

10. ARISTOTLE'S CONCEPT OF *OUSIA*

The concept of *ousia* is among those for which Aristotle finds in Book V of the *Metaphysics* a plurality of meanings. After the investigation of unity in Chapter 6 and being in Chapter 7, he analyses *ousia* in Chapter 8. He first distinguishes four meanings and then regroups these into two. In the first meaning *ousia* is ascribed to the elements, to the earth, water, air, fire, ether, and in general to material bodies, to what can be composed from them, namely living beings and *daimones* in such a way that the organic parts of living beings can already be characterized as *ousia*. In the second meaning *ousia* is the name given to whatever it is that causes being in the elements of the first meaning. For example, the soul considered as the cause of being for animals is called *ousia*. In the third meaning *ousia* is a name for those parts which are present in the elements, giving them form and being by limiting them, as the body is limited by the plane and the plane by the line. Finally, in the fourth meaning, *ousia* can refer to the essence of each thing. Aristotle then regroups these four definitions into two, by joining together the second, third and fourth and characterizing them more generally as *eidos*. This allows Aristotle to claim that *ousia* is used in two fundamental meanings. In the first it means the ultimate substratum, which is never predicated of anything else, but is rather the recipient of all predicates. In the second meaning *ousia* means shape and *eidos* (form). They are called *ousia* because they cause being in those things named in the first meaning.[1]

In Book II of the *Physics*, one can find a parallel investigation of *ousia* in the first sense. The first Chapter of this Book is, as Aristotle expressly says, an analysis of the meaning of *physis*. But the compass of the analysed term and the result of the analysis make it clear that Aristotle really has *ousia* in mind. The compass is the same as in the analysis of the *Metaphysics*, except that the enumeration is given in the reverse order. Thus Aristotle gives the term *physis* to animals and their organic parts, to plants and to the elements. The four elements are named explicitly: earth, fire, air and water. The *daimones* and composite bodies mentioned in the *Metaphysics* are here left out, while plants are added.[2] Aristotle invites comparison with the *Metaphysics* by adding, '. . . and all these are *ousia*.'[3] The characteristic definition of this domain is given by Aristotle when he says that all these things have in themselves a principle of motion and rest.[4] Something is named *physis* because it has within itself the capacity to begin and to end its motion, its growth and its change.

The most important thing for us is the reduction of the plurality of meanings to two main ones: *ousia* as individual being and *ousia* as *eidos*. In other places Aristotle speaks of individual beings as primary *ousia*, and *eidos* as secondary *ousia*.[5] The question, how these two meanings are related and which of them is the pre-eminent meaning is a difficult and much disputed problem in the interpretation of Aristotle.

It is to be noticed that the Aristotelian distinction of the two main meanings both continues and ends the Platonic development. We saw that originally *ousia* designated only the Idea, this was quite clear in the *Phaedo*. The meaning of *ousia* then develops to include, in a manner not yet fully clarified, individual beings. This explains the emergence of the two meanings in Aristotle's work. We have decided, on historical and systematic grounds, to consider *ousia* in the sense of individual beings as the pre-eminent meaning. We will also adopt this Aristotelian doctrine, so interpreted. The plan and the execution of our investigation is based on this interpretation.

47

CHAPTER II

THE GREAT THEORIES OF BEING

II. PLATO

By a theory of being I understand, in company with Heidegger,[1] a complex of basic ontological concepts and propositions, as they have taken particular shape in the thinking of some philosopher. If the philosopher makes a distinction between different modes of being, as will usually be the case, then this distinction will be contained in the theory of being. In that theory we must find some indication of how these modes of being should be distinguished and whether one of the modes is pre-eminent.

The basic form of a theory of being is given by Plato in the theory of Ideas, and this theory is decisive for the subsequent development of Western philosophy. Plato himself recognizes the importance of his theory of being; already in the *Phaedo* he coins the clear formula: the two modes of being.[2] We saw already how Plato distinguishes the two modes of being ontologically and epistemologically. The Ideas are eternal and unchanging, they are grasped through pure thought; sensible things are changing and perishable, they are grasped through the senses. The Ideas are the pre-eminent, the true being. Plato never abandoned this basic proposition, and the proposition remains decisive for all philosophizing in Plato's sense and for all his successors. Of course, Plato himself already raises questions about the meaning of this basic proposition. One can sharply formulate Plato's expressions in the *Phaedo* by making use of a strict Eleatic disjunction. The Ideas are, sensible things are not. But we also saw that Plato could not and in the end did not want to maintain a strict Eleatic disjunction. He came rather to recognize the necessity for ascribing being in some way to sensible things. When Plato's antagonists, in particular Nietzsche,[3] represent Plato's theory of being as a two-worlds theory, the representation is clearly a simplification, but one that finds support in many places of the Platonic texts. Yet Plato was the first to recognize the problematic which his theory engenders. How are we to understand the thesis of two modes of being? How understand the thesis that the being of Ideas is true being? How characterize the relation between the two modes of being? How is each one separately to be characterized? For the present it may suffice to point out the problem. The discussion of the problem and its consequences will constitute the major part of our investigations.

12. ARISTOTLE

Aristotle enters directly onto the path of Platonic thought and advances it. He takes over the distinction between the Ideas and sensible things, both developing it substantively and giving it precise linguistic form.[1] He defines the two modes of being in the terms of his own logic as the general and the individual, and in agreement with Plato he distinguishes them further as primary and secondary ousia.[2]

In his continuation of Plato's struggle with the problem of the mode of being proper to sensible things, Aristotle arrives at a thesis which is flatly opposed to that of Plato. For Aristotle the individual thing is the true being. The being of individuals is for him true being, and the eidos, the general, has for him a derivative being.[3]

In this way is the relation between primary and secondary ousia determined in Aristotle's ontology. We noticed already that the substantive distinction is already found in Metaphysics V, the terminological clarity is found less often.[4] Clearly secondary ousia is a development of the Platonic Idea. And it is thus not surprising that the attempt should have been made to so define the relation between the two substances, that secondary ousia would be true being for Aristotle.[5] Then Aristotle would have remained a Platonist in his interpretation of the general and the individual. There is no denying that there are places in Aristotle's writings which can be understood in this sense, when taken out of context. But against this interpretation stands Aristotle's explicit explanation that the general can never be *ousia*.[6] This explanation must be read in context, for it can only mean that the general can never be primary *ousia*. Quite clearly, the general is secondary *ousia*, for this is given as the explicit definition of secondary *ousia*.[7] Taking into consideration the writings of Aristotle in their totality, the large chorus of commentators, and the unanimous opinion of Aristotle's students, one can only conclude that for Aristotle individual being is the true *ousia* and thereby the true being. We will also assume this standpoint and we therefore have, together with Aristotle, two tasks before us. We must explain the grounds and the consequences for this thesis, that the individual being is the true being. This will be done in this first Part. Once this fundamental proposition has been accepted, the question then arises: what is the general? The question thus posed then becomes the theme of the second Part.

Thomas Aquinas, whom we reckon as belonging fundamentally to Aristotelian philosophy, provides considerable support for our decision. Of course it is not correct to think of Aquinas as an Aristotelian in every respect. It was Aquinas who completed the shift in medieval thinking from the Platonic to the Aristotelian philosophy. We still lack wholly satisfying accounts of the reasons for this shift, its meaning and significance. One can immediately see at least this much, Thomas did not intend to have this shift understood as a one-sided partisan declaration against Plato and for Aristotle. He is much more interested in their connexion than in their opposition. His example ought to be followed. The historical and systematic connexion between the two philosophers is so narrow that one will have to regard Aquinas' way of representing their relation as well-founded.[8]

The significance of Aquinas' attitude is in no way lessened because of the fact that for him theological as well as philosophical reasons are decisive. This holds also for the acceptance of

Aristotle's fundamental thesis, that individual being is the true being. The Greeks as well as the Romans did not have a high regard for individual men and therefore also no high regard for individual being. This makes Plato's inclination towards the general understandable, but it also makes it remarkable that Aristotle should have arrived at this ontological priority of individual being and therefore individual men. However the Greeks may have decided on the question of value, Christianity regards the value and the right of individual men as intrinsic and inalienable. It is the individual on whom everything now turns.

13. DESCARTES

In the *Principia Philosophiae* Descartes gives a summary representation of his theory of being. In Par. 48 he says: '*Quaecunque sub perceptionem nostram cadunt, vel tanquam res, rerumve affectiones quasdam, consideramus; vel tanquam aeternas veritates, nullam existentiam extra cogitationem nostram habentes*'.[1] Leaving the *affectiones rerum* aside, we obtain the first fundamental distinction of being into *res* and *aeternae veritates*, that is, into things and eternal truths. *Res* corresponds to the Aristotelian substance, in particular to substance in the sense of primary *ousia*. It is things which underly and constitute all reality. Of eternal truths Descartes says explicitly that they exist only in our thinking: *nullam existentiam extra cogitationem nostram habentes*. This sounds more nominalist than he intends. It must be read in context since for Descartes the eternal truths are also the thoughts of God.[2] They are therefore closely related to Augustine's interpretation of Plato's theory of Ideas.

The concept of *res* coincides with the concept of substance for Descartes. He uses the terms *res* and *substantia* interchangeably, although he generally prefers the term *res*. He further distinguishes three modes of being for *res*: God, *res cogitans*, *res extensa*. In the *Principia* the following definition of substance is given: '*Per substantiam nihil aliud intelligere possumus, quam rem quae ita existit, ut nulla alia re indigeat ad existendum*'.[3]

In this strict sense only God can be called a substance. A created substance must be regarded as one that needs the assistance of God for its existence. '*Possunt autem substantia corporea et mens, sive substantia cogitans creata, sub hoc communi conceptu intelligi, quod sint res, quae solo Dei concursu egent ad existendum.*'[4] This means that existence, and correspondingly, being, cannot be asserted in the same sense of God and of created substances: '*Atque ideo . . . non convenit Deo et illis univoce, ut dici solet in Scholis, hoc est, nulla ejus nominis significatio potest distincte intelligi, quae Deo et creaturis sit communis.*'[5] In these theses, which represent the individual being as the true being, and assert that being is not an univocal concept, Descartes joins himself directly to the Aristotelian-Thomistic tradition.

We are chiefly concerned with the *res creata*. Descartes calls it both *res* and *substantia*, he speaks of the *res cogitans* as well as the *substantia cogitans*, of the *res corporea* as well as the *substantia corporea*.[6] Each of the two substances is characterized through its essential attribute, the *res cogitans* through *cogitatio*, the *res corporea* through *extensio*.[7]

The main point for us is that the *res extensa*, the purely material thing, is understood both as *res* and as *substantia*. It is also in the strict sense actual and real. It is the material body that is said to exist independently for itself and needs no other for its existence except the assistance of God.

In the atomism of antiquity a similar conception was maintained. For Democritus and for his successors, particularly Lucretius, the atom, the material thing, is true reality, true being. But this view was not typical of antiquity. For Aristotle, as we saw already, the elements, earth, water, air and fire are substances, but they are substances because they are living. The material bodies composed of them, such as wood or marble, are also living. Descartes, on the contrary, attributes true being also to the purely material body, in its very materiality, and to this body, *res extensa*, neither thought nor life is attributed.

Descartes is rightly numbered among the founders of the modern age because of the importance he attached to man as subject. But it is just as decisive for the modern age that Descartes attributes substantiality and true being to the purely material thing. If one ponders the importance of Descartes for the modern age one will have to consider that this Cartesian thesis was not universally accepted. At the beginning of the modern age Leibniz rejected it and in more recent times both Heidegger and White-head have rejected it. Of course these rejections refer to different aspects of the Cartesian thesis. Leibniz[8] and Whitehead are primarily attacking the interpretation of *res extensa* as substance and true being. Whitehead maintains that the material body as such represents only an abstraction, an idealization.[9] The purely material body is of course an abstraction of the highest importance, yet it is an abstraction, not a reality, let alone the true reality. Heidegger primarily attacks the *res cogitans*. He begins by pointing out[10] that the concept of *res* as such, contained in the concept of *res cogitans*, is taken from the *res extensa*. If that is so, the interpretation of man as *res cogitans* means that man is in the last analysis understood from the standpoint of the *res extensa*, from material things. There are good grounds for these objections, and it would therefore seem doubtful to consider the philosophy of Descartes without qualification as the authentic expression of the modern age.

14. LEIBNIZ

Leibniz's theory of being must be understood as a synthesis of Plato and Aristotle. This would correspond well with the basic attitude of Leibniz, which is one of harmonizing and mediating. But it conflicts somewhat with the manner and form of Leibniz' self-understanding. Leibniz understands himself primarily as a Platonist.[1] But one should not overlook the strength of the Aristotelian influence in his thought. It consists in the fact that the monads, individual beings, represent true being.[2] The Platonic influence, which came to Leibniz largely in an Augustinian form, rests in the interpretation of all concepts and the truths resulting from them as Ideas, the Ideas in turn being understood as the thoughts of God.

The Aristotelian influence was probably acquired very early

from his teacher, and it stands out clearly in the early works of Leibniz.[3] For example, Leibniz says in his *Dissertatio de stylo philosophico Nizolii*, '*Nam concreta vere res sunt, abstacta non sunt res sed rerum modi, modi autem nihil aliud sunt quam relationes rei ad intellectum, seu apparendi facultates*'.[4] In this thesis that only the *concreta*, and not the *abstracta*, have true reality, the basic Aristotelian proposition is perhaps more sharply expressed than in any formulation of Aristotle himself.

Step by step, in the elaboration of this theory of monads, Leibniz achieves his own philosophical standpoint. As a person I am myself the prototype of a monad.[5] God is also a monad, though a monad *sui generis*.[6] In the infinite series of monads, higher beings stand above man, perhaps also on other stars.[7] Beneath man stand the animal and the plants in an infinite series of monads.[8] They are much simpler beings, much simpler monads than man. They have only *perceptio* and lack the *apperceptio* of man and with it the knowledge of the eternal truths.[9] Though there are many simpler beings than man, they are all alike living beings. As living beings they are in principle similar to what I myself am, as living beings they are bound up with man, and therefore with me, through the basic characteristics of all monads, *perceptio* and *appetitus*.[10] The world of monads contains ever simpler monads in an endless series. How far this really goes, and how Leibniz imagines it to appear, this is not easy to say. Supposedly there are no monads which would be the simplest and the most primitive; supposedly there is behind every monad, however simple, one still simpler. Hegel seems to interpret this to mean that Leibniz regarded crystals, salts, and the like, as monads.[11] It seems to me, however, that Leibniz restricts the concept of monads to living things. In that case the crystals must either be regarded as something living or they would not be monads, and would belong rather to the phenomenal realm of material nature.

On the basis of the theory of monads Leibniz can formulate his fundamental determination of being more sharply. Towards the end of his life, in 1716, he writes to Dagnicourt: '*Les véritables substances ne sont que les substances simples ou ce que j'appelle*

Monades. Et je crois qu'il n'y a que de monades dans la nature, le rest n'étant que les phénomènes qui en résultent.'[12]

This theory of being recognizes only monads and phenomena; its main problem is the definition of phenomena. What does the concept of phenomena include and how do we define the mode of being proper to the phenomena? All relations belong to the phenomena. Leibniz also subsumes the categories of quality and quantity under the category of relation, first the secondary qualities and, after some hesitation, also the primary qualities.[13] Space and time also belong to the phenomenal realm.[14] Here too belong the concepts and laws of arithmetic, geometry and physics; these are all relations and systems of relations.

The ontological definition is based on a strict disjunction. The monad is the *ens reale*, the phenomenon is the *ens mentale*. The explicit formulation is found in a letter to des Bosses: '. . . *sed relationem communem utrique esse rem mere mentalem* . . .'[15] But this reference of all relations and hence all phenomena to thinking is found in many other place as well: for example, in the *Nouveaux Essais*.[16] This theory of being is in the strict sense a dichotomy, and in a certain respect also a two-worlds theory. In such a two-worlds theory Leibniz finds his particular agreement with Plato.[17] But the agreement does not go nearly so far as Leibniz himself may have thought. The actual, the underlying reality which supports the phenomenal being, is for Plato the Ideas, for Leibniz the monads, that is, individual beings. This is a difference that appears greater to me than it did to Leibniz himself.

This dichotomy in his theory of being, so closely connected to a two-worlds theory, Leibniz later modifies by introducing intermediate steps.[18] But this late modification was not completely carried out and it is, for that reason, not easy to follow. The basis for the modification was no doubt the ever increasing importance which Leibniz attached to the *vis activa*, what we today call energy.[19] The *vis activa*, or energy, does not really fit into a dichotomized theory of being. It is certainly not a monad. But Leibniz rightly hesitated to relegate it to the phenomenal sphere. Leibniz attempted a solution by further expanding the concept of a *phenomenon bene fundatum*.[20] The consistent development of this modification would have to lead to a continuous series of infinitely many modes of being. And there are hints of this conclusion. Leibniz had always been inclined toward continuity. The reality of the monads is in an infinitely graduated and continuous series. But it must be left undecided whether such an extreme view of infinitely many modes of being is intrinsically possible and whether Leibniz himself really intended to assert the view.

15. KANT

For us, the most important feature of the Kantian theory of being is the distinction between appearance and thing-in-itself, between the phenomenon and the noumenon, between the *mundus sensibilis* and the *mundus intelligibilis*. This distinction is bound up with all manner of historical and systematic difficulties of interpretation. One would expect that the historical presuppositions of this distinction lie in Plato. But instead it seems that no direct confrontation of the Platonic texts occurred, but rather a confrontation with the texts of Leibniz. The relationship to Leibniz becomes particularly clear when Kant treats of the phenomenality of space and time. But it must be borne in mind that Leibniz himself refers explicitly to Plato and that Kant perhaps regarded that relation as sufficient.

At the end of the Transcendental Analytic of the *Critique of Pure Reason* Kant treats the problem of the distinction of being. The third major section of the second book bears the title: 'On the Ground of the Distinction of all Objects in General into Phenomena and Noumena'. In this investigation Kant distinguishes between a noumenon in the negative sense and a noumenon in the positive sense:

'If by "noumenon" we mean a thing so far as it is *not an object of our sensible intuition*, and so abstract from our mode of intuiting it, this is a noumenon in the *negative* sense of the term. But if we understand by it an object of a *non-sensible intuition*, we thereby presuppose a special mode of intuition, namely, the intellectual, which is not that which we possess, and of which we cannot comprehend even the possibility. This would be "noumenon" in the *positive* sense of the term.'[1]

In this definition, all the emphasis is laid on the noumenon in the negative sense. One of the most fundamental questions in the interpretation of Kant's philosophy is whether Kant only makes use of the noumenon in the negative sense throughout his philosophy or whether he has progressed to the noumenon in the positive sense. In the *Critique of Practical Reason* we find an explicit investigation of this point. It constitutes the second section of Book I, Chapter 1 of the Analytic of Pure Practical Reason and bears the title: 'Of the Right of Pure Reason to an Extension in its Practical Use which Is Not Possible to It in Its Speculative Use'. Here Kant explains that the fundamental results of the *Critique of Pure Reason* depend on the distinction between thing-in-itself and appearance. He puts the problem of causality in the foreground. It is the result of the Transcendental Analytic that causality can only be applied to appearances and that its validity *a priori* can only be established for appearances. Thus Kant can ask the question: 'But how lies it with reference to the application of this category of causality . . . to things which are not objects of possible experience but lie beyond its boundaries?'[2] This question leads to the noumenon[3] and in particular to the *causa noumenon*.[4] Can such a *causa noumenon*, a noumenon in the positive sense, be allowed? Kant answers affirmatively and says in conclusion about the concept of an empirically unconditioned causality:

'Even though I have no intuition which would determine its objective theoretical reality, it nevertheless has a real application exhibited *in concreto* in intentions or maxims; that is, its practical reality can be pointed out. All this is sufficient to justify the concept even with reference to noumena.'[5]

Kant establishes two connecting links to the treatment of the same theme in the *Critique of Pure Reason*. First he says that the *Critique of Pure Reason* has established the possibility of the noumenon, that is the noumenon in the positive sense, by showing that this concept is free of contradictions, and therefore possible.[6] Secondly, the treatment of the noumenon in the *Critique of Practical Reason* does not go beyond such a concept of possibility.[7] We might ask in this connexion whether the use of the concept of the noumenon in the Dialectic, especially in the solution of the fourth antinomy, does not already contain an extension, as is explicitly admitted in the *Critique of Practical Reason*.[8]

The distinction between thing-in-itself and appearance, between noumenon and phenomenon is one of the chief difficulties in the interpretation of Kant. Soon after the appearance of the *Critique of Pure Reason* Jacobi pointed out the difficulty when he said: '. . . that *without* this presupposition I cannot get into the system, and *with* it I cannot remain in the system.'[9] We will discuss in detail the difficulties of the distinction between appearance and thing-in-itself in the eleventh chapter; we will hope to show that we are dealing with an authentic Kantian doctrine, which is capable of a reasonable interpretation.

16. NICOLAI HARTMANN

In the return of German philosophy to ontology, Nicolai Hartmann has a great importance. Hartmann comes from the Marburg school of neo-Kantianism, which was marked by an extreme idealism. His own formulation of realism must be understood against the background of his polemical stance against this extreme idealism.

The basic position is first given in the *Grundzüge einer Metaphysik der Erkenntnis*.[1] Some fifteen years later Hartmann published a systematic ontology in several volumes. The first volume, appearing in 1935, bears the title: *Zur Grundlegung der Ontologie*.[2] In 1938 followed the presentation of the problems of modality under the title: *Möglichkeit und Wirklichkeit*.[3] Finally, there appeared in 1940 the third volume, an outline of the general theory of the categories under the title: *Der Aufbau der realen Welt*.[4]

The theory of being is based on the distinction between real and ideal being. The thematic treatment of real being is found in the third part of the *Grundlegung* under the title, '*Die Gegebenheit des realen Seins*'.[5] The treatment of ideal being follows in the fourth part under the title, '*Problem und Stellung des idealen Seins*'.[6]

Real being is always individual being. Hartmann says explicitly: 'Now it is clear that what "is present" and in its presence has real existence "is" in a sense which is different from and truer than that which is not present'.[7] To that extent Hartmann takes over the basic Aristotelian position. The individual is being in the true sense. But one must not restrict being as such to individual beings, as Aristotle himself does not. Such a restriction leads to the mistake of nominalism which denies any being to the general as a non-individual being.[8] In the realm of ideal being Hartmann distinguishes four regions, the mathematical, the logical, essences and values.[9]

The distinction between real and ideal being results from categorical analysis. Real and ideal being are determined through different categories in different ways, this is seen most clearly in the modal determinations, but can also be seen in the true categories.[10] Here Hartmann rightly claims a fundamental philosophical achievement through his explicit clarification of a method which has always been used.[11]

Two questions arise from this distinction of being. Firstly, how is the relation between real and idea being to be determined? Secondly, what about the knowledge of real and ideal being? The relation between real and ideal being is determined first of all by the fact that the two modes of being overlap. There is ideal being which ranges over real being. Hartmann points to mathematical being as an example.[12] Conversely there is real being, which is not determined through ideal being, and which therefore ranges over ideal being.[13] On the whole one gets the impression that for Hartmann real being represents the more authentic being and that ideal being is regarded in some imprecise sense as the weaker mode of being.[14]

Epistemologically, the same strict realism holds good for both modes of being, the real as well as the ideal being. 'Being is independent of being-known.'[15] Hartmann often emphasizes the point that this basic thesis holds for both real and ideal being. And yet one might suppose that this strict formulation of realism is not the happiest aspect of Hartmann's ontology. The formulation seems understandable as a reaction to the extreme idealism of the Marburg School. But one misses any aporematic element in this dogmatic formulation. It might possibly have been a great gain for Hartmann's ontology if he had leavened the strict dogmatic of his thesis of realism through aporematic elements.[16]

17. HEIDEGGER

For our consideration of Heidegger's theory of being we will draw primarily on his main work, *Being and Time*, which appeared in 1926. Only the first half has so far appeared. Heidegger presents therein a sketch of the whole work. According to the sketch the second part would deal with the 'Basic Features of a Phenomenological Destruction of the History of Ontology, with the Problematic of Temporality as Our Clue'. This second half was to be divided into three sections containing confrontations with Kant, Descartes and Aristotle.[1] Presumably the work appearing in 1929 under the title *Kant and the Problem of Metaphysics* may be regarded as in some sense the first of the promised sections, the promised confrontations with Descartes and Aristotle are still lacking. Still, certain indications in the published first half show the direction which his planned interpretation of Descartes might take.[2]

Being and Time represents one of the most important steps in the revived interest in ontology among German philosophers. Heidegger himself understands this work as a fundamental ontology.[3] Nevertheless it is almost impossible to determine clearly what theory of being underlies this work. The term '*Seinsentwurf*' (theory of being; literally, projection of being) stems from this work[4]; and yet the theory of being which underlies this work remains largely obscure.

The obscurity stems in good measure from the fact that the reflection on method in this book is quite unsatisfactory. The method is phenomenological and Heidegger himself says: 'With the question of the meaning of Being, our investigation comes up against the fundamental question of philosophy. This is one that must be treated *phenomenologically*.'[5] The relation to Husserl's phenomenological method is therefore asserted and adhered to. But it becomes clear in the course of the investigations as well as in the particular reflection on method in par. 7 that Heidegger does not at all adopt the phenomenological method as Husserl himself had treated it.[6] But if the phenomenological method is here understood in some other sense, what is that sense? Heidegger says, 'Thus the term "phenomenology" expresses a maxim which can be formulated as "to the things themselves!" '[7] This formulation is thoroughly unsatisfactory and the subsequent analyses of the concept of phenomenon, the concept of *logos*, and the preliminary conception of phenomenology do not satisfy one's questions about method.[8] Heidegger seems to sense this himself, for in referring to the maxim: 'to the things themselves!', he grants that it could be regarded as completely obvious.[9] But this explanation also fails to satisfy. The deep uneasiness remains that Heidegger's turn towards *Dasein*, care, and temporality, for example, is regarded as a turn towards 'the things themselves'.

Nor does any clarity on the methodological problem emerge in the course of the investigations. Heidegger emphatically attacks the concept of eternal truths and says 'That there are "eternal truths" will not be adequately proved until someone has succeeded in demonstrating that Dasein has been and will be for all eternity. As long as such a proof is still outstanding, this principle remains a fanciful contention which does not gain in legitimacy from having philosophers commonly "believe" it.'[10] And shortly before this passage Heidegger says by way of example: 'Before Newton's laws were discovered, they were not "true"; it does not follow that they were false, or even that they would become false if ontically no discoveredness were any longer possible'.[11] This thesis is advanced with great emphasis and yet it remains only a negative thesis. One would like to know what positive thesis it implies. In what sense, one would like to ask, are Newton's laws tied to their discovery by Newton?

This question becomes the more obvious since it can also be raised in relation to Heidegger's assertions about the being of *Dasein*. Heidegger's assertions about the being of *Dasein* are, according to their sense, according to their methodological importance, and according to Heidegger's explicit claim, *a priori* and essential assertions. An example of such an assertion is the definition of the being of Dasein as care.[12] Heidegger says expressly that being-in-the-world is essentially care,[13] and he also emphasizes explicitly the *a priori* character of this definition.[14] If the truth of Newton's laws depends on their discovery by Newton, must not the truth of this existential-*a priori* assertion also depend on its discovery by Heidegger? But in what sense this dependency should be understood, and how such a dependency can be squared with its apriority—on these points one finds no precise information in *Being and Time*.

With respect to the question posed by our investigation then, Heidegger's book remains primarily a *philosophia negativa*. Heidegger expresses this point himself when he develops the historical task essentially as the task of destroying the history of philosophy,[15] and when he assigns to the second half of the work (not yet published) the task of destroying the history of ontology. If one turns this line of thought into a somewhat more positive form, one comes to a formulation which Heidegger chooses in his discussion of Descartes, one comes to a hermeneutic discussion.[16]

The importance of this hermeneutic is great and Heidegger rightly relates it to Plato and Aristotle. The essential determinations here are also negative but this might well lie in the problems themselves.

The negativity is seen first in the determination of man. Man is not a thing, not a substance.[17] Here Heidegger refers to Husserl[18] and Scheler[19] and this provides important help in understanding his meaning.

In general, the central thesis affirms: 'Being is not an entity'.[20]

Heidegger would have provided considerable assistance to the questioning reader if he had also here made explicit references to antecedent philosophy. In a certain sense he does provide this when he reminds us of Kant's thesis: 'Being is not a real predicate'.[21] But a further reference to Aristotle would also have been very helpful. One might suppose that the basic thesis: 'Being is not an entity' would be translated into Aristotle's conceptual language as: being is not *ousia*. Then it would correspond to the doctrine of Aristotle, when the latter says, 'If, then, no universal can be a substance, as has been said in our discussion of substance and being, and if being itself cannot be a substance in the sense of a one apart from the many . . .'[22] If this supposition is correct the thesis: 'Being is not an entity' would gain considerably in clarity through the reference to Aristotle.

18. WHITEHEAD

The metaphysics of Whitehead must be described as one of the most important events in the philosophy of our century. It is difficult to understand and the struggle over its interpretation has barely begun. The course of his life was quite deliberate. Whitehead always lived under strong philosophical impulses. Yet he devoted his early years and his maturity essentially to physics, mathematics and logic. In collaboration with Bertrand Russell, Whitehead developed the *Principia Mathematica*, the classic work on logic and the foundations of mathematics.[1] In his later years Whitehead turned entirely to philosophy. Now metaphysics, seen from the standpoint of Plato, became the centre of his thinking.

The very course of his life already affords an important decision for the understanding of metaphysics and the understanding of Plato. One often hears the thesis that the modern sciences, in particular, modern mathematics and modern logic, have definitively shown the impossiblity of metaphysics and the philosophy of Plato. Many may perhaps make this claim and perhaps in very lively style. But there can be no assertion that the thesis has been demonstrated or that it is generally recognized. The reference to

Whitehead suffices in order to recognize the insufficiency of the thesis, and on the German scene, one obviously thinks of Heinrich Scholz who always understood himself as a committed Platonist.[2] I have always marvelled at the levity, not to say irresponsibility, with which especially logicians and theoretical scientists of our time continually proclaim their own standpoints as demonstrated and generally recognized. One might have supposed that it would especially suit logicians and theoretical scientists to exercise caution and discretion in these questions.

The fundamental distinction in Whitehead's philosophy, from our point of view, is the distinction between actual entity and eternal object.[3] The eternal object corresponds to Plato's Idea, the actual entity to Aristotle's individual being. Considering first the actual entity, we find that Whitehead often emphasizes the relation to the basic conception of Aristotle's thought and to its further development by Leibniz. The living individual being in Aristotle's sense is obviously the prototype of the actual entity.[4] This applies also to the development of Aristotle's basic conception in Leibniz' doctrine of monads.[5]

In agreement with Aristotle and Leibniz, Whitehead defines the actual entity as a being of infinitely great complexity,[6] as a being which is in continual movement,[7] and as a being which is related in its movement to every other being.[8] Whitehead uses the term process to designate this idea, and he therefore says that the actual entity is not a thing, but a process.[9] This puts Whitehead into marked opposition to Descartes, as much to Descartes' concept of *res extensa* as to his concept of *res cogitans*. *Res extensa* is not actual being but an ideal concept, though one which is usable in many ways.[10] *Res cogitans*, the individual thinking being, is of course actual, but it is not a *res*, not a substance, not a thing.[11] In this ontological discussion with Descartes there is revealed a relation between Whitehead and Heidegger, not much noticed to date. It shows up not only in the polemic against Descartes but also in many positive aspects, in particular in the valuation of time. This substantive relation is all the more remarkable since neither author seems to have been aware, so far as we know, of the other.

The relation with Plato shows up in the theory of eternal objects, which Whitehead often identifies with the Ideas. To the eternal objects belong naturally all mathematical objects, but also qualities and among them also the secondary qualities, such as colour.[12]

In this theory of being the question arises about the relation between the eternal object and the actual entity, the old question about the relation between Idea and individual thing. In many places Whitehead speaks of two realms, alluding obviously to Plato's expression of two modes of being. For example, he says: 'It is the foundation of the metaphysical position which I am maintaining that the understanding of actuality requires a reference to ideality. The two realms are intrinsically inherent in the total metaphysical situation.'[13]

In determining the being of these two realms Whitehead opts for the Aristotelian basic thesis: '. . . the general Aristotelian principle . . . that, apart from things that are actual, there is nothing—nothing either in fact or in efficacy.'[14]

If in this sense the being of actual entities, and that means, in the terminology of this book, the being of individual things, represents true being, what is the being of the eternal objects? In a few places one finds Whitehead's attempt to distinguish the two modes of being through actuality and potentiality: '. . . the Type of Actuality, and the Type of Pure Potentiality. These types require each other, namely Actuality is the exemplification of Potentiality, and Potentiality is the characterization of Actuality, either in fact or in concept.'[15] Ivor Leclerc has investigated the problem that arises here;[16] one gets the impression from him that Whitehead himself did not arrive at a final solution. This has contributed essentially to the conviction underlying this book, that apodictic solutions cannot be achieved in the fundamental ontological problems.

CHAPTER III

INDIVIDUAL BEING
AND ITS DETERMINATIONS

19. SUBSTANCE

In modern times the concept of substance has frequently been attacked. Is the concept really quite useless? Already Locke claims this.[1] But Leibniz replied that such scepticism went too far and that the term substance should be retained.[2] In fact, it depends on the meaning one wants to give to the term 'substance', and for a carefully considered meaning it seems advisable not to break unnecessarily with usage in the history of philosophy.

We encounter first a very abstract meaning of substance, particularly developed in the Aristotelian-Scholastic philosophy. We can for the moment put aside the question whether it corresponds to the intention of Aristotle. The starting point of the Aristotelian-Scholastic theory of substance is the question about the relation between substance and accident. The relation is defined from the side of substance as a subsisting and from the side of accident as an inhering.[3] In spite of the abstract formulation this view rests on very pictorial representations. A stone is regarded as a substance, which supports warmth, and warmth is regarded as an accident which is supported by the stone. Colour is understood in a similar way. A coloured body is a substance, which supports colour. The colour is an accident supported by this body. This representation is then generalized into the concept of the *ultimum subsistens*, the *ultimum substratum*. The question which now arises, how the distinction between substance

66

and accident is to be understood, will be discussed in the following paragraphs. Here we will consider the concept of substance as such.

It is the question whether this concept of *ultimum subsistens* still has a definite content or whether it is a completely empty concept, which first receives content and meaning through a concretization in some direction. Most philosophers who have discussed the problem seem to have taken the second alternative; this seems to have been Aristotle's meaning too.

Such a concretization is afforded, for example, by Descartes. The true definition of substance for him is not the *ultimum subsistens*, but the *esse a se*.[4] Of course this applies strictly, as we saw, only to God. The *substantia creata* is an *ens a se* in the restricted sense that it requires nothing other than the divine assistance. On the contrary, accident—Descartes often says *'modus'*—is a being which fundamentally requires a substance for its being. Although this definition of substance as the *ens a se* is seen from the standpoint of the substance-accident relation, an expansion of the concept of *ultimum subsistens* has also been introduced.

That the abstract concept of substance as the *ultimum subsistens* is empty and that it needs a concretization in order to be capable of any application was formally expressed by Kant. His doctrine of the Schematism, generally regarded as the most difficult and obscure part of the *Critique of Pure Reason*, is the elaboration of this thought. In Kant's interpretation the categories as such are empty, an additional temporal determination is necessary before they can be applied. This means that, for substance, the concept of *ultimum subsistens* as such is empty, the concepts of *constans* and *perdurabile* must be added. The concept of substance becomes usable only by being schematized. Kant expressly says:

'Substance, for instance, when the sensible determination of permanence is omitted, would mean simply a something which can be thought only as subject, never as a predicate of something else. Such a representation I can put to no use, for it tells me nothing as to the nature of that which is thus to be viewed as a primary subject.'[5]

If the schematizing first obtains a usable meaning for the category of substance through the determination of permanence, it also restricts the schematized category to appearances and thus leads to the concept of a *substantia phaenomenon*.[6]

This Kantian doctrine of schematized substance removes from the category much of its old meaning. To begin with, substance has lost the preferential status assigned to it by Aristotle. It is no longer the first category and it no longer renders the primary meaning of being. This point is expressed in the fact that in Kant's Table of Categories substance is subsumed under the category-group of relation.[7] In the Kantian Table of Categories there is no pre-eminent category in the true sense. One can speak in a certain sense of the primacy of unity, but the unity thus singled out is not the category of unity, it is the original synthetic unity of apperception,[8] which Kant also calls the transcendental unity of self-consciousness.[9]

From the careful development of the Kantian doctrine of substance a second restriction emerges. Kant determines the schematized substance through the concept of permanence. Now material substance in the Cartesian concept of *res extensa* is something permanent, but not everything permanent is for that reason a material substance. The Kantian determination requires only a permanence of some kind, it requires only, to single out one definite realm, that a constant quantity must underlie the physical understanding of the world. About the particular form of this constant quantity Kant says nothing. Kant himself already considered the possibility that the concept of energy, energy taken as a constant quantity in the world, would satisfy the requirement of substance.[10] From this point of view the Kantian concept of substance would be considerably removed from the Cartesian, but it would continue to preserve the relation with the definitions of Aristotle and Leibniz.

As we have seen, Aristotle gives in the *Metaphysics* an analysis of the meaning of the term '*ousia*'.[11] He works out two main meanings, which in other places he distinguishes as primary and secondary *ousia*.[12] Primary *ousia* designates individuals, secondary *ousia* designates the general. I hold fast to the claim that individual being is true *ousia*.

First we ought to clarify the compass of everything that falls under primary *ousia*.[13] We can characterize as individual beings everything that falls under the Aristotelian concept of primary substance, and in Aristotle's sense they could also be characterized as living beings.

Among the more detailed determinations of primary substance we find mentioned already in the analysis of meaning in the *Metaphysics* the determination which became dominant in the Aristotelian-Thomistic tradition, *ultimum subsistens*. Aristotle speaks there of the ultimate substratum, which is no longer predicated of anything else.[14]

Next follows the further determination of the enduring character of substance as against the changing character of accident, the same determination which Kant took over as the concept of permanence in the concept of schematized substance. Aristotle notes this determination in an important passage of the *Metaphysics*: substance remains, every change refers to its modifications.[15]

The third determination, which seems the most important to me, Aristotle treats in the *Physics*. First he distinguishes natural being from everything which has another origin, for example, artifacts made by men. The compass is already familiar to us: animals, their organic parts, plants and the elements. Aristotle then gives the general determination: 'All the things mentioned present a feature in which they differ from things which are *not* constituted by nature. Each of them has *within itself* a principle of motion and of stationariness.'[16] The concept of motion is taken very broadly here to include not only change of place but also growth and decay and qualitative changes. Aristotle then says once again that products of art, he names as examples a bed and a coat, have as such no principle of motion. Aristotle concludes these determinations by saying expressly, all these things are *ousia*.[17]

It is interesting to notice that in this definition the concept of cause is applied to the end of a motion as well as to its beginning This is of course the Greek outlook. Everything living has its own size which belongs among its essential attributes. When it has achieved its size it will grow no more. Thus the Greek state has a definite size and when it has reached that size it should not strive for a further enlargement.

Aristotle's doctrine of elements gives a pregnant example of this Greek outlook. Each element has its own place. The earth belongs in the middle of the cosmos, water follows it, then air, then fire. Each element has within it an impulse towards its natural place. Once it has reached that place, it remains there at rest.[18] But Aristotle's determination emphasizes the beginning of motion. In this respect his determination is related to that of Plato in the *Sophist*[19] and both lead to the fundamental determination of spontaneity.

Leibniz's concept of substance must also be understood in terms of the dynamic conception here being developed. That Leibniz should name substance as an example for the assertion that metaphysics works with obscure and poorly-defined concepts[20] is quite understandable. But, as we have seen, Leibniz hangs on to the concept of substance, both in his discussion of Descartes[21] and in his discussion of Locke.[22]

In Leibniz too we find the three Aristotelian definitions of substance. Leibniz first describes substance as *ultimum subjectum*.[23] He also emphasizes that, as against the changing accidents, substance represents the permanent.[24] Finally, he considers substance in a third definition as that which has power. He presented this definition in a generally accessible form in an essay appearing in the *Acta Eruditorum*.[25] In a second essay, appearing in the same journal in 1698, four years later, he attempted to express the same point more precisely: '*quibus addi potest, quod alibi a me explicatum est, et si nondum fortasse satis perceptum omnibus, ipsam rerum substantiam in agendi patiendique vi consistere.*'[26] This becomes the true definition of substance and thus Leibniz can say in the *Theodicy*, '*Ce que n'agit point, ne mérite point le nom de substance.*'[27]

According to the doctrine of monads, only the monad is a substance. Leibniz establishes this definition immediately in the first paragraph of the *Monadology*,[28] and the definition means that only the individual, the living individual being, is a substance.[29]

In these definitions Leibniz is closely related to Plato and Aristotle. The relation to Plato was stressed by Leibniz himself.[30] He was perhaps thinking of the definitions in the *Sophist*. There Plato had defined being as *dynamis*[31], and there he specifically laid down the requirement that all true being must be living.[32] That the fundamental definitions of the doctrine of monads are closely related to Aristotle is obvious.

On the basis of these definitions Leibniz registers a sharp opposition to Descartes' theory of substance, and we may well suppose that the decisive insights of the doctrine of monads grew out of his confrontation with Descartes. Leibniz's basic definitions of substance, conceived in the spirit of Plato and Aristotle, do not allow the *res extensa*, mere extended matter, to be considered a substance. When Descartes defined *res extensa* as substance he misunderstood the concept of substance and created many difficulties: '*quorum causa fuit non intellecta substantiae natura in universum.*'[33]

When Descartes understands *res extensa* as substance, two alternatives are presented. One can insist that a false concept of substance is being used and attempt to rectify the mistake. This is the path Leibniz and Kant took. One can also surrender the concept to its Cartesian employment and renounce substance entirely. To some extent Heidegger has taken this path, and Whitehead has taken it quite deliberately.

In the confrontation with Descartes, Heidegger first gives a careful analysis of the text. Heidegger is not primarily concerned with the correct or false use of the concept of substance; he raises the question historically. Descartes applied the traditional determinations of ontology to modern mathematical physics and its transcendental foundations.[34] This historical interpretation seems at first to be illuminating but its correctness must nevertheless remain doubtful. The analysis of the Cartesian text is supposed to clarify the analysis of the question as such and the analysis of the question as to being, in particular. Where must I look when I ask, what is being? We have tried to make it clear that Aristotle looks to the living when he asks about being. Descartes looks to material bodies, more exactly, he looks also to material bodies and one sees from the result how much that result is already determined by the realm within which the question is raised. If from the outset I consider the material body in the sense of physics as true being, I have introduced a pre-judgement fraught with consequences. Implicit in Descartes' initial orientation, as Heidegger shows, is a prejudgement about the faculty through which true being becomes accessible: '. . . the only genuine access to this being lies in knowing (*intellectio*), in the sense of the kind of knowing we get in mathematics and physics.'[35] In this analysis the Cartesian theory appears as the fundamental idea of the modern period, though at the same time as the fundamental mistake in so far as the possibilities of mathematico-physical knowledge have been raised in the modern period to the highest criterion of both knowledge and being. This makes it understandable that Heidegger for the most part avoids the concept of substance so interpreted.

If we ask positively, what is true being for Heidegger in *Being and Time*, we will do well to consider the question and the answer of this work in their relation to Plato and Aristotle. We may regard a proposition from the beginning of the positive interpretation as setting the theme: 'We are ourselves the entities to be analysed.'[36] This is definitely not a subjectivism, on the contrary, being-with others is constitutive of our being, according to this work. But the being of others is primarily understood from one's own point of view. I must look to myself when I ask the question about the meaning of being. I am true being and everything which is like me is true being. This gives another indication of why Heidegger avoids the term substance. I am not a thing, I am not a substance, these negative formulations seem understandable. The positive formulation which Heidegger prefers is also understandable: I am *Dasein*.[37] In spite of all the polemic against previous ontology, and that means against Plato, Aristotle,

Leibniz and Kant, and in spite of all the destruction of traditional ontology, Heidegger's positive formulation implies an agreement with the tradition on the basic thesis that individual living beings and primarily the self represent true being.

Whitehead too puts up considerable resistance to the concept of substance which is also based on his resistance to Descartes' use of the term. Whitehead understands the Cartesian metaphysics as a bifurcation[38] of being, which he regards as a basic error. Whitehead seeks a confrontation with Descartes not so much in an analysis of the ontological foundations, as Heidegger does, but rather in an analysis of his basic orientation in physics. The result is the same. The objects of physics together with the related faculties of knowing were falsely posited as absolutes, Whitehead claims. Whitehead is convinced that the basic mistake of scientific materialism was also Descartes' basic mistake.

Whitehead also assumes that the Cartesian concept of substance is seen from the standpoint of *substantia corporea*. There will then always be the danger that in some later use of the term Descartes' original orientation will shine through. This is also the reason why Whitehead makes practically no use of the term 'substance' and why he usually prefers to put 'actual entity' in its place.

The question must now arise whether we should continue to use the old term 'substance' at all. This concept has led to so many dead ends of thought that it is understandable when Heidegger and Whitehead turn away from it. Nevertheless it seems to me that the attitude of Leibniz deserves to be preferred. As we saw Leibniz too stands in sharp opposition to Descartes on the problem of substance. But he retains substance as such both in his systematic orientation and in his confrontation with Locke.

Prescinding from the question of terminology, one finds common ground among the positions. For Aristotle, for Leibniz, for Kant, for Heidegger and for Whitehead, the individual living being is the true being. In the development of this line of thought the point that was made at the very beginning emerges with ever greater clarity: that I myself am the true centre of this domain. In a certain sense one can say that Plato already began with that thought. Already in the *Phaedo*, the thinking being, the thinking I, stands in an original relation to the Ideas. In a cautious sense then, one can say that, for all philosophers, living being is true being and that in a development whose lineaments become increasingly clear the I becomes the prototype of the living and thereby the prototype of true being.

20. QUALITY

The ontological question about quality is the question of its reality. The fact that the history of this question consists almost entirely of detours and blind alleys is very instructive for the understanding of the ontological question as such.

How should we understand the reality of a quality? It seems obvious to ask whether a mythological understanding of the world or a naïve modern understanding of the world has not already produced definite modes of representation. And looking at beauty and anger, for example, one would have to answer yes. In fairy tales when the good fairy lays the gift of beauty in the cradle of the newborn girl, this is not to be taken as a mere metaphor. Beauty is imagined as something which as such can be given as an additional gift. Such a representation is clearly evident in Homer. In the *Odyssey* Athena bathes Penelope's face with ambrosian beauty 'like that, with which Cythera bathes herself'.[1] The interpreters differ on the meaning of this passage but I believe that Passow is right when he says: 'Homer regards beauty as something bodily, subsisting in its own right, like a garment, with which the gods can dress or undress men.'[2]

In my opinion, anger can also be represented in a similar way both in folk interpretations and in the mythological understanding of the world. Many forms of expression support this opinion: anger seized him, anger penetrated him, anger left him. These expressions are not mere metaphors. They are to be taken literally. We must assume that anger is here imagined as a demon or a goblin, which can enter into men and then leave them again. For that reason the man possessed by anger no longer appears to be himself in the true sense.

What happens to these images in philosophical reflection? For Plato the theory of Ideas originally and in its primary scope designates qualities understood in a narrower or a wider sense. This is doubtless true of the great trinity of Ideas: the beautiful, the good, the just. It is also true of the logico-mathematical Ideas, as can be readily seen in Plato's example of equality. By contrast the Ideas of generic concepts, for example the Idea of man, only later claim Plato's attention. Thus the problem of the hypostasis of Ideas and the problem of the *chorismos* between Ideas and sensible things is focused primarily on qualities. There can be no doubt that in the *Phaedo* beauty is presented as a subsistent reality. But how shall we understand this quality of being-beautiful in a man, a horse and a garment? This raises the question of participation, in this case the participation of beautiful things in the Idea of beauty. But as we have already seen, we are thereby led into the aporias of the theory of Ideas, which must still be discussed in detail. However the reality of individual qualities, say the beauty of this beautiful horse, is represented, Plato has no doubt about the reality of the quality itself, the Idea of beauty.

The issue is more complicated in Aristotle. Does Aristotle regard a quality as an independent reality? If so, what does Aristotle mean by an independent reality in this case? Among the categories of Aristotle is numbered the category of *habitus*,[3] and as examples of it he lists being-clothed,[4] being-shod,[5] and being-armed.[6] The inclusion of such conditions among the categories and also among the accidents is curious. Certainly being-armed is not only the possession of weapons but also a condition of security. In the same way being-shod and being-clothed means not only the possession of shoes and clothes but also a condition. But the condition does rest on the possession of definite things like weapons, shoes or clothes. If one could infer from the category of *habitus* back to the other accidental categories, being-beautiful would then be a possession of beauty just as being-armed is a possession of weapons. These questions were not pursued. It would seem that Aristotle did not explicitly formulate such a thesis of reality in the strict sense. On the other hand, it is not impossible that such a representation, closely paralleling the folk intuition, could have played a role in Aristotle's thinking.

In the Scholasticism of the Middle Ages each category was regarded by the realists as a *res*.[7] Scholastics of all persuasions were in agreement that this designation should hold for substance; *substantia prima*, the individual being, is a *res*. The differences among them begin with the question whether all the other categories are to be understood as *res*. But this depends naturally on the question of what meaning that thesis should have, that every category represents a *res*. In what sense then can quality, quantity and relation be regarded as a *res*? Thomas Aquinas understands the *res* of an accidental category as a *res addita*.[8] Ockham extends this to the thesis that the *res* in question must be regarded as a *res realiter distincta*.

The decision on the kind of reality proper to accidents is, in the Middle Ages, bound up with the problem of transubstantiation. It was a requirement for any metaphysics in that period to give an ontological account of transubstantiation. All the thinkers of the period are bound by the dogma of transubstantiation, but the dogma does not itself lay down any particular ontological interpretation. The given element in the dogma is the transformation of the substance of bread and wine into the substance of the flesh and blood of Christ and also the phenomenal fact that the appearance of the accidents of bread and wine remain unchanged. The abstract ontological possibility of letting the accidents of bread and wine inhere in the substance of the body and blood of Christ is scarcely acceptable theologically. The supposition that the accidents of bread and wine would continue to inhere in the substances of bread and wine is difficult to reconcile with the dogma. There remains then only the possibility that the accidents of bread and wine exist without any subsisting substances. And this can be conceived in several ways. One could suppose that all individual accidents without exception have a subsistent existence. One could suppose that certain foundational relations remain intact or are newly created. The doctrine of Aquinas moves in that direction. He assumes that only one accident, quantity, inheres directly in the substance, while all the other accidents in their turn inhere in quantity. This is for Thomas the *quantitas continua*.[9] With respect to transubstantiation this leads to the consequence that only the *quantitas continua* is an *accidens sine subjecto*, while for all other accidents the normal inherence in the *quantitas continua* remains intact. The existence of this *accidens sine subjecto* can be conceived in different ways. One can suppose that such an *accidens sine subjecto* receives in the transubstantiation the character of a subsisting substance through divine intervention. But one can also suppose that such an *accidens sine subjecto* simply exists as such. The reflections of the Scholastics move in these and in similar directions without any one thinker achieving a definitive solution. In any case with respect to the problem of transubstantiation the Scholastics must lay great stress on the reality of all accidents or at least on the reality of one. This reality must be great enough to permit accidents to exist without substance either in general or through divine intervention or, again, great enough to permit accidents to acquire the subsistence character of substance through divine intervention.

This problematic must be borne in mind when Thomas determines every category as *res*[10] and when he further develops the meaning of *res* through the concept of *res addita*.[11] But since Thomas undoubtedly defines some relations as *relationes rationis*, his position must be regarded as qualified. As far as I can see, Thomas did not achieve a final and definitive solution.

If I see the matter correctly, Ockham was the first to pose the problem as a theme. He is explicitly concerned with the question of what it means to define an *accidens* as a *res*. But, as we will see, Ockham broadens the problem considerably. Ockham refuses the *res*-character for almost all accidents, recognizing it only for certain qualities.[12] These allow him to interpret the transubstantiation, a possibility he would lose if he rejected the *res*-character for all accidents. Ockham arrives at the following result: When one defines something as a *res*, one considers it as a *res realiter distincta*. The concept of *res realiter distincta* is equivalent to the concept of the *distinctio realis*. This concept had great importance for Scholastic philosophy but is itself in need of clarification. Ockham comes to the conclusion that the *distinctio realis* was originally asserted of two substances and that this provides the key to its meaning. If one calls an accident *res* then, according to Ockham, one is saying that this accident is different from its substance and from every other real accident through a *distinctio realis*, and this in turn means that it differs from them in the way that one substance differs from another substance.

A metaphysics which defines every accident as a *res* in this sense could be regarded as a theory of building blocks. The substance and all its accidents lie like building blocks on top of and alongside one another. Certain foundational relations may exist, as we for example encountered in Thomas' theory. But at bottom an accident is something that is added to a substance and to other accidents as a new reality. Thomas expressed this very clearly in the concept of *res addita*.

The Scholastic discussion about the meaning of the reality of accidents has great methodological importance. Yet the problem has lost some of its interest because the concept of quality involved has forfeited more and more of its meaning in the development of the natural sciences, in particular in the development of physics. One could of course deny the competence of physics for this question, but then one must not forget that for Aristotle as well as the Scholastics qualities belong essentially in the domain of physics. Aristotle defines the elements through the conceptual pairs warm–cold, dry–moist.[13] Colours too he always relegates to physics.[14] But since warmth and colour have always been the paradigmatic examples for the metaphysical treatment of quality and hence for accidents, metaphysics cannot overlook the fact that these concepts have undergone important changes through the development of physics. The changes were caused by the fact that modern physics begins with atomistic suppositions and that these suppositions have remained the indispensable means for physical thinking. But atomistic suppositions stand against the independent reality of warmth and colour, they leave no room at all for an independent reality of qualities. This is already evident in the theories of Greek atomism. In reality there are only atoms and the void, but the atoms are characterized through their size, their form and their movement.[15] Evidently colour cannot be a real quality on this view.[16] There remains only the question whether at least form, size and movement can be regarded as real qualities or whether they can be regarded as qualities at all.

One can say generally that for Descartes the problem of real qualities has receded to the background. The ancient Atomist concept of the size of atoms appears here as the *extensio* of the *res extensa*. But Descartes does not recognize a real distinction between the *substantia* as substrate and *extensio* as quality, however one wants to define such a real distinction in detail. The *extensio* is rather the direct definition of the *res extensa*, it is what essentially constitutes the *res extensa*.[17] In the atomistic construction of the Cartesian physics every possibility is lacking for interpreting the form and the movement of atoms as real qualities, and still less is there such a possibility for warmth[18] and colour.[19] Newton's view is no different. In his great methodological caution, Newton is prepared for both an atomistic and a continuum theory. For our purposes we will consider Newtonian mechanics in the form of a mechanics of material mass-points.[20] In this mechanics there are mass-points distributed at finite distances in empty space, each one endowed with a definite mass. In a limiting case, the concept of substance is here idealized into the concept of mass-point. In the process the concept of form from the ancient definition of the atom is completely lost, the concept of size is transformed into the concept of the quantity of matter, and it is clear that here mass cannot be a quality really distinct from substance. It is noteworthy that the durability of substance is retained in the constancy of mass. The third determination of atoms, their motion, also acquires a new aspect. In such a system of mass-points there is a whole series of impulses, of which the clearest are velocity, acceleration, and kinetic energy. If one likes, they can be called qualities of the mass-points, but one cannot interpret them as really distinct qualities, not even in the sense of the building-block model. Their relative character forbids that. But also forbidding it is the fact that out of the equations of motion very many and very different such 'properties' can be and have in fact been distinguished.[21]

It is thus understandable that Locke should put into the foreground the already much discussed distinction between primary and secondary qualities.[22] The primary qualities are the ancient atomist determinations: size, form and movement. All other qualities are secondary qualities. Only the primary qualities are real, the secondary qualities are relative to subjective perception. The ancient basic qualities, warmth and colour, belong to the secondary qualities. Thus they can no longer be considered as res. The primary qualities, the ancient atomist determinations, were never accommodated to the res-model; this already holds for size, still more so in the case of form, and completely so in the case of movement.

With this in mind it becomes understandable that one finds hardly any mention of the ancient ontological meaning of qualities in Leibniz and Kant. For Leibniz, the qualities are reduced to determinations of monads, appetitus and perceptio.[23] But the ancient theory of qualities had also never understood these determinations as distinct qualities. Kant retains from the category of quality only the concept of a continuously changing size and with it only a small fragment of the ancient conception of quality.[24]

Whitehead assigns a somewhat greater importance to the problem of quality, but he is obviously not concerned with their reality in the ancient sense, he assigns them rather an ideal existence. Red is for him an eternal object.[25]

Not the least important condition for this development was the fact that nineteenth century physics, through the kinetic theory of gas, had successfully concluded the frequently attempted definition of heat as a form of motion. This made a reality out of one of the ancient dreams of atomism. For our own century one can say that in relation to colour the same result is now within reach. It is thus understandable that for an ontology which wants to take account of the course of the natural sciences, the qualities have lost their ancient importance. This does not mean that physics is not always speaking of properties or that it will not continue to do so. But these are not qualities in the sense of medieval metaphysics, they are not accidents which are really distinct from a substance and from each other. They are relations, and the subject matter of physics therefore belongs, from the standpoint of categorial analysis and ontology, not under quality but under relation.

21. RELATION

The problem of relation is one of the most fundamental for ontology. This becomes clear when one considers how much the standpoints of logic, categorial analysis and ontology are here interrelated. For the same reason the opinions on this problem also confront each other with particular sharpness.

One opinion affirms that all true being is contained in substances and in a certain sense in their qualities and quantities, and that relations represent only an incidental addition. Descartes can be understood to hold this. Whether he speaks of the *res cogitans* or the *res extensa* he speaks always of substance and in a certain sense of its quantities and qualities. For him, relations are obviously an unimportant addition.

On the other side stands the bold thesis that there are only relations. It is possible, as we considered earlier, that this was the position of the Pythagoreans. If one considers numbers to be relations, then the Pythagorean thesis leads into the general thesis: everything is relation. At least for certain domains the thesis has often been advanced. Leibniz considers nature as a network of relations.[1] Kant expressly says that nature consists in nothing other than pure relations.[2]

It is the relations themselves that give this broad scope to the concept of relation and that draw out thereby the great divergence of theories. One only needs to think of kinship relations. They range from the fundamental relation of a man to his parents, his siblings or his children up to the loosest degrees of kinship.

Insight into the importance of the problem of relations was achieved only with difficulty. For Plato, relation has only a slight importance. Even so, of the five highest genera of the

Sophist, at least two, identity and difference, are pure relations.[3] The relation of knowing to the known and the relation of Idea to sensible things lead to the fundamental problems of the theory of Ideas. But Plato lacked the general concept of relation and therefore also lacked any definite term for it. Aristotle was the first to achieve this. He first explicitly coined a new term.[4] The term is formed in contrast to ordinary usage and in this respect is quite fit to stand alongside many other carefully formed terms of philosophy. Relation appears as the fourth category and is given detailed treatment in both the *Organon* and the *Metaphysics.* Yet one has the impression that for Aristotle relation does not have the same importance as substance, quality and quantity.[5] In some places one begins to suspect, as Aristotle himself may well have done, that the investigation of relation requires a deeper treatment than he has provided. We may conclude that Aristotle had an inkling of the possibility of a logic of relations.

The difficulties of the theory of relations arise from the fact that so many aspects are mutually conditioning. With respect to formal logic, it was noticed very early that the logic of Aristotle, both in the theory of propositions and in the syllogistic, is concerned almost exclusively with the relation between substance and quality. The logical thesis that every proposition is defined through its subject and predicate corresponds to the ontological thesis that all being is defined through substance and quality. This seems particularly obvious in Leibniz. With great emphasis he claims that every proposition must have the form: subject, copula, predicate.[6] His theory of analytic judgements is based on this presupposition.[7] But in his own work in logic Leibniz moved considerably beyond this presupposition. He came to see that a logic based on the relation between substance and quality and therefore on the relation between subject and predicate was not sufficient. Instead he saw the possibility and the necessity of a logic of relations,[8] and himself made the first important contributions to it.

New difficulties turn up from the standpoint of categorial analysis. By this term I understand the investigation of the categories with special attention to the question, which categories do or do not occur in a certain domain.[9] If one considers mathematics from this standpoint then, following the Aristotelian schema of four categories, mathematics would be defined through quantity, arithmetic through *quantitas discreta* and geometry through *quantitas continua*. Now Aristotle himself saw that this orientation is too simple. He recognized the importance of the general theory of magnitudes.[10] The general theory of magnitudes obviously goes beyond the distinction between *quantitas discreta* and *quantitas continua* and evidently has a strongly relational character. It becomes understandable then that thinkers should attempt to do away with quantity as an independent category and subsume it under relation. Ockham carried this out at least with respect to ontology,[11] and Leibniz carried it through to completion both in categorial analysis and ontology.[12]

One could say that subsequent developments have confirmed Leibniz in this interpretation and that today nearly all experts share his view. For example, if one considers the arithmetical proposition, $7 + 5 = 12$, one sees that it represents an identity and therefore a relation. The addition that appears in the equation is also a relation. What about the natural numbers appearing in the equation? Plato understood them as Ideas. However one may judge this determination, it does not imply a categorial decision since among the Ideas one also finds obvious relations like identity in the *Phaedo*[13] and difference in the *Sophist*.[14] The modern development of logic and the theory of relations have confirmed the relational character of numbers.[15]

In geometry too, one immediately encounters propositions which obviously have a relational character. For example, the proposition about the point of intersection of the three altitudes of a triangle is obviously a relational theorem. So also the Pythagorean theorem, which asserts an equality and therefore a relation. Thus, summing up, one can say that mathematics is a theory of relations. And in the opinion of most experts, the designation applies to the essence of mathematics.

If one pursues the problem into physics it will be likely from the outset, given the importance of mathematics for physics, that the relational character of mathematics will be carried over into physics. Viewed from the standpoint of a categorial analysis it is significant that physics formulates its results in equations, which are relations. And this confirms the standpoint of Leibniz. Quantity loses its categorial independence and is absorbed, here too, into relations.

The scope of relations, when considered from the standpoint of categorial analysis, makes for sweeping and difficult onto-logical problems. First one must distinguish between real and merely imagined relations. That some relations, at least, rest only on the conceptions of men has always been noted, and thus the distinction between *relatio realis* and *relatio rationis* is quite old. The concepts right and left offer an old example. They obviously depend on someone who characterizes directions as right and left. The example occurs in Plotinus as a case of merely con-ceptual relations,[16] and we find the same example used over and over again.

But there are other relations which evidently do not have this character; kinship relations are the old example, Socrates as the son of Sophroniscus. There is a good point in calling such relations real, and the ontological problem is the question: in what does the reality of relations consist? One is easily led to interpret the reality of these real relations in the same way as the reality of qualities. They would then be understood under the schema substance-quality. This is already suggested by forms of language. In the sentence, 'Socrates is different from Cebes' we have a predicate attributed to a subject and the sentence seems to have the same form as the sentence, 'Socrates is brave'. But in reality the relation is built into the predicate. A more correct form would be, 'Socrates and Cebes are different'. In this form one sees immediately that the substance-quality schema has to run into difficulties. If one is influenced by the first form and if one defines quality as an accident in the strict sense, then rela-tion also becomes an accident in the strict sense, it becomes a *res*. Take difference as an example. If difference is a real relation in the sense of being interpreted as a *res*, then the relation consists in two real accidents: Socrates has the real accident: different from Cebes, and Cebes has the real accident: different from Socrates.

Whether such a determination of real relations as *res* is held by Aristotle seems doubtful, even unlikely. Aristotle would then have had to regard quality as a real accident, and even this cannot be safely determined. The determination which Thomas Aquinas makes of relations is also not fully clear. His interpreters hold different opinions. Some interpreters say that Thomas defined the real relation as an accident in the strict sense.[17] Others contest this, among them such an expert interpreter as Suarez.[18]

An ontological determination of relation as an accident in the strict sense quickly encounters systematic difficulties. For certain relations, at least, it leads to a *regressus in infinitum* and, further, it merely postpones the problem. The emergence of a *regressus in infinitum* is obvious in the case of difference. Consider the predicate in our example 'different from Cebes' as an accident in the strict sense and therefore as a *res*, and then this *res* 'different from Cebes' must be in turn different from the substance Socrates as well as from all other real accidents of Socrates. But this is a new difference which must be in turn a *res*, and so on indefinitely. But even if one could get around the *regressus in infinitum* through some additional determination, the result would be an agglomeration of being very difficult to understand. Socrates would than have not only the real accident 'different from Cebes', but also the real accidents 'different from Simmias', 'different from Crito', and so forth. With respect to every other being and every other real accident of every other being, he would possess the real accident 'different from . . .'. This would be confusing enough. But since the substances and their accidents are conceived to be in an unceasing flux, this unavoidable accumulation of real differences in Socrates must also be found in the same unceasing flux. None of this can be entertained, of course, and Ockham's razor[19] would here perform a useful service.

It may have been such difficulties which have repeatedly prevented thinkers from defining difference as a real relation. The very same difficulties may have led Thomas to define identity[20] and difference[21] in terms of *relatio rationis*. But that definition raises other difficulties. Difference is evidently a relation with a reality unlike that of fancying oneself stronger than some other man. Duns Scotus resolved the problem by applying to relations the threefold articulation of being which arises in connexion with the problem of transcendentals, discussed below. In the ontological sense he distinguishes three kinds of relation: *relatio realis*, *relatio transcendentalis* and *relatio rationis*.[22] All the relations in the domain of the transcendentals he assigns to the transcendental relations, but for Duns Scotus this also includes difference. The real relation he considers an accident in the strict sense.[23] The transcendental relation is a real relation, but does not have the *res*-character of a strict accident.[24] Against this Ockham raised the question whether it was necessary or even possible to distinguish two different kinds of real relations.[25] If the transcendental relation is a real relation, then it is a temptation to regard all real relations as transcendental, and this is what Ockham does.[26]

An interpretation of relations in terms of quality must be regarded from the outset as dubious. Further consideration quickly shows that such an interpretation completely misses the proper character of relations because it misjudges fundamental differences between quality and relation. If one interprets a relation, say the equality between A and B, in such a way that A has the real accident 'equal to B' and B, correspondingly, has the real accident 'equal to A', then nothing has been gained, the problem has only been postponed. Equality presents a connexion and the interpretation is supposed to clarify this connexion. Instead of that one has posited two real accidents, one in A and the other in B, and now one faces the question, how these two are connected. This consideration leads to the insight that relation as such is already a connexion, that is, a unity in a multiplicity. An individual relation is therefore in a certain sense something general. This point is already expressed in everyday speech, as we have seen. One can say naturally: A is equal to B and B is equal to A. But one can also say in everyday parlance: A and B are equal to each other, and this form of expression meets the specific problems of relation much better.

Leibniz saw the problems we have been discussing with a clarity never surpassed. In the fifth letter to Clarke he writes:

'The ratio or proportion between two lines L and M can be represented in three ways: as a ratio of the greater (L) to the smaller (M), as a ratio of the smaller (M) to the greater (L), and lastly as something abstracted from both of them, that is, as the ratio between L and M, without considering which is anterior and which posterior, which is the subject and which the object. . . . In the first way of considering them, L the greater is the subject and in the second M the smaller is the subject for this accident. But what will be the subject in the third way of considering them? We cannot say that the two taken together, L and M, constitute the subject for such an accident, for then we would have an accident in two subjects, which would stand with one foot in one subject and the other in another subject, and this contradicts the concept of accidents. Thus we have to admit that the relation in this third way of considering it is indeed outside the subjects; but that since it is neither substance nor accident, it must be a purely ideal thing, which it is none the less very fruitful to consider.'[27]

Leibniz makes his train of thought clearer by referring to tonal relations in music, in which the relational character is generally recognized.

In fact there is no better way to express the point that the interpretation of relation in terms of substance-accident (and that means in terms of substance-quality), misses the specific concept of relation. Relation as such is already a unity that binds together a multiplicity. This is more clearly seen when instead of restricting oneself to dyadic relations, one considers polyadic relations, for example the relation: A lies between B and C.

Thus a nominalistic interpretation of the problem of relations is particularly tempting. In terms of our example it would mean that Socrates as well as Cebes, each for himself, would possess certain properties and that a third person would regard these as greater or less or just the same. The relation would then consist only in the conception of the observer. Such an interpretation would be suggested by the fact that there are undoubtedly some relations which only exist in the conception of the observer. Such a nominalistic interpretation of relations is found in the Greek Sophists, and later in the nominalism of the middle ages and modern times. But this interpretation also contains a mistake. It presupposes that individual beings with all their properties exist independently. Relations represent only fleeting externals which do not affect the true being of the individual. This is probably the way Descartes regarded the problem. The *res cogitans* and the *res extensa*, each with its own properties, exist independently; all relations which may accrue to them mean nothing for their true being. Such an interpretation does not see the constitutive significance of relations. I may perhaps refer to Russell, [28] Whitehead, [29] and Heidegger, [30] who have from quite different starting points impressively brought out the constitutive significance of relations.

Given the importance of relations it is understandable that syntheses should be attempted which, however, nearly always give rise to new problems. Leibniz treats relation as an *être de raison*, [31] as a *chose idéale*, [32] and as a *res mentalis*. [33] But for him the *esse in mente tantum* is also an *esse in mente divina*. [34] To construe the *esse in mente* as occuring only in the mind of an individual person, on the contrary, would be to raise difficulties in understanding how relations hold and are valid *in general*. This difficulty of extreme nominalism Leibniz avoids. But he must then assume the consequence, that all theories of relations, logic, mathematics and physics, are primarily thoughts of God. [35] This he is disposed to do on many grounds, yet because of the discursive character of these theories he encounters not a few difficulties.

When Kant annuls this theological foundation, he is forced to refer all relations to men. But it is not easy for Kant to say which man it is who establishes all relations. This leads him into irresolvable difficulties which we must discuss later.

22. THE TRANSCENDENTALS

The theory of transcendentals has had a varied fate in the history of philosophy. It has sometimes been considered peculiar to scholastic thinking, but this is an error. Even Kant, who designated his own philosophy a transcendental philosophy, was not able to reconcile himself with the transcendental philosophy of the ancients, as he called it.[1] We will detach the theory of the transcendentals from its association with Aristotelian-Scholastic philosophy and find its true meaning in the basic assumption that the concepts of being and unity have a special character but also bring with them a special problem. In this broader interpretation we are in agreement with an essay of Ryle's on Plato.[2] In fact the concepts of being and unity constitute the centre of transcendental philosophy, even though their connexion is quite variously perceived. For Plato and Kant unity stands in the foreground, while Aristotle gives the priority to being. Plato clearly recognized the special difficulties of unity, the dialogue *Parmenides* shows that. And Aristotle expressly says that the questions about being and unity belong to the highest and most difficult questions of metaphysics.[3] Thomas Aquinas widens the scope of the theory of transcendentals by adding to *ens* and *unum* the further concepts of *bonum*, *verum*, *res* and *aliquid*.[4] And he also considers a still further broadening. Duns Scotus continues the expansion,[5] and Ockham goes one step further, at least in relation to the ontological interpretation.[6] We will disregard these questions of expansion and concentrate on being and unity. Considering first unity, one immediately sees that the interpretation of unity as an Idea and its interpretation as a *res* in the sense of a real accident both remain unsatisfying. This was perceived early on and has led to the insight that the disjunction: something is either real or a mere conception, is insufficient. Instead it proves to be necessary to regard transcendental being as a new, intermediate possibility of being. What is primarily involved is the unity of individual beings. How far am I myself one?—thus Plato formulates the question in the *Parmenides*.[7] We are now concerned with this unity of individual beings; the unity of the general will be taken up in the second Part.

If one interprets being and unity as Ideas and then interprets Ideas as independent realities, one encounters the aporias of the theory of Ideas, which Plato developed in the *Parmenides* and which we will discuss in the second Part. These difficulties are known under the name τρίτοσ ἄνθρωποσ. Plato exhibits them in connexion with the Idea of size. For systematic reasons we prefer to develop them in connexion with the Idea of unity. If the Idea of unity, which establishes the unity of Socrates, were in turn an independent reality and as such a unity, then a new Idea of unity would be required, to establish the unity between Socrates and the Idea of unity, and one sees immediately that a *regressus in infinitum* has started. Then we would require not only an Idea of unity, but an infinite series of Ideas of unity. Of course, such an infinite regress is not itself a proof of impossibility, but such an infinite series of Ideas in every case is still more than improbable.

If the attempt to define being and unity as Ideas leads to difficulties, one could attempt to escape the difficulties by defining being and unity as accidents in the strict sense and thereby as *res*. It is the express opinion of Scholasticism that this is not possible. We will pursue the ontological discussion first among the Scholastics and then turn back to Aristotle.

Thomas discusses the question as to the ontological status of unity in a whole series of passages. The most instructive is surely the *Quaestio XI* of the first Part of the *Summa Theologica*. There Thomas poses the question: *Utrum unum addat aliquid supra ens?*[8] Referring to Aristotle's *Metaphysics X*, Thomas revives the opinion of Pythagoras and Plato that number and therefore also unity is the substance of all things. What is meant by this is that Plato defined number and unity as Ideas and further defined Idea as substance. But Plato and Pythagoras have been led into error by the unity which is the principle of number. By contrast to them, Avicenna has, so Thomas continues, understood unity as an accident and therefore a *res*. On this interpretation the unity of a man would be understood in the same way as his colour. But his colour, his *esse album*, is an accident in the strict sense and therefore a *res*; thus his *esse unum* is also an accident and therefore a *res* in the strict sense. According to the report of Aquinas, which is correct, Avicenna teaches: '. . . *credidit, quod unum quod convertitur cum ente, addat rem aliquam supra substantiam entis, sicut album supra hominem.*'[9] But this definition of transcendental unity, Thomas objects, must be wrong, for it leads to an infinite regress. If one understands the individual thing as a multiplicity of realities and the unity of these many realities as being in turn a new reality, then there arises in fact a new multiplicity which requires a new unity.[10] If the unity of many things is itself of the same ontological character as the things of which it is supposed to be the unity, then an infinite regress is unavoidable. From this Thomas concludes that the *unum transcendens* cannot be a *res*.

Thereby arises the problem of the mode of being of transcendental unity. If a strict disjunction were to be used: something is either real or it is a mere conception, then it would have to follow that transcendental unity is a mere conception. This is certainly not the opinion of Thomas. Transcendental unity is neither a reality in the sense of *res* nor is it a mere conception. It has a reference to *ratio* but its being is not exhausted in being-conceived. The problem that arises here is one that we will have to recur to again and again. For the present we will only hold on to the point that we see here emerging a new, a third mode of being, which transcends the old disjunction between *ens reale* and *ens rationis*.

It is Duns Scotus who further clarifies the problem, earning on this ground alone his title of *Doctor subtilis*. Leibniz refers to this doctrine in one of his very early writings: '*Distinctio formalis . . . tribuitur communiter Scoto, ut media inter realem et rationis, unde ejus sectatores dicti Formalistae.*'[11] In fact Duns Scotus distinguishes *ens reale*, *ens formale* and *ens rationis*. To the *ens reale* belong substances and accidents, to the *ens rationis* belong mere conceptions, and to the *ens formale* belong the transcendentals.[12] The scope of the transcendentals is considerably broadened. For example Scotus reckons difference as one of the transcendentals.[13]

Through this concept of *ens formale* Duns Scotus fixed the problem. But the question of how to understand the being of the *ens formale* does not receive a decisive answer even from the *Doctor subtilis*.

The philosophical work of Ockham on the problem of transcendentals first appears as a broadening of its scope. For Ockham substance remains, naturally, the true reality, it provides the meaning of *res*. Of the accidents only a few of the qualities retain this character. All other accidents Ockham considers, at least ontologically, as transcendentals. This applies in particular to quantity and relation, but also to many of the qualities.[14]

As for the further question, how Ockham understands this considerably enlarged transcendental being, I have not been able to find a decisive answer in his writings. There are places which could be understood in the sense of a purely nominalistic interpretation.[15] But there are other passages which do not lend themselves to such an interpretation.[16] My own investigations into Ockham's writings have led me to the conviction that he cannot be regarded as a pure nominalist.[17] For Ockham, too, transcental being has an essential reference to *ratio*, but one cannot say that he defined the transcendental properties and among them particularly *ens* and *unum* finally and exclusively as *entia rationis*, mere conceptions.

If from the standpoint of Scholastic transcendental philosophy one refers the question of the transcendentals to Aristotle's philosophy, there is no doubt that Aristotle understood the special problems surrounding being and unity. The true counterpart, however, the interpretation of the category as a reality in the sense of *res* is lacking. We have already seen that it cannot be clearly decided how Aristotle conceived the reality of accidents. Aristotle's expositions of the transcendentals are so brief that it is impossible to tell what grounds were decisive for him and what consequences he drew in particular cases.

It is certain that Aristotle recognized the peculiar generality characteristic of being and unity. They are the most general concepts, but do not form a genus.[18] From this follows their transcendental character, although Aristotle lacks a fixed term for this idea. The *transcendere* of the transcendentals, for Aristotle and the Scholastics, does not mean transcendence in our sense, it means rather that these concepts surpass every categorial classification and every classification of being in general. Aristotle says explicitly that being and unity cannot fall into any one of the categories, they surpass every category and yet also accompany every category.[19]

It is less easy to see what ontological consequences Aristotle will draw. In Book X of the *Metaphysics* he says explicitly that unity does not signify an additional predicate.[20] The point is made negatively, and Thomas formulates it as a thesis: *unum non est res addita*.[21] In Book IV of the *Metaphysics* Aristotle says that being and unity are the same *physis* but that they are not brought to light through the same *logos*.[22] If one translates *physis* with *res*, one comes close to the Scholastic definition. In order fully to reach the Scholastic definition one would have to assume that Aristotle also regarded an accident as a special *physis*. This is perhaps not impossible. *Physis* seems to have a very broad meaning in this section of the fourth Book. We will not find a definite decision in the brief Aristotelian tests, not even in this place in Book IV which represents the chief Aristotelian text on the transcendentals.

How is *logos* to be understood in this text? Is *logos* what is thought or the act of thinking, a concept or what is conceptualized? It could be the case that being and unity differ in our mode of thinking them, and this could be understood in extreme nominalist fashion, so that here thinking would mean the subjective exercise of a single act of thought. But being and unity could differ also by being presented through concepts of objective difference. This could be conceived in such a way that there would be different definitions of being and unity. It must be remembered of course that strictly speaking there can be no definitions of being and unity. A final decision about Aristotle's meaning is not to be had, by reason of the brevity of the text. But it is also not to be expected on systematic grounds. According to the interpretation we are presenting in these investigations, being and unity have a reference to *logos*, but about the kind and manner of this reference no apodictic answer is possible for systematic reasons. This is shown already in Plato. No doubt the reference of the Ideas to *nous* is very important for him. The Ideas are fundamentally characterized as νοητόν.[23] But what does this expression mean? Is *nous* a merely passive faculty, and does it merely contemplate the independently existing Ideas? Or is *nous* an active faculty, a spontaneous faculty, and is the being of Ideas connected with this spontaneity? Aristotle refers being and unity to *logos*, but we have just seen that it remains obscure what manner of reference is involved. Thomas interprets the transcendentals in relation to *ratio*, but this definition only exposes the difficulties. Leibniz reduces all reality to the reality of the monads; all categorial and transcendental determinations (Leibniz does not distinguish them) belong to thought. But the thought that primarily thinks all these determinations is the thought of God. God's thought is *actus purus* and to this extent the *esse in mente divina* of all categorial and transcendental determinations means for Leibniz a special mode of dependence on thought for these determinations, even though it is the thought of God.

The problem is instantly complicated when Kant annuls the reference of these determinations to the thought of God and refers them solely to human thought. For Kant the question then arises, which man it is who thinks all these determinations, and for us the question proves to be one of the most difficult in the interpretation of Kant.

If we were to attempt a summary of the first part of our investigations, two points could be regarded as secure. Being has many meanings and individual being provides the authentic meaning. Individual being is primarily living individual being, and one may follow here the lead of Leibniz: I am myself a living individual being and the prototype of living individual beings. With reference to being this implies that I am myself a being and the prototype of all being. I myself am, and whatever is like me, also is. By contrast, we were unable to give a final answer to the question as to the being of properties. Under properties we understand both categorial accidents and the transcendental determinations. Both exhibit a reference to *logos*. Among the categories this is most evident for relation, and among the transcendentals most evident for the difference between being and unity. This reference to *logos* is noted by all thinkers, but none of the individual thinkers has succeeded in arriving at consistent definitions nor is it possible wholly to reconcile the definitions of the various thinkers. Relations and transcendentals, one could say in summary, obviously have a reference to *logos* but the reference cannot be clearly defined. The relations and the transcendentals thereby lead into the question about the being of the general. And in the question about the being of the general the reference to *logos* will prove to be the central problem.

PART II

THE GENERAL

Section I

LOGICAL PROBLEMS ABOUT THE GENERAL

CHAPTER IV

THE UNITY OF THE GENERAL

23. THE LOCATION OF THE GENERAL

The general is the true battleground of metaphysics, the battle-ground upon which the attack on the possibility of metaphysics is launched, and the battleground, upon which the different metaphysical standpoints struggle against one another.

The extreme opponents of metaphysics refuse to accept the general in any sense whatever. The refusal is, to be sure, quite ancient. According to a Greek anecdote, it was objected to Plato that one could only see a horse, not horseness. Against this objection we will ourselves follow a suggestion of Aristotle's. As he begins to consider the being of numbers in the 13th book of the *Metaphysics*, he coins the neat formula: Not whether there is number, but how there is number, that alone is the philosophical question.[1] We will apply this consideration to the general as such and say: Not whether there is the general, but how there is the general, that alone is the philosophical question.

The general shows itself first in language. Often languages can designate a strict individual only by referring to spatial and temporal aspects of a definite situation. Most linguistic expressions in fact designate something general from the outset. Thirst designates—under the burning August sun of Magna Graecia—something which I had yesterday, have today and will have again tomorrow. Wine designates something which in its many kinds is excellently suited to quench this thirst. That there are many kinds of wine is from the first included in the word and the concept.

99

It is quite understandable, then, that Socrates, the discoverer of the general, constantly recurs to language. When he is concerned with the definition of courage, he insists on the fact that we use one word to name many and different actions: the word 'courageous'.[2] This is a phenomenon which cannot be questioned. Particularly clear is the case of numbers, where the phenomenon of the general appears in different ways. Three-score eggs designates 60 eggs. The numerical word is here bound up with definite things; there are still many such expressions though less used today than formerly. But then the numerical word is separated from this conjunction with definite things and becomes a pure number. Whitehead once remarked with justice that it was one of the greatest achievements of human thought to have achieved the insight that seven days and seven fish have something in common: the number seven, thereby discovering the general concept of the number seven.[3] The contemporary investigations into the foundations of arithmetic show that this process of ascending to abstract concepts of number is still by no means finished.

If language is the place where the general first shows itself, then another phenomenon immediately shows itself in the same place. To be thirsty is the same whether I express it in German or in Italian. And within one language the same thing can be said in different ways. In the case of numbers this is shown in many ways. They are the same numbers whether I write them in Greek, Roman or Arabic numerals, whether I pronounce them in Greek, Roman or German words. Of all the ways to write numerals the Arabic has achieved the widest currency. Throughout the world the number seven is written or at least understood through the Arabic numeral 7. The same numeral is then pronounced in a great variety of ways in the countless different languages. Here we see different levels of the general, one after the other. The English word 'seven' refers to a general in contrast with seven days, seven fish and seven houses. The Arabian numeral 7 refers to a general in contrast to the many different words in the different languages. The general concept of seven refers to a general independent of its expression in Greek, Roman or Arabic numerals. Finally, there is once again the general concept of the natural number in contrast to five, six, and seven.

The characteristic of generality in language is a simple phenomenon, and anyone who wants to treat of the general must constantly recur to it. But two different considerations are frequently confused herein. It is an important task to exhibit the phenomenon of the general, and it is a totally other, and also important, task to infer ontological consequences from it. Bolzano has shown this with admirable clarity. He develops the theory of the concept-in-itself and the proposition-in-itself, but he expressly opposes any attempt to impute ontological claims to his theory of in-itself without further qualification.[4]

It is important to distinguish the phenomenon of generality from the ontological interpretation of generality. The systematic difficulties and the many differences of philosophical standpoints begin with the question of interpretation. The ontological interpretation raises the question: What is the general? We have seen how the question arises in a relatively concrete form with Socrates, who asks about courage and piety. With Plato and Aristotle the question becomes abstract and general, it has been raised to the questions: What is being? What is unity? What is the general?

In our own times, by contrast, research into the foundations of mathematics and linguistic philosophy has led to the thesis: all metaphysical questions are meaningless questions and the answers given to them meaningless claims.[5] But such a thesis is easier to formulate than to prove. It may be generally conceded, from the outset, that there are propositions which are meaningless because grammatically incorrect.[6] In this sense the following is a meaningless proposition, if it can be called a proposition at all: 'Seven is not or.' More is meant by the thesis, of course. It implies that there are propositions which are grammatically correct and yet meaningless.[7] We are concerned, for example, with propositions like: 'Seven is drunk' or, to take a somewhat less drastic example, 'Seven is green.' That such propositions are not and could not be true is beyond doubt. But what are they then? One could consider them false propositions, but this leads to many difficulties. Thus one might well concede that such propositions should be called meaningless. From this point of view one could consider as meaningless the question: 'What is the general?' and every answer to it, for example: 'The general has objective reality'. Then the battle against metaphysics would have ended victoriously. But one has to ask what assumptions may be used in order to characterize a proposition as meaningless. The general battle against metaphysics will be successful only if there is a general criterion which allows us to distinguish all the grammatically correct propositions—we are concerned only with these—into meaningful and meaningless propositions.[8] One would apply this criterion to metaphysical propositions and it would then be evident that they are meaningless, and thereby the long attempted goal would have been reached.

The difficulty is, however, that there is no such general criterion and cannot be one. We have no choice but to enter into the investigation appropriate to each proposition. And this is in fact quite possible for the examples we have been using. One quickly sees that a category mistake is involved.[9] The predicates 'drunk' and 'green' cannot be brought together with the subject term 'seven'. To do so would be a category mistake, and the resulting proposition would then be justly considered meaningless. The point of this solution, one quickly sees, is that the discussion must be pertinent to the particular problems concerned. One cannot show by general criteria that the concepts 'green' and 'drunk' cannot be predicated of the concept 'seven', one recognizes this only by pertinent discussion of these three concepts.

The case is no different for the general. Suppose we take a relatively concrete question: 'What is the number seven?' and two relatively concrete answers: 'The number seven exists' and 'The number seven is an Idea'. These answers may be good or bad, we are not now concerned with that. The question we are now raising is whether it is possible to regard these answers together with the question as, in general, meaningless. How could this be possible? Is it not clear that one must rather enter into a concrete and pertinent discussion. If the answer is given: 'The number seven exists', one must ask what 'exists' means in this case. If by 'existence' one means the existence of an individual being in space and time, the answer is obviously not correct, and one can regard it as meaningless. Bolzano, a determined supporter of the in-itself status of the general and hence also of the number seven, was unequivocal in defending himself against a naïve concept of existence. And a similar defence must be made for the Platonic thesis: the number seven is an Idea. One's estimate of this answer obviously depends on what meaning one wants to give to the concept of an Idea. If the Idea is naïvely considered as like a thing, the proposition then becomes more than questionable. This will have to be shown in detail, particularly the point that it was Plato himself who saw the problems arising here.

It is unlikely that the question: What is the general? together with all the answers which can be given it can be regarded, quite generally, as meaningless. Instead the general question and all possible answers must be judged on the basis of concrete discussions of the problems. In this sense we may be allowed to repeat: Not whether there is the general, but how there is the general, that alone is the philosophical question.

24. THE GENERAL AS CONCEPT, AS JUDGEMENT, AS THEORY

When we ask about the being of the general, we must first ask, whither we should look in order to be able to speak pertinently about the general. That question leads to different possibilities, and it is clearly no accident that linguists have had the same experience. They too must ask themselves which is the true phenomenon of language? Three answers have resulted: The basic phenomenon of language is the word[1] or the sentence[2] or speech.[3] It seems obvious to consider the word as the basic phenomenon of language. Then the sentence becomes a combination of words and speech a combination of sentences. Part of the reason for this obviousness is that in some cases single words can be used as complete sentences or even as complete speech. 'Give!', 'Speak!', 'Help!', 'Fire!' are old examples. But generally speaking the individual word does not have a complete function of expression. It asserts nothing, according to Aristotle's interpretation.[4] This consideration suggests that the sentence must be regarded as the first independent formation of language. But the consideration leads on further to the realization that speech represents the first truly independent formation of language. I adopt this third interpretation and, more particularly, I adopt it in the form given it by Walter Porzig.[5] There are of course examples of speech consisting of a single sentence or even of a single word. But in general speech is composed of several sentences, this basic character of speech is made clear by just that speech-function of individual sentences and words.

Philosophical interest in the general is concerned with similar differences. The general can be understood as concept, as proposition, and as theory. For that reason it is possible to choose different starting points and yet arrive at the same conclusions. This will be revealed most clearly by a historical consideration. In the theory of Ideas, Plato considers primarily concepts: the good, the true, the beautiful, identity, the number three. Only in the later dialogues does the problem of their inter-relations occur. Plato seems uninterested in propositions. This could be sharply formulated by saying that, for Plato, only Ideas, that is, only concepts have an ideal being, not propositions. Among Plato's successors, this holds also for Leibniz. He also holds that concepts, particularly the basic concepts, have true being in the realm of the ideal.[6] For him, propositions are explications which clarify the relations between concepts. This is the meaning of Leibniz's theory of the analytic judgement. Against the radical completion of this theory of analytic judgements, however, stands the fact that principles appear which cannot be fitted into the analytic schema, such as the *principium contradictionis*[7] or the *principium rationis sufficientis*.[8] For this reason, one can say that, beginning with Leibniz, the proposition begins to acquire a meaning of its own. But, on the other hand, Leibniz attaches no importance to theory. For him, all propositions lie more or less on the same plane, this is already implied by his rejection of the axiomatic method.[9] This viewpoint becomes especially clear in the case of mathematical propositions, which according to

Leibniz arise one and all from the principle of contradiction.[10] Thus all mathematical propositions constitute a unity, and their division into theories is meaningless for Leibniz.

With Aristotle one can say that, in contrast to Plato, a certain balance has been achieved between concepts and propositions. Concepts continue to have their great importance. One cannot fail to notice that in the *Logic*, but also in large parts of the *Physics* and the *Metaphysics*, concepts form the primary theme. But the problem of the proposition does appear in Aristotle in its full significance. Propositions are regarded as important according to their content, especially the principle of contradiction.[11] The form of propositions also becomes a theme of philosophical interest, not just in the hermeneutics, but quite generally in the logic. Plato had often reflected on theories, in particular, on arithmetic,[12] geometry,[13] and astronomy.[14] Aristotle attempts to go further and to achieve an insight into the grounds for distinguishing among theories, into the grounds, for example, which constitute arithmetic, geometry and astronomy as different theories.[15]

There is even more reason to speak of a balance between concepts and propositions for Kant. Of the four chief tables in the *Critique of Pure Reason*, two refer to concepts and two to propositions. The first two are the tables of the categories[16] and the schemata,[17] the other two are the tables of judgements[18] and of principles.[19] Following them, one can express the theme of the *Critique of Pure Reason* in terms either of concepts or of propositions. In terms of concepts the basic question has to do with the objective reality of the categories,[20] in terms of propositions the basic question runs: How are synthetic *a priori* judgements possible?[21]

Hermann Cohen has made an important contribution toward the understanding of this structure in the *Critique of Pure Reason*. He does not assign ultimate systematic significance to the subdivision in these four tables. Basically, the four tables occur because the *Critique*, like all other books, had to be written step by step. According to Cohen the true theme of the *Critique* is not these four tables; whether they treat of concepts or propositions, the true theme is a theory, Newtonian physics. This is the reason why Cohen gave his interpretation the title: *Kant's Theory of Experience*. From the analysis of Newtonian physics as experience in its pure form there grew, in Cohen's opinion, the analyses of the judgements, the categories, the schemata and the principles.[22] If that is so, a theory constitutes the true subject of investigation of the *Critique* and thus the notion of theory has a much greater importance for Kant than it had for either Plato or Aristotle.

We can now take the reflections of linguistics together with those of the history of philosophy. In the problems of linguistics, I follow the standpoint of Porzig and consider speech to be the true basic phenomenon of language. By analogy, in the onto-logical interpretation of the general, I consider theory as the true basic phenomenon of the general. One can do this more readily since theory encompasses judgements and concepts, just as speech encompasses sentences and words. A viewpoint directed from the outset at theories must therefore also be directed at proposi-tions and concepts, while a viewpoint which begins with concepts must attempt to construct propositions out of concepts and is then faced with the further task of constructing theories out of propositions.

With this viewpoint I will waive any attempt to formulate a general notion of theory as such. There are important studies devoted to this, our investigations too will lead us to very general reflections about theories as such. Nevertheless, it must remain questionable whether a notion of theory as such, however con-structed, could achieve a truly encompassing meaning. Instead, I will begin with a few concrete theories and, following Wittgen-stein, I will define theory as something which is like these concrete theories. In this sense I will pick out four theories, firstly, logic or rather that part of it constituted by two-valued propositional calculus, which in turn can be regarded as a formal presentation of a part of Aristotelian logic.[23] Secondly, elementary arithmetic in the limitation which Gödel has given it.[24] Thirdly, Euclidean geometry and fourthly, Newtonian mechanics. These four theories, which will determine the scope for our questions about the general, will be defined more precisely in the following investigations. Quite apart from considerations of principle this way of proceeding has marked advantages. It is possible to get a comprehensive view of these four theories, they are fundamental, their epistemology has been thoroughly explored, and they may reasonably be regarded as representative of theory as such. Moreover, they are the theories with which Plato, Aristotle, Descartes, Leibniz and Kant have been concerned. It is reasonable to hope, then, that by beginning with these four theories, one will get some grasp of the essential problems of theory as such and thereby also of the essential problems of the general as such.

This way of proceeding raises, of course, some questions of method. Is the focus too narrow? Shouldn't biological theories or those from the humane sciences be considered as well? Aristotle and Leibniz did that. But against this objection is the fact that the four theories we have singled out have achieved an exceptionally pure form, something that cannot be claimed for the biological or psychological theories. Moreover, an epistemological and ontological discussion of a theory is meaningful only if one is thoroughly acquainted with the theory in question. But the quantitative development of the sciences has made it impossible for an investigator today, unlike Aristotle and Leibniz, to have a comprehensive view of the complete spectrum of theories. One can only hope, therefore, that those theories with which the investigator is familiar are fit to stand for the complete spectrum of theories.

A second consideration brings further difficulties. Doesn't this manner of proceeding narrow the investigation from the beginning to the theoretical general, and isn't the existence of an ethical or an aesthetic general thereby placed in question? This is not at all our intention. Our question: What is the general? can be formulated in Plato's manner as the question: What is the Idea? How could such a question imply a denial of the Idea of the beautiful, the Idea of the good, and the Idea of justice? Our way of proceeding limits the investigation to a part of the Platonic Ideas, to the logical-mathematical Ideas. These are certainly important Ideas and it is surely no accident that Plato, when he introduces the theory of Ideas in the *Phaedo*, so strongly emphasizes the Idea of equality. But the logical-mathematical Ideas are only a part of the Ideas. If we restrict ourselves to this part, we do so for two reasons. The first reason has already been mentioned. This area is better known and more thoroughly investigated. The second reason is that this area is largely free from differences in standpoint, which unavoidably appear with ethical and esthetic Ideas. One must surely ask: What is the good? What is the beautiful? But here differences about the substance of these questions at once appear. We will limit our investigation to the theoretical general. But we are doing this not because we wish to deny the generality of the good and the beautiful, we are doing this because we hope, by a peaceful consideration of the true, to prepare the way also for insight into the good and the beautiful.

25. UNITY HAS SEVERAL MEANINGS

That, generally speaking, the meaning of a word is developed in everyday language, is a fact important also for unity. But the connotation of this word varies considerably in the different languages. Special complications appear in German because here the linguistic forms and the meanings of the indefinite article are directly bound up with the linguistic forms and the meaning of unity in the true sense.

In many languages, among them Greek, the situation is simpler. In Greek therefore investigations proceed directly to the development of the meaning of unity in the true sense. Plato himself seems to have stumbled onto the problem. It is worthy of note that Cornford constructs his interpretation of the second half of the *Parmenides* entirely on the thesis that here different meanings of unity are being developed.[1] It may seem questionable whether Cornford is not forcing his thesis somewhat in order to cover all the texts. But for many of these, Cornford's interpretation is convincing. Read this way, Plato has already discovered the development of the meaning of unity.

Aristotle gives a thematic treatment of the plurality of meaning of unity. We find two explicit investigations, one in Book V, the other in Book X, of the *Metaphysics*. The two investigations agree substantially and to a large extent even in the form of expression.

Aristotle first excludes as accidental those unities that are formed solely by the occurrence of different properties in the same subject.[2] Among authentic modes of unity we find first mere being-together,[3] whether, to cite an example often repeated later, we are dealing with a mere heap,[4] or with unities which arise from binding[5], glueing[6], or nailing[7] things together, as for example a bundle.[8] Next, Aristotle considers those unities which consist in a mere coherence of material[9], such as the unity of a plank.[10] Then follows the unity resting on form[11], such as the unity of a marble ball.[12] The unity of a living being represents the last in this series.[13] The highest example of this type of unity is the unity of the cosmos,[14] which has both the unity of a living being and, because of its spherical shape, the unity of a form. All these are forms of unity for individuals. To them must be added an entirely new mode of unity, that of the general, the unity of logos,[15] as Aristotle rather cautiously expresses it. This is primarily a matter of the unity which is expressed in a concept, for example the unity of the human race as the unity of the concept 'man'.

The Aristotelian theory of the plurality of meanings for unity played a great role in Scholastic philosophy. But I am not able to discern any substantive development in this epoch.

This same theory occurs again as an explicit theory in the writings of Leibniz. But it appears there in an abbreviated form, since there are only two modes of unity,[16] the unity of the living,[17] in Leibniz's terminology the unity of the monads, and the unity of mere aggregates.[18] In this sense Leibniz distinguishes the *unum per se* and the *unum per accidens*.[19] In not a few places this distinction acquires a systematic importance for Leibniz. Thus, for example, the world as a whole is for Leibniz only an aggregate,[20] an aggregate of monads. Also the totality of natural numbers is only an aggregate.[21]

Kant distinguishes in practice different modes of unity, but does not reflect further on his distinction. The highest unity,[22] the unity of apperception, must be distinguished from the category of unity.[23] Also, the Kantian theory of the antinomies in fact presents an investigation about unity, in so far as it deals with the unity of the world.[24]

26. THE UNITY OF THE GENERAL

Since there are several meanings of unity, the question arises: What unity has the general? Aristotle speaks of the unity of the logos, is this different from the unity of the general? In our opinion, this is the direction in which the discussion should move. An initial differentiation appears when the general enters as concept, as judgement or as theory. In what sense is a concept a unity? What is the relation of the general concept man to the individual men, who fall under this general concept? In what sense is a judgement a unity? What is the relation between the general proposition $7 + 5 = 12$ and the individual cases which fall under it? In what sense is a theory a unity? What is the relation between the Newtonian mechanics and the individual cases which fall under it? Beyond these, there are further questions at what amounts to a second level, and we are particularly concerned with them. What is the case with the totality of all concepts? This is, as it were, the concept of concept. What is the case with the totality of all propositions, meaning here the totality of all true propositions? Here we encounter propositions which assert something about all propositions. What kind of unity is this? What is the case with the totality of all theories? Here we would obtain a theory of theories. But what kind of unity has this totality of all theories, and in what sense can one speak here in general of a totality?

If we once again attempt an historical orientation, then as we already saw, for Plato, concepts stand in the foreground. The totality we are concerned with at present, the totality of concepts, Plato would represent as the totality of all Ideas. One will not find in Plato an explicit term for the totality of all ideas. But the problem is very much recognized in the middle and late dialogues.

It may be that Plato had originally thought of the Ideas essentially as individuals. In a sense, the Idea of the beautiful stood for itself alone, the Idea of equality likewise. But in subsequent reflection Plato must have asked himself the question of how the Ideas are related to one another. What binds them together, what distinguishes them? Here difficulties arise which caused Plato to consider various possibilities. One alternative is to accept a highest Idea. Plato does this in the *Republic*, where the Idea of the Good is regarded as the highest Idea.[1] A consistent development of this would mean that the so-called Platonic pyramid of concepts represents the unity of Ideas.[2] The pyramid of concepts would be the fundamental result of Platonic philosophy, this was the meaning Leisegang saw in it.[3] From the systematic standpoint this would not be very satisfactory. Furthermore, one doesn't get the impression that Plato himself had arrived at a final decision in the question about a highest Idea. The Ideas of being and unity would also be obvious candidates for such a highest Idea, if there were one. It is support for the Idea of unity that Neoplatonism, and the interpretation of Plato influenced by it, have considered this Idea as the highest. The importance which the Idea of unity has in the *Parmenides* gives good reasons for such a decision.

Another alternative is presented in the *Sophist*. At the outset Plato does give examples for the pyramid of concepts. But in the course of the dialogue he seeks the connexion of Ideas not in the logical construction of a pyramid of concepts, but in the connexion of a net. And he speaks explicitly of a community of Ideas.[4]

The Ideas singled out for attention in this dialogue, in particular the Ideas of identity[5] and difference,[6] make it clear that at least for these Ideas the interpretation using a logical analysis of the pyramid of concepts is not satisfactory. One must therefore conclude that Plato did not arrive at a final decision in the question about the unity of all Ideas. And the drift of the *Parmenides* and the *Sophist* allows us to conclude that, in Plato's opinion, contradictions are contained in the totality of Ideas.

Leibniz repeatedly turned his attention to the question of the totality of possible concepts as well as to the question of a possible occurrence of contradictions in this totality. In the *Meditationes* he points out that concepts which at first appear wholly unsuspicious often turn out to contain contradictions on closer inspection. He gives as an example the concept of a highest velocity,[7] which is in fact contradictory under the assumptions of classical physics. One could also discuss the concept of *ens perfectissimum*, which might be non-contradictory in form, but according to Leibniz is not in fact so. At any rate, it has not been proved that the concept is non-contradictory and thus there is a gap in Descartes' proof for the existence of God.[8] From such considerations Leibniz arrives at a simple criterion of existence. All concepts which are free of contradictions exist, those which contain contradictions do not exist. And this leads him further to a relatively simple notion of the totality of all concepts. The concepts with which we are ordinarily concerned are compound. At the basis of these compound concepts lie simple, elementary concepts.[9] The totality of all compound concepts arises from the combination of all elementary concepts. Thus, the totality of all concepts is represented as the totality of all basic concepts and the totality of compound concepts generated from them by combinatory modes. This totality is more encompassing than that of Plato's Ideas, since Leibniz also recognizes concepts of individuals, for example, Alexander the Great.[10] Of course, Leibniz realizes that the problem is not at all so simple as it appears in this outline. To begin with, he is quite careful about the totality of elementary concepts, which ideally one should be able to organize into a table. It seems that Leibniz has not definitively claimed of any one concept that it is elementary. In any case, no table of all elementary concepts appears in any of his publications nor did he promise to give one.

The question as to what constitutes freedom from contradiction is difficult for him. On his assumptions, Leibniz must prove the existence of a compound concept by proving that it is free of contradictions.[11] But such a proof is not easily carried out and in practice it is consequent upon a recourse to actual existence.[12] The totality of all true concepts and the true propositions resulting from them Leibniz calls the realm of eternal truths. The term is quite old, it occurs in Augustine;[13] surprisingly, neither the term nor its equivalent occur in Plato. Most often Leibniz uses the expression 'la région des vérités éternelles',[14] and this is the form used in the *Theodicée*.[15] Through that book the term received widespread currency.

Kant takes over from Leibniz the idea of a distinction between simple and compound concepts. The simple concepts are represented by the categories, of which Kant claims that he has faithfully reproduced all in his twelve-fold table.[16] From the categories as simple concepts the compound concepts arise, more or less in the way indicated by Leibniz.[17] Leibniz's structure is changed, however, in that Kant separates spatial and temporal appearances, in so far as they are *a priori*, as pure intuitions. Between the pure concepts and the pure intuitions relations appear which, among others, lead to the difficult chapter on the schematism.[18] Finally, in the Dialectic Kant sums up a series of conceptions which contain or lead to contradictions. The most important of these for our purposes is the concept of the world.[19] It is Kant's conviction that we have here only a few, exhaustively enumerable conceptions.[20] The contradictory conceptions of the Dialectic have important functions in spite of their contradictory status.[21] Their indispensable importance can be rendered intelligible.[22]

With respect to our question, Kant's opinion is that contradictions appear within the realm of the general. These contradictions can, however, be represented and made comprehensible. In the philosophical sense, therefore, they can be resolved.[23] These are the only contradictions in the realm of the general. With these isolated, the realms of logic, mathematics and physics in the narrow sense remain free of contradictions.

With respect to our question about the realm of eternal truths, Hegel takes a peculiarly ambivalent position. On the one hand, he teaches that every concept is contradictory,[24] and on the other hand, he teaches that the totality of concepts constitutes a necessary[25] and rational[26], though dialectical, set of relations. First Hegel says expressly in the *Logic* that every concept is in itself contradictory. It must be admitted, however, that Hegel still owes us a proof for this sweeping claim. His reference to ancient scepticism[27] does not of itself constitute a proof. That the elementary concepts of mathematics contain contradictions, that, for example, the concept of two or the concept of the circle contain contradictions, has not been shown by Hegel or by anyone else up to the present. Until we have such a proof, Hegel's claim that every concept is contradictory must remain in abeyance.

On the other hand, this claim functions constitutively in Hegel's systematic thought. The contradiction contained in every concept releases the dialectical movement, which leads from this concept to another one. Thus arises the interconnexion of all concepts. This interconnexion exists in its pure form in God's thought, and is therefore rational in God's thought.[28] But this interconnexion of all concepts is also accessible to our understanding.[29] It is not easy to represent this interconnexion perfectly and Hegel does not claim perfection for his own presentation.[30] But the interconnexion as such exists, and with it the totality of all concepts as a necessary and rational totality. The fact that the interconnexion is dialectial does not remove its existence, its necessity or its rationality. In fact Hegel claims that his dialectic is an actual dialectic.[31] We will have to test this claim in the third Part.

The same assertion of the existence of a totality of all true concepts, all true judgements and all true theories, even though built on a diametrically opposite standpoint, is found in the line of philosophical development that leads from Bolzano to Husserl. In this sense, Bolzano teaches the existence of conceptions in-themselves[32] and the existence of propositions in-themselves.[33] Of course one must not confuse this mode of existence with that of spatial-temporal existence.[34] All conceptions in-themselves and all propositions in-themselves are continually thought by God, although this is not constitutive of their being.[35] The encompassed realm is considerably wider than for Leibniz since Bolzano considers also 'false' propositions[36] and 'false' conceptions[37] as propositions and conceptions in-themselves. And so Bolzano cannot follow Leibniz in using the principle of contradiction as a criterion of existence for the totality of concepts.

Husserl, in the *Logical Investigations* at least, takes the same point of view as Bolzano. In Chapter 11 of the first volume

Husserl turns expressly to the question of the unity of science. He first defines the concept of theory as such: 'The systematic unity of the ideally closed totality of laws, which rest on *one* fundamental lawfulness as on their ultimate foundation and are derived from it through systematic deduction, is the unity of *systematically complete theory*. The fundamental lawfulness consists either in a fundamental law or in a union of *homogeneous* fundamental laws.'[38] In the *Ideas* this is made explicit once again. A theory is a totality of propositions, in which for each one in a finite number of steps from a finite number of axioms, either the truth of the proposition itself or the falsity of its contradictory can be proved. This holds particularly of mathematical theories.[39] Between the theories interconnexions exist, there are theories which describe species[40] and others that, in a sense, describe individuals.[41] As an example of the latter Husserl mentions the three-dimensional Euclidean geometry,[42] as an example of a theory which includes this and others in a species he mentions n-dimensional geometry.[43] Thus the theories fit together into a totality, and for this totality there also exists a theory of all possible forms of theories.[44] Although Husserl does not, so far as I know, expressly speak of a totality of all theories, his presentation may be reasonably taken in this sense. There are close parallels here to the *scientia universalis* sought by Leibniz, and Husserl is well aware of them.[45]

Husserl noticed this property of theories and called such a theory a definite manifold.[46] I will use a somewhat more general term and will call such a theory a classical theory or will say that such a theory has a classical structure.

The structure which Husserl works out for mathematical theories is transferable to the totality of all theories. Although Husserl does not say this in so many words, as far as I can see, one can hardly understand the concluding remarks of the first volume of *Logical Investigations* in any other sense. There theories link up into a highest unity, which is grounded in the idea of theory as such,[47] and Husserl considers it a great task of logic to make theory as such an object of its investigation.[48] This concluding passage may permit us to summarize Husserl's teaching as follows: the totality of all theories exists and has a classical structure. This means, therefore, that the totality of all theories is free of contradictions, decidable and capable of axiomatization. To say that a theory is capable of axiomatization is to refer it back to a finite number of axioms. How Husserl applies this to the totality of theories I have not been able to determine from the texts. If there were infinitely many theories—on this too, I find nothing definite in Husserl—then it would be possible to have infinitely many axioms for infinitely many theories, while still having a finite number of axioms for each individual theory. This classical character of the totality of all theories is transferable to the totality of all the true propositions and all the concepts contained therein. The totality of all concepts must then acquire the property of being free from contradiction from the totality of all theories. It could be said that Leibniz had already asserted much of this, although his formulations lack the exactness Husserl gives to his.

Thus we come to a fundamental opposition between Husserl and Plato and we must seek a decision. What character is possessed by the totality of all theories and the totality of all concepts contained therein? Does it have a classical structure and, in particular, is it free of contradictions, or does it have some other structure and is it, in particular, burdened with contradictions? In the *Logical Investigations* Husserl claims that the totality of all theories is free of contradictions. Plato claims in the *Parmenides* that the totality of all Ideas contains contradictions. We believe that the investigations of the last hundred years on the problem of foundations has yielded a decision for Plato and against Husserl. And we turn therefore to a discussion of the problem of antinomies as it occurs in the research into foundations, which we will consider only in those aspects which are most important for our investigations.

27. RUSSELL'S ANTINOMY

An event stands behind Russell's work on the antinomies, an event which shows that even in discussions of pure mathematics and logic, tragic developments may occur. Russell's point of departure was the investigations of Frege. Frege was deeply convinced that arithmetic has a classical structure in the sense explained above. Every proposition of arithmetic is therefore either itself an axiom or it must be proved. This applies particularly to the elementary propositions of arithmetic, for example, to the proposition $1 + 1 = 2$. This proposition, too, must be shown to be an axiom or it must be proved.[1] Frege recognized this task very clearly and devoted all his life's energies to its achievement. Today Frege's importance is recognized, but in his own times he acquired, understandably, little fame. This was because Frege published his results in a symbolic language having little apparent use, and thus we can well appreciate the fact that in his own lifetime Frege had few readers. One of these few, however, was the young Bertrand Russell. He quickly recognized the great possibilities which the investigations of the foundations of arithmetic, particularly of its elementary concepts and propositions, had opened up. Russell applied himself at once to intensive work on these possibilities, and he had soon realized that from the foundations of arithmetic developed by Frege contradictions could be constructed. Russell wrote to Frege reporting his discovery of contradiction. Frege had received practically nothing except silence in response to his lifework and it strikes me continually as tragic that one of the few answers he did receive, Russell's letter, placed in question Frege's entire lifework. Frege begins his answer with the exclamation: 'Alas! Arithmetic totters'. Frege himself describes the event in the second volume of his work,[2] and Whitehead has given us a second report. Whitehead adds: 'Arithmetic tottered and totters still',[3] and in fact the discovery of Russell's antinomy cast doubt upon the classical character of logic and mathematics.

Russell published his antinomy in 1903[4] and later gave a more extensive statement in the *Principia Mathematica*:

'Let w be the class of all those classes which are not members of themselves. Then, whatever class x may be, "x is a w" is equivalent to "x is not an x". Hence, giving to x the value w, "w is a w" is equivalent to "w is not a w".[5]

A little later the antinomy is put into formulas:

'. . . there would be a class of all classes satisfying the function "$a \sim \epsilon a$". If we call this class κ, we shall have

$$a \epsilon \kappa \, . \equiv . \, a \sim \epsilon a$$

Since, by our hypothesis, "$\kappa \epsilon \kappa$" is supposed significant, the above equivalence, which holds with all possible values of a, holds with the value κ, i.e.

$$\kappa \epsilon \kappa \, . \equiv . \, \kappa \sim \epsilon \kappa$$

But this is a contradiction.'[6]

To better understand this antinomy it is often compared with antinomies already known. The relation to the well-known liar paradox of the Greek sophist tradition was recognized by Russell himself.[7] The relation to the Platonic antinomies, in particular those brought out in the *Parmenides,* have been investigated by Ryle[8] and Gregory Vlastos.[9] Hessenberg[10] has worked out the relation to Kant's antinomies, from the standpoint of set theory.

Although Russell's antinomy is not the only one in this field, we may fairly regard it as characteristic. We will turn immediately to its consequences for epistemology and ontology. The appearance of antinomies forces a new reflection on the basic concepts of logic and mathematics. In the light of the antinomies the original construction of set theory seems naïve.[11] Georg Cantor believed in the existence of sets in the sense of a naïve Platonism, he saw no difficulties either in the concept of sets as such or in the concept of the set of all sets. One must admit, however, that without such a naïve faith he could never have undertaken his great journey of discovery. Comparison with the discovery of the infinitesimal calculus leaps to mind. From the vantage point of the foundations for the infinitesimal calculus, as laid in the nineteenth century, the original thought processes of the great discoverers, Newton and Leibniz, seem quite naïve. But just because of the admitted necessity for a naïve beginning, the later reflection on the foundations of what has been discovered grows greatly in importance. That the initiative for such a reflection followed upon the discovery of the antinomies was, in a certain sense, accidental, but it was also useful, since the antinomies had made such a reflection immediately pressing.

We will discuss now the logical and epistemological consequences, later we will take up the ontological consequences. This will make it clear that our investigations are determined to a considerable extent by the contemporary situation of logic, mathematics and physics. This will be counted as untimely, at least in Germany. It sometimes seems as if today in Germany, history, whether in the true sense or in the sense of history of being, were the only theme for philosophy. We will take no pains to avoid the charge of being unfashionable. We will instead hold to the fact that always in philosophy, for Plato, Aristotle, Descartes, Leibniz, Kant and Whitehead, the problems of logic, mathematics, and physics have belonged to the great tasks set for philosophy. On the other hand, one must also call in question the conviction, widespread in Anglo-Saxon countries, that a particular ontological standpoint necessarily follows from the contemporary situation of these sciences, or that out of this same situation the impossibility of metaphysics follows.

Let us turn back to what is generally recognized: the appearance of antinomies makes a new reflection on the foundations necessary. What can we strive for? What can we hope to achieve? Evidently, a considerable goal, a solution in principle. One can strive for that foundation of logic and mathematics in which contradictions do not arise and in which it can be proved that contradictions do not arise.

That the totality of all true propositions is free of contradictions was, as we have seen, the opinion of Leibniz[12] and Husserl.[13] Logic and Mathematics are of course included in this totality of true propositions. David Hilbert[14] and Heinrich Scholz[15] might also be mentioned as supporters of this view. According to the view, contradictions can only appear if mistakes have been made in the definitions or in the inferences. These mistakes must be removed and then the contradictions will be removed also. The problem comes with the question whether this absence of contradiction can be proved and whether it must be proved. Husserl and Scholz do not seem to have regarded a proof as necessary. Leibniz, as we have seen, required such a proof for every concept, except for the basic concepts, for which consistency was intuitively given.[16] He reflected on the possibility of such a proof but encountered considerable difficulties.[17] David Hilbert made the proof of the consistency of mathematics one of the great goals of his life,[18] and he believed several times that he had practically achieved his goal. But Hilbert's failure to reach the goal was one of the decisive events in the research into foundations during the first decades of the present century. Today we know that the proof of consistency can be carried out only for relatively simple theories and that a proof of consistency for the whole of mathematics is not to be looked for. (This will be discussed below.) The great goal must therefore be given up and we find ourselves driven to the second possibility. When a specific contradiction turns up, one must go back to rearrange the definitions and axioms of logic and mathematics in such a way that the contradiction will be avoided. This task can be clearly illustrated in the case of Russell's antinomy.

Russell's antinomy would be eliminated if the concept of the set of all sets could be got rid of. Of course, one cannot simply eliminate the concept *ad hoc*. Instead one must restrict the conceptions which at first appear possible in such a way that the dangerous concept of the set of all sets can no longer appear. Foundations of logic and mathematics which meet this requirement have often been given, their logical significance and success have been variously judged. Obviously, such great efforts would not have been repeatedly made had it not been assumed possible to eliminate such antinomies as occur. The basic question thus rises again: is it possible to avoid every antinomy, can it be shown of every antinomy that it rests on false definitions, false axioms or false inferences? It is improbable that such an ambitious goal could be achieved, since it would in fact amount to a proof of consistency for the whole of mathematics. One might undertake the lesser task of resolving the antinomies presently known. Russell's antinomy will do for a start. To resolve it, one must show that the antinomy rests on false definitions, false axioms or false inferences. Whether this can be done or whether it has in fact already been done—these are disputed questions. Logicians who have provided a solution will claim this. But none of the suggestions offered to date has received general recognition. We may restrict ourselves to the consideration of two solutions, the one given by the theory of types and the intuitionist solution.

As a remedy against the antinomy he discovered, Russell himself developed the theory of types. He gave the first presentation in 1903[19], and the classical presentation is found in the *Principia Mathematica*. The theory of types divides sets and functions into various levels, or types, as Russell calls them. For example, among the sets, type T_0 contains the elementary things, type T_1 the sets of elementary things, type T_2 the sets of sets of elementary things, and so on, in an infinite series of types. The theory of types then regards all sets and all functions as assignable to some definite type. This means that for any given set, all elements of that set must belong to the same type T_n, and that the set itself must be of the next higher type, that is, of type T_{n+1}. Furthermore the theory of types requires that every assertion in order to be valid must be referred to a definite type.[20] Thus, for example, it follows that the principle of contradiction is not valid generally, but must be claimed or proven for each new type,[21] and it follows likewise, that there can be no general concept of two, the concept of two must be given anew for each type.[22]

One easily sees that in a logic and mathematics restricted according to the theory of types, Russell's antinomy is no longer possible. On the basis of the theory of types the concept of the set of all sets is no longer possible. That concept and all the assertions which can be formulated about it would cut across all types, thereby destroying the whole point of the theory of types. The concept of a set which contains itself would also no longer be possible. Such a set would contain its own members as well as itself. Its members, however, are of type T_n, while the set itself is of type T_{n+1}, and therefore this set also violates the theory of types. The concepts, upon which Russell's antinomy rests, cannot be constructed and the antinomy itself therefore cannot appear. The principle of the solutions becomes clear: by a revision of the foundations, to exclude all those concepts from which the antinomy arises.

It has gradually emerged, however, that the first formulation of the theory of types is insufficient, certain refinements are needed. Russell himself provided some refinements, and later Quine suggested others.[23]

The question then arises whether the theory of types can be regarded as the solution of all antinomies or whether it is only a solution to Russell's antinomy. The question is not easy to answer. Russell himself[24] and Quine[25] are sceptical. Whitehead's attitude seems particularly important. Whitehead lived through the discovery of the antinomy and the development of the theory of types together with Russell, who was then Whitehead's student. He may certainly be regarded as an expert judge. Towards the end of his life, Whitehead summed up his position on this question. He said:

'Russell was perfectly correct. By confining numerical reasoning within one type, all the difficulties are avoided. He had discovered a rule of safety. But unfortunately this rule cannot be expressed apart from the presupposition that the notion of number applies beyond the limitation of the rule. For the number "three" in each type, itself belongs to different types. Also each type is itself of a distinct type from other types. Thus, according to the rule, the conception of two different types is nonsense, and the conception of two different meanings of the number three is nonsense. It follows that our only way of understanding the rule is nonsense.'[26]

In my opinion, one may summarize the judgement of the experts by saying that a satisfactory construction of the theory of types has not yet been achieved.

The second solution we have to consider is the intuitionist foundation of mathematics. While the theory of types is intended directly as a solution of the antinomies, the intuitionist foundation is aimed from the outset at the basic concepts of mathematics. The solution of the antinomies is only a partial result, although one expressly intended. Brouwer regards arithmetic as the true centre of mathematics and logic. And in arithmetic the immediately given is the series of natural numbers.[27] Here Brouwer goes back to the conceptions of the Greeks, as they were represented in the previous century, especially by Kronecker.[28] The natural numbers are truly given, all other numbers are only auxillary constructions. This leads Brouwer into a definite opposition to Cantor, whose express goal it was to go beyond the infinity of the natural numbers. Brouwer's standpoint can be formulated by saying that only the infinity of the natural numbers, the 'numerable infinite', can be admitted. The resulting infinite realm may therefore be admitted, all higher infinities must be rejected. Brouwer further requires that only processes which can be actually carried out may be admitted. This excludes indirect proofs. The principle of excluded middle, which is the foundation of indirect proofs, is held to be invalid.

The operative logic of Paul Lorenzen[29] takes an old idea and makes of it the central point of logic. It has always been understood that certain concepts of logic can be represented as actions, as *operari*. The great importance of the operative logic of Lorenzen consists in actually carrying out this old suggestion, presenting us with a logic in which everything is understood as an action. At the moment we are not intending to exhaust the significance of Lorenzen's operative logic nor that of Brouwer's intuitionist standpoint, we are only asking whether they represent a satisfactory solution of the antinomies.

One must hold fast to the point that in intuitionist mathematics or in operative logic a proof of consistency cannot be conceived, according to their presuppositions such a proof cannot even be asked for. As a matter of fact, according to Brouwer and Lorenzen, logic and mathematics restricted in this way are consistent, and no one has yet succeeded in finding contradictions in the restricted theories.

A weighty objection against the intuitionist theory is raised by many mathematicians. And this objection is recognized as such by the intuitionists. Between the infinity of the natural numbers and the infinity of points of a straight line there is a difference, some would say an abyss. The classical interpretation of mathematics bridges this difference by assuming the existence of a new class of numbers, the real numbers. Cantor went further along this way and created the conceptual means by which to express precisely the relations in question, whether they in fact exist or are merely assumed. Cantor asserts that, beyond the infinity of the natural numbers, there exists an incalculably large realm of infinities. He is particularly concerned with the infinity of real numbers which, if they exist, cannot be unambiguously modelled on the infinity of the natural numbers. The infinity of the real numbers is of a higher power than the infinity of the natural numbers; it is, however, equivalent to the infinity of the points in a straight line. Cantor's solution becomes impossible when intuitionism contests the existence of any infinity other than that of the natural numbers. But since the possibility of understanding geometrical problems with arithmetic means is indispensable, the intuitionists find it necessary to resort to auxillary constructions, which create a rather artificial impression. The artificiality of these auxillary constructions is, in the eyes of most mathematicians, not unfairly, a strong argument against the intuitionist interpretation.

These considerations increase in weight when one recurs to the philosophical problems. Then we are concerned with existential questions in the realm of the infinite. It was early recognized and Hessenberg has shown formally that there is a relationship here to the old antinomies, especially to Kant's antinomies.[30] The introduction of an infinity of real numbers means that one particular infinity, that of the natural numbers, is taken as a unity, and then regarded as an element of a higher infinity. The intuitionists have noticed that this introduces a critical step, one which they regard as inadmissible. The infinity of the natural numbers may not be regarded, in its turn, as an element. It will be noticed that the intuitionists impose, very early on, a prohibition which does become necessary at some point. There is today general agreement that the set of all sets should not be itself regarded as a set, which could therefore become an element of another set. But the intuitionists forbid even the recognition of the set of natural numbers as a set in the strict sense, lest it be understood as a new element. The question is whether the prohibition has been imposed too early.

Leibniz had already seen that there is a problem here and that one can ward off many difficulties with a strict decision. We have already pointed out that, for Leibniz, the infinity of the natural numbers is not a *totum* but only an *aggregatum*.[31] Kant took an important further step. He saw that it is the interplay between infinite progression and an ever recurring, necessary conclusion, new infinite progression and new necessary conclusion, which constitutes the true irritant in the problem of infinity and is also the source of contradictions. The intuitionist solution means that one rejects this interplay at its very first occurrence; already the first infinity, the infinity of natural numbers, may not be understood as a unity in the full sense. It is thus easy to see how the intuitionists exclude antinomies, since they exclude the irritating aspect of the infinite. But this sacrifice might turn out to be too large. Kant himself looked for another way out. He lets the interplay between progression and conclusion stand. He seeks an understanding of this process and is convinced that in that understanding the contradictions, though not removed, are resolved by being understood.[32] If one considers this philosophical background of the problem it seems clear that the intuitionist solution cannot be regarded as wholly satisfactory.

Neither the solution offered by the theory of types nor the solution of intuitionism can count as a final solution. A similar judgement could be reached if one were to test the other known solutions under the same point of view. The carefully reserved summary judgement of Fraenkel and Bar Hillel should be considered important.[33] No truly satisfactory solution has yet been given, which will exclude the antinomies logically, and it is difficult to anticipate that this will one day happen. It is more likely that Kant's view will prevail: one cannot exclude the antinomies, one can only understand them; we resolve them only in so far as we understand them.

28. GÖDEL'S THEOREM OF UNDECIDABILITY

In the first decades of the present century, experts in logic and foundations were very disturbed that Hilbert's large-scaled attempts to prove the consistency of mathematics had failed. Gödel's theorem of undecidability brought the weighty knowledge that this goal is unattainable, because too comprehensive. Gödel published his discovery in 1928.[1] The importance of his discovery was soon recognized and a large literature grew up around it. Gödel's treatment was primarily formal, but before long informal presentations were also given. Every investigation presented in a strict, formalized language can also be presented in an informal language, if one is willing to waive the precision of the formalization. I have in mind particularly Rosser's presentation,[2] which is expressly characterized as 'informal', as well as the summary treatments of Mostowski,[3] Stegmüller,[4] and Bar Hillel.[5]

Gödel first restricts the area under investigation. The area shall contain the natural numbers and the operations which can be performed on them: adding, multiplying, and raising to a higher power, also the relevant theorems of elementary number-theory together with the logical means necessary to work out these concepts and theorems, in particular, the propositional calculus and the first-order predicate calculus.[6] In these investigations, when I speak of elementary arithmetic, or simply of arithmetic, I mean the system as thus defined by Gödel: the natural numbers and their laws. The unrestricted operation of subtraction and division is not required, and hence the existence of negative and rational numbers is not asserted. This is also the area which Plato, Aristotle and Euclid understood as arithmetic.

Within this area Gödel is able to define the concept of proof and provability. An arithmetic proof means a certain chain of arithmetic theorems. A particular theorem is proved when such a chain has been found, and it is provable when such a chain exists within the restricted area.[7] Within this restricted area, then, are contained not only arithmetic theorems but also theorems about their provability, for example, not only the theorem '$7 + 5 = 12$' but also the theorem '$7 + 5 = 12$ is provable'. After Gödel has shown this, the next step is to assign a number to all theorems. The theorem '$7 + 5 = 12$' receives a definite number, as well as the theorem '$7 + 5 = 12$ is provable'. After these preliminaries, Gödel succeeds in showing that a theorem with the number n can be constructed, and that theorem n asserts: theorem n is unprovable.[8] The theorem asserts its own unprovability and it is clear that this theorem can be proved neither true nor false.[9]

Initially, it is a purely mathematical question whether such a theorem can be constructed using only the means limited by Gödel. Until now, Gödel's claim has withstood all tests. Once the purely mathematical claim is accepted, one can ponder the significance of Gödel's theorem. Gödel himself observed that the old paradox of the Cretan liar has, in effect, been set up within elementary arithmetic.[10] The Greeks had raised the question: what is to be thought of the Cretan who stands up in the market-place and asserts that all Cretans are liars. The assertion is taken to mean that everything a Cretan says is a lie. One sees at once that the assertion, so understood, cannot possibly be true. If it were true, then it would be a lie, and hence false.[11] In the same way, the therem constructed by Gödel cannot possibly be prov-able, for if it were provable, it would have to be unprovable. This shows that within elementary arithmetic there is at least one unprovable theorem.[12] Such a result was not thought possible in the two-thousand year history of arithmetic, logic and philo-sophy. Furthermore, the arithmetic of natural numbers has always been regarded as the standard example to show that every theorem must be either true or false and that the truth of every true theorem and the falsity of every false theorem can be proved. In this sense, Husserl takes arithmetic as the standard example for a definite manifold.[13] He has no doubt that every theorem of arithmetic is either an axiom or can be proved or contradicted from a finite number of axioms. Using the terminology we introduced above, we can say that, according to Husserl, elementary arithmetic as a theory has a classical structure. The astonishing result of Gödel's discovery is that even such an elementary theory as the arithmetic of natural numbers no longer has the classical structure envisioned by Husserl.

Gödel's work contains a further, philosophically important result. The undecidability of a theorem can be postponed. Through appropriate arrangements, an undecidable theorem can be made decidable, but behind it, so to speak, another undecidable theorem appears.[14] The undecidability is therefore not an absolute fact; rather, it has, in a certain sense, a dynamic character.

Gödel shows further that the consistency of a theory cannot be proved using only the resources of the theory itself, consistency can be proved only by using the resources of a superordinate theory.[15] Thus, the consistency of a theory can only be achieved in a reflection upon the theory, this result of Gödel's is also quite understandable from the philosophical point of view.

29. GEOMETRIES AND THEORIES OF PHYSICS

We could continue our reflections by showing how Gödel's results have been extended by logicians and mathematicians. But we prefer to take another path. We will discuss problems which have not been widely investigated formally, and in any case are more accessible to an informal investigation like ours.

We ask first about the totality of possible geometries. From the standpoint of philosophy, this question is burdened with many difficulties. For the Greeks there was only one geometry. They did not doubt, and had no grounds for doubting, that the geometry, which we call Euclidean, is the only geometry and also the true theory of actual space. Leibniz had the same opinion, for he held that geometry, like all mathematics, rested solely on the principle of contradiction.[1] Thus, any other geometry which one might conceive would have to be contradictory. Leibniz seems occasionally to have considered the possibility of other geometries; they would be, however, mere schemata for calculating, and as such consistent, but incapable of validity in the real world.[2]

The first doubts appeared in the eighteenth century in connexion with the investigations about proving the parallel axiom. Saccheri tried to prove the parallel axiom with an indirect proof. The Euclidean parallel axiom requires that, through a given point, one and only one parallel can be drawn. In order to prove this indirectly, it must be shown that the alternative assumption: through a given point more than one parallel can be drawn to a given straight line, contains a contradiction either in itself or in its consequences. To his great astonishment, Saccheri had to pursue a large number of consequences before he hit upon the desired contradiction.[3] In later verifications, however, it was shown that the inferences he had used to exhibit the contradiction were logically objectionable.[4] Thus the supposition became more conceivable that the alternative axiom: through a given point more than one parallel can be drawn to a given straight line, together with its consequences, represented a non-Euclidean geometry. But mathematicians were slow to draw this conclusion. Lambert recognized that such a geometry represented the metric of a sphere with imaginary radius.[5] In his early writings, Kant expressly claimed geometries with more than three dimensions, and he thought of them as true geometries.[6] In his later reflection, he begins, in my opinion, with the assumption that the Euclidean parallel axiom cannot be proved from the principle of contradiction and that other consistent geometries are therefore conceivable. At the beginning of the nineteenth century, almost simultaneously, Bolyai[7] and Lobaschevski[8] published the geometry later named after them. It has been shown that Gauss had already developed this geometry but deliberately kept it hidden in his desk.[9] Riemann added a geometry in which it is assumed that no parallels exist.[10] These non-Euclidean geometries remained at first mere formalisms, and mathematicians drew attention to the absence of a proof of consistency. The proof was then obtained through the discovery of the so-called Euclidean model of non-Euclidean geometry. Poincaré,[11] in particular, was able to show that in Euclidean geometry there are figures which follow the laws of non-Euclidean geometry. If the non-Euclidean geometry were to contain a contradiction, it would then carry over to the Euclidean geometry. The last step in the development came with Einstein's introduction of Riemannian geometry into physics.[12]

The resistance of mathematicians, logicians and philosophers to the non-Euclidean geometries was strong. But the continuing successes of work in these geometries gradually brought the resistance down. A last way-out was attempted by allowing the non-Euclidean geometries but declaring that only the Euclidean should be called a geometry, while other names should be chosen for the non-Euclidean geometries. But, of course, this is only a matter of terms, not affecting the facts.

If the existence of non-Euclidean geometries can no longer be doubted, then one has to ask how this affects the concept of geometry as such. In particular, the question arises about the number of possible geometries. One sees quickly that the number of possible geometries cannot be finite. This follows immediately from the fact that the number of n-dimensional geometries cannot be finite. But the number of Riemannian geometries (and the same holds for Lobaschevskian geometries) cannot be finite. Riemann saw this[13] and Poincaré emphasized it also.[14] The transformation of other axioms, in addition to the parallel axiom, and the use of other logics open up areas for new geometries, the number of which can also not be finite.

Hence, the question arises, what character this totality of possible geometries has. Are there, for example, laws which must apply in any theory that deserves the name geometry? If there are such laws, it should be possible to gather them together into a system of axioms or, as it would be called from the standpoint of philosophy, a system of principles. This was Husserl's opinion. His reflections in the first volume of the *Logical Investigations* are determined by his admission of non-Euclidean geometries. Husserl teaches the existence of a highest genus of geometry, under which the individual geometries stand in different gradations. Just as every theory is defined by a system of principles, so this highest genus is also defined by a system of principles or axioms, though it is of course possible that the system should be comprised of only one principle or axiom.[15]

Husserl's assumption seems to us unprovable. For one thing, one must remember that the transformation of the axioms of Euclidean geometry rather quickly leads to quite alien theories. We have all got used to the non-Euclidean geometries already mentioned. But if, for example, one were to annul the Archimedean axiom of continuity,[16] the result would be a very peculiar geometry, and we would understand why the strongly reduced geometries are designated pathological. The existence of a highest system of axioms would mean that the process of transforming geometries runs up against an outer limit, which cannot be exceeded. Such a limit has not yet been found. As long as this is the case, one must consider the other possibility that the process of developing new geometries can expand without limit. There is an important difference here from the series of numbers. The series of natural numbers can also be continued without limit, but one always knows what numbers will be reached, since the process of expansion is determined by a law. No such law of expansion is known for the development of new geometries, and one cannot therefore know what geometries will be reached. I will call such a totality an open totality, using a term which has gained currency in recent decades, being used, for example, by Gonseth,[17] Bernays,[18] Hasenjäger[19] and Fränkel-Hillel.[20] I am thus accepting a view contrary to Husserl's conception of a classical totality. By the term classical totality I understand, following Husserl, a totality, which is defined through a highest system of principles and by an open totality I understand a totality which lacks such a highest system of principles. I am here considering only totalities of theorems, that is, a set of theorems or a theory. My thesis is, then, that the totality of geometries is not a classical totality, but rather an open totality.

There is less clarity in the question of possible systems of physics. The discovery of atomic physics has profoundly influenced our century, not only by its applications in war and peace, but also in the purely theoretical problems of the new discipline. We must, however, set aside the shock and go over to a cool, epistemological analysis. What kind of theory is atomic physics? How is it related to classical physics? Are other systems of physics possible? At present we know little about the relation of atomic physics to classical physics. The sarcastic remark is still characteristic that atomic physics is valid on Mondays, Wednesdays and Fridays, classical physics on Tuesdays, Thursdays and Saturdays. If the finite amount of the energy quantum approximates zero, and if the dimensions correlated with the energy quantum vary accordingly, then one comes to classical physics. This limiting condition, which is supposed to show the connexion between atomic physics and classical physics, has only one drawback: such a continual change is not at all possible according to the basic theorem of atomic physics.

Another possibility of representing the connexion between the two systems of physics would be to suppose that certain theorems hold in classical physics but that in atomic physics either these theorems do not hold or some variant of them holds, possibly even their contradictories. This would then correspond to the axiomatic way. One such theorem would be the principle of causality and the replacement of that principle through statistical laws. But this point has not been sufficently clarified. The physicists are by no means unanimous in their attitude towards the causal principle. Many physicists, today perhaps the majority, would eliminate the causal principle entirely in atomic physics. This is the opinion, for example, of Niels Bohr[21] and Werner Heisenberg[22]. Highly respected persons take the opposite side, for example, Planck[23] and Schrödinger[24], who maintain that it is not at all impossible that a causal lawfulness underlies the course of atomic processes, now understood only statistically. At least this impossibility has not been proved and would be very difficult to prove. The discussion is hindered by the fact that no one is sure just what the causal principle asserts or is supposed to assert. Future reflections must first seek a clarification of this point. The most promising direction for future research seems to me the reasoning of De Broglie.[25] De Broglie regards as too simple the disjunction that the causal principle either does or does not hold in atomic physics. He admits that the causal principle in its classical form does not hold in quantum physics, but he asserts that it is possible a weakened form of the causal principle holds in quantum physics. An analogue for this would be the laws of multiplication, which hold in their strong form for the natural numbers, and hold in an analogous form for other classes of numbers. When this idea of De Broglie's is further developed we will presumably arrive at the result that a series of laws of classical physics remain valid also in quantum physics, while other laws are not wholly eliminated, but rather remain valid in an analogous form.

If the question about the connexion of these two systems of physics remains open, the question about the possibility of other systems of physics has not yet been clarified. Do classical and atomic physics exhaust the possible realm of physics or is there perhaps behind or under these a third physics, perhaps several systems of physics or even an infinite series of possible systems? The opinion has been repeatedly expressed in the past that a particular science at a particular time is in full possession of its basic characteristics. D'Alembert was the first, so far as I know, to make this claim for mathematics, when in the foreword of his *Encyclopedia* he expresses his concern that mathematics will soon be exhausted.[26] In the nineteenth century we find a similar interpretation of mathematics by Hankel.[27] Given the condition of classical physics during the second half of the nineteenth century, it is quite understandable that it should have been thought complete in its basic characteristics.

It is possible now that the discovery of quantum physics exhausts the principal possibilities of physics, regardless of how much remains to be discovered within the framework already staked out. Such a question cannot be answered *a priori*. One can only reflect on the events known to us. Planck discovered the basic concept of quantum physics when he recognized that for certain processes energy could not be transformed continuously. Now this continuous transformation of energy was a wholly plausible presupposition of classical physics. No one could suppose and no one did suppose that this assumption could be changed. It was only new experimental findings, which could not be fitted into the old conceptual schema, that made the introduction of the quantum concept necessary. After this experience, no one will want to eliminate the possibility of a repetition. In quantum physics itself, as in any physics whenever and however developed, basic concepts may be hidden, seemingly self-evident and yet, when changed, capable of leading into an entirely new physics. Of course we cannot know what such a physics will look like, we cannot know whether and which of the contemporary basic concepts could be changed. But if one holds this possibility open, then the totality of possible systems of physics is not a classical totality but an open totality.

30. ARITHMETICS AND LOGICS

In arithmetic and logic we know a little more about these problems than in geometry and physics. In arithmetic the problem turns first on the classes of numbers. These are the extensions of the arithmetic of natural numbers, which lead to negative, rational, irrational, and complex numbers. Here it is quite customary to speak of an arithmetic of natural numbers or an arithmetic of complex numbers. For a long time, two interpretations have opposed one another. One interpretation begins with the conviction that there is a general concept of number, under which, in a way still to be defined, stand the concepts of natural, whole, rational and complex numbers. The other interpretation considers the natural numbers alone as numbers in the true sense, all other numbers are extensions which must be referred back to the natural numbers. The first interpretation is defended by Husserl. He asserts explicitly the existence of a generic concept 'number', under which the individual classes of numbers are arranged as species.[1] In a somewhat different form this interpretation is already found in Hankel. Hankel sees the extension of the natural numbers as a process in which, at any given time, an unrestricted completion is demanded of operations which, in a certain area of numbers, can only be completed in restricted form. Hankel regards this as a fundamental law.[2] This attempt to set up a systematic connexion between the classes of numbers is very impressive at first, but it does not stand up under close scrutiny. For one thing, Gauss had already shown that after the complex, two-dimensional numbers, new phenomena do not appear which would remain intact under the previously valid laws even when the dimension of the number is raised.[3] The interruption of the development at this point remains inexplicable in Hankel's system. But the most important objection is that the real numbers cannot be reached along the trail set out by Hankel. If the real numbers are to be reached by the operative route, entirely new operations must be devised, for example, the set-construction of sets of natural numbers.[4]

The other interpretation was advanced by the Greeks. The Greeks regarded only the natural numbers as numbers. Zero does not belong to them, the Greeks did not use it until the time of Diophant and, in a certain sense, one does not belong to them either.[5] The old Greek interpretation was revived in the nineteenth century by Kronecker[6] and in our own century by Brouwer and his followers. According to this view, a systematic connexion of the classes of numbers in the strict mathematical and logical sense does not exist. The first view claims the existence of such a connexion, for example in the form of a highest genus 'number', but to date no satisfactory development of this view has been given.

One should also not overlook the doubts that can be raised against the interpretation of Hankel and Husserl from the standpoint of axiomatics. The achievement of the axiomatic standpoint in geometry has run into many difficulties, and the development in arithmetic has been still slower. Kant was perhaps one of the first to consider an axiomatic construction of arithmetic.[7] In the latter half of the nineteenth century the axiomatising was pursued earnestly and Peano was one of the first to present arithmetic as an axiomatic system.[8] If a theory can be axiomatised, then derivative theories can be developed from it. By analogy with non-Euclidean geometries, I will call them non-classical theories. Such variations are formed when, for example, the commutative or associative laws are suspended for certain operations, and it is

in fact easy to give examples of operations which are not commutative. The suspension of the axiom of infinity reaches deeper
into arithmetic,[9] although finite number-classes, somewhat
differently conceived, have always played an important role.
More radical still are the suspensions of Archimedes' axiom of
continuity[10] or Zermelo's axiom of choice.[11]

The question whether a systematic connexion can be found
for these possible variations obviously depends on the question
whether the axioms themselves have a systematic connexion.
One would imagine that the possible arithmetics would represent
the possible axiomatic variations of a particular arithmetic,
presumably the arithmetic of natural numbers. This would presuppose, in turn, that the axiomatic system of the natural numbers
is completely known or at least systematically knowable; but this
is not the case. We come thus to the result that the totality of
possible arithmetics is not a classical totality, not a definite
manifold in Husserl's sense, but an open totality.

It is not different in the case of logic, although here opinions
are more sharply opposed. Many philosophers, and also many
logicians, emphatically assert that there is only one logic. This
was certainly the opinion of Aristotle, Leibniz and Kant. Kant
even thought that logic could be completed, indeed that in a
certain sense it had already been completed by Aristotle.[12]
Leibniz saw more clearly on this point; he considered logic a
science capable of the same development as mathematics.[13]
Modern logic has adopted the view of Leibniz.[14] Even so, many
logicians hold fast to the conviction that there is only one logic.
The actual development of logic, however, has assumed a different
appearance; today a whole series of different logics, bearing fixed
designations, is recognized. Thus the terms 'classical' or
'Aristotelian', on the one side, and 'non-classical' or 'non-
Aristotelian' on the other, have received a definite and recognized
meaning. The development to date has followed three main
directions: the development of many-valued logics, the development of model calculi and the development of intuitionist logics,
although these three lines of development do not exhaust all that
has already been achieved.

The development of many-valued logics is owing to Lukasie-wicz. In modern presentations an important part of Aristotelian logic has been formalized in the two-valued propositional calculus. It was advanced and applied by Frege in his *Basic Principles of Arithmetic* and by Russell and Whitehead in their *Principia Mathematica*.[15] In general an axiomatic construction is used. Wittgenstein recognized that one could substitute matrices for the axiomatic construction.[16] The matrices are two-valued, and they present the possibility of a further development through many-valued matrices. Lukasiewicz saw the possibility and studied in particular three-valued logics.[17] In many-valued logics all the theorems which hold in two-valued logic might conceivably remain valid, generally however only a part remains valid.[18] The development of many-valued logics is still in flux.

Lukasiewicz pondered the connexion of many-valued logics with Aristotelian logic. He regards it as incorrect to call them 'non-Aristotelian' and suggests instead 'non-Chrysippian' Lukasiewicz refers explicitly to the methodological connexion with the non-Euclidean geometries.[19] Although the designation 'non-Chrysippian' is more accurate for those many-valued logics which Lukasiewicz investigated, it is advisable to characterize the general problem as the problem of non-Aristotelian logic. The problem of non-Aristotelian logics, here in particular of the many-valued logics, is now at the stage in which the non-Euclidean geometries were found in the first half of the nineteenth century. At that time the formal schemata for calculating these geometries was known, and today the formal schemata for calculating the many-valued logics is known. In the first half of the nineteenth century no application was yet known for non-Euclidean geo-metries, and today no generally recognized application of many-valued logics is known. Applications have been suggested. For example, Reichenbach has suggested that atomic physics should be interpreted as an application of three-valued logic,[20] and Guenther has suggested that the philosophical theses of German Idealism could be understood as an application of three-valued logic.[21] The fact that, until now, generally accepted application of many-valued logics have not been found is no argument against the possibility of such logics. The lack of applications is a defect, to be sure, but one that could be removed tomorrow.

Furthermore, the basic requirement of an application is questionable. To recognize mathematical or logical concepts only when they have an application would constitute an indefensible rigorism. It is difficult to make application an existential requirement for mathematical and logical concepts. In the question of many-valued logics, Linke has followed the way often considered in the case of non-classical theories. He does not want to call the many-valued systems logic, preferring instead the term 'calculi'.[22] It is very questionable whether anything material is changed by the change in terminology.

Since these logics are defined by matrices and since there are infinitely many matrices, there are also infinitely many logics. And if one admits matrices with infinitely many values, the problem of the infinity of non-Aristotelian logics will be greatly increased.

The modal logic, developed by Lewis and Langford, has also proved significant.[23] It began with the assumption of three modalities, corresponding to the classical modalities of possibility, actuality and necessity. Modal calculi were also defined through matrices, and the classical modal calculus was therefore defined by a three-valued matrix. An axiomatic definition is also possible. One sees immediately that, by continuing on this path, modal calculi with more than three modalities could be reached. The investigations of Oskar Becker on higher modal calculi seem to me especially significant.[24] Resistance against higher modal calculi and the possibility of finding more modalities than the classical three is also very strong. But one should not forget that Nicolai Hartmann already recognized a larger number of modalities.[25] Hartmann, however, explicitly rejected higher modal calculi obtained on formal grounds. He was instead convinced that there is one and only one modal theory, his own, and that this theory represented the existing modal relationships better than any other. And yet one may be allowed to suppose that the development of modal theory will follow the development of non-Euclidean geometries.

The intuitionist and constructivist logics have developed along other lines. Brouwer made the decisive beginning. But he thought of arithmetic as the true centre of the theoretical sciences. Logic is, for him, only an auxiliary science.[26] Thus, the deliberate construction of an intuitionist logic had to wait until Heyting.[27] The principle of intuitionist logic and its true difference from classical logic is the rejection of the principle of excluded middle. This leads to the rejection of the indirect proof. It is against these two rejections that the main objections have been directed.

But to counter these objections it must be remembered that at all times an indirect proof has been valued less than a direct proof. Greek mathematicians preferred the direct, constructive proof, for example, of the prime numbers. An indirect proof is conceivable which could show that a finite number of prime numbers is contradictory. By contrast, Euclid's constructive proof[28] sets out a procedure by which an infinite series of prime numbers can be calculated, even though the procedure does not yield all the primes.

Even if one were less disposed to prefer the direct proof to the indirect, it would still be an important question, which theorems of logic and mathematics are dependent on the principle of excluded middle and which can be proved without this principle. By distinguishing these theorems the proponents of intuitionist mathematics and logic have made a useful contribution. But it is something else again when these proponents claim that intuitionist arithmetic and logic is the whole of arithmetic and logic. Such a claim requires much more support than has yet been given, and until then we will use intuitionist logic, against the intention of the intuitionists themselves, as a proof for the possibility of different logics.

The situation is much the same in the operative logic of Lorenzen, which in not a few aspects can be regarded as a continuation of intuitionist logic.[29] Lorenzen interprets logic as a set of thought-operations, and the laws of the elementary operations of thought are the laws of logic.

A question in no way decided by Lorenzen's construction is his claim of absoluteness. If I understand Lorenzen correctly, he is claiming that operative logic is logic as such. I am considering operative logic as one more item of evidence for the possibility of different logics, though this is diametrically opposed to Lorenzen's view. But I cannot see that Lorenzen has supplied good reasons for his claim to absoluteness. I prefer to follow the lead given by the development of geometry. From Euclid to Leibniz, mathematicians, logicians, and philosophers were convinced there was only one geometry, the three-dimensional geometry of Euclid. Today the possibility of many geometries is generally recognized. I believe that one must understand the actual appearance of many logics in our own day along the same lines. In my opinion, the point is not to find the correct logic after so many attempts, but rather to admit that there are in fact many logics. It cannot be denied that the problem in logic is much more fundamental than in geometry. It can be imagined easily that someone would be prepared to accept the possibility of many geometries but balk at the idea of many logics. One must also admit that, at the moment, the question is by no means decided. It will be decided only when there has been success in finding interpretations for different logics. The contemporary situation in logic, however, forces us to take seriously the possibility of many logics.

31. THE TOTALITY OF THEORIES

The questions discussed in the last two sections dealt with logical and epistemological, not ontological, problems. They were given a rather detailed discussion and we will continue analogous discussions in the next chapter, since the logical status of the general must influence the ontological status of the general. For the ontological status of the general it is not a matter of indifference whether the realm of the general is without exception determined by strict principles or whether such a crystalline clarity is questionable for the general as a whole. And then, one must remember that the realm of the logical, arithmetical, geometrical and physical theories we have discussed is only a part of the realm of the general. The general contains not only theories, but also propositions and concepts. Of the theories we have investigated only a small part. From the natural sciences we have considered only physics. Chemistry, geology, biology—to name only a few—have been omitted. The humane sciences have been left entirely out of account, although for the theory of theory as such it is obviously necessary to give careful attention to historical and grammatical theories, again mentioning only examples. But our goal has been to show that the realm of the general as a whole cannot have a classical structure, and for that purpose, it is enough to show this of a partial region. We hope that our claim about this region can be made thoroughly reasonable.

Plato and Kant perhaps started from similar considerations. In the first part of the *Parmenides* Plato discussed the ontological status of the Ideas and in the second part he developed the antinomies which emerge with the Ideas of unity and being. Apparently he assumed that it was enough to exhibit contradictions for two Ideas. The second part is explicitly designated an exercise in dialectic,[1] but not a complete presentation. Plato must have assumed, then, that contradictions can also appear in the other Ideas. The connexion between the two parts of the dialogue can only be understood by assuming that the appearance of antinomies in the Ideas must influence the ontological status of the Ideas.

Kant took a further step along this path. He hoped to restrict the antinomies and dialectic in general to one particular realm. The objects in this realm have a special ontological status. They have objective reality but not in the same sense as the categories;[2] they are, one and all, transcendental ideals,[3] and therefore have the objective reality[4] appropriate to transcendental ideals.

If one asks about the totality of theories, certainly the simplest and clearest solution is that given by Leibniz: there is only one logic, one arithmetic, one geometry, and one physics. An axiomatic construction of these is not basically necessary. Logic and mathematics rest solely on the principle of contradiction, physics and the other theories rest on other principles and on *a posteriori* facts.[5] In this sense the totality of consistent concepts, the totality of true theorems and the totality of theories, all exist for Leibniz.[6]

This solution is placed in doubt by the non-Euclidean geometries. The discovery of the non-Euclidean geometries in the narrower sense was basically enough to cast doubt on the position represented by Leibniz and the same discovery was thus enough for the wider discussion we wanted to start. We could have dispensed with the investigation of logic, arithmetic and physics. But the expansion of the area under discussion may perhaps have served to clarify the significance of the problem.

If one grants the existence of non-Euclidean geometries in both the narrower and wider senses, and attempts nevertheless to hang on to the classical standpoint so far as possible, one reaches the standpoint of Husserl. There are different geometries,[7] but these geometries unite in an intelligible way to form one general geometry.[8] The unity of each special geometry,[9] as well as the unity of general geometry,[10] are both constituted by a system of principles. The system of principles which underlies general geometry must also be valid for every special geometry when expanded by the appropriate special principles. All theories are thus united into one general theory. In the next chapter we will return to this point once more. What is here claimed in this general form for Husserl's viewpoint will not be found expressly in his works, it is, rather, a consequence of his writings. I have not been able to find in Husserl's works an explicit affirmation that the totality of all theories comprises a definite manifold. Husserl did not succeed in carrying through even in geometry the theoretical foundation he demanded in all areas. It would be useful for the understanding and evaluation of Husserl's thesis if at least in geometry the system of principles valid for all geometries were to be set forth. This has not been done and could only be done with great difficulty so long as an upper limit has not been found to the construction of new possible geometries.

This in no way implies that the totalities we are here discussing make all structure and every general definition superfluous. When Leibniz claimed that there could be only one geometry, one logic, one arithmetic and one physics, he was claiming too much, and when Husserl claimed that every such field is defined by a highest system of principles, this is also claiming too much. It would be much more justifiable to assume that every such region is defined by a central theory and that all other theories of the region arise through variations of the central one. This would imply, for example, that Euclidean geometry was central and that all other geometries were derived from the Euclidean through variations. In arithmetic, presumably the arithmetic of natural numbers would constitute the central theory. Now the relationship of the classes of numbers can be seen, in a certain sense, as a relation of general to particular. In this sense, Husserl[11] as well as Natorp[12] place a general concept of number above the concepts of individual classes of numbers. In the interpretation just discussed this relationship would be reversed, and the natural numbers would be understood as the constitutive region of numbers. And this would entail the old interpretation that the natural numbers are the only true numbers. This is what the Greeks thought, and in our day, Kronecker and Brouwer. That implies, for example, that fractions are not to be interpreted as numbers, but rather as relations between natural numbers, as the Greeks did. The logical foundation of fractions, as we know it today, reaches the same result. One must presuppose the natural numbers and then define fractions as relations of natural numbers. But since fractions can be defined and have been defined as the more general in relation to natural numbers, such a construction would define the general through the particular, quite against the old maxim: *definitio fit per genus proximum et differentiam specificam*. The logical construction of the theory of complex numbers must also be made in this way. One can therefore reckon as justifiable the conception which posits a central theory at the basis of the totality of all geometries and the totality of all arithmetics. It may be supposed that analogous relationships exist among the various systems of logic and physics, but for considerations of principle this can be left undecided. It is sufficient that the interpretation can be shown for the totality of geometries and for the totality of arithmetics. The open structure of these totalities must necessarily imply the open structure of the totality of all theories.

If that is so, it becomes understandable that the inevitable idea of one system of mathematics has never proved fruitful in the long run. Repeatedly it has been possible to create systematic presentations of limited regions of mathematics. And it is thus inevitable that a systematic presentation of the whole of mathematics, at least in its principles, should have been aimed at. Such attempts have been made repeatedly but have never led to a final success. In my opinion, this is now quite clear; it affords, however, no grounds at all for pessimism. That we can never complete mathematics and the theoretical realm in general, that we cannot even complete the number of principles, but must rather consider that mathematics and the theoretical realm in general contain unimagined and immense possibilities—this should constitute for us the real attraction of mathematics and the theoretical realm in general. We are convinced that today mathematics and the theoretical realm in general have now and will always have immense possibilities open before them.

CHAPTER V

THE EXACT DEFINABILITY
OF THE GENERAL

---

32. DEFINITIONS AND DEFINABILITY

Every concept must be defined. The definition of a concept must show what the concept is supposed to mean. Nothing seems to be clearer and more obvious than this demand, yet not a few difficulties stand in the way of its satisfaction. One needs for this purpose a definition of definitions. It is obvious that there are many good, exact and precise definitions. But such definitions become possible in a certain theory only when other steps have already been taken. The difficulties lie in the elementary concepts. For example, one can define very exactly even and odd numbers, to use an example that was very important for Pythagoras and his students, for Plato, for Aristotle and for Euclid. But the definition of number as such presents great difficulties.

The question of what can be defined obviously depends on what one means by definition. A definition implies the referral of a concept to other concepts and it also often implies the referral of compound concepts to their components. Here one may refer to the agreement between Plato, Aristotle and Leibniz. Plato introduces a genus-species analysis. Its result is sometimes called the Platonic pyramid of concepts[1] or the *arbor porphyriana*.[2] The procedure probably played an important role in the Academy, but we have only a few examples of it, in the *Sophist*,[3] for example. In this procedure a concept is divided up into its component concepts. The aim is to find two subordinate concepts

145

which, between them, exhaust the concept to be defined. In the ideal case the division is between a property and its negation. Aristotle also provided a systematic treatment of definition,[4] his results are summed up in the formula: *definitio fit per genus proximum et differentiam specificam*.[5] Aristotle's procedure was given a further formalization by Leibniz. Leibniz regards a definition in correct form as the analysis of a compound concept into its constituent concepts.[6]

Whatever procedure one chooses, the question will always arise whether the defining procedure goes on into infinity or whether it is concluded after a finite number of steps. All three thinkers follow the second alternative. By different ways they arrive at the same result: not all concepts can be defined.

The Platonic method of analysis obviously depends on the highest point in the pyramid. That cannot be arbitrary or the whole procedure would become arbitrary. The ideal solution would be for all conceptual pyramids to be nested in one and the same highest point. That highest point of the analytic procedure, then, would presumably be identical with the highest Idea. Here Plato encountered difficulties and in the theory of Ideas as well as in logic he rightly avoided a definitive theory.

In Aristotle's view, those concepts over which a superior genus no longer stands cannot be defined.[7] Here belong, for example, the concepts of unity and point, but also the concepts of the categories, such as substance, quality, quantity, relation. Among the concepts which, according to Aristotle, can no longer be defined, the concept of the general may well be included.

Leibniz admits concepts of infinitely high complexity. Here belong the concepts of individuals, for example, the concept of Alexander the Great.[8] Infinitely complex concepts are not wholly resolvable for a finite understanding. But in general concepts are of a finite degree of complexity. They can be resolved into their constituent concepts and, after a finite number of steps, the resolution comes to an end in unresolvable basic concepts. According to Leibniz's concept of definition, the non-compound basic concepts can no longer be defined. For Leibniz, therefore, it can never be the case that all concepts are definable. Difficulties arise for Leibniz's theory, however, when it turns out that non-compound basic concepts cannot be reached and thus cannot be presented. Leibniz complains expressly that no one has yet succeeded in pursuing a conceptual analysis back to the basic concepts and thus to its end. But he is convinced that at least the number concepts lie very near the basic concepts. It remains a serious defect in Leibniz's theory that not a single basic concept can be truly presented. Even if this defect were removed, many concepts would remain undefinable on the basic of Leibniz's theory of judgement: on the one hand, the concepts of individuals, on the other, the basic concepts.[9]

Whatever method one may choose, the result remains always the same. Aristotle put it this way: One cannot prove everything, one cannot define everything.[10]

These difficulties are especially conspicuous in the case of the basic concepts of mathematics. Euclid begins his *Elements* with a long series of definitions, among them one finds the definitions of point,[11] straight line[12] and plane.[13] But one soon notices that in the subsequent development Euclid makes no use of his definitions. So if one were to exchange the definitions of straight line and point, nothing would be changed in the construction of the geometry, since the definitions are not used. This unsatisfactory situation has often been noticed, Leibniz also pointed it out.[14]

Hilbert attempts to find a way out of the awkward situation. He gives up explicit definitions entirely and regards ə system of axioms as an implicit definition of the concepts contained therein.[15] For example, the straight line is defined by the axioms in which the concept occurs. But it is difficult to say that Hilbert's implicit definitions have led to a truly satisfactory result. One reason for this is that a system of geometrical axioms cannot be clearly referred to the basic geometrical forms. But the true difficulty does not lie therein. The true difficulty lies in the fact that an existence proof must be supplied for such a system of axioms. And this brings one up against the old Aristotelian problem of the correct definition. Now one could attempt to get get around this difficulty through a purely pragmatic standpoint. Build up any system of axioms you like and then pick out the one that suits Euclidean geometry. But there are limits set to the free invention of systems of axioms. At the least one must require that a system of axioms be consistent, that must be regarded as a minimal requirement for the existence of a system of axioms. Now the consistency of systems of geometrical axioms can be reduced to the consistency of systems of arithmetical axioms, but that only postpones the problem. A complete solution is faced with those difficulties which become visible in Gödel's proof.

Even with the definition of elementary arithmetical concepts the situation is not so favourable as one might suppose or hope. Three problems lie one upon another: the definition of number as such, the definition of natural number, and the definition of individual natural numbers, of one, two, three, and so forth.

With respect to the definition of number as such, we have already seen in the previous chapter that Husserl presupposed the existence of such a definition. But he did not present the definition itself, and it must remain questionable whether such a definition exists.

For the Greeks, the definition of natural numbers is identical with the definition of number as such. Euclid defines number as a set of unities.[16] The same definition occurs in Aristotle,[17] and the substance of it is already found in Plato.[18] The definition doesn't help much since it merely substitutes for the difficult concept of number the certainly much more difficult concept of set. In modern times, from Leibniz to the present, different methods have been suggested. One can continue to follow the old method of definition *per genus proximum et differentiam specificam*. One can adopt a constructive definition. Finally, there is the possibility of an implicit, axiomatic definition.

For the traditional approach, the concept of set appears as the proximate genus; this is the concept Euclid used. Cantor also followed this approach. One has to assume the existence of the totality of all sets and achieve, by successive limitations on that totality, a set which corresponds to the concept of natural number. But since it has been shown that the idea of a totality of all sets leads to antinomies, this approach has become dubious.

The implicit definition through a system of axioms runs up against difficulties in its existence proof, which we must consider below.

The approach through constructive definition remains. Here, the individual natural numbers must first be defined, so that one can gradually ascend to the concept 'natural number'. The Greeks looked for a definition of the number one; definitions of two, three, and the following numbers they held to be either unnecessary or impossible. In any case, such definitions are not known. That these definitions of one, two, three, and the following raise special problems was, as far as I know, first seen by Duns Scotus. If one were to use the traditional definition *per genus proximum et differentiam specificam*, the *genus proximum* 'natural number' would be divided into infinitely many species: one, two, three, and so forth, and this would be unusual, to say the least. But one would also need an infinite series of specific differences, and it is not to be expected that this infinite series of specific differences would look very different from the infinite series of natural numbers themselves.[19]

Leibniz made the first decisive advance. He recognized that one can construct the series of numbers by the operation of addition, that one can build up a chain of definitions: $2 = 1 + 1$, $3 = 2 + 1, 4 = 3 + 1$, and so forth.[20] From this chain of definitions one must first consider separately the beginning, because special problems arise about the numbers one and two. Apart from the problems of the beginning, this could well be the correct approach, and the elementary definitions in arithmetic today ordinarily use it. This means that the concepts of the natural numbers are referred back to the concepts of addition, equality and unlimited succession. Unlimited succession is expressed by the phrase 'and so on', the phrase constitutes an indispensable part of the definition. One sees that the concepts of addition and equality will not be easy to master, and that the difficulties lying in the infinity of the series of numbers are only postponed, trivially, in the concept of infinite succession.

The initial definitions of one and two, and perhaps also of zero, underlie this chain-definition. The definition of the number one is an old problem. Aristotle says: πανταχοῦ δὲ τὸ ἓν ἢ τῷ ποσῷ ἢ τῷ εἴδει ἀδιαίρετον.[21] It is debatable whether Aristotle intended this description as a definition in the true sense, although that was the opinion of Thomas Aquinas.[22]

The definition or the possible definition of the number one plays a great role in the foundations research of the last hundred years. One can distinguish three approaches: a set-theoretical definition, recourse to reality, and a purely logical definition. The set-theoretical definition stems from Cantor. Out of the set of all sets one can first separate those sets which contain only a finite number of elements. These sets can be ordered according to size and all the ones with the same number of elements grouped together. In this way one obtains the series of finite cardinal numbers and, at the beginning of this series, the numbers one[23] and two.[24] This definition, therefore, does not rest on a construction, but it runs into difficulties because it makes use of the set of all sets as a starting point.

Frege attempts a purely logical definition of natural numbers. His starting point is the definition of zero. A zero set is a set which contains no element. Such a set can be defined by a contradiction. One defines a set which, for example, contains all those elements which are not identical with themselves.[25] After this it is easy for Frege to define a set which contains only one element and thereby to obtain a definition of the number one.[26]

The exceptional position of the numbers zero, one and two is expressed in the *Principia Mathematica* by the fact that they are treated already in the first volume, while the general discussion of cardinal numbers follows in volume two. One can, of course, assume that this exceptional position was not expressly intended but was instead called for by substantive reasons. The *Principia Mathematica* dissolves the connexion suggested by Frege between the numbers one and zero, they are defined independently.

The null class is defined in 24.03 as the opposite of the universal class. The universal class, in turn, is defined as the class of all those elements, which are identical with themselves. In essence this is Frege's definition.[27] But the authors of the *Principia* take another approach to the definition of the number one. First the cardinal number one is defined as the class of all unity-classes.[28] Then the unity-class is defined as the class of all those elements which are identical with a given element.[29] This definition presupposes the definition of identity. This is given formally in 13.01. The formal definition is then rendered in everyday language as follows: 'This definition states that x and y are to be called identical when every predicative function satisfied by x is also satisfied by y . . .'[30] This implies, as the authors of the *Principia* clearly see, that Leibniz's *principium identitatis indiscernibilium* is being used.

The ordinal numbers[31] and the cardinal numbers[32] are defined in the second volume. The definitions rest not on addition, but on the concept of two-termed relations. The definition of the cardinal number zero is given in 54.01.

It is evident that two basic concepts have emerged. First one encounters the concept of unity as such, then the combination of two unities into a new unity. Plato had already taken these as basic elements, for his doctrine of unity and the indefinite dyad can hardly be interpreted in any other way.[33]

Summing up the result of this long and intensive work, one finds that it is not very satisfactory from a strictly logical point of view. Generally recognized definitions have not been found. It is thus understandable that from an intuitionist or operative standpoint the series of natural numbers is regarded as originally given. There is no need to doubt that certain analyses are possible here, the results of which can be set down in definitions. Yet, after a few steps, one encounters concepts which are not further definable: the concept of set, the axiom of infinity, the concept of the connexion of two unities into a new unity. One finds that Leibniz's insight is confirmed: the natural numbers are very close to undefinable concepts if they are not so regarded from the outset. The consideration of the elementary concepts of mathematics thus ends with the old insight of Aristotle: one cannot define everything.

33. THE AXIOMATISING OF THEORIES

The basic characteristic of axiomatics was recognized by Aristotle. To prove means to show that a theorem follows from another theorem as from its presupposition. The referral of a theorem to its presuppositions either goes on endlessly or it comes to rest in an ultimate presupposition.[1] In the second case the ultimate presupposition must be reached in a finite number of steps. In this sense, Euclid gave his *Elements* an axiomatic construction. Leibniz turns against the axiomatic construction of mathematics, in particular of geometry,[2] but his position is better characterized by saying that mathematics rests on one sole axiom, the principle of contradiction.[3] This position has not been confirmed. Mathematics cannot make do with the principle of contradiction alone. It seems that Leibniz himself, in some problems, went beyond his own expressed position.

If a theory needs several axioms, the next easiest possibility is that a theory has a finite number of axioms. This is Husserl's opinion,[4] and he seems to have thought that the finite number of axioms could be completely formulated. From what we know today, this thesis must be rejected. Only a few theories can be axiomatised in a finite number of formulable axioms. For some quite simple theories this is no longer the case, and Tarski has shown that only a small fraction of known theories can be axiomatised.[2]

First one must grasp the point that, in contrast to Aristotle's opinion, a theorem's property of being an axiom is not an absolute property. This was made clear very early for geometry. In the Euclidean framework, if the parallel axiom is adopted then, for example, the theorem about the sum of the angles of a triangle is a provable theorem. But one can also take the latter theorem as an axiom, and then the parallel axiom is a provable theorem.[6] These relations are quite apparent in the two-valued propositional calculus, which can be considered as in many respects the standard example of a theory. The two-valued propositional calculus is easily axiomatised, the *Principia Mathematica* gives a system based on five axioms.[7] Tarski was the first to show that the system of two-valued propositional calculus can rest on one sole axiom.[8] This is not to be confused with Leibniz's standpoint, since the axiom in question goes far beyond the principle of contradiction.

In order to decide whether every theory must follow the condition laid down by Husserl, we will first consider the actual discoveries of some fundamental axioms. There are fundamental axioms, which have already been used implicitly and only relatively late have been recognized explicitly as axioms. A good example is Archimedes' axiom. It is found in two places. In the *Squaring of the Parabola* it runs: 'If two areas are unequal, it is possible to multiply the ratio by which the smaller is exceeded by the larger so often that any finite area will thereby be exceeded.'

In the text *On the Sphere and the Cylinder* Archimedes lists five axioms. The fifth runs: 'Also for unequal lines, surfaces and bodies, the excess of the larger over the smaller is of such a magnitude that through repeated multiplications it can become larger than any given magnitude of the sort under comparison.' The axiom describes such an obvious fact that it has always been in use, as Archimedes himself remarks. In Euclid the axiom occurs as a definition,[11] in Aristotle as a theorem.[12] Archimedes' axiom is often called the axiom of continuity. It does not hold for all quantities. The best known example is the angle of contact between the circle and its tangent. If one inscribes contiguous circles of different radius through the same point on a straight line, different angles of contact occur. The difficulties of their treatment have always been noticed, they rest on the fact that angles of contact are not Archimedean quantities. Once the significance of Archimedes' axiom is known, it is easy to construct non-Archimedean geometries and non-Archimedean arithmetics. Hilbert gives several examples.[13]

The peculiar problem lies in the fact that the axiom had always been in use and that its function as axiom was discovered relatively late by Archimedes. But this leads us to consider the possibility that lurking in our theories are axioms, for which an explicit presentation is possible and necessary. This interpretation is strengthened by the fact that the explication of implicit pre-suppositions has occurred several times.

Perhaps the clearest example is Pasch's axiom. It states that a straight line which enters into a triangle must also come out of this triangle.[14] This axiom also has always been applied, Pasch's achievement is to make it explicit.

As a further example I will mention the axiom of infinity. That there are infinitely many numbers has always been known since the beginning of mathematics, and many proofs rest on this presupposition. But it is not easy to grasp this point axiomatically. Peano divides the point into two axioms.[15] The first asserts the unlimited continuation of a successor relation, the second forbids such an unlimited succession from returning to itself. It cannot, for example, run in a circle. The difficulties of the axiom of infinity appear clearly in *Principia Mathematica*. The treatment begins in section 120 with the introductory remark: '. . . mathematical induction was treated as a kind of self-evident axiom.'[16] The authors first define the concept of inductive cardinal number.[17] Then the axiom of infinity is defined.[18] In section 123 the authors give a series of definitions, which are equivalent to the axiom of infinity, which show for example that the axiom of infinity is equivalent to the existence of a numerable infinite.[19] Then they say expressly: ' "Infin ax", like "Mult ax", is an arithmetical hypothesis which some will consider self-evident, but which we prefer to keep as a hypothesis, and to adduce in that form whenever it is relevant.'[20] And the authors of the *Principia* adhere to this procedure.[21] This was, as a matter of fact, a possibility often considered in the nineteenth century: to interpret all axiomatic theories hypothetically. For example, the parallel axiom would appear only hypothetically in Euclidean geometry: if there is one and only one parallel to a given point, then the sum of the angles in a triangle amounts to two right angles. But such an hypothetical interpretation is no longer possible if logic itself is axiomatised. Thus we have in the *Principia Mathematica* the remarkable irresoluteness that logic itself is axiomatised while the axiomatising of arithmetic is retracted to the extent that the axiom of infinity and the axiom of choice are introduced only hypothetically. I do not believe that a separate treatment of logical and arithmetic axioms is grounded in reality. It is easier to suppose that the different treatment arose from the wish to reduce arithmetic and all mathematics to logic.[22] Whatever the treatment one decides to give these two axioms, they were long in use before being explicitly recognized and formulated.

This applies particularly to Zermelo's axiom of choice. Zermelo discovered it as he was attempting to find an axiomatic foundation for set-theory.[23] According to the usual interpretation the axiom of choice is necessary only for infinite domains. Given an infinite set of sets, each containing more than one element, the axiom of choice guarantees the existence of a set containing one and only one element from each of the infinitely many sets. Russell's example strikes me as the clearest. Think of a set of infinitely many pairs of shoes. Then there is a set which contains only the right shoe from every pair.[24] The property chosen, 'right shoe', is illuminating. Whether such a property exists in every case is questionable, and it is the function of the axiom of choice to guarantee that this will be so. The axiom of choice has a wide-ranging significance; without it, very simple operations, such as the multiplication of two sets, cannot be carried out in general.[25] Thus the axiom of choice reaches deeply into the structure of a theory; domains in which the axiom of choice is not valid are as a rule still quite odd.

Reflections on these four axioms lead to the same result. Each time fundamental facts are formulated. They are facts that have always been implicitly required, they cannot be dispensed with in the construction of the relevant theories. One must therefore reckon with the possibility that further such fundamental axioms will be discovered, and each of these discoveries belongs to the great deeds of intellect. There is at least no possibility of proving that further such discoveries will not be made. With respect to such fundamental axioms, theories remain always open.

Although this fundamental question cannot be answered by reason of its nature, there are certain partial questions which can be answered. Skolem has shown that even elementary arithmetic cannot be completely axiomatised, in the sense that all axioms have been completely presented.[26]

But one can go on to ask the further question whether every theory as such can be axiomatised. Of course this depends on what one understands by a theory. Certain reflections are possible about the propositional calculus which will also prove relevant in this epistemological discussion. The theorems of two-valued propositional calculus can be regarded simply as a set of theorems. Then, for example, the three-valued logics which Lukasiewicz investigated become partial sets which can be defined axiomatically as well as through matrices. One can then consider any partial set of the theorems of two-valued propositional calculus and name such a partial set a theory. For example, one could remove only one theorem from two-valued propositional calculus, and name the remaining partial set a theory. One could not expect to be able to axiomatise such a partial theory. Further one must consider that two-valued propositional calculus also depends on rules of inference, and that it would be changed through any changes in the rules of inference. One would expect that the logics which arise in these different ways could not generally be axiomatised. The logics which can be axiomatised constitute a distinctive but perhaps only a very small part of the possible logics.[27] The capacity for being axiomatised would then be a distinction applying to only a small part of the immense number of possible theories.

34. CLASSICAL THEORIES AS IDEAL THEORIES

We have been pursuing the concept of a classical theory, a theory which Plato and Aristotle presupposed as self-evident, and which Leibniz, Bolzano and Husserl have made ever more exact. Of such a classical theory three properties are required: consistency, decidability, the capacity to be axiomatised. We will reproduce here Husserl's clear exposition:

'. . . the variety of spatial formations generally has a remarkable logical basic property, to indicate which we introduce the name *"definite"* manifold or *"mathematical manifold in the pregnant sense of the term."*

'It has the following distinctive feature, that a *finite number of concepts and propositions*—to be drawn as occasion requires from the essential nature of the domain under consideration—*determines completely and unambiguously on lines of pure logical necessity the totality of all possible formations in the domain*, so that *in principle*, therefore, *nothing further* remains *open* within it . . . Every proposition constructed out of the designated axiomatic concepts, and in accordance with any logical form whatsoever, is either a pure formal implication of the axioms, or formally derivable from these as the opposite of what they imply, that is, formally contradicting the axioms; the contradictory opposite would then be a formal implication of the axioms.'[1]

In the preceeding investigations we have, however, raised a series of valid objections to the classical concept of theory. But this in no sense implies that we are rejecting the classical concept of theory as such. We would like to summarize once again those objections and then attempt a positive interpretation of the classical concept of theory.

The first objection is about the classical requirement of consistency. The requirement is not only that every theory should be consistent, but that this consistency should be capable of proof. So far as I know, Leibniz was the first to make an explicit demand for consistency. But we have seen that consistency cannot be proved generally, in any case not in the general sense attempted by Leibniz and Hilbert. But is the actual requirement of consistency generally justified? The mathematicians and logicians are concerned that from one contradiction any other contradictions can follow. A theorem corresponding to this can be easily proved in two-valued propositional calculus. But this theorem holds only with the logical expedients available in two-valued propositional calculus. These expedients can be limited in appropriate ways. In that case theories are conceived in which only one contradiction appears, or alternatively, in which a delimitable group of contradictions appears, and the rest of the theory is kept free of contradictions. For such theories the understandable hesitation of mathematicians and logicians against the appearance of contradictions would no longer hold. An example of the first interpretation is given by Plato and Hegel. They were of the opinion that the appearance of one contradiction led to all others. An example for the opposed interpretation is given by Kant. For him, contradictions are restricted to the transcendental dialectic; logic, mathematics and physics remain consistent.

To accept the principle of contradiction as a universally valid principle would be to deny the possibility of any dialectic. One would then have to reject the dialectic of Hegel, but also the dialectic of Kant and the dialectic of Plato. It is hard to believe, however, that all these investigations of dialectic should correspond to nothing in reality.

Against the general validity of the principle of contradiction stand also the investigations into intuitionist and operative logic. It is true that the principle of contradiction is retained in these logics and in the mathematics built on them, but the suspension of the principle of excluded middle which is so closely bound up with the principle of contradiction considerably affects the old self-evidence of the two principles.

The thesis that every theory must be consistent can thus neither be proved nor, in my opinion, intuitively grasped from the pure essence of 'theory as such'. The same applies, as we have seen, to the requirement of complete decidability and to the requirement of complete axiomatisation.

But it does not follow from this that the classical concept of theory as a system of propositions which is consistent, completely decidable and capable of complete axiomatisation is meaningless or even superfluous. We believe such a conclusion would be over-hasty. One must instead regard the classical theory as the ideal for all theories. The ideal is even achieved by some few theories, for example, the two-valued propositional calculus. At least this holds when one prescinds from the difficulties concealed in the metatheoretical definitions of every theory and therefore also of two-valued propositional calculus. Among the meta-theoretical definitions of two-valued propositional calculus are, for example, definitions about the correct use of signs. It is not to be expected that such definitions can be put into an ideal logical form. Other theories, for example elementary arithmetic, closely approximate the classical ideal of a theory. Perhaps the often lamented imprecision of biological theories or of theories in the human sciences is owing to the fact that factual theories are, as a rule, a good distance removed from classical theory and that this distance in the case of biological theories or of theories in the human sciences is particularly conspicuous for reasons hitherto not considered.

In the interpretation presented here, that most theories are not definite manifolds and that, in particular, the totality of all theories is not a definite manifold, the author has been strongly reinforced by the fact that Husserl himself towards the end of his life reflected again on the classical standpoint. His famous formulation: 'The dream is now ended'[2] signifies his final interpretation. The bitter formulation is reminiscent of Frege's deeply felt complaint. Nevertheless I believe that Frege and particularly Husserl have considered things too pessimistically. On the contrary, it seems to me that Husserl's great merit was to have expressed with special precision the conviction which mathematicians, logicians and philosophers have had for more than two thousand years. All have believed, in fact, that every theory as such and also the totality of all theories constitute definite manifolds. The exact formulation remains an indubitable merit. The pure idea of a theory retains its meaning, and one must always test how far a theory meets or falls short of these ideal requirements. This is only possible if the ideal requirement has been precisely formulated, and to that extent the concept of the definite manifold is in no sense a dream, but a concept of great and enduring significance.

35. PRINCIPLES AND AXIOMS AS FOUNDATIONS

We are accustomed to designating principles and axioms as foundations. But this expression, for which incidentally there is no Greek equivalent, suggests misleading errors. The foundation of a house must be laid first, only then can the house be built. But if one characterizes the principles and axioms as foundations, this interpretation suggests that one must first have the principles and axioms, in order to build a theory upon them. The Greeks were more careful in their expressions. The Greek temple did have a strong substructure. But the Greek house did not ordinarily have such strong foundations. In their systematic construction of theories as well as in the logical and ontological interpretation of theories, the Greeks avoided a term which would be equivalent to 'foundation'. Euclid used the term αἰτήματα.[1] The term ἀξιώματα is found in Aristotle.[2] In logical and ontological discussions the usual term is ἀρχή. Its primary meaning is 'to stand at the top', and Plato can therefore use it to designate the highest Ideas.[3] Gradually, the meaning 'to stand at the beginning' became stronger, and this is ordinarily the meaning Aristotle attaches to the term.[4]

If one reflects on the relation of a theory to its principles, Plato's interpretation is undoubtedly that mathematics does not begin with its principles. A long and difficult ascent to the principles is necessary. As a rule mathematicians will not undertake this ascent, but will instead make do with the pragmatic application of current assumptions.[5]

Subsequent developments have shown that Plato correctly interpreted the function of principles. We have just seen that in the case of four fundamental axioms, the axioms themselves had always been used but were only discovered at a relatively late stage of the theory and then placed at the top.

The Platonic interpretation is confirmed through the history of mathematics as a whole. Geometry certainly did not begin with axioms, but with intuitive properties, in particular, with the intuitive properties of symmetry. The theorem on the sum of the angles of a triangle was, as Geminus reports, first proved for particular cases, only at the end was the general proof formulated. The historians of mathematics have convincingly explained that the sum of angles in the triangle was first discovered for the equilateral triangle and was initially read off the equilateral triangle from its properties of symmetry.[6] And, in fact, the equilateral triangle can be inscribed six times within a circle. This yields a figure of great symmetry from which the sum of the angles can be easily read off. In an analogous way the Pythagorean theorem was first discovered for the triangle which has sides with dimensions of 3, 4 and 5. It is just the same in the case of arithmetic. Peano, in the nineteenth century, was the first to set his mind to the axiomatising of arithmetic, while the theory itself was already in large measure present in Euclid. One may suppose that this is not a matter of historical accidents, but that the systematic construction of mathematical theories also had its beginning in concrete and intuitively grasped facts.

For these reasons the interpretation of axioms as foundations seems to me thoroughly misleading, at least when the original meaning of foundation as something which must be there first is retained.

If one wants an image for the relation of theories to their principles, the image of a tree would serve better. The higher a tree grows, just so much deeper do its roots reach. The construction of a theory is also a process in two directions. On the one hand, the theory will be continually extended, and on the other hand, its principles will be continually discovered and explored. Part of the reality is also expressed in the terminology of foundations, when one says that the foundations of a theory must be more deeply dug. Strictly speaking, this expression is in conflict with the concept of foundation. One cannot lay the foundations of a temple more deeply without tearing down the temple. But nothing is further from the intentions of those working on questions of foundations than tearing down the theories.

We believe, therefore, that the construction of a theory in some sense always moves in two directions. In the one direction a theory is built up towards ever more abstract and general theorems, and the process ordinarily has no end. In the other direction one searches for principles and axioms, and this work too never comes to an end. In this interpretation of principles and axioms we hope to have correctly formulated the convictions of the great explorers, for example, Zermelo and Gödel.

In this sense we consider the discovery of a new principle and a new fundamental axiom as one of the great achievements of the human spirit. But we think that one understands this work incorrectly if one believes that it could be finished today or tomorrow. Work on the foundations, in the nature of the case, must always be regarded as an open possibility, only then does one see it in its true significance.

PART II

Section II

THE ONTOLOGICAL DETERMINATION OF THE GENERAL

CHAPTER VI

THE GENERAL AS IDEA: PLATO

36. THE TASK OF THE ONTOLOGICAL DETERMINATION OF THE GENERAL

In this metaphysics we have allotted such a considerable space to the logical problems of the general because the logical status of the general is closely connected with its ontological status. The ontological determination of the general, to which we now turn, encounters in striking fashion the plurality of philosophies. And it is particularly in ontology that the question becomes especially pressing: why are there so many philosophies? To answer this we will follow Hegel's conviction that the plurality of philosophies does not constitute a defect, philosophy must necessarily be expressed in many philosophies.[1] We will discuss Hegel's conviction in detail in Part Three, on method. We will there attempt to show that Hegel is right in his conviction about the necessity of many philosophies, but that he cannot be followed in his opinion about the kind and manner of connexion between the philosophies. We are also not able to follow him in taking up the plurality of philosophies in their full historical content. Instead we will concentrate the historical content under systematic headings into three great possibilities: Plato, Aristotle and Kant. Even so, we already have with these three a plurality which must be affirmed. It is not the task of ontology to take sides with one of these philosophical parties. It cannot be the first task of ontology to defend Platonism or Aristotelianism or Kantianism. Such a Platonism ordinarily tends towards a naïve Platonism, which is certainly not in the spirit of Plato. It is just the same with Aristotle and Kant. Once the plurality of philosophies is recognized the primary task is to understand each of them in its ontological design. The investigation must show what is intended in each philosophy and in what way its assertions are grounded in reality. A second investigation must then assess whether the particular approach can be carried through without qualification or whether it encounters difficulties or perhaps even leads to aporias. Finally the question must be discussed whether and how the three philosophies we are considering are interconnected. Our first goal is in a certain sense stated by Hegel's thesis: philosophy is the totality of philosophies, this totality being restricted, for our reflections, to three great philosophies. The result will then be investigated in the third Part, in relation to method as such.

37. ARITHMETIC

Plato's theory of number and hence of arithmetic is so complicated that it will perhaps never be fully clarified. Today we have begun to understand that these complications have systematic causes. But his theory does contain a core which is beyond debate and sufficient for our reflections. This core consists in the theory that the numbers are Ideas, though number must of course be understood here in the Greek sense. This part of the theory of Ideas is unassailably fixed in examples, there is an Idea of two,[1] of three,[2] of eight,[3] of ten.[4] There is an Idea of ἕν,[5] and to the extent that ἕν is regarded as a number, that is, as the number one—which is not in every respect valid for the Greeks—it too belongs here. This much is certain, everything else is difficult and questionable. Are there Ideas for the larger numbers as well? Aristotle's report implies that Ideas were assumed only for the first ten numbers,[6] and this seems highly probable. It is understandable that many things should remain open in this question. If one assumes Ideas only for the first ten numbers, it becomes difficult to assign a reason why there is no Idea for the numbers from eleven on. If one assumes Ideas for all numbers, we then have infinitely many numbers and this is not easy to reconcile with the basic conception of the theory of Ideas.

Plato evidently further attempted to derive the plurality of numbers systematically from principles. Aristotle comments on this,[7] and in the *Parmenides* one finds a derivation approximating to this.[8] Stenzel has studied it,[9] and Becker has considerably advanced our insight into the problem.[10] A final clarification can hardly be expected from such meager material, and only in modern times do we have a true appreciation of the systematic difficulties of such a problem, some of which were discussed in the preceding paragraphs.

In his old age Plato apparently sought for a particular connexion between numbers and Ideas. On this too we have a report by Aristotle,[11] and the lecture 'On the Good'[12] given by the aged Plato must have been intensively concerned with this question.[13] Here also one can expect no final clarification. It must remain in doubt whether Plato in fact ever formulated a definite and final theory. For our reflections it is enough that there are Ideas of the numbers.

What is the meaning of this thesis? What does Plato intend to say when he explains that the number three is an Idea? This is the ontological task which we see as primary: not to take sides immediately, not to argue for Plato or against him. For both positions there would be good reasons. But the philosophical task is to understand the ontological meaning of the theory of Ideas, in the first instance with the thesis: the number three is an Idea.

In my opinion, there are two considerations which led Plato to understand the numbers as Ideas and which also determine in general every ontological interpretation of number: the general normative character of number for all thinking and the quality of precision. This is probably the point of strongest influence of Pythagoras and his students on Plato.

The general normative character of numbers and their laws is, in fact, a simple given, which may be called either a fact or a phenomenon. There is no need to doubt that in some remote time there were men who did not yet recognize number and that there may be such men today. It is, however, not easy to demonstrate this. There seems to be no known language which does not recognize the number two; in some cases there is an explicit numeral, in others the number is expressed in a special linguistic form, for example as a dual. The connexion of numbers with definite objects is also a feature of early linguistic formations. However that may be, when men come to the consideration of number—and by number I mean here, as ordinarily in these investigations, the natural numbers—they then always see number in the same way. Natural numbers and their laws are the same for all men at all times and in all places. Arithmetic is the same for the Greeks, for the Romans and for the Germans, if we may extend a formula which, as we will later see, Leibniz applied to geometry.

The second consideration which probably led Plato to regard numbers as Ideas is their quality of precision. In the equation $3 \times 4 = 2 \times 6$, the one side is truly equal to the other, not nearly equal, not equal to the nearest approximation, but truly equal. This argument, which plays such a great role in the *Phaedo*,[14] is there referred to equality. But it can be varied for the Ideas as a whole in ever new ways.

These two arguments, in particular that of the general normative character, are difficulties for an extreme empiricism, and it is not easy to see how they can be overcome from that standpoint. Certainly there are empirical aspects within the domain of the general and particularly in arithmetic, geometry and logic; we will have to discuss them thoroughly at a later stage. But these empirical aspects do not authorize any attempt to dispute away the general normativeness of the arithmetic of natural numbers, and at least with respect to logic such an attempt has hardly ever been made.

If one tests the meaning of the two arguments for the theory of Ideas, one sees that at least for the general normativeness, we are dealing primarily with an epistemological problem. This is because we are considering a very special domain. In fact, one can say with justice: It is the Idea of beauty which makes beautiful things beautiful. But one will not want to say with the same emphasis: It is the Idea of three which brings it about that three things are each three.

From the standpoint of methodology one can ask generally: what reasons are there for assuming the existence of Ideas? The question is independent of one's final evaluation, it can be raised both when one wants to accept the theory and when one wants to reject it. One can ask: With what arguments can the theory of Ideas be proved? On what presuppositions do these proofs rest? How much do they prove? Do they prove less than the advocates of Ideas desire? Or do they perhaps prove more? If the proofs were to prove too much this would be presumably just as bad as if they proved too little. The problem took on this methodological form already in Plato's time, perhaps through the work of his students and friends, perhaps through his own work. In any event, Aristotle had a clear conception of the problem; he considered the structure of the existence proof for the theory of Ideas[15] and of one particular proof he says expressly that it proves too much.[16] It is regrettable that the methodological problem did not remain on this high level. The advocates of Ideas are usually so directly preoccupied with questions of content, that they devote little time to questions of method. This applies even for thinkers well trained in method, such as Bolzano and Husserl. It seems to us necessary to detach the investigation of proofs of existence from the ontological standpoint of the investigator, and to test these proofs under purely methodological criteria. Of course we are quite clear on the point that in these investigations towards a general metaphysics we can really only give a programme, not carry it out. This is all the more the case since the methodological requirement holds not only for the philosophy of Plato but for those of Aristotle and Kant as well.

As a fundamental principle we must keep two things carefully distinct in the theory of Ideas. The thesis that, for example, numbers have an ideal being, must be separated from the question how this ideal being is to be understood. To this extent we apply a variation of the Aristotelian formulation: Not whether there are Ideas, but how there are Ideas, that alone is the philosophical question.[17] As long as one in this sense keeps open the question of what is to be understood by the ideal being of numbers, and so long as one wants to understand by the thesis: number is an

Idea, only that numbers and their laws are generally binding for all thinking men, just so long is the theory of Ideas simply a description of fact. We do not mean to imply that, for Plato, the problem arises in this general normativeness. The reverential cult of number among the Pythagoreans, of which we have such an impressive example in Philolaus,[18] certainly exerted a profound influence on Plato. But the significance of number in arithmetic as a pure science probably influenced Plato even more than the significance of number for the cosmic harmony of the spheres. In any case, of all the reasons which may have moved Plato to the interpretation of number as an Idea, the general normativeness of numbers and their laws for all thinking beings has been the most important historically and the one richest in consequences.

38. GEOMETRY

The objects of geometry are Ideas, the theorems of geometry are ideal theorems, geometry is an ideal science—all this is undoubtedly true for Plato. But also for Plato, as in the issue itself, great difficulties spring up.

The difficulties begin in the strange fact that Plato only rarely refers explicitly to geometrical concepts as Ideas. In the *Phaedo* interest is focused on the ethico-aesthetic Ideas, the beautiful, the good, the just. Nevertheless, even in this dialogue, a whole series of logical and mathematical Ideas do appear. The Idea of equality is used as example when the theory of Ideas is introduced, the Idea of three is expressly named, and Ideas of other numbers also appear in the discussion. But geometrical Ideas are lacking in the *Phaedo*. By contrast, the theory of Ideas is introduced in the *Seventh Letter* by means of the Idea of circle.[1] In the *Republic* we find the Idea of square and the Idea of diagonal.[2] But, so far as I know, the Idea of point, the Idea of straight line, and the Idea of flat surface do not appear in the Platonic dialogues. Aristotle discusses such Ideas when he systematically assesses the interpretation of mathematics in the theory of Ideas.[3] Of course one quickly sees the difficulties which must occur in an Idea of point.

In geometry too the true foundation is probably given by the general normativeness. Geometry, says Leibniz,[4] is the same for Greeks, as for the Romans and the Germans, and there can be no doubt about this. Now the empirical aspect is easier to see in the case of geometry, than in arithmetic. The name 'art of measuring land' clearly expresses this and it is thus understandable that repeated attempts have been made towards an empirical foundation for geometry. But a purely empirical foundation for geometry is always wrecked on the reef of geometry's general normativeness, and it always will be wrecked thereon. The fact of geometry's general normativeness is also not eliminated by the discovery of non-Euclidean geometries. We regard the discovery of non-Euclidean geometries as a fundamental phenomenon for epistemology and for ontology. But the general normativeness of geometry must be understood precisely in this connexion. For Plato things were much easier. For him there was only one geometry, and for him geometry is one of the great steps leading up to the entrance into the theory of Ideas.[5]

In geometry the second basic phenomenon, the precision of ideal being, becomes more evident than in arithmetic. Only the circle of geometry is a real circle, only it is a line all points of which are equidistant from a centre point. No circle in actual reality is a circle in this precise sense. The flat surface of geometry is the only exact flat surface. The art of the mechanic and the optician goes a long way, they can manufacture surfaces smooth as glass, but they will never manufacture a flat surface in the exact sense. The distance between the most perfect forms of actual reality and the absolutely perfect forms of geometry is a traditional example for the distance between the Idea and the actual thing. It is thus clear how markedly the characteristics of general normativeness and precision influenced Plato in interpreting the objects of geometry as Ideas.

39. PHYSICS

For Plato, physics is essentially astronomy, and in a certain sense this is also true for Aristotle, although both go beyond this limitation in their theories of the elements. The turn to astronomy is understandable because the discovery of lawfulness in nature began with the discovery of lawfulness in the heavens. In a certain sense celestial mechanics remains even for Newton the core of mechanics and thus the core of physics.

In his interpretation of astronomy Plato comes to a distinction which at first sight appears strange. In the *Republic* he says:

'These sparks that paint the sky, since they are decorations on a visible surface, we must regard, to be sure, as the fairest and most exact of material things, but we must recognize that they fall far short of the truth, the movements, namely, of real speed and real slowness in true number and in all true figures both in relation to one another and as vehicles of the things they carry and contain. These can be apprehended only by reason and thought, but not by sight.'[1]

Plato compares this ideal astronomy to geometry, which may certainly not be guided by models, though the models be made by Daedalus himself. Then he emphasizes once again that the numerical proportions of days to months and months to the year are unsatisfactory.[2] In fact the revolutions of the heavenly bodies, here in question, are not at all related by integers. This is, however, what Plato demands. He obviously supposes that the proportions of the revolutions should be related only through integers. Furthermore, in his opinion these integers should also be special numbers, for example, perfect numbers in the arithmetic sense. So, for Plato, the great year, in which all stars will return again into the same constellation, is determined by a number marked out by purely arithmetical properties.[3] Today this sounds rather absurd, but it has not yet been established whether certain fundamental determinations of physical reality do not flow out of simple mathematical regularities. In this way Plato had to distinguish between an ideal astronomy and a factual astronomy, in which for him only the ideal astronomy could be a science in the true sense.[4] Plato was led to make this demand not only by his theory of Ideas, but probably also by the

Pythagoreans. For the Pythagoreans the determination of the universe through number could only mean that the cosmos is determined through integers, indeed, through special integers. In this vein Aristotle reports, and his report is probably true, that the Pythagoreans had to add one more to the nine known, moving celestial bodies, in order that the cosmos could be ordered under the number ten.[5] Although Plato's distinction between an ideal and an empirical astronomy may seem alien, it is based on reality. Theoretical astronomy is in fact an ideal theory, because it treats of ideal objects, and every theory is an ideal theory.

This can be clearly seen in Newton's work. Firstly, physics is here essentially astronomy. Newton discovered his laws of motion as laws of the movements of heavenly bodies, and only in a second, bold step did he extend the validity of these laws to all bodies and hence also to terrestrial bodies. If one inquires about the basic character of Newtonian physics, the *Philosophiae Naturalis Principia Mathematica* then proves to be a very mixed work. It is in no sense limited to mathematical principles, it also treats problems which largely depend on empirical data, for example, the theory of tides.[6] Of course this mixed character of text-books even of theoretical physics continues down to the present day. Presentations of theoretical physics as a completely pure theoretical system or even attempts to do this are rare, though Hertz's presentation and Hermes' attempts towards an axiomatising of Newtonian mechanics might be mentioned.[7] If one separates theoretical physics from its connexion with the empirical, it then appears as a purely theoretical system, and one can regard it for example in the Newtonian form as a mechanics of mass-points. In this domain one can operate largely with the principles of mechanics, taking some of them as presuppositions and others as derivable theorems.[8] In the same domain one can also use laws other than Newton's law of gravitation.[9] This clearly reveals the ideal character of the system. In the real world there are no discrete mass-points. There can also be no question of asserting that real movements describe ellipses in the exact sense. Continual disturbances from the other heavenly bodies already render this impossible. The ideal character of Newton's mechanics of mass-points is revealed still more clearly in his first axiom. The axiom asserts that a body continues its motion in the same direction and with the same velocity so long as no other forces act upon it. This can never occur in reality because the condition is unreal. In reality other bodies are continually acting upon any given body. The Newtonian mechanics of mass-points treats therefore of ideal objects and in respect to this idealization it is intimately connected with geometry. This makes it clear why theoretical physics was formerly regarded as a joint task by mathematicians and physicists and why the great researchers: Archimedes, Newton and Gauss, to name only a few, worked with both physics and mathematics, regarding them as a unity. That in the Newtonian mechanics of mass-points we have an idealization, that at bottom every theory represents an idealization, at least those which are presented in mathematical form— these two points have often been made. I will mention only Mach,[10] Niels[11] and Whitehead.[12]

If one attempts to get clear about Newton's own interpretation of his laws of motion, the usual opinion is that he adopted a markedly Platonic standpoint. But this is not at all certain. It seems to me that the theological aspect had considerable importance for Newton, so that his view would at least have to coincide with the further development which Augustine gave to the theory of Ideas. In this sense one can say that Newton thought of the laws of motion primarily as God's thoughts. God has laid down these laws by his free decision. He could have laid down others, He can also change these at any moment.[13] This consideration allows Newton to solve a problem that evidently gave him much trouble. One can ask whether the system of planets will not come to a standstill and hence a collapse, because of its continual loss of energy. But God gave energy to the system of planets in a free decision and he can therefore at any moment freely restore the lost energy.[14]

Newton says all this, however, with great caution and only in passing. The situation can be more clearly grasped in Leibniz. Here the connexion between Plato and Augustine is clearly evident, and Leibniz himself frequently alludes to it. Natural laws are, for Leibniz, spatial-temporal systems of relations and, like all relations, particularly relations of space and time, they exist primarily *in mente divina*.[15] The distinction between necessary and non- necessary truths is, in a certain sense, retained. The necessity of the *principium rationis sufficientis* holds generally. It holds for all finitely existing things as well as for the decisions of God. But there is in addition the necessity of the *principium contradictionis*. The laws of logic, arithmetic, and geometry are necessary by reason of the principle of contradiction. The laws of physics, on the other hand, are also necessary but only by the principle of sufficient reason.[16] Thus, other laws of motion with other exponents are both consistent and possible,[17] but in this actual world there can be only one law of attraction, that of the second power, because of the principle of sufficient reason. Other laws exist as possibilities in the mind of God, but there is a sufficient reason why in the best of possible worlds there should be a law of attraction of the second power, and it is just this reason which is invoked in God's creation of this world with this law of attraction. With these considerations Leibniz rejects any arbitrary intervention of God into nature and guarantees the thoroughgoing validity of the laws of nature.

Taking all these considerations together, the laws of nature are determined as Ideas, by Plato in a somewhat indefinite form, and by the great scientists of early modern times, who represented the Ideas and therefore the Laws of nature primarily as God's thoughts. Two reasons for this emerge, and they are the same that appeared for geometry and arithmetic: the general normativeness of mechanics and its precision.

Limiting ourselves again to classical mechanics, there can be no doubt that we all have the same mechanics, just as we all have the same arithmetic and the same geometry. This general normativeness is not eliminated by the fact that atomic physics restricts the classical mechanics in certain ways which are not yet wholly clear. One thing is clear: atomic physics does not cancel out classical physics, it sets limits to it and thereby brings it for the first time into its own true domain.

Just as clear in classical mechanics is the character of precision which attaches to the aspect of idealization. That two bodies move in ellipses of which the focal point is the centre of mass—this is as far removed from the real world as the geometrical theorem that the tangent which touches the circle has one and only one point in common with it.

40. LOGIC

If we attempt to look at logic from the standpoint of the theory of Ideas, we are doing what Plato himself could not yet do, for it is to Aristotle that we owe the first construction of logic as an independent discipline. On the other hand, quite a number of distinguished representatives of logic take a markedly Platonic standpoint, among them Leibniz, Bolzano, Frege, Husserl, Scholz, Whitehead, Church, Gödel, Fitch, and many others.

Discussion is made difficult by the fact that opinions differ about what constitutes the object of logic. Is logic a theory about the art of thinking or a theory about what is thought? If the former option is taken, then logic is often built up as an art which teaches how the results of thinking are best presented. If logic is taken as a theory about what is thought, it develops of itself into a theory of the thinkable, the thinkable regarded in reference to certain formal structures.

These difficulties are already to be found in Aristotle. The content of the *Organon* is extraordinarily diverse. It contains linguistic investigations, the Aristotelian theory of categories, the Aristotelian syllogistic, an epistemology, instructions for convincing an opponent, and also instructions for merely persuading him.

We may leave the discussion about the object of logic to one side, since we are considering only a part of logic, in which matters are somewhat simpler: the two-valued propositional calculus. This can now be presented with great precision, we are thinking in particular of its presentations in the *Principia Mathematica*,[1] and in Quine[2] and Scholz.[3] It belongs to the theories which have been most carefully explored epistemologically; we already saw that it is consistent,[4] decidable[5] and capable of axiomatisation in a finite number of steps.[6] It is one of the few theories which correspond to the requirements laid down by Husserl for all theories.

Because of the logical simplicity of two-valued propositional calculus the question about its ontological status is relatively clear. Two-valued propositional calculus has an ideal being, that is the thesis maintained by those logicians who represent a Platonic standpoint. Of course, many logicians, particularly those of the empirical and analytic school, regard this thesis as incorrect, but their objections are not very convincing at least for the two-valued propositional calculus. That theory presupposes such a definiteness in its objects that one cannot see to what empirical domain two-valued propositional calculus could be adequately applied. It is no different when one refers the theory to language, as many logicians are now inclined to do. With respect to two-valued propositional calculus, at least, it seems difficult even to articulate what this frequently expressed opinion is supposed to mean. If the opinion means that two-valued propositional calculus is a part of language, in so far as it must be spoken, that is trivial, since every theory must be spoken. And to the extent that the theory must be spoken, it is so markedly different from all ordinary languages that it must at least be regarded as a *sui generis* language. If the opinion means that two-valued propositional calculus treats of language, then its proponents must first say what this language is. In any case, it is not any of the known ordinary languages. There can be no doubt that the known ordinary languages are not two-valued. It becomes understandable then that Scholz, in his dispute with Kaila, claimed he could find no meaning in his opponent's thesis.[7]

The two reasons we have already worked out for the acceptance of an ideal being: general normativeness and precision, are revealed just as clearly in two-valued propositional logic. Two-valued propositional calculus is only a part of logic and is also only the formal presentation of a part of the Aristotelian syllogistic. To that extent it can be regarded as an arithmetic of the numbers one and two,[8] it is a part of arithmetic. In either way of regarding it, the two-valued propositional calculus remains a generally normative theory, binding on all men and obvious to them. When particular theorems, such as the principle of excluded middle, are challenged in intuitionist and operative logic, this is not a challenge against the general normativeness of the theory as such, but rather a challenge against the claim that a certain theorem belongs to this generally normative theory.

One can perhaps debate whether the ideal being of the two-valued propositional calculus follows from its general normativeness, and in our systematic considerations this is the essential question, but one cannot contest the general normativeness of logic.

Just as great is the precision of two-valued propositional calculus. The theory presupposes absolutely that all propositions which can be formulated in its propositional variables, are either true or false. But in the real world there are very few two-valued facts. It is certainly true that in February of this year 1963, in this place and at this time, it is unmistakeably cold, but the question whether it is warm or cold cannot be so clearly answered in every place and at every moment. Bolzano mentioned as example the blossoms of a tree, and it is clear that he wrote this paragraph in a beautiful Spring hour.[9] But the very example Bolzano uses seems to me to prove the incorrectness of the underlying opinion. There are always forms on this tree of which one cannot say whether they are still buds or already blossoms, and there are always forms of which one cannot say whether they are still in bloom or already wilted. The discrepancy between the continuity of process and the discreteness of our determinations, first noted by Zeno, makes it impossible to interpret the world with its continually changing processes as a manifold of two-valued events. Here too one must say that two-valued propositional calculus is just as removed from the real world and just as removed from real language, as the relation of a tangent to the circle is removed from the relation of a rod to the wheel of a locomotive. In the two-valued propositional calculus we have, without doubt, an ideal theory.

CHAPTER VII

THE GENERAL AS LAW OF NATURE: ARISTOTLE

———

41. PHYSICS

If one wants to sum up Aristotle's opinion in a short formula, it is not easy to find a suitable term. One can choose between two versions: the general is a law of being or the general is a law of nature. In their German senses, the first expression is too broad, the second too narrow. The expression 'law of nature' in German is pretty generally tied to physical laws, sometimes even to mechanical laws, and this is too narrow for Aristotle. Among the general concepts which we want to investigate in their Aristotelian interpretation is also found, for example, the concept of unity or the concept of man. On the other hand, the term 'law of being' is too broad, since the term 'being' in the terminology of Nicolai Hartmann also includes ideal being. Nevertheless, this meaning as ideal being is already a certain extension of the term, and the German word '*Sein*' remains strongly tied to real being. If one keeps this primary trait in view the term 'law of being' corresponds pretty exactly to what Aristotle intends.

That in physics the general is represented as a law of nature and that physics deals with nature, hence with real being—this seems to be a triviality. Aristotle too in many places regards this as self-evident. But things are not so simple. What does that mean: treats of the real world? We have just seen that the Newtonian laws of motion stand much closer to the laws of geometry than to an empirical description of actual events. In order to understand Aristotle on this point, we will attempt a brief summary of his theory of nature.

From our point of view the relevant parts of Aristotle's theory of nature can be divided into three groups: the theory of the cosmos as a whole, the theory of the movements of the stars and the theory of the elements.

The theory of the cosmos in general represents a rational cosmology in the sense of Christian Wolff.[1] Aristotle teaches that the cosmos is a sphere[2] with a finite extension[3] and with the earth, at rest, as its centre.[4] Around the earth there lie in concentric spherical shells water, air and fire, and then as a fifth element, the ether.[5] The ether constitutes the heaven of the fixed stars.[6] This heaven makes one revolution daily around the earth.[7] This motion is unchangeable, without beginning and without end.[8] The cosmos of Aristotle is therefore spatially finite and temporally infinite.

The theory of the motions of the heavenly bodies constitutes astronomy. Here Aristotle departs essentially from Eudoxus.[9] There are seven celestial bodies in motion: the sun, the moon, and five planets. Their visible motions are composed of circles.[10] The whole constitutes a rather complex system of circles,[11] the model for which was in Aristotle's own time still undergoing frequent changes. Aristotle himself assumes 47 circles.[12]

The Aristotelian theory of elements is based upon the idea of motion and qualities derived from it: light and heavy.[13] This approach would be characterized nowadays as physics. A second starting point is furnished by the qualities warm, cold, moist and dry.[14] And this would be regarded today as chemistry. Of these three domains, the cosmology and the theory of elements are specifically Aristotelian, while in astronomy Aristotle could base himself upon already developed theories. Understandably, then, Aristotle turned primarily to astronomy for epistemological and ontological reflections. Aristotle also gave some attention to optics[15] and acoustics.[16] Of course these two sciences were still in their first beginnings, although the Pythagoreans had already achieved some remarkable insights into acoustics.[17] But it remained for Aristotle's intuition to recognize what possibilities had been opened up in these two new sciences.

The three sciences, particularly astronomy, treat of the real world. This is important for Aristotle in his debate with the theory of Ideas. The substance of the debate concerns the argument for the existence of Ideas, which Aristotle calls the argument from the sciences.[18] A science, the argument asserts, can deal only with Ideas, and since astronomy is a science it must deal with Ideas. We have seen with what determination Plato draws this consequence. But if Plato is correct here, there must be in fact an ideal sun and an ideal moon, and astronomy would deal with them.[19] Aristotle finds it preposterous that astronomy should not deal with this visible heaven.[20] According to the argument for the theory of Ideas astronomy must be related to an ideal heaven, which exists alongside the visible heaven.[21] For Aristotle this is absurd, and one may well assume that it was particularly the assertions in the *Republic* which struck him as absurd.

Aristotle's interpretations have always been regarded as a form of empiricism. Kant, for example, remarked that Aristotle can be regarded as the chief of the empiricists.[22] In a certain sense this is no doubt correct. But this should not lead one to overlook the *a priori* aspects which considerably shape Aristotle's theory of nature. An important part of the theory of nature is deduced *a priori* and it can be achieved in no other way, since the claims in question, for example the spherical shape of the cosmos, are in no way accessible to empirical experience. And these *a priori* elements bring again a certain ideality into the Aristotelian physics, as we will see. This prevents us from interpreting it as a pure empiricism.

42. GEOMETRY

Astronomy, geometry and arithmetic have the same great significance for both Plato and Aristotle. They are important to Plato when he sets up his theory of Ideas, and they are important for Aristotle when he comes to consider the theory of Ideas. Plato and Aristotle are fully justified in assigning so much significance to these three disciplines, and no investigation into the being of the general can afford to overlook them. Aristotle speaks of them in detail in Book XIII of the *Metaphysics*. He succeeds here in giving a quite clear presentation of his position both as to its affirmations and its denials. Here Aristotle's polemic against Plato becomes particularly intelligible, and here his theory on the being of the general finds one of its most intelligible presentations.

Book XIII of the *Metaphysics* is a full-scale investigation of the being of the general. Werner Jaeger points out that here, apart from a few paragraphs, we find methodical and terse metaphysical investigations.[1] I can only concur in Jaeger's praise for Book XIII. The book begins with a short presentation of the object and plan of the investigation.[2] According to the plan, the investigation is divided into three parts. In the first part Aristotle asks about the being of mathematical objects,[3] in the second he asks about the being of the Ideas as such,[4] and in the third he investigates the connexion between the mathematical objects and the Ideas.[5] We are concerned with the first part, in which the theme is the being of mathematical objects. As guiding principle for the investigation Aristotle employs the beautiful formula we have already cited: Not whether there are numbers, but how there are numbers, that alone is the philosophical question.[6]

In Chapter III Aristotle presents his theory about the ontological status of astronomy, geometry and arithmetic. In the same place he also discloses his opinion about their mutual relations. As we have already seen, Aristotle regards it as self-evident that astronomy treats of the heavens as we observe them. Astronomy considers the heavens, however, not in their full perceptual content but only in their observable motions. Here begins the fundamental moment of abstraction for Aristotle, on the basis of which one can rightly characterize the Aristotelian theory as a theory of abstraction. For example, astronomy does not regard the sun in its full perceptual content. The sun warms and illuminates, it brings the Spring, it determines the course of the year. Astronomy abstracts from all of this,[7] it regards the sun only as a body in motion. Such an interpretation can only be considered an abstraction. For this it is not necessary to accept the existence of motion as an ideal being in the sense of the theory of Ideas.[8] It is also not necessary to assume—Aristotle is here perhaps thinking of certain derived forms of the theory of Ideas—that there is in visible things a special Idea of motion existing for itself.[9] The fact of astronomy as a science does not therefore necessarily lead to the acceptance of Ideas existing for themselves;[10] in Aristotle's opinion it can be better explained through his theory of abstraction.

Aristotle holds that geometry is to be understood in the same way. To do this one must imagine that the abstraction, on which astronomy rests, must go a further step. The orbital paths are now no longer regarded as orbital paths, but only according to their geometrical form as curves, the basis of which is the circle. In the same way, the sun is now no longer regarded as a light-giving and warming heavenly body, and also not as a moving heavenly body. Instead it is considered solely as to its form, that is, as circle. Even here the decisive thing is the as-function of the abstraction. Geometry considers the real, perceivable world, but it touches the world only in a definite abstraction, it touches the world only in its spatial form.[11]

Finally, according to Aristotle's conviction, arithmetic should be understood in the same way. Once again the abstraction goes a step further. Arithmetic also deals with the real world perceivable through the senses. But it considers the world solely in relation to its numerability, it takes all things solely as numerable.[12] Now the celestial bodies are no longer interpreted in their full brilliance, as they show themselves, but also no longer in their motions, as in astronomy, and no longer in their form, as in geometry, but only as numerable. Now the sun is no longer the warmth-giver and light-bringer, no longer the self-moving, no longer the circle, but only one among the seven moving celestial bodies.

According to Aristotle's conviction, then, in the real world different structures lie one upon another, and these structures can be separated out through abstraction and each represented in a special way.

In this sense geometry treats of the real world, of course taken in a special way. Aristotle says this in many places. Geometry, he says once sharply, deals with the straight lines which occur in nature.[13] Geometry is thus the theory of the space of the real world and of the forms which occur therein.

Aristotle's theory of geometry as a science of the real world has been repeatedly adopted, although we are not here concerned with the question of direct connexion with Aristotle. For Newton, geometry, as well as arithmetic, are only auxiliary sciences of physics.[14] It is thus understandable that Newton's infinitesimal calculus is introduced not as a purely mathematical theory, but rather as a theory of motion, and therefore constitutes a part of physics. If Newton thus builds geometry into physics or, to use his preferred terminology, into *philosophia naturalis*, then it follows that geometry deals with the real nature which forms the subject of *philosophia naturalis*.

Among mathematicians an empirical interpretation of geometry has repeatedly been advocated, I might refer in particular to Pasch[15] and Helmholtz.[16] Of course an empirical foundation for geometry has been made more difficult because of the axiomatising which must necessarily lead to non-Euclidean geometries both in the narrow sense and in the wider sense. As long as only one geometry was known, one could well imagine that this one geometry represented the theory of the one space of the real world. But difficulties arise when one recognizes the existence of several geometries. One is then led to ask which of the many geometries holds for the real world. Poincaré rejected this question, it was his opinion that every geometry could be transformed into every other and that it is therefore a question of expediency which one uses to describe the real world.[17] Einstein, on the other hand, maintains the thesis that the world has a definite spatial structure. He allows the question to be put, which is the correct geometry, and he decides that the world has a Riemannian space. So, for Einstein, only Riemannian geometry refers to the real world.[18]

43. ARITHMETIC

According to Aristotle arithmetic treats of the real world. It treats of real things, however, not in the fulness of their perceivable qualities, but only in abstraction, in so far as they are numerable.[1] We have just seen how Aristotle shows, on the instructive example of the celestial bodies, that the abstraction from the sensible properties of celestial bodies pushes on beyond astronomy and geometry to arithmetic.

To this extent Aristotle understands arithmetic as a theory about real things, taken in their numerability. We have characterized this feature of arithmetic and of the general as such as its general normativeness. The general normativeness is especially clear in the case of arithmetic. The laws of natural numbers are generally normative for real things. Five pennies and seven pennies makes twelve pennies. They are exactly twelve pennies, not more and not less; this proposition seems completely clear and this is where Aristotle's interpretation begins. But things are not so simple as they at first appear. If arithmetic is a theory it must have a certain distance from the real world. This distance in the case of geometry cannot be missed. For numbers and their laws, however, the distance seems at first inconceivable. But the Aristotelian idea of abstraction can be followed a long way also for arithmetic. The theory of abstraction presupposes that the things, upon which the abstraction of numerability is made, are already in themselves discrete and fixed. But in the real world this basic presupposition is often not realized. The example of the pennies is from a domain in which the requirements of discreteness and invariance are realized in the dimensions normal in human existence. But, in general, there stretches an unbridgeable gap between the discreteness and invariance of things, as presupposed in arithmetic, and the real world of things which are continually being altered and transformed into one another.

The Pythagoreans came upon this gap for the first time when they discovered that the diagonal of the square cannot be measured by the sides of the square, and that there is therefore no natural number and no proportion of natural numbers which measures the diagonal.[2] One can understand that this recognition struck the Pythagoreans like a catastrophe.[3] Although in modern times numbers have been developed and refined so far that the connexion between arithmetic and geometry can be constructed again, the fundamental problem remains the same.

The things of the real world are not numerable in the strict sense. Of course Bolzano claimed the opposite. In his example which we have already mentioned, the number of blossoms on the pear tree, which no one certainly has counted, nevertheless is a definite and discoverable number. But this same example seems to me to show the incorrectness of Bolzano's interpretation. The number of blossoms on this pear tree at this moment is not a fixed number, in my opinion. This comes not from the fact that no one has counted the blossoms, but rather from the fact that the processes of blooming and withering are continuous processes. On many places of this beautifully blooming tree it is therefore not objectively fixed whether a blossom is already there or no longer there.[4]

Whitehead clarifies this problem in a thought experiment.[5] He supposes that a man is transformed into the dimensions of an atom. At the same time his measurement of time is so transformed that a thousand years is only a second for him. After this transformation, the pennies (Whitehead speaks of chairs, but we may retain our example) lost their discreteness as well as their invariance. Taken spatially the penny would be a very large set of atoms, a kind of cloud of atoms, and this cloud would change steadily. Many atoms leave the set, others are added, and this change would proceed unabated before our eyes. In such a way the ever-changing cloud would shortly be wholly transformed, whether, seen in our time dimension, through attrition, through shattering or through melting down. And quite apart from the relative invariance of the penny coins, in a hundred thousand years only a very few of the ones now existing will still exist.

Also, it is very easy to give examples of domains that are not countable. The clouds in the Spring sky, the waves in the moving sea are not countable, not because no one has the time or the inclination to count them, but because they are not in themselves countable given their continual changes. The things of the real world are not countable in their plurality because the definiteness and exactness necessarily required of the objects of arithmetic are lacking in them.

Nevertheless since the time of Aristotle this reference to the real world has had a great importance for the ontological interpretation of number. The medieval formula: *numerus est res numeratae*[6] does not necessarily have to be understood in the sense of an extreme nominalism. This was probably the intention of Petrus Aureolus,[7] but in the case of Ockham one can suppose that the formula is to be understood in the sense of a conceptualism.[8] A thoroughly Aristotelian foundation of number upon the numbered things is found in Leibniz. For him numbers are always numbers of monads or of the perceptions and strivings of monads. To that extent we find the numbers in ourselves.[9] The specific existence of numbers, for Leibniz, consists in their being conceived, by us,[10] or, in the last analysis, in the mind of God.[11] Thus numbers, as well as the whole of mathematics, before the creation of the world would exist only in the mind of God as possibilities.[12] This is for Leibniz an unreal hypothesis, however, since the world was not created at some finite time, but has always existed. In this sense the imaginary numbers are nothing real for Leibniz, because they do not designate anything real.[13] Gauss was the first to find a foundation for the imaginary numbers when, taking his stand on ontological questions with Aristotle and Leibniz, he proposed that imaginary numbers and all complex numbers in general could be interpreted as representations of real relations.[14]

The difficulties Aristotle has with the infinite number series, which we will consider below, pose no problem for Leibniz. For him there are infinitely many monads[15] and therefore an *actu infinitum*,[16] this means that the infinity of the number series is guaranteed by objects. In addition, the Aristotelian interpretation plays an important role in Leibniz's existence proof. We have seen that Leibniz requires an existence proof for all concepts, and that it consists in a proof of consistency. But a proof of consistency is usually not available.[17] It is here that Leibniz makes use of the Aristotelian interpretation to prove the existence of numbers. The number two exists, because there are two things.

The number three exists, because there are three things. Thus the ontological interpretation of number also preserves its logical meaning.

The same problem arises in the *Principia Mathematica*. There the problem is to guarantee the existence of classes. We saw already that the *Principia Mathematica* abandons Frege's purely logical construction and that it presupposes the existence of at least one class through the existence of at least one thing. One thing at least must exist, hence there is also a set, which contains this thing.[18] The existence of further sets, including among them the existence of numbers, can then be proved, according to the *Principia*, by purely logical means.[19]

It can therefore be said that Aristotle's idea that numbers refer to actual reality and that numbers can be understood as numbers of things, has had a great influence. An extreme empirical interpretation of arithmetic does not seem fruitful, however. In any case, I have not been able to find, either in Comte or in Mill, a convincing interpretation of arithmetic from an extreme empiricist standpoint.

44. LOGIC

Aristotle is the founder of logic as an independent discipline. It cannot therefore present itself to him in the same way as astronomy, geometry and arithmetic. This explains why one encounters very few ontological reflections on the nature of logic in Aristotle's writings. We have already seen that Aristotle's *Organon* in the form in which it has come down to us contains a great variety of topics. The scope of the work ranges widely, from hermeneutics to the fallacies of the sophists.

Within the broad compass of the *Organon* there are, however, parts which constitute a logic in the strict sense. They are, in particular, formal logic in the narrower sense contained in the *Prior Analytics* and epistemological investigations contained in the *Posterior Analytics*. Although Aristotle did not publish an ontological determination of logic as a whole, we do find explicit ontological reflections on partial problems. The most notable is on the principle of contradiction and, understandably, this investigation is found in the *Metaphysics*.

Aristotle deals with the principle of contradiction in Book IV of the *Metaphysics*. The book begins with the explanation, already referred to above, that there is a science which treats of being as such and the properties which are ascribed to being as such.[1] This is the context within which the discussion of the principle of contradiction must be seen. Chapter 2 provides epistemological discussions about such a philosophy, first repeating thematically the theory of the plurality of meanings of being.[2] In Chapter 3 and throughout the rest of Book IV, Aristotle treats expressly of the principle of contradiction and the problems connected with it.[3] Here it emerges clearly that the principle of contradiction has a double function. The principle says that a being cannot possess an attribute and its contradictory at the same time,[4] it also says that we cannot think and maintain as true both a proposition and its contradictory.[5] The principle of contradiction is therefore at the same time a law of being and a law of thought. This double function has often been emphasized.[6] In so far as the principle of contradiction is a law of being, it makes clear the reference of Aristotelian logic to the real world.

Leibniz's way of emphasizing this connexion is to assert that the principle of contradiction also holds for God's thought. Augustine had already insisted that God's thought must be *rationabiliter*.[7] But in the discussions of the Middle Ages this was often disputed. Leibniz deliberately returns to the standpoint of Augustine.[8] All truths, in so far as they are primarily God's thoughts, are determined by the principle of contradiction. The infinity of possible worlds, in so far as their being consists in being thought by God, is determined by the principle of contradiction. Therefore the real world too, in so far as it is first conceived by God and then created by God, is included in the scope of this principle. Thus one can say that Leibniz continues the Aristotelian approach, for Leibniz too the principle of contradiction is both a law of being and a law of thought.

We also find this double function in Wittgenstein's *Tractatus* in a most interesting way. For the purpose of our ontological reflection, we divide the *Tractatus* into two levels: the theory of the elementary propositions and the theory of the logical propositions. The two levels pose different ontological problems. The elementary propositions express what is the case,[9] and the totality of all elementary propositions summarize everything which is the case.[10] We do not need to enter now into a discussion about the existence of elementary propositions, we will follow Wittgenstein's own assertions. Initially, the elementary propositions refer directly to what is the case. But then, in a meta-theoretical sense, it is asserted that there cannot be two elementary propositions which contradict one another. In this meta-theoretical sense the principle of contradiction in the *Tractatus* is initially an assertion about the totality of elementary propositions, about the character of the assertions made in these propositions, but it is at the same time an assertion about reality.

CHAPTER VIII

THE GENERAL AS
ACTIVITY OF THOUGHT: KANT

45. ARITHMETIC

Kant defines the general as an activity of thought. In the *Critique of Pure Reason* he says:

'But the combination (*conjunctio*) of a manifold in general can never come to us through the senses, and cannot, therefore, be already contained in the pure form of sensible intuition. For it is an act of spontaneity of the faculty of representation; and since this faculty, to distinguish it from sensibility, must be entitled understanding, all combination . . . is an act of the understanding. To this act the general title "synthesis" may be assigned, as indicating that we cannot represent to ourselves anything as combined in the object which we have not ourselves previously combined, and that of all representations *combination* is the only one which cannot be given through objects. Being an act of the self-activity of the subject, it cannot be executed save by the subject itself.'[1]

Our summarizing formula for the Kantian standpoint—the general as activity of thought—has been drawn from this text, for here Kant speaks explicitly of combination as an activity of the understanding. There can be no doubt that we have here the fundamental thesis of Kant's thought. Cohen has summarized it in the thesis: All unity is combination[2] (*Vereinigung*), and Heidegger has shortened this to: All unity is unification (*Eini-*

gung).[3] We will attempt to clarify Kant's basic approach[4] by using the four theories which we have selected as *exempla metaphysicae*.

With respect to arithmetic, Kant was not at first clear as to where this theory fits in the construction of the Critical Philosophy. The appropriate arrangement is clear for geometry. Kant treats geometry in the Transcendental Aesthetic with the theory of space, and he says there explicitly that every theory of space must explain the possibility of geometry and that, in fact, only the interpretation of space as pure intuition in the sense of transcendental philosophy could really do this.[5] It would seem obvious, then, to interpret arithmetic as a theory of time, and Kant considered this possibility on occasion. But later Kant located number essentially with the schematism, where number appears as the schema of quantity.[6] In this connexion Kant says expressly: '*Numerus est quantitas phaenomenon*.'[7]

Two aspects of number especially interest Kant: first, the summation of a manifold into a unity, in particular the summation of two into one, and secondly, the capacity of this operation for unlimited continuation. For Kant all the emphasis lies on the first aspect; the capacity for unlimited continuation, and therefore the infinity of the number series, recedes into the background. The significance of this accentuation is seen when one notices how often the accent is placed on this second aspect in the interpretation of Kant. Among the interpreters—Natorp is a case in point—the infinity of the number series is the most important, indeed in a certain sense, the only important aspect.[8] Nevertheless I believe that Kant is right when he concerns himself primarily with the summation of a finite multiplicity into a unity. In this sense, he says:

'But the pure *schema* of magnitude (*quantitatis*), as a concept of the understanding, is *number*, a representation which comprises the successive addition of homogeneous units. Number is therefore simply the unity of the synthesis of the manifold of a homogeneous intuition in general, a unity due to my generating time itself in the apprehension of the intuition.'[9]

Here there is no mention of a capacity for the unlimited continuation of such a synthesis, and thus of the infinity of the number series. At least, there is no claim that the manifold could also contain infinitely many elements. It is also improbable that this could be intended implicitly, for such an operation would require an actually infinite time. This summation, which constitutes number, is an activity of thought. Kant describes it as a synthesis and refers back to the meaning of synthesis explained in the beginning paragraph of the transcendental deduction just cited.[10] Finally, he says expressly that I engender not only number but also time itself in this activity. We do not now need to discuss the thesis about the engendering of time, we are here concerned only with number. Kant's opinion in this quotation, as in many parallel quotations, is unambiguous: I engender number in an activity of thinking.

Such a reference of number to counting has often been made in the history of ontology. The history begins with a quotation in Aristotle's *Physics*.[11]

'Whether if soul did not exist time would exist or not, is a question that may fairly be asked; for if there cannot be some one to count there cannot be anything that can be counted, so that evidently there cannot be number; for number is either what has been, or what can be, counted. But if nothing but soul, or in soul reason, is qualified to count . . .'

This passage has often been discussed, although no wholly satisfactory interpretation has been reached. It is difficult to reconcile this passage with the Aristotelian theory of abstraction.

The referral of number to an enumerating thinking played a large role in medieval nominalism, and it is understandable that the passage from Aristotle's *Physics* was repeatedly discussed. The most instructive presentation I know is found in Petrus Aureolus. He first contrasts the two opinions. The realists, he seems to be thinking primarily of Thomas, claim: there is number in things even when every activity of thinking is eliminated (*circumscriptio omni actu intellectus*). This means that number brings to the things of which it is predicated, to extension therefore, a real entity. But this is contradicted by the other thesis, Petrus Aureolus is probably thinking of Duns Scotus or Henry of Ghent. They claim: There is no true number outside the understanding. It is rather in the soul in an intentional manner: *sed est tamen in anima objective.*[12] Petrus Aureolus himself agrees with the second thesis. The ten of ten stones consists only in the fact that a mind counts these stones. Thus every number is only an enumeration, a summing-up, and of every enumeration it must be true that it takes place not in things but only in the mind. '*Constat enim, quod summatio non est in re extra, sed tantum in mente summante.*'[13]

This medieval discussion of number reaches its highest level, in my opinion, in the writings of Ockham. Ockham first rejects the extreme interpretation of number as an *accidens* in the strict sense and he can refer for support to numerous considerations of his predecessors, in particular, of Duns Scotus and in a certain sense also of Thomas.[14] Positively, he interprets number in terms of transcendental being, thereby continuing a development begun by Aquinas.[15] In his *Logic* Ockham coins the terse formula: '*numerus nihil aliud est quam res numeratae.*'[16] Ockham's discussions on the problem of number are characterized by great subtlety, and the categorial-analytic definition of number is always more important for him than the ontological definition. Ockham makes clear that number must be seen from the standpoint of relation and that, with relation, it belongs to the problem of transcendentals.

It is not easy, however, to specify how the ontological determination of this domain which contains the transcendentals, relations and numbers is to be interpreted. We have raised this question already in the first Part. Nearly all interpreters are agreed that it does not present an extreme nominalism. The objects of this domain are not *flautus vocis*. Many interpreters hesitate to call Ockham's ontological position a nominalism, they prefer to call it a conceptualism.[17] But this distinction perhaps means only that everyone senses a difference here but cannot specify in what the difference consists. My own investigations make it seem probable, at least to me, that Ockham never achieved a clear and definitive decision between the different ontological possibilities.[18]

After a brief period of vacillation, Leibniz found his basic ontological position in his earliest years. Thus he writes in 1770: '*nam concreta vere res sunt, abstracta non sunt res sed rerum modi, modi autem plerique nihil aliud quam relationes rei ad intellectum seu apparendi facultates.*'[19] This holds true especially for numbers, as the continuation of the text shows. In the *Monadology*, Leibniz says that the eternal truths exist in the thought of God,[20] and that must also hold true of numbers. He has in mind the biblical passages also, according to which God has ordered all things in measure and number[21] and that God has numbered the hairs on our heads.[22] From this primary existence of numbers in God's thought is derived their secondary existence in our thought. If one attempts to imagine this concretely, it means that numbers exist by reason of the fact that a thinking being numbers the monads and their real properties. When Leibniz says in the *Nouveaux Essais* that I find numbers within me,[23] he imagines this in such a way that I, as a monad endowed with *perceptio* and *appetitus*, represent these acts to myself and in particular count them.

This is also the direction in which Dedekind's views emphatically point, even though his historical presuppositions have not yet been clarified. Dedekind says expressly: 'I consider the whole of arithmetic as a necessary or, at least, natural consequence of the simplest arithmetical act, counting.'[24] Of number in general he says: 'Numbers are free creations of the human spirit.'[25]

In more recent work on foundations, the standpoint of intuitionism can also be reckoned as in agreement with this direction. It was noticed early on that the three great directions taken in regard to foundations in the first decades of the present century are closely related to the old philosphical directions. So formalism is related to the basic vision of Plato, logicism to that of Aristotle and intuitionism to that of Kant. The intuitionist, like Kant, admits pure intuition as a constitutive element. Kant and the intuitionists agree also in the recognition of a constructive aspect. The constructive interpretation requires that in mathematics only those objects should be admitted, of which it can be shown how they are to be constructed. Greek mathematics is very strongly determined by constructivist interpretations. We will see in the next paragraph how this applies to geometry. For arithmetic too one can give an instructive Greek example. Euclid proves the proposition that there are infinitely many prime numbers by proving that for every prime number there is another larger prime. The proof consists in Euclid's method for constructing a larger prime number.[26] It was Kant who, in sharp contrast to Leibniz, deliberately revived the constructive character of arithmetic, and coined the important concept of symbolic construction.[27] The intuitionists have once again insisted on the requirement of constructibility. This forced them to subject a whole series of mathematical concepts to a critical examination. The higher powers of set theory proved to be especially problematic from this point of view. And the nineteenth century hopes of bridging the discrepancy between the discreteness of numbers and the continuum of geometry proved to be unfounded after critical examination. The problems of constructibility are in no sense finally clarified and we agree with Bar Hillel that it is in any case a merit of such investigations to show what can be achieved with particular presuppositions and particular means. The intuitionists have been rather reserved about an ontological interpretation of arithmetic, but it is understandable that the strong emphasis on constructive elements should lead to an operative interpretation of arithmetic.

We return now to the analysis of Kant and this time to the second aspect. The operation of counting can always be taken up again, it goes on into the endless, and thus engenders the infinity of the number series. In this infinity of the number series is revealed a basic concept of mathematics, but it must remain an open question whether the concept of infinity constitutes mathematics as such and in general. That this is so explains why Kant gives little play to the concept of infinity in arithmetic. For Kant the basic phenomenon of arithmetic is the summation of two into one. The synthesis of a manifold is for him always the synthesis of a finite manifold. One reason for this is that in the Transcendental Analytic the concept of infinity has a very small significance. Kant's decision to regard the summation of two into one as the basic phenomenon of arithmetic has support in reality. In the *Principia Mathematica* too, it is demonstrated that an essential part of logic and mathematics can be treated before the introduction of the concept of infinity. This was probably also Leibniz's opinion since he wanted to treat the general theory of manifolds and the general theory of relations before the introduction of the concept of infinity.

Finally, it is possible that Plato's reflections are also to be understood in this sense. Aristotle reports that Plato saw the principles of numbers in unity and the dyad.[28] Here unity stands obviously for the summation of a manifold into a unity, and the dyad for the capacity for unlimited continuation of this or some other process, for example doubling or halving. If one were to attempt to weigh these two principles in the scales, the more important for Plato would probably be unity, the summation of a finite number into a unity. Thus, from historical as well as systematic considerations the Kantian interpretation appears well-founded. In summary that interpretation is: to regard the summation of a finite manifold into a unity as the basic phenomenon of number, and to regard this summation as an activity. From one particular aspect of this activity of the understanding, from its capacity for unlimited continuation, there then results the infinity of the number series.

46. GEOMETRY

Kant interprets geometry also as an activity of thought. To imagine a straight line is to draw a straight line; to imagine a circle is to describe a circle. Kant says explicitly:

'To know anything in space (for instance, a line), I must *draw* it, and thus synthetically bring into being a determinate combination of the given manifold, so that the unity of this act is at the same time the unity of consciousness (as in the concept of a line) . . .'[1]

This operational interpretation of geometry obviously has a real basis in the constructive, axiomatic and synthetic character of geometry.

The constructive interpretation of geometry is best revealed in Euclid's *Elements*. It is not known what induced him to undertake this strictly constructive interpretation, but there is no doubt that the structure of the *Elements* is strongly constructive; Zeuthen was the first to make this clear.[2] The constructive interpretation of geometry means that a geometrical form is recognized as existing only when it can be constructed, and when this is guaranteed either by an axiom or by a proof. Euclid permits himself to speak of the half of a line only when he has shown how the middle point can be constructed.[3] Only then does he use the concept of half a line. This same procedure is followed for any further subdivision of a line. First Euclid gives the method by which a line can be subdivided into the desired number of parts,[4] and only then does he make use of the concept. The problem is still more sharply focused with angles, where the ratio is differentiated. Any angle you please can be divided in half,[5] and so Euclid may use the concept of half an angle. But with Euclid's means it is not possible to divide any angle into as many parts as one pleases, it cannot for example be divided into thirds and so Euclid may not use the concept of a third of an angle. A constructive interpretation must list the means available for the construction. Epistemological investigations have clarified this question in the *Elements*. Only constructions using compass and ruler are permitted. In purely geometrical terms, only straight line and circle are used,[6] and in fact Euclid has guaranteed the unlimited feasibility of these two basic forms in his axioms.[7] This question of permissible means is very difficult to answer for a general constructive interpretation of mathematics. If one defends a constructive standpoint also for arithmetic it becomes difficult to say how the circle of constructive means is to be limited.

Kant himself goes further than Euclid in this question of

admissible means, he speaks generally of a construction in pure intuition.[8] As we saw, he also interprets the procedure of arithmetic as a symbolic construction.[9] This is considerably more than Euclid allows. Thus, for example, the ellipse and the parabola are constructible for Kant, but not for Euclid, for they cannot be constructed with compass and ruler.[10]

Such a constructive interpretation is at first an epistemological problem. It amounts to the question of what presuppositions a given form and a given proposition depend upon. In this restricted form it is a purely mathematical task which is still independent of any ontological standpoint. Nevertheless it cannot be denied that a constructive interpretation in the epistemological sense is very close to an operational interpretation in the ontological sense.

The same thing can be done with the axiomatic interpretation of geometry. One may assume that Kant was fully acquainted with the axiomatic character of geometry. He recognized that the axioms of Euclidean geometry cannot be proved from the principle of contradiction alone,[11] as Leibniz believed.[12] Kant therefore probably regarded other geometries as possible, even on the basis of the principle of contradiction. His opinion probably was that other consistent geometries are also possible but that the Euclidean geometry is the only one which can be constructed in pure intuition. Presumably Kant was reserved on this problem because the alternatives had not yet been sufficiently clarified. His reserve was probably correct, as the later debates on this question have shown.

In reality, Euclid's *Elements* have a certain axiomatic construction,[13] and this axiomatics has naturally always been efficacious. We saw in Part I how great the possibilities of the axiomatic method are. There are no limits as far as we know to the articulation of a given theory, in particular of a given geometry, along axiomatic lines. This immense abundance of possible geometries is perhaps not completely unintelligible from a Platonic standpoint. Husserl reckoned, as we have already seen, with the possibility of non-Euclidean geometries, he interprets them as genus and species.[14] Moritz Geiger also comes to grips with the axiomatic method from a Platonist standpoint.[15] It seems to me that this much of Geiger's basic idea is correct: from a Platonic standpoint all the alternative theories must admit of a systematic presentation. But we hold that the number of possible geometries is immense. The great possibilities of the axiomatic construction suggest that the axiomatic construction should be interpreted as activities of our spontaneity. The appearance of new systems of axioms is usually described in this way: one builds or constructs a new system of axioms. Such an interpretation is found in Hilbert,[16] and it is certainly no accident that Hilbert should choose a citation from the *Critique of Pure Reason* as the motto of his *Foundations of Geometry*.[17] The flexibility of axiomatics has encouraged an interpretation of geometry that goes considerably beyond Kant, often to an extreme nominalist position. Kant himself binds the axioms to pure intuition and thus arrives at only one geometry and only one arithmetic.

To these two grounds for the Kantian interpretation of geometry one may add as a third the characteristic of activity so peculiar to this science. Draw a line, inscribe a circle, raise a perpendicular, bisect an angle, make two triangles coincide, everywhere the geometrical terminology is permeated by active verbs which express an activity. When Plato mentioned the circle as an example of an Idea he was probably ignoring this aspect of activity completely. For him a circle is a being resting in itself. But it is a good question whether this relatively static interpretation of the circle by Plato really articulates all its aspects or whether the dynamic interpretation, already implied in the terminology and emphasized by Kant, does not come closer to the essence of geometrical forms.

47. PHYSICS

Kant's conviction about the operational character of science is clearly expressed in his interpretation of physics. Understanding prescribes laws to nature, that is Kant's famous, deliberately provocative formulation.[1]

In physics is clearly revealed the different forms of the general which we discussed at the outset. To make immediately the case of causality, we find alongside one another: concept, judgement and theory; the concept of the causal, the judgement of the causal law, and the theory of Newtonian physics determined by the causal law, and the theory of Newtonian physics determined by the causal law. In the *Critique of Pure Reason* appear one after another the category of causality, the schema of causality and the fundamental principle of causality. It is a much discussed question how properly to understand this triple manifestation, which is in reality a quadruple manifestation, since the corresponding judgement appears first before the three other determinations. In my opinion Hermann Cohen sees the issue correctly.[2] One uniform phenomenon is involved: the Newtonian physics, therefore a theory. This uniform phenomenon is resolved into four aspects solely for methodological reasons. In the Kantian construction the fundamental principle seems to be placed in the foreground, as Cohen understands it. This allows us to say that, for Kant, the general is represented primarily as a law of nature. The question: what is the general? takes on for him the concrete form: what is the law of nature?

Kant regards the Newtonian laws as the fundamental laws of nature.[3] He defines nature as conformity to law.[4] In Kant's terms then the basic question: what is nature? means: what is the lawfulness of nature? All of this has been reasonably worked out by Cohen and the title of the work in which he interprets the *Critique of Pure Reason, Kant's Theory of Experience,* appropriately characterizes the goal and the result of his interpretation. Does Cohen's interpretation imply a narrowing-down of Kant's achievement? Kant himself summarized the main interest of philosophy in the four questions:

What can I know?

What ought I do?

What may I hope for?

What is man?[5]

Heidegger's interpretation of Kant can then be placed under the heading: what is man?, and Heidegger himself makes reference to Kant's formulation.[6] Cohen's interpretation is essentially directed at the question: what can I know? To refine it further one can narrow it down to the question: what is nature? Are not these two fundamental questions of interpretation: what is man? what is nature? diametrically opposed? Nevertheless one should not overlook the connexion of the two fundamental questions. It is the conviction of Kant, and one he shares with Plato and Aristotle, that science represents one of the greatest possibilities of man. Perhaps Kant would not go so far as Aristotle has gone in the beginning of the first book of the *Metaphysics*.[7] Kant would place the action of the simplest man, when he follows the voice of his conscience, over the science of the best physicist.[8] But this limitation does not eliminate the point that for Kant science remains one of the greatest possibilities for man. But then the two questions: what is nature? what is man? are at bottom only two sides of one and the same question. A reflection on the possibilities of science, if it only goes deep enough, must meet the original possibilities of man. We will follow Kant's lead on this point. We have selected science in the form of four very concrete disciplines as the domain from which metaphysics wins its answers. Heidegger has, to be sure, attempted to characterize science as a deficient mode and has laid stress on an alleged decay in science.[9] Now it can definitely not be denied that the sciences especially in our time are in danger of being exhausted in a hectic hustle and bustle. But this dangerous possibility of decay they share with all human undertakings, with art as well as with language, and Heidegger himself has elaborated on the decay that affects language. I therefore believe that Heidegger's doubts do not have a conclusive effect and that instead one may and must maintain with Socrates, Plato and Aristotle, but also with Descartes, Leibniz, and Kant, that science is one of the great possibilities of man.

One might formulate this as follows: man, by nature, strives after science, and that means that man is by nature a physicist. But then one must also turn this around and say that the physicist, by nature, is a man. And then spontaneity appears as an original property of man even in physics.

A very instructive expression for these connexions was found by Johann Schultz in his commentary on the *Critique of Pure*

Reason,[10] and one may well suppose that this commentary, written by a friend of Kant's and with Kant's knowledge, was influenced in large measure directly by Kant.[11] It is the same man who pursues mathematics and physics. Physics is necessarily referred to mathematics, mathematics is the language spoken in physics. But in that case the same basic determinations must appear in mathematics and in physics.

Physics is not mere description, on this there can be no doubt. This holds for experimental physics as much as for theoretical physics. To describe experimental physics Kant found the beautiful expression: the scientist can be compared to a judge who compels nature to answer the questions he poses.[12] It is the isolation of the material to be studied both in the posing of the question and the carrying out of the experiment, which can only rest on the spontaneous activity of the physicist. This explains why it was particularly of the experimental part of physics that Bridgman thought when he developed his operational interpretation of physics.[13] The Vienna Circle attempted to counter this interpretation with the principle of protocol propositions. But it must not be overlooked that the protocol proposition presupposes all the apparatus needed for experiments, and that this apparatus is a world constructed by the physicist and not a protocol proposition. Furthermore the principle of the protocol proposition is itself a principle. One can dispute whether it is a good principle or a bad one, but it is a principle none the less and not a protocol proposition.

The activity of the physicist is just as marked in theoretical physics. We have already pointed out that the first Newtonian axiom is anything but the description of an empirical state of affairs. This holds also for the Newtonian mechanics as a whole. One will have to agree with Heinrich Hertz when he says that the fundamental principles which appear here are synthetic *a priori* principles in Kant's sense.[14] Einstein too, who certainly had a clear perception of the empirical aspects of physics as of mathematics, stresses the fact that the Kantian interpretation is grounded in reality.[15] And it is a philosophically gratifying result of atomic physics that the character of activity in physics, already visible to the sensitive eye in Newtonian physics, is now made fully clear to all.

48. LOGIC

In the discussion of logic in Plato and Aristotle we encountered difficulties, which had their ground in the fact that in Plato's case logic did not yet exist as a theory and that in Aristotle's case it was in process of formation. We will now consider the ontological interpretation of logic from the Kantian standpoint and again we will encounter difficulties, difficulties of a different kind but serious difficulties none the less.

Kant distinguishes between transcendental and formal logic.[1] Transcendental logic, in its two sub-divisions of transcendental analytic and transcendental dialectic, constitutes the true core of Kantian ontology. Kant distinguishes general logic from this transcendental logic. It is this general logic which Kant expounded in his lectures on logic in connexion with the textbooks in general use at that time.[2] It covers pretty much the same ground as Aristotle's *Organon* and contains, as one of its most important parts, the syllogistic.[3] We have been concentrating our attention on the two-valued propositional calculus and we now have before us essentially the part of Kant's logic which corresponds to that theory.

Kant considers general logic a fixed and completed theory. In a certain sense this was always true of the syllogistic and is true today of the two-valued propositional calculus. But Kant holds that the scope of formal logic goes beyond syllogistic. In particular, general logic must develop a table of judgements which is systematically constructed and therefore complete.[4] And in connexion with this systematic table of judgements one should also be able to discover, in Kant's opinion, a systematic table of categories.[5] He also regards the systematic completeness of these two tables as a requirement in principle.[6] Klaus Reich has pursued this problem and interpreted the Kantian reflections.[7] Whether the Kantian reflections are grounded in reality and redound to his fame is, of course, another question.

It is not quite clear how Kant intended to interpret general logic with his epistemological basic concepts. I believe, however, that in terms of the distinction between analytic and synthetic propositions one must say that for Kant formal logic is an analytic science. It would therefore be interpreted in the same way as the general theory of magnitudes. The general theory of magnitudes is arranged according to formal logic and Kant says of it explicitly that its propositions are analytic.[8]

In my opinion Kant is inconsistent here. After he had taught the synthetic character of mathematics, and therefore of geometry and arithmetic, he should for the sake of consistency have also characterized the theory of magnitudes and general logic as synthetic.

The development of formal logic in the last hundred years has revealed the inner homogeneity between logic and mathematics and it has also shown that formal logic in Kant's sense must be regarded as a synthetic science. Logic and mathematics are either both analytic or both synthetic. This holds even for that restricted part of logic we have been considering, the two-valued propositional calculus. The two-valued propositional calculus cannot be derived solely from the principle of contradiction, this is a finding of modern logic which is beyond all doubt. The principle is, however, a fundamental condition for all analytic propositions. It is contained in their definition that they can be derived from the principle of contradiction alone'[9] But two-valued propositional calculus also needs formulas in the same sense in which arithmetic requires formulas. In Kant's sense then it is constructed in pure intuition. Formal logic is therefore in Kant's sense a synthetic science and it would not have been impossible for Kant, in his own time, to recognize this.

One can also view the problem historically, and then Kant's attitudes are seen to be related to Leibniz. For Leibniz, logic, arithmetic and geometry are sciences which are analytic in Kant's sense, because they can be proved from the principle of contradiction alone.[10] Kant saw that this did not prove true for arithmetic and geometry, and in consequence of this doubt he recognized the synthetic character of these sciences. But in his interpretation of logic he continued to follow Leibniz. When Kant therefore, in contrast to Leibniz, contests the analytic character of arithmetic and geometry and claims instead their synthetic character, and when, in agreement with Leibniz, he retains the analytic character of logic, this latter point is not in line with his true intentions. If I understand Kant's intention correctly, he should have taken the further step and gone on to recognize logic too among the synthetic sciences.

These considerations make it clear why, particularly in more recent times, logic has been reckoned among those sciences which must be understood in terms of the activity of our own thinking.

We have already pointed out that in the interpretation of logic quite different standpoints have always been presented. It becomes understandable then that in our time nominalism draws new support from the formal construction of mathematical logic. One might mention here Goodman[11] in particular, although Quine[12] also inclines strongly to a nominalist view. On the other hand, to date no one has succeeded in carrying through without remainder a purely nominalist standpoint in formal logic,[13] and it seems doubtful whether this will ever be possible. There are even formal reasons against it. This may be disturbing for an extreme nominalism, but for our dialectical standpoint it is not at all surprising. On the contrary, one can both expect it and understand it as soon as one reflects on the question of what standpoints as such can achieve.

Wittgenstein's approach is very instructive. He begins with the conviction that the content-part of the sciences can be precisely separated from the logico-formal-part. The content-part is shown in states of affairs[14] and the elementary propositions which correspond to them.[15] The logical part is shown in the combination of elementary propositions[16] and in the logical laws referring to them.[17] This is logic, a domain which, in contrast to the elementary propositions, devolves upon language and thought alone. Wittgenstein receives the necessary support from his investigation of negation. An assertion can be negated. How is this to be understood? Certainly only by saying that it is we who negate it. The capacity of negation for repetition yields an important argument. A single, a three-fold, a five-fold negation is a denial; a double, a four-fold, a six-fold negation is an affirmation. This endless chain of negations, which first becomes clear in formal logic, cannot easily be conceived as an endless chain of objective realities in the sense of a Platonic interpretation. This would invite a piling up of being, having little sense. If one tries to think of the 238th or 239th negation, their interpretation as objective reality becomes patently absurd. This is why Wittgenstein interprets negation as a negating.[18]

This interpretation becomes more convincing when we consider that negation is an ancient source of philosophical difficulties. The history begins already in Plato. Justice is an Idea, the good is an Idea. But what of injustice? and evil? Are there Ideas of negations? Plato himself was evidently made uncomfortable by the difficulties which crop up here,[19] and Aristotle explicitly drew attention to them.[20] In light of the basic foundations of the theory of Ideas only one solution is possible but, so far as I know, only Bolzano followed the principle through: one must accord to negations the full status of ideal being. For that reason Bolzano considers not only true propositions but also false propositions as propositions in themselves.[21] Because of the repeatability of negation and the variability of actual circumstances one arrives at a heaping up of propositions which is difficult to countenance. But Bolzano may not have considered this unhappy consequence in its full scope.

All of this inclines one to understand negation as an operation. But one can then go further and assign an operational character to the whole of logic. This has already been done in intuitionist logic, particularly in the form given it by Heyting.[22] And Lorenzen has constructed an operative logic intended to cover its entire scope.[23] Here basic concepts are understood as basic activities of thought. The part of operative logic which corresponds to the two-valued propositional calculus does not, however, wholly correspond to the theory we are considering as *exemplum metaphysicae*. This is because the principle of excluded middle is lacking in operative logic. Operative logic has perhaps not achieved its ultimate refinement in the form presented by Lorenzen, but his presentation shows impressively how far the operational interpretation reaches in logic.

CHAPTER IX

THE APORIAS OF THE
PLATONIC STANDPOINT

---

49. NEW TASKS

It was the goal of the last three chapters to show that each of the three great standpoints is grounded in reality. Now we encounter the question how the three great standpoints are related to one another. We thereby explicitly take up a question which we have repeatedly touched upon. The simplest solution would be to say that one of these standpoints was correct and the two others, along with all other possible philosophical standpoints, false. This interpretation is widespread and it is the characteristic of philosophical schools, such as Platonism, Aristotelianism and Kantianism. But philosophical schools, which easily become narrowed into philosophical sects, are peculiar things. The more obstinately a certain standpoint is defended, the narrower becomes the vision of the defender. This also applies to those schools named for systematic rather than historical considerations. Schools like realism, nominalism, idealism, and analysis nearly always dim the vision they were supposed to sharpen. Schools are necessary but they readily incline to a naïve extremism, and in philosophy the naïve and the extreme are from the outset false paths. What people generally think of as Platonism will usually turn out to be naïve Platonism. And then the old joke will be in place: Plato was not a Platonist, and of course the same joke applies to the Aristotelians and the Kantians. We do not intend to defend a particular standpoint in these investigations, we will instead try to understand the plurality of standpoints. We are thereby following a conviction of Hegel's and one represented before him by Aristotle and Plato.

In the *Sophist* Plato considers the opposition between Parmenides and Heraclitus. Parmenides will recognize only a strictly identical being, he rejects thereby all becoming. Heraclitus recognizes only becoming and rejects all identity and permanence. Plato understands that the philosophical task here is not to take sides with one of the views, to adopt Parmenides and reject Heraclitus or to adopt Heraclitus and reject Parmenides. Instead one must press on to the insight that each of the viewpoints, taken alone, is impossible, because each of the viewpoints, taken alone, cancel themselves out. The philosophical task, one must see, is to find a combination.[1]

Aristotle regards a confrontation with the preceeding philosophies as one of the essential tasks of philosophy. It was justifiable then for the compositor of Aristotle's *Metaphysics* to place his confrontation with his predecessors as the first book. This book is both systematic and historical. Its intention is to show that the course of Greek philosophy leads up to the philosophy of Aristotle. The guiding thread of the presentation is the theory of principles. The early thinkers first encountered the principle of *hyle*,[2] then the Pythagoreans followed by Plato discovered *eidos*.[3] There are also some glimmerings of the principle of the origin of *kinesis*.[4] But the summation and the completion comes with Aristotle's introduction of the principle of *telos*.[5] In general Aristotle's opinion is that every philosopher has said much that is correct and much that is false. The task is therefore to separate the correct from the false, and after this separation the Aristotelian philosophy will appear, in the opinion of its founder, as the totality of what is correct.

Leibniz was strongly influenced by this basic conviction of Aristotle. Leibniz's many attempts at conciliation and his successes are, at bottom, based on his conviction that every claim has some truth in it.[6] The task then is to understand and accept all these correct elements. Once this task is completed the oppositions between philosophers will disappear, according to the convictions of both Aristotle and Leibniz. These oppositions represent only an imperfect, indeed they are in a certain sense only an appearance.

In Hegel just this opposition between philosophers becomes a positive thing. The plurality, the multiplicity of philosophies is not an imperfection, not a defect, not an evil. It is essential and necessary for philosophy to appear in many philosophies. The true task for philosophy is to understand its own plurality.[7] We fully accept Hegel's demand; it is the fundamental task of philosophy to understand its own plurality. The understanding of this plurality may not be sought—and here we join Hegel in opposition to Aristotle and Leibniz—by attempting to separate the true from the false and then fitting the acceptable pieces together into a whole, the kingdom of truth. The connexion between the many philosophies must preserve the oppositions and the contradictions, it must be, as Hegel showed, dialectical.

We will attempt to make a start on this fundamental task by asking about the structure of the individual philosophies. We have shown that each of the three great standpoints is grounded in reality. But what about their development? Does any of the three great standpoints find a consistent development or do all three encounter difficulties, even perhaps aporias? This is the question to which we now turn.

50. THE BEING OF THE IDEAS IN THE *Phaedo* AND THE *Republic*

We have already touched upon the aporias of the theory of Ideas several times, now we shall discuss them systematically. For this purpose we consider the *Phaedo* as the true dialogue of the theory of Ideas, more exactly, of the early theory of Ideas, and we will draw upon the *Republic* as a supplement.

The *Phaedo* presents a fundamental distinction of being. Plato says explicitly: δύο εἴδη τῶν ὄντων.[1] It is not easy to find an exact German expression. Schleiermacher translated it as: two species of things.[2] This suggests that Plato was thinking of a division of being into genus and species, but this is hardly supported by the context. It seems more careful to translate it as: two modes of being. While genus reflects the Aristotelian-Scholastic distinction, mode of being is derived from the Latin '*modus*'. This term was given a variety of uses in modern times, particularly by Descartes[3] and Wolff,[4] the term being chosen just because it is so general that it does not imply the genus-species distinction. In the *Phaedo* the two modes of being are the Ideas and sensible things. The examples of Ideas in the *Phaedo* are, as we saw, nearly all ethico-aesthetic or logico-mathematical. Among the ethico-aesthetic Ideas there stands in the foreground the great trio of the beautiful,[5] the good,[6] and the just.[7] Among the logico-mathematical Ideas we find the Ideas of numbers, of two,[8] three,[9] eight,[10] ten,[11] but also the Ideas of even[12] and uneven.[13] And the Idea of the equal[14] has a special, not yet explained meaning. One will not suppose that Socrates himself had already asked: what is the equal? But then there must be a systematic reason why Plato has Socrates introduce the theory of Ideas by means of the Idea of equality. Interpreters have not yet discovered a truly convincing reason for this.

With respect to the other mode of being, we are accustomed to speak of sensible things. The corresponding Greek expression: τὰ αἰσθητά occurs only seldom in Plato,[15] it becomes the usual term only in Aristotle. Plato himself prefers the expression τὰ ὁρατά.[16] For him, seeing is still the prototype of sensory perception in general. We prefer the terms used in the tradition of Aristotle, Thomas and Leibniz, 'individual being' and 'individual'.

If this distinction is to be apt, Plato must first characterize the two modes of being in their differences. The Ideas are eternal and unchanging,[17] sensible things are continually changing and perishing.[18] A series of examples is listed for sensible things: beautiful men, beautiful horses, beautiful clothes,[19] as an example of equality Plato lists equal sticks and stones.[20] The distinction then leads up to the task of distinguishing the two modes of being in their being. Plato speaks of *ousia*,[21] of being,[22] and in many places even of true being.[23] In the *Phaedo* this being is expressly attributed to Ideas. The Idea is *ousia*, it is being, it is true being. In his *History of Philosophy* Hegel found the apt formulation which we have already mentioned above: 'The Ideas are, and they alone are, being.'[24] This conception of being is very forcefully stated in the *Phaedo* and the *Republic*, and the historical influence of Platonism is essentially rooted here. Nevertheless, the conception of being contains all sorts of problems. In particular, two main questions arise. The first has to do with the meaning of the thesis, the second with its evidence.

The Idea is *ousia*, the Idea is true being, what meaning does this thesis have, what does it intend? It has often been understood in the sense of what is customarily called Platonism. Attention is focused on the *Phaedo* which is then interpreted as a two-worlds theory. This is the way Nietzsche understood Plato,[25] and he himself understood his polemic against Plato as a polemic against Platonism. As far as I know, the term 'two-worlds theory' was expressly introduced into philosophy by Lask.[26] A two-worlds theory can contain two different claims. First, it can merely say that beyond this world there is another world. But it can also claim that this other world is the true world and that our visible world is only an appearance or whatever, in any case not true being. The *Phaedo* is particularly understood in this way. According to such a two-worlds theory then, the *Phaedo* teaches that behind and beyond the world of sensible things there is a world of Ideas, that this world of Ideas represents true being, and that the world of sensible things is only an appearance.

Now there are certain passages in the *Phaedo* which support such an interpretation. An example is those passages where Socrates characterizes the body as a prison,[27] which hinders all genuine knowledge and therefore also every genuine philosophical life. But still one may not escape this prison by suicide. But if he is freed from this prison, even by means of an unjust condemnation, the philosopher will rejoice to be able to enter a better world.[29] Also in the myth of the sun in the *Phaedrus* a two-worlds theory is unmistakably expressed. The philosopher joins the ascent of the gods. And when that journey has reached the summit of the arch that supports the heavens, he views the Ideas in their heavenly dwelling place.[30] It has often been remarked that nearly all the passages which imply a two-worlds theory occur in the context of a myth. And in the myth of the sun in the *Phaedrus* serious intent and irony are mingled together in a manner which is not easy to penetrate. When the journey is ended the horses are unharnessed and given nectar to drink.[31] One cannot help thinking that this playful ending works against the elevated style of the journey. Not only from this single detail, but from the overall impression it always remains doubtful how far one should go in giving an ontological evaluation to the mythical passages and to what extent one should understand the expressed flight from the world as a two-worlds theory in the full ontological sense.

The two-worlds theory amounts to a doubling of the world, this reproach was first made against Plato by Aristotle. He says explicitly that Plato has assumed so many Ideas, probably implying that he had to assume so many, that this world here below is reproduced up there.[32] Now Aristotle's criticism of Plato has often been attacked. Natorp in particular claims quite simply that Aristotle never understood Plato, that Aristotle regarded the Ideas as things, an unparalleled misunderstanding.[33] But the problem is not so simple. Natorp opposes to the Aristotelian critique the thesis: the Ideas are not things, but laws.[34] But in order to make this reasonable one has to know what laws are. Natorp has in mind primarily the laws of logic, mathematics and physics. These laws are so obvious for him that the cool ontological question: what then are laws? would strike him as having little sense. But so long as this question has not been raised and answered, his thesis: the Ideas are not things, but laws, does not carry us much further.

But it must be recognized that we are dealing here with a fundamental problem. If one says for example that Aristotle reified the Ideas, the formula already appears convincing. Who would want to run the risk of having reified the general? But if one says, on the other hand, that there is an enduring inclination to interpret the general as an individual being to some extent picturable, then one has at least an opportunity to see the problem. Immediately a great variety of connexions emerge. As a matter of fact general concepts are imagined as perceivable individual beings when they are personified. Thus death is abundantly represented in saga, myth and art as an individual being, for example as a skeleton armed with a scythe.

Such pictorial representations have considerable force for Plato. Thus, for example, Hygeia is for Plato an Idea, but she is also a demi-goddess in the popular Greek conception. She has her temples, is revered in a cult, generally together with Asclepius. Art was represented in a great variety of images for the Greeks.[35] It must be supposed that Plato's representation of Hygeia as an Idea was influenced by the popular Greek representation of Hygeia as a demi-goddess.

There is in fact a series of passages which can only be understood in this sense. The journey with the gods in the *Phaedrus*, which we recalled a moment ago, leads to the Ideas, which can be viewed by the philosopher in their location above the heavens. But how can they exist in this dwelling place if they are not individual beings? How can the philosopher view them there if they are not individual beings?

It is the same in Plato's argument in the *Symposium*. The beautiful is first glimpsed as beautiful bodies, but the gaze ascends by steps until at last the beautiful itself is glimpsed. It becomes evident in this ascent that the Idea of the beautiful is itself something beautiful, indeed that it is the true beauty.[36] Certainly the connexion with sensible bodies is lost in the ascent. But in a certain sense the connexion with a concrete individual is retained; in a certain sense at the end of this ascent the Idea of beauty is seen not as an abstract concept, but with Greek eyes as a concrete image of the gods.

If one takes all these passages together one has to recognize that the passages in the *Phaedo* cannot be left out of account. Some such representation must lie at the basis of the theory of anamnesis. This theory asserts that men viewed the Ideas in an earlier life.[37] But if they were viewed in an earlier life then the Ideas must certainly be in themselves capable of being viewed, and this they can be only if they stand there for themselves. They can be viewed as individuals only if they stand there as individual beings.

This hypostasizing of Ideas is in no sense a mere blunder on Plato's part. We are rather dealing with one of Plato's presuppositions and, in a certain sense, even quite generally with an inner, systematic necessity. Aristotle was the first to see the systematic problems involved here and we will follow his interpretation of the theory of Ideas in pursuing them. But quite independently of this systematic problem, one will not be able to believe that a naïve two-worlds theory was Plato's persistent and final opinion.

51. THE IDEA AS EXCLUSIVE BEING

The Idea is *ousia*, the Idea is being, the Idea alone is being, the first two expressions are used by Plato in numerous passages,[1] the third is Hegel's appropriate summary.[2] Once again two questions arise: What is the meaning of this assertion? What is the evidence for it?

In the *Phaedo* Plato evidently regarded the assertion as self-evident. In the *Sophist*, as we have already seen, he says with reference to the *Phaedo*: 'Previously we knew what being means, now we are at a loss.'[3] This description: 'previously we knew what being means' is exactly the situation of the *Phaedo*. Plato has in mind his own assertion: The Idea is *ousia*, the Idea is being. Support for this assertion strikes him as unnecessary. In the *Phaedo* it does not even seem necessary to him to reflect on the meaning of this assertion, so reasonable, so self-evident did it appear to him then.

Plato assumes in the *Phaedo* that there is an original intuition of the Idea. The Idea of the beautiful, the Idea of the good, the Idea of the just, all are seen in a direct intuition. The solution which Plato in the *Phaedo* regarded as satisfactory, the theory of anamnesis, poses great difficulties for us. Even if one were prepared to admit such an original intuition of the Ideas, this would still not mean that the ontological status of the Ideas was given in the same or in an analogous intuition. The ontological thesis that the Idea is *ousia* is certainly not itself seen in an intuition.

In this situation one might suppose that Plato would admit an Idea of being which could be intuitively grasped. And Plato does have an Idea of being,[4] but only in the later dialogues. It is also quite understandable that the Idea of being should appear later. As soon as the Idea of being appears the question of the connexion of Ideas must also appear, for it lies in the nature of Ideas that every other Idea should have a share in this Idea of being. But in the *Phaedo* Plato is still far removed from the question of the inter-connexion of Ideas with its attendant difficulties. In the *Phaedo* it is self-evident that the beautiful in itself, as every other Idea, is true being.

In the *Phaedo* we do not get beyond this self-evidence. Thus one is inclined to ask about prior philosophical assertions with which this Platonic principle could be connected. Aristotle noted that a close connexion with the Pythagoreans presents itself[5] and that the basic principle of the Pythagoreans is closely connected with the early assertions of the philosophers of nature. We have already discussed the possible interpretations of the Pythagorean thesis: all is number. We saw that there are two possible interpretations. One can imagine that alongside the Pythagorean numbers there are things and that the thesis then implies: all order in things, all lawfulness in things is number. And we saw that Aristotle interpreted the Pythagorean thesis in this sense. But we also saw that there is another possible interpretation of the Pythagorean thesis. One can interpret the thesis: all is number as being like the thesis: all is water. Then there would not be things alongside numbers, things which would be ordered and enumerated by numbers; number would be truly everything and there would be truly nothing other than number. Putting this in the form which Hegel gave to Plato's basic principle, one could say: numbers are and they alone are being. Of course, Aristotle and also Hegel himself interpreted the Pythagorean thesis otherwise. Yet it seems to me that the Pythagoreans themselves interpreted the thesis in the extreme sense.

We have already touched upon the possibility of such an assertion and we may perhaps discuss it here once more in relation to the Ideas. To do this we will advance to a concept which is closely related to both the Pythagorean numbers and the Platonic Ideas, namely the laws of nature. Then our thesis takes the form: there are only the laws of nature, the laws of nature are and they alone are being. Again we will take a very simple conception of being as a basis for discussion, mechanical materialism. On this theory there exist only atoms moving in empty space according to the Newtonian laws. Here Newton's laws are regarded as the laws of nature. Can it be said on the basis of mechanical materialism that the Newtonian laws are and they alone are being? In the beginning of our study we weighed this question. Mechanical materialism is certainly a very simple, one might even say, primitive conception of being. But it already quite clearly contains a distinction of modes of being. On the one hand, the atoms, on the other, the laws of nature according to which the atoms move. It is indifferent here how one defines the being of the laws of nature. For mechanical materialism at all events they are real. This conception of being is simple, concrete and plausible. But is the distinction between atoms and laws of nature necessary? Or is it possible that there are only laws of nature? In our preliminary considerations we come to the conclusion that the thesis: there are only laws of nature cannot be proved contradictory. Now the Aristotelian-Scholastic philosophy maintains that a material substratum must underlie the laws of nature, which have the character of relations. But to date at least this thesis has not been proved by showing the impossibility of its contradictory. From this one has to conclude that the thesis, there are only laws of nature, is not in itself contradictory. There are of course certain difficulties in the fact that we cannot imagine the thesis concretely. This is the direction in which Kant's considerations move.

This applies not only to the Pythagorean thesis: there are only numbers, but also to the Platonic thesis: there are only Ideas, if the Platonic thesis be understood in that way. In so far as the theory of Ideas claims, for example, the existence of an Idea of the number three, and the number three is contained both in the Pythagorean numbers and the laws of nature, the two theses are closely related. If one were to interpret Plato's basic principle in

Hegel's sense: there are Ideas and they alone are being, it would presumably not be possible to prove that the thesis was self-contradictory. Nevertheless very serious doubts arise from the fact that the thesis, so understood, cannot be concretely imagined, indeed in a certain sense cannot be imagined in any way.

The difficulties are increased when one considers the ethico-aesthetic Ideas. Plato teaches the existence of the Idea of beauty and in such a way that one has to understand: the Idea of beauty is and it alone is being. That means therefore: the Idea of beauty is and beautiful things are not. This is the Eleatic disjunction which we worked out at the beginning of our study. If one puts it at the basis of the theory of Ideas, all the objections which arose against the Eleatic disjunction will arise against it, including the ones Plato himself raised. The Eleatic disjunction consistently thought through eliminates all thinking and thereby eliminates itself as soon as one attempts to think it.

This general objection against the Eleatic disjunction acquires a special weight in the theory of Ideas as can be seen in the case of the Idea of beauty. In fact, the Idea of beauty would lose its meaning if only the Idea of beauty existed and not beautiful things. The Idea of beauty would lose its meaning if it did not appear and shine forth in beautiful things. If this did not happen, what would the Idea of beauty then be?

All considerations lead to the result that the theory of Ideas, if interpreted in the sense that the Ideas are and they alone are being, is not in itself impossible because of some inner contradiction, but that a theory of Ideas, so interpreted, is in itself meaningless.

52. THE IDEAS AND SENSIBLE THINGS

We have considered two possibilities for the interpretation of the theory of Ideas and have seen that in both Plato would encounter difficulties. Both possibilities rest on a univocal concept of being. The first possibility recognizes only one mode of being and it therefore attributes this same being both to the Ideas and to sensible things. This leads to a two-worlds theory in the sense that the Ideas are also reified. I cannot believe that this could have been Plato's real opinion. The second possibility was the Eleatic disjunction. Then the only possible meaning of being is accorded to the Ideas, and sensible things cannot be, just as Parmenides said: being is and non-being is not. But this reasoning leads into aporias, which quickly show it to be untenable.

The third possibility is the one which Aristotle made explicit, although it was already implicitly present in Plato. Being belongs to the Ideas, but it also belongs in a certain sense to sensible things, and this means that the being of Ideas and the being of sensible things differ in sense.

Although the ontological determinations of the *Phaedo*, to the extent that they are made explicit, move essentially in an Eleatic direction, I none the less find reasonings which point toward an appropriate being for sensible things. It is not merely the relation between the Ideas and sensible things which we are now raising, for in the *Phaedo* itself the being of sensible things is to a certain extent already recognized. If we reduce the *Phaedo* to the Eleatic disjunction we are sacrificing the richness of the work to an extreme interpretation. Even the examples which Plato uses for beautiful things: beautiful men, beautiful horses, beautiful garments,[1] show that Plato was not willing to consider the being of sensible things as wholly nugatory, in the sense of Parmenides. It is the same with equal things. Plato's example was equal sticks and stones.[2] Certainly they are not exactly equal, certainly they are far removed from the Idea of equality. But in order to stand so far removed from the Idea of equality, they must exist in some way. When therefore Plato speaks in the *Phaedo* of two modes of being[3], meaning thereby the Ideas and sensible things, he is already according a certain being to the sensible things.

This becomes wholly clear in the *Timaeus*. This dialogue presents Plato's cosmology. The demiurge looks to the Ideas for a model in his engendering of sensible things.[4] This cosmology presupposes that these engendered things are not nothing. Certainly they do not have the being of Ideas, but they must have being in some sense, how else could they be engendered according to their model, the Ideas?

That this presents him with the task of distinguishing the being of sensible things from the being of Ideas was not explicitly seen by Plato. Aristotle was the first to see this explicitly. But Plato already sees that the question of the relation of sensible things to the Ideas has become inescapable.

Following Aristotle, who fixed the terminology of Plato, this is known as the problem of *methexis*. Plato's struggle with this problem begins with a remarkable passage in the *Phaedo*, to which attention has often been drawn. Socrates tells the story of a young man who asks himself whence comes the order and beauty of the cosmos. Materialistic explanations do not satisfy him. He takes up the book of Anaxagoras because he knows that this philosopher assigns a great significance to *Nous*. But Anaxagoras also disappoints him because he makes no use of *Nous* in working out his ontology.[5] Among the interpreters it is still disputed whether this picture of youthful development refers to Socrates or to Plato himself. Whoever is meant, it is clear that the theory of Ideas appears after this disappointment as the correct solution: when something is beautiful it is so through the Idea of beauty. Here the materialist solution is rejected. To say that something is beautiful because it has a beautiful colour, or because it has a beautiful form, is insufficient. Only the theory of Ideas can bring a solution. Everything that is beautiful is so because it participates in the Idea of beauty. Now this of course leads to the question how one should imagine such a participation. The participation of all beautiful things in the Idea of beauty presents itself, from the standpoint of the Ideas, either as a presence of the Idea in the beautiful things or as a community of the Idea of beauty with beautiful things, perhaps also in some other way. Socrates waves off the difficulties of this participation, almost, one might say, with a show of anger. He repeats three times that he takes his stand simply, artlessly, one might even translate it as ingenuously, on the belief that all beautiful things are beautiful through the Idea of beauty.[6] One can only understand the passage to imply that at the time of writing the *Phaedo* a discussion on the problem of participation was already in process. One cannot discern in this brief passage what form the

discussion took. It could well be that Plato weighed these difficulties in an inner dialogue but it might also have been the case
that his friends or students came upon the difficulties and
presented them to Plato in open discussion.

A thematic discussion of the problem is found in the first part
of the *Parmenides*. Parmenides and Zeno are discussing the theory
of Ideas with the young Socrates. Parmenides is referred to as
65 years old. Zeno is in his forties and Socrates is a young man.[7]
The theory of Ideas appears as the teaching of this youthful
Socrates; Parmenides and Zeno take up their stands on the basis
of this theory. In the interpretation of the dialogue nearly everything is disputed. Since Socrates' birthdate is known, the conversation must have taken place about the year 450. It is first of
all questionable whether Parmenides, Zeno and Socrates could
have met at all; that depends on Parmenides' dates which are not
known exactly. Even if the conversation did take place it is
questionable whether it had the content which Plato presents to
us. Taylor says that he finds nothing in the conversation which
could not have been said at the putative time of the conversation.[8]
But to me and to many others it seems impossible that in the year
450 a discussion on the theory of Ideas of this type could have
taken place. The *Parmenides* is a reflection on the theory of Ideas
as it was presented in the *Phaedo*. It seems incredible that the
theory of Ideas, as presented in the *Phaedo*, was already
developed in the lifetime of Socrates, we have already touched
on this. But it seems completely incredible that Socrates could
have discovered the theory of Ideas as a young man around the
year 450. Furthermore it seems impossible that already at this
time the whole problematic of the theory of Ideas was already
known. There is nothing of all this in the early Platonic dialogues,
which can largely be interpreted as reproductions of Socratic
conversations, nor in any other of the sources. It seems advisable
therefore to set the discovery of the theory of Ideas and the
discovery of its problematic each in the times in which the
relevant dialogues were written. This need not hinder Plato's
conviction that the theory of Ideas was what Socrates really
wanted to assert and that, moved by this conviction, Plato might

very well have let the theory of Ideas be presented by Socrates in the way he has done.

The discussion in the first part of the *Parmenides* raised first the question: of what things are there Ideas? We will come back to this question shortly. The discussion then moves on to the question of the being of the Ideas and their relation to sensible things.

One might first suppose that the Idea is a mere representation in our soul.[9] But Plato rejects this interpretation with rather artificial arguments.[10] It seems possible, however, to find better arguments.

If one gives up the notion that the Ideas are only our own representations and accords them their own reality, then new difficulties arise for which Plato found no solution and for which, indeed, no solution is to be found.

If we regard the relation of sensible things to the Ideas as a sharing, we can then attempt to ascertain the possible modes of sharing, in order to ask whether one of them might fit the relation of things to the Ideas. Children can have a share in the inheritance of their parents, in that the inheritance remains undivided and each child has his share in the undivided inheritance. But the inheritance can also be divided and each child receive his own special share. If there is sharing only in these two modes[11] and one applies this to the relation of sensible things to the Ideas, then using beauty again as example it can be the one and undivided Idea in which the many things are, or the Idea of beauty is divided into pieces and in each beautiful thing there is a piece of the Idea of beauty. Neither of these two modes is possible. If the first were the case, then one and the same thing would be present in different places at the same time, something obviously not possible.[12] If the second were the case, then the Idea of beauty which in its essence is one would be fragmented in many parts.[13] Socrates objects that there is perhaps another way in which the same thing can be present in different places at the same time. And he introduces a beautiful example: one and the same day which is in many places at the same time and nevertheless not divided.[14] One might think that Plato would now expand on this conception. In the *Republic* the Ideas are compared to the sun[15] and to light.[16] But on the contrary Plato introduces a grossly material image. Parmenides begins to compare the relation of the Ideas to sensible things, to a sail which is spread out over many people.[17] It is obvious that over each of the individuals only a piece of the cloth is spread, and thus the image of a sailcloth leads back into the fragmentation-interpretation. The problem of disintegration permits a witty interlude when one compares the Ideas of large and small, and Plato does not let the opportunity pass.[18] The difficulty of participation proves to be insoluble, at least along this path.

As a second possibility of understanding the relation of Ideas to sensible things Plato discusses the concept of similarity. The individual things are similar to the Idea, or the Idea is the pattern and sensible things are copies.[19] But it is easy for Plato to show that this interpretation also fails to advance us.

The worst difficulty for the theory, Plato says explicitly, is still ahead of us.[20] This worst difficulty, like all the others, rests on admitting a unique reality for Ideas. The formulation Plato found for this must be regarded as excellent, but it is not easy to translate. Cornford has: 'I assure you, then, you have as yet hardly a notion of how great the difficulties will be, if you are going to set up a single form for every distinction you make among things'.[21] But one might paraphrase the passage as follows: '. . . how great the aporias when you describe an Idea in such a way that you separate it as a unity, but also as an individual which exists independently for itself among all being'. Here the reality of the Idea is understood in such a way that every idea is separated from all other being, it exists as an individual, just as each sensible thing exists as an individual. When one defines the reality of the Idea in such a way that it exists as an individual thing like all other individual things, then it becomes impossible to understand how an Idea can be a general of many individuals. The worst aporia which Plato announced consists in the fact that such an existence of Idea as an individual thing would eliminate every connexion between Ideas and, in particular, the knowability of the Ideas.[22] This would in effect also eliminate the theory of

Ideas as such. The young Socrates does not know how to eliminate these difficulties and yet all of them notwithstanding he holds fast to the theory of Ideas.[23]

How should this discussion be understood? One can first regard the whole discussion as unintelligible. To aid one in this opinion the dialogue could be regarded as spurious. A few scholars in the nineteenth century took this decision.[24] But this only postpones the problem. Even if one holds that the *Parmenides* was written by another author, the systematic interpretation of its meaning would still remain a problem.

A second interpretation is the puzzle-theory, especially as developed by Natorp.[25] For Natorp the difficulties of the dialogue are soluble and the reader should find the solution by his own mental effort. But if this interpretation is to be accepted Natorp and his followers must present the solution. As long as this does not happen, the puzzle-theory must be regarded as unacceptable.

Our investigations follow the interpretation, which we will have to make good in our reading of the second part of the *Parmenides*, viz., that we are dealing here with genuine antinomies which cannot therefore be wholly resolved. These antinomies underly metaphysics as such, and they must therefore be looked for whenever a philosopher has penetrated into the basic problematic of metaphysics. This will lead us to read the antinomies as Plato wrote them, and to regard them as an appropriate expression of systematic difficulties.

This interpretation also has consequences for understanding the relations of Aristotle to Plato. The debate with Plato and the criticism of Plato play a great role in Aristotle's works, and we will treat this debate thematically in the next chapter. Plato's followers are often inclined to regard the criticism of Aristotle as worthless, indeed as wholly false. Natorp is typical. In his opinion Aristotle did not understand Plato at all.[26] But things are not so simple. Along with many other interpreters, I will mention among more recent ones Cherniss,[27] I have come to hold a positive interpretation of this debate. One does not need to deny that Aristotle in many passages pays an unphilosophical tribute to the Greek love of argument and that this tempted him not infrequently into a delight in mere dispute and obstinacy. But perhaps this delight in obstinacy is not confined to the Greeks or to philosophers. If one sets these excesses down to human failing, there still remains a penetrating critique of the Platonic theory of Ideas which lays bare the inner difficulties of Platonic philosophy, indeed the inner difficulties of philosophy as such. We will entertain some of Aristotle's objections here and in the next chapter consider the critique once again as a whole.

Aristotle's criticisms can be grouped under four main headings: the problem of *methexis*, the problem of *chorismos*, the problem of the τρίτοσ ἄνθρωποσ and the significance of the proofs. With respect to the *methexis* problem Aristotle says explicitly in the first book of the *Metaphysics*, where he is giving a summary presentation of the theory of Ideas, that individual things insofar as they have the same name as the Ideas exist on the basis of a *methexis* (participation). There can be no doubt that Aristotle is here reproducing Plato's explanations correctly. Against this theory Aristotle raises the objection that Plato has not explained how this *methexis* is to be understood. We have just seen that Plato presents this same question in the *Parmenides*,[29] and thus Aristotle's doubts are the same as those raised by Plato himself.[30]

Aristotle's second objection is to the *chorismos* (separation). Aristotle says that Socrates regarded the general as existing in things, but that Plato, on the other hand, regarded the Ideas as existing apart.[31] According to Aristotle's interpretation the *chorismos* has a two-fold meaning. First it separates the Ideas from sensible things, and this line of thinking leads to a two-worlds theory. The world of Ideas then becomes a second world. But the objection to the *chorismos* has also another meaning. He criticizes the theory of Ideas for positing an isolated being for the Ideas, a being like that possessed by the independently existing individual things.[32] In this sense Aristotle accuses Plato of reifying the Ideas. But here the relation of Aristotle's criticism to the texts of Plato is somewhat more difficult. While there are presentations of the idea of *methexis* in many of the dialogues, there is mention of *chorismos*, strictly speaking, only in one dialogue, the *Parmenides*. Here, however, the term χωρίσ is used six times.[33] And one does find the notion of *chorismos* if not the term in those passages in the main dialogues on the theory of Ideas which are commonly designated myths. I may perhaps refer again here to the well-known passage in the *Phaedrus*. Plato says expressly that the Ideas exist there ἐν ὑπερουρανίω τόπῳ.[34] We conclude then that Aristotle can support his critique of the theory of Ideas by both the content and the terminology of the Platonic dialogues.

The third part of Aristotle's critique is the objection of τρίτοσ ἄνθρωποσ (the third man).[35] This objection too has been strongly contested. Unfortunately we do not have the detailed presentation of the objection, which was located in an early essay on the Ideas, now lost. Only a few excerpts survive. In the first book of the *Metaphysics* Aristotle merely draws attention to the τρίτοσ ἄνθρωποσ, he presupposes that his hearers and readers are familiar with the problem.[36]

The paradox of the τρίτοσ ἄνθρωποσ assumes that the basic principle of the theory of Ideas is that the unity of many men is only guaranteed if there is an Idea of man, and therefore that Man as such must have a unique reality. If one accepts this presupposition, then many men and Man as such form a pair of different realities and, according to the basic presupposition of the theory of Ideas we need another Idea, which as the τρίτοσ ἄνθρωποσ, will support this new unity, and this must once again have a new reality different from the others. One quickly sees that a *regressus in infinitum* arises here, and that behind every required additional Idea a further Idea must be required.

For a long time the problems of the τρίτοσ ἄνθρωποσ were not taken seriously. But now a more penetrating interpretation of Plato and the appearance of antinomies in the foundations of logic and mathematics have reawakened interest in the old problem.

It was first noticed that the paradoxes of logic and mathematics are closely related to the τρίτοσ ἄνθρωποσ. To my knowledge, Ryle was the first to draw attention to this connexion.[37] About the same time a more penetrating interpretation of Plato had brought to light that Plato himself had seen the problem. It is developed in the Parmenides,[38] but is also to be found in a series of other passages which is perhaps not yet complete.[39] As far as we can now see, Plato never referred the problem to the Idea of man. Limiting ourselves to the basic discussion in the *Parmenides*, we find that there Plato uses the example of largeness.[40] The reasoning run as follows: there are doubtless many large things. According to the basic assumption of the theory of Ideas, their unity can only be accounted for by an Idea of largeness, therefore by a Largeness in itself. But then this Largeness itself and the many large things constitute a new pair, which in its turn needs to be unified. Therefore a new Idea of largeness as an independent reality becomes necessary and we are launched immediately on a *regressus in infinitum*. There are two oddities in Aristotle's treatment of the problem, which have not yet found a satisfactory explanation. The first oddity consists in the fact that Aristotle knows the solution of the paradox and presents it formally, although in a somewhat concealed passage.[41] We do not know why he made no use of this solution in his critique of the theory of Ideas. A second oddity is that Aristotle, so far as we know and in any case in the writings available to us, does not say that the problem was already known by Plato. Aristotle refers in so many passages expressly to Plato, and in many passages even to particular dialogues by name, that his silence on the problem of τρίτοσ ἄνθρωποσ is not easy to understand.

To sum up the problem of these aporias in Plato: Plato himself clearly recognized the aporias of *methexis*, *chorismos*, and τρίτοσ ἄνθρωποσ. They are all given a special presentation in the first part of the *Parmenides*. There is no unanimous opinion among the philosophers and logicians on whether the aporias are systematically soluble. Our study rests on the conviction that they are not soluble. What Plato himself held on the question cannot be clarified with certainty from the few passages dealing with it. We will postpone the systematic discussion of the three Aristotelian objections and all discussion of his fourth objection to the next chapter.

53. PLATO AND THE TWO OTHER STANDPOINTS

In these three chapters we are pursuing the same two tasks in the thought of Plato, of Aristotle and of Kant: we wish to show that each of these philosophies in its own development comes upon aporias which it cannot master from its own standpoint. But we also wish to show that in no one of these three philosophies is its own standpoint presented in extreme form and in absolute strictness. In each of these three philosophies there are aspects of the two other standpoints. These two problems are so important, that we will discuss them in detail for each of the three chosen philosophies. We have just presented the aporias for the Platonic standpoint and will now consider the relation of the Platonic philosophy to the two others.

No one will doubt that the theory of Ideas is the middle point of the Platonic philosophy. But we have seen that the unreflective form of the theory of Ideas, as found in the *Phaedo*, did not satisfy Plato himself. Plato saw the difficulties which result when one begins to ask what the ideal being of Ideas really means.

We have already seen that the Ideas have a necessary relation to the real world, and this means that in a certain sense they must necessarily have the function of laws of nature in Aristotle's sense. Certainly Plato attempts again and again to screen off the Ideas from sensible things. When he, understandably, comes into difficulties, he makes distinctions. There are different numbers, the numbers with which the mathematician has to do, and the numbers, with which the practical man, the general, the tradesman, the craftsman have to do.[1] On the whole, the distinction is not completely reasonable. Aristotle says that Plato had distinguished three kinds of numbers: numbers as Idea, the mathematical numbers and the sensible numbers.[2] The reports are not, however, wholly unambiguous. Nevertheless we would say that the distinction between pure and applied numbers emerges very clearly from the *Republic*. But however Plato wants to distinguish them he will certainly not deny a connexion. To the laws of pure numbers, with which the mathematician has to do, for example that $7 + 5 = 12$, there are corresponding laws of numbers for sensible things, with which the practical man has to do.

We have seen that Plato drew a similar distinction in astronomy. There is a pure astronomy in which the revolutions of the stars are determined through pure numbers. Also the periods, in which these revolutions lead back to the same state of the cosmos, are determined by whole numbers. This number of the great year is a very large number but still a whole number, and it is determined by simple arithmetical laws.[3] In contrast to this stand the actual courses, and it was recognized already in Plato's time that the course of the moon through the month and the course of the sun through the year deviate considerably from whole numbers, that they are determined by fractions in which a mathematical lawfulness is not to be found. Empirical astronomy, to the extent that Plato is still prepared to accept it as a science, rests on empirical data.[4] However Plato chooses to distinguish these two geometries—and the distinction will not be counted among his happiest thoughts—he cannot deny the connexion between pure astronomy and empirical astronomy. Pure astronomy determines actual reality by revealing the lawfulness of nature, and it is owing to matter, so Plato thought, that the Ideas do not unfold their pure validity in this material world.

In the *Timaeus* the function of the Ideas as laws of being comes fully into view. In the engendering of the world, the Demiurge looks towards the Ideas,[5] he engenders the real world after the pattern of the Ideas,[6] this is especially the case for the Ideas of the elements.[7] Of course it remains true that the Ideas do not prevail completely in the actual world. Fire here below does not represent the pure Idea of fire, it is only like fire. And the various kinds of earths do not represent the Idea of earth as an element in its purity, they are only 'of the nature of earth'.[8] But for all this, it is not to be doubted that the pure elements in the *Timaeus* are Ideas and that they function as such and as laws of being, that is, as laws of nature in this special domain.

In his interpretation of Plato, Natorp gave particular attention to the function of Ideas as laws of nature. He says simply that the Newtonian laws represent the true example of a Platonic Idea.[9]

One will recognize the exaggeration in this claim but one will also recognize that a genuine aspect of the theory of Ideas is expressed in this interpretation.

That the Ideas function widely as laws of nature and therefore have an Aristotelian aspect is thoroughly understandable, given the fundamental connexion between Plato and Aristotle. The connexion with Kant is subtler and harder to see. It might seem completely absurd on first consideration that the Ideas could be regarded as activities of thought. The problem depends on what meaning is given the term νοητόν. It is indubitable that the reference to *Nous* contained therein is a fundamental characteristic of the Ideas. One can regard *Nous* as a purely passive capacity that contemplates the independently existing Ideas in pure receptivity; but one can also understand *Nous* in its relation to the Ideas as, in a sense, an active capacity, an activity, a doing. We cannot exhaust this question, we can only make it understandable. Perhaps the following consideration will give us a point of entry. The interpretation of nous as a purely receptive capacity rests on a comparison with seeing. Just as we see visible things, so *Nous* contemplates Ideas. One can then raise the question whether seeing itself is a purely passive capacity and this, I think, must be denied. Seeing is not a purely passive receiving but rather to a certain extent an active operation. This was one of Goethe's great insights and he speaks expressly of an 'action and counteraction' of the eye.[10] But if seeing itself is not a purely passive capacity, then the interpretation of *Nous* as a purely passive capacity cannot rest on this comparison, and the way to the consideration of other possibilities is open.

One cannot object here that this is a consideration wholly alien to the Greeks. As we will see, Aristotle recognized that already for us *Nous* contains an aspect of *energeia*, and that the divine *Nous* represents pure *energeia*, pure activity. One can imagine that Aristotle here too develops a Platonic initiative and it is thus understandable that in the interpretation of Plato our attention has been drawn to this aspect of spontaneity in *Nous*.

Among contemporaries, Bruno Liebrucks has again emphasized the aspect of spontaneity. He says: 'It is a question of the reality of all those things which we stamp with the seal of αὐτὸ ὅ ἔστιν. Here we have again the active aspect!'[11] Liebrucks supports himself with the evidence that Plato paraphrases knowledge of the Ideas with the expression: upon which we impress the seal.[12] Liebrucks' observation corresponds to great and very old interpretations of Plato. Augustine understood the Ideas as God's thoughts.[13] It must be conceded that this interpretation in this form is not to be found explicitly in Plato, it is however well suited to Plato. But there can be no passivity in the mind of God, God's thinking like His being is an *actus purus*. The Ideas must share the pure act-character of the divine thinking. And, following Plato and Augustine, this is just what Leibniz formally claims. For Leibniz too, the Ideas are God's thoughts and the being of Ideas is determined by the pure activity of divine thinking.[14] We arrive then at the result that Ideas have on the one hand a relation to nature and, on the other, a relation to *Nous* as to an active capacity for spontaneity. But these are the two basic aspects of the Aristotelian and the Kantian approaches.

CHAPTER X

THE APORIAS OF THE
ARISTOTELIAN STANDPOINT

54. ARISTOTLE AND PLATO

Aristotle was engaged in a constant debate with Plato, and the debate is fundamental for his own philosophy. We will have to examine two questions. The point of the first question is whether Aristotle's critique of the Platonic theory of Ideas is grounded in the facts. The point of the second is whether Aristotle succeeded in developing on his own an ontological interpretation of the general which will withstand criticism. Or does Aristotle's interpretation of the general lead to new criticisms and new aporias? In order to discuss these two questions we must first discuss once again summarily the historical relation of Aristotle to Plato.

If one looks at Aristotle's writings with a view to his relation to Plato, the fundamental importance of this relation quickly emerges. Aristotle says of himself that he had been a student of Plato for twenty years.[1] Then it must have been around 367 that he entered the Academy. This fits very well with Aristotle's dates, he would then have been about 17 years old. Aristotle knows the Platonic dialogues exactly. In his index Bonitz lists about 200 citations from the Platonic dialogues and references to them,[2] and this list is by no means complete. Aristotle also knows much of Plato's lectures and the discussions in the Academy, which we know only by second-hand reports, most of them by Aristotle himself. Aristotle is also one of the few to have heard Plato's lectures on the Good, which he gave in his old age.[3]

The representation of Plato's philosophy and the debate with it occupies a large space in Aristotle's writings. But the details of this debate are by no means clear. This is also understandable since we are dealing with the subtlest debate in the history of philosophy. Only the debate of Kant with Leibniz can be to some extent compared with it. Werner Jaeger attempted to present and interpret Aristotle on developmental and historical principles.[4] And he uses for his guiding thread Aristotle's relations with Plato, certainly a legitimate criterion. But as a whole this interpretation cannot be considered an unqualified success. One may be sceptical whether the developmental and historical method can serve in the interpretation of a philosopher to the extent that Jaeger allows for. Even if one were to grant this, Jaeger's interpretation suffers from being based on an over simple schema. He assumes that Aristotle first agreed entirely with the Platonic theory of Ideas and sees his development in a gradual withdrawal, ever more extensive, from that theory.[5] Such a schema is not *prima facie* appropriate, it might be all too simple. Kant's debate with Leibniz, for example, took an entirely different form. Kant first takes a decisive stand on the basis of the Leibnizian philosophy, and this is clearly expressed in the early writings.[6] There then ensues a second phase in which Kant becomes critical of Leibniz and moves far away from him or at least believes that he does. In the *Critique of Pure Reason* Kant emphasizes his differences with Leibniz.[7] In a third phase, however, characterized perhaps by the *Metaphysical Principles of the Natural Sciences*, Kant arrives at a new understanding of Leibniz on the basis of his own philosophy, now securely established. Now Leibniz is for example the one who anticipated the fundamental Kantian distinction between analytic and synthetic judgements with his distinction between the two great principles: the principle of contradiction and the principle of sufficient reason.[8] Here the debate takes a new turn and makes one wonder whether Jaeger's hypothesis of a steadily diverging path is really correct. Two difficulties are especially noticeable. It is difficult to find the proper chronology of Aristotle's writings, and still more difficult to give an unambiguous characterization of the Platonic philosophy. With respect to the chronology of Aristotle's writings there is danger of circular reasoning. The chronology of Aristotle's writings is supposed to yield the temporal course of his relations with Plato. But, on the other hand, this debate, or more exactly, a hypothetical form of this debate, is supposed to yield the chronology of his writings. But considering the special nature of the Aristotelian writings, one must say that to date no method is known to determine their temporal sequence. with satisfactory accuracy. Werner Jaeger's approach cannot be regarded as satisfactory, and perhaps the special nature of the Aristotelian writings makes it completely impossible to order them temporally. There is also a special difficulty here. Another series of Aristotle's writings is known, of which one can say with certainty that they were written in his youth. But these early writings survive only in fragments. To infer from these fragments a definite claim about Aristotle's philosophical position at the time, as Jaeger does, is hardly possible. If the *Phaedo* or the *Critique of Pure Reason* existed only in fragments, a satisfactory interpretation would not be possible. Even the interpretation of the books that have come down to us intact makes for difficulties upon difficulties; no one could infer the totality of these works from fragments. These methodological difficulties are not resolved by Paul Wilpert's discovery that the number and scope of these fragments can be increased[9] and that further increases are likely. For all that, it must be maintained that thorough philosophical interpretations can only be attempted when the work to be interpreted exists intact.

The difficulties of assembling integral pieces out of the Aristotelian writings correspond to the unprecedented richness of the Platonic dialogues. Werner Jaeger says that the young Aristotle was a Platonist.[10] But what does that mean? It is correct that the theory of Ideas is presented in the *Phaedo* in a compact, though somewhat naïve, form. But then Plato himself later dissolved this all too compact form. It has been a source of no little trouble for the interpreters of Plato to have realized that the late dialogues reflect on the early dialogues and that, in particular, the *Sophist* and the *Parmenides* reflect on the *Phaedo*. But given this lively movement of Plato's thought, what does it mean to say that Aristotle was a Platonist? One might assume hypothetically that the Academy took its stand on the *Phaedo* in those first years after Aristotle had entered it, perhaps between 367 and 360. But this hypothesis would not be provable and not very probable. In any case, during the twenty years in which Aristotle belonged to the Academy, there must have been lively discussions about the meaning of the theory of Ideas. And at some point, either before or after Aristotle's entrance into the Academy, the *Sophist* and the *Parmenides* were written, in which these discussions received a partial expression. What then does it mean to be a Platonist?

The problem is further complicated by the fact that we do not know how Aristotle's critique of the theory of Ideas is related to Plato's own critique, in particular that expressed in these two late dialogues. Aristotle's criticisms are in many places identical with those advanced by Plato himself. To the obvious question, why Aristotle says nothing about this, we have to date no satisfactory answer. How did Aristotle stand with respect to the theory of Ideas during his twenty years in the Academy? What was his position on the criticism which Plato himself directed to the theory of Ideas or, more exactly, to a naïve interpretation of the theory of Ideas? To date we have not been able to find satisfactory answers to these questions. I cannot convince myself that Werner Jaeger's answer does justice to the systematic-philosophical difficulties. If one attempts to imagine various possibilities of how it might have been, one will certainly have to assume that Aristotle had taken a very intense part in the discussions about the theory of Ideas during his twenty years in the Academy. And one could further assume that part of the objections were first made by Aristotle. One might consider the possibility that the young Aristotle with all the impetuousness of youth took up the objections made against the naïve theory of Ideas and that he then took up a decided opposition against the theory of Ideas. Only gradually would the possibility and the necessity have arisen in his mind of understanding the theory of Ideas in a deeper sense. In the *Posterior Analytics* there is an impetuous sally against the theory of Ideas. One might translate it bluntly as: devil take the Ideas![11] It is of course impossible to assign an exact date to this individual outburst. It might have been written in a very early manuscript, but it could just as well date from a late one. I will only say that the possibility which Werner Jaeger developed is certainly not the only one, one can imagine quite different possibilities.

We should therefore strive for an interpretation which takes into account the whole relation of Aristotle to the Platonic theory of Ideas. We can say that his relation to the theory of Ideas was always critical. But then so was Plato's later relation. And Aristotle also follows the late Plato in never leaving the standpoint of the theory of Ideas in all his criticism of it. There may well have been fluctuations in Aristotle's relation to Plato, fluctuations which we cannot exactly date, at least not at the present time. But all fluctuations and all criticisms apart, Aristotle always was a Platonist and always remained one. This assumption strikes me as more fruitful than Jaeger's hypothesis of development. We will adopt the counter thesis: In the critical sense in which Aristotle was a Platonist, he always remained one. But then Plato himself, particularly Plato, was only in this critical sense a Platonist.

55. SYSTEMATIC PROBLEMS OF THE ARISTOTELIAN CRITIQUE

In the previous chapter we began to discuss Aristotle's critique of the theory of Ideas, we will now continue the discussion under systematic points of view. We are not now concerned with the historical question of what critique Aristotle in fact made, but rather with the systematic question whether this critique was grounded in the facts. We will divide the discussion into three groups: the question of the difference of being between Ideas and sensible things, the question of the provability of the theory of Ideas, and the question of the difference of meaning between the being of the Ideas and the being of sensible things.

The first question is, then, whether and how the being of sensible things can be distinguished from the being of Ideas. On this question depend the problems of *methexis*,[1] *chorismos*,[2] and the τρίτος ἄνθρωπος.[3] Aristotle expressly raises all three objections against Plato but Plato himself had already raised them, particularly in the first part of the *Parmenides*. The objections in effect assert that a being different from the being of sensible things has not been found for the Ideas, and that one must therefore ascribe the same being to the Ideas as one does to sensible things.[4] The Ideas are considered like sensible things; as Natorp rightly says, they are reified. This objection lies at the basis of the *chorismos* problem. When Aristotle says that Plato claims a *chorismos* between the Ideas and sensible things,[5] he means to say that Plato has distinguished Ideas from one another and from sensible things in the same way as two sensible things are distinguished from one another, namely by spatial difference. An analogous objection underlies the τρίτος ανθρωπος. We have seen how, in the usual form of the argument, behind the Idea of man must lie another Idea, the so-called 'third man', and how in the Platonic form of argument a further Idea of largeness must stand behind the Idea of largeness.[6] The confusion rests on the fact, pointed out by Aristotle,[7] that the Idea of man is itself regarded as a man, the Idea of largeness as itself large. But if the Idea of man is itself a man, then it also contains the being of man, and if the Idea of largeness is itself large, then it also contains the being of largeness.

We have seen that this difficulty does not occur in the Eleatic form of the theory of Ideas. If one submits the theory of Ideas to the Eleatic disjunction—we will ignore here the question of how far Plato himself did this—then sensible things have no being at all. The problem only arises when both sensible things and the Ideas are accorded being. One does not need to doubt that Plato wanted to distinguish the Ideas from sensible things, the question is rather to what extent such a distinction is possible. In terms of the *chorismos* problem the question takes on a more definite form: to what extent is such a distinction possible without bringing spatial imagery into play. Now the great Platonic Ideas, the beautiful, the good, the just, are burdened with so many difficulties that they render an ontological discussion unnecessarily ponderous. We will therefore choose a very simple conception of the world, one we have already used, the conception of the world in mechanistic materialism. For mechanistic materialism there exist only atoms in empty space and the laws of nature which govern the motions of the atoms. Although space plays an important role in this conception, we will ignore it for the moment and ask only about the difference between atoms and laws of nature.

A purely nominalist solution would seem indicated in as much as the laws of nature are interpreted as mere imaginings. But in general this is just the point that is strictly denied by the defenders of mechanistic materialism. Instead they regularly insist on the objective reality of the laws of nature. But if this is to be maintained, the difference between atoms and laws of nature must be clarified, and this task leads to difficulties analogous to those which obscure the distinction between the Ideas and sensible things. If one pursues the problem, one will everywhere find personifying and reifying formulations which are all liable to Aristotle's objection of *chorismos*. One says the laws of nature govern the motions of atoms. But this is a personification, for a governor is a man who has other men, the governed, under him. If one says: the laws of nature represent the motions of atoms, this is no better. An actor represents Henry IV. But in the world of mechanistic materialism where are the representer and the represented? If one says: the laws of nature describe the motions of atoms, the case is still no different. I stop someone on the street and he describes for me the way to the train station. But what are the laws of nature that they could describe something in this sense? Moreover, it is the defenders of mechanistic materialism themselves who like to use personifying modes of speaking. They like to talk about the majesty of the laws of nature. But what is majesty here? Is it the majesty of God? The defenders of mechanistic materialism would reject such an interpretation indignantly. Is it then the majesty of some great governor? But in that case the laws of nature are strictly speaking personified. The defenders of mechanistic materialism are here obviously in the same situation as Plato. Both want to make distinctions, the distinction between Ideas and sensible things, and the distinction between atoms and laws of nature. But our thinking and our language do not yield such a distinction without concrete imagery, and that means in general, spatial imagery. One could of course fall back on the mere concept of difference, but even here it must remain an open question whether a concrete, perhaps even a spatial, aspect is not lodged in the concept of difference, and it must also remain an open question whether this concrete aspect can be wholly eliminated.

If from this vantage point we now look back at Aristotle's objection of *chorismos*, we see that it contains both a positive and a negative aspect. The positive aspect reveals the difficulties of a distinction between Ideas and sensible things in as much as it shows that spatial imagery is contained in these distinctions. The significance of the objection is not diminished by the fact that Plato himself already saw the problem. The explicit reference in the *Parmenides* to a *choris* between the Ideas and sensible things can only be understood in this sense. But it remains an achievement of Aristotle to have raised the question formally.

The negative aspect of the Aristotelian critique lies in the fact that Aristotle apparently thought he was dealing with a problem capable of an unqualified solution. Aristotle, it seems, assumes that one must work out in a critical analysis this spatial aspect of the distinction between Ideas and sensible things, so that it can then be wholly eliminated. This, he thought, would remove the aporias of the *chorismos*. In particular this would mean that his own solution, growing out of the critical analysis, would be free of aporias and final. We will pursue the question whether the Aristotelian solution is free of aporias. Nothing in the history of philosophy suggests that it is the final solution.

The second phase of Aristotle's critique of the Ideas also gives rise to substantive difficulties. Aristotle asks about the scope of the arguments advanced to validate the theory of Ideas. What do the proofs advanced for the existence of Ideas actually prove? Do they perhaps prove too much? The proofs rest on the existence of the sciences and on the existence of the general. Where there are sciences there must also be Ideas, and where the general is, there must also be Ideas, so assert the proofs. But then, says Aristotle, there must be Ideas wherever there are sciences and Ideas for all those things for which there is a general. Now there are scientific knowledge and general concepts both of relations and of negations. And therefore there must also be Ideas of relations and negations, but the defenders of the theory of Ideas do not want to admit this. Therefore something must be wrong with the proofs for the existence of Ideas.[8]

To date it has remained unintelligible what Aristotle intended when he said that the defenders of the theory of Ideas were not willing to accept Ideas of relations. Quite the contrary, concepts of relations play a large part in the theory of Ideas. In the *Phaedo* the theory of Ideas is introduced by means of the Idea of equality.[9] Difference is named in the *Sophist* as one of the five highest concepts.[10] In the enumeration of Ideas in the *Parmenides* equality is again explicitly mentioned.[11] I cannot myself suggest a satisfactory interpretation for Aristotle's claim and I do not find a satisfactory answer among the interpreters.

The problem of negation, on the other hand, is very important. We have already looked into this problem during our discussion of Kant's logic. As we saw at that time, the problem depends on the arbitrary repeatability of negations. If one admits an Idea for any negation, an Idea then evidently becomes necessary for each subsequent negation, and hence for an unending chain of negations. This problem has harassed every theory of Ideas and, as far as I know, Bolzano has been the only one to draw the conclusion already mentioned: to assign an independent being to all negative concepts and all false propositions. Plato saw the problem very clearly. In the exposition of the theory of Ideas there are, as a rule, Ideas only of positive concepts, one need only think of the great trio, the beautiful, the good and the just. But in the first part of the *Parmenides* Plato discusses the problem at hand. He asks there: of what things are there Ideas? As a first group logico-mathematical Ideas are named: likeness, unity, plurality. As a second group he names ethico-aesthetic Ideas: justice, beauty, goodness. As a third group biological Ideas are named, which did not yet play a role in the *Phaedo* and the

Republic, the Idea of man, the Idea of fire, the Idea of water. Finally the question is raised whether there are also Ideas of trivial and undignified things such as hair, mud and dirt. Socrates says that he can't make up his mind about these. Sometimes he thinks there may be, at other times he rejects them for fear of falling into a bottomless pit of absurdity. But Socrates does express in this passage the fear that what may be true in one case is true in all, and Parmenides, here defending the theory of Ideas, predicts that Socrates will one day be fully experienced in philosophy and will not then despise any of these objects.[12] Although this passage does not explicitly mention negations, its relevance for Aristotle's objection is readily grasped. One wonders why Aristotle did not point out this relevance, a part once again of the remarkable fact that the dialogue *Parmenides* seems not to exist for Aristotle.

That this is a case of systematic difficulty is shown by the fact that Kant has a similar problem. In Kant the proofs for the existence of the *a priori* correspond to Plato's proofs for the existence of the Ideas. The two situations are much the same. The Kantian proofs for the *a priori*, for example the first argument for space, prove not only the apriority of Kant's *a priori* concepts; when exactly analysed they prove the apriority of every concept. To this extent the unlimited apriorism of the German Idealists is a legitimate consequence of the Kantian method of proof. One may assume that a similar state of affairs holds for all proofs in which the existence of Ideas or the existence of an ideal being is supposed to be proved. In all cases, except for a very few truly consistent thinkers, the proofs of existence probably prove more than they are supposed to. Thus Aristotle has revealed a radical weakness of these proofs with his objection.

The third aspect of the Aristotelian critique of the theory of Ideas treats of the problem of plurality of meaning. At the end of his debate with Plato in the first book of the *Metaphysics*, Aristotle says expressly that it is impossible to search for the principles of being until one has recognized the plurality of meanings for the fundamental ontological terms.[13] This is particularly true of *ousia*. One must carefully test the plurality of possible meanings of the term *ousia*, and ask in particular whether it has the same meaning 'here and there' (i.e. in the realm of Ideas).[14] We have already pointed out that Aristotle in his analysis of the plurality of meaning of *ousia* in Book V of the *Metaphysics* also enumerates certain meanings which he himself rejects, but which the proponents of the theory of Ideas accept: for example, the plane, the line and numbers. There is therefore an inner connexion between Aristotle's critique of the theory of Ideas and his theory of the plurality of meanings. We can even go further and say that the Aristotelian theory of the plurality of meanings grew out of his critique of the theory of Ideas. We have already seen that the question: what is being?, could only grow out of the Platonic distinction between Ideas and sensible things. One may hazard the further thesis that the Aristotelian theory of the plurality of meanings could only grow out of the theory of Ideas. Now it may be that the contemporary judgement of Aristotle's theory of the plurality of meanings is not always favourable, but that judgement may be prejudiced. In any case this theory remains one of the foundations of metaphysics. The possible hindrances, particularly through theological questions, were the reason why we have made repeated use of the difference between atoms and laws of nature in these investigations.

We have seen how the meaning of *ousia* undergoes development, already in Plato. Originally, *ousia* characterizes only the being of Ideas. In a development which is easy to overlook the meaning of *ousia* is later extended so that the term can also refer to sensible things. We have also seen how this development in Plato influenced Aristotle's use of *ousia*; the Aristotelian distinction between primary and secondary *ousia* grows out of the Platonic development. Finally, we saw that this question is by no means undisputed among the interpreters; we ourselves maintain nevertheless that for Aristotle primary *ousia*, that is, the individual being as *ousia*, represents the preferred meaning of *ousia* and that secondary *ousia* receives its meaning from the primary.

In this connexion too, the Aristotelian critique reveals important aspects of the theory of Ideas. But at the same time it

brings new difficulties to light. It has been the guiding theme of
our reflections on the theory of Ideas that a theory built on the
strict Eleatic disjunction would lose its meaning, that a theory of
Ideas must naturally assign true being to the Ideas but that it must
also assign being in some sense to sensible things. Plato himself
recognized this, but Aristotle was the first to grasp the problem
in its full methodological significance. We will follow Aristotle's
insights in pursuing these questions. To summarize in strict
Aristotelian form: both the Ideas and sensible things have a being,
but each in a different meaning.

This Aristotelian interpretation now leads into new difficulties,
if one draws in the further Aristotelian thesis, that the meanings
of being do not stand alongside one another without connexion;
they are connected and one of them is the pre-eminent meaning.[15]
Now here Plato and Aristotle stand diametrically opposed. Plato
considers the being of Ideas as true being and the being of sensible
things as derivative at best. Aristotle on the contrary regards the
being of sensible things as primary and the being of the Ideas as
derivative. This conclusion of course contains our interpretation
that for Aristotle primary *ousia* is pre-eminent and secondary
ousia derived.

Now one may consider the Platonic or the Aristotelian standpoint, both present difficulties. If one follows Plato and regards
the being of Ideas as true being and this meaning as pre-eminent,
then one does not see how the being of Ideas is grasped by us.
In the *Phaedo* and even in the *Republic* it is presupposed that the
being of Ideas is given through a self-evident insight, perhaps
through an original intuition. Still today, many Platonists consider the being of Ideas self-evident in such a way that they are
unable to grasp the point of the questions which arise about it.
But it is Plato himself who raises the questions. In agreement with
many interpreters, we have understood the *Sophist* as self-
criticism. When Plato asks about the meaning of being and goes
on to say: I knew it formerly, but now I have encountered an
aporia,[16] we have referred the 'formerly' to the *Phaedo*. In fact
if a naïve form of the theory of Ideas is adopted one has to hope
for an original intuition. No doubt every theory of Ideas claims

the being of Ideas. But then one can only interpret all sensory experience as deception, and one has to claim an original experience of the being of Ideas. But it is not apparent how this can be conceived, and it was Plato himself who pointed out the difficulties of this approach.

The difficulties of the Aristotelian approach are no less serious. If one supposes that the being of Ideas and the being of sensible things have different meanings, and if one supposes further that of these two meanings the being of sensible things is the preeminent and original meaning, then one has to explain how one passes from the being of sensible things to the being of Ideas. The Aristotelian thesis, taken in its purest form, asserts that it is individual things perceived by the senses that are originally experienced, and from them by ontological analysis the original meaning of the concept of being is reached, and that the ontological analysis in a further stage can rise to the being of Ideas or, in stricter Aristotelian terms, to the being of the general. But the difficulties begin with the first supposition: individual things perceived by the senses represent the original experiences. In that case the tree, the stone, the house would be the original experiences. One would then have to show, however, that hunger and thirst, joy and pain are secondary experiences. It is obvious that we must first clarify what is meant by primary and secondary. If one has recourse to language, the thesis would then mean that certain substantives, like 'tree', 'stone', 'house', are the original words and, by contrast, certain verbs like 'to be hungry', 'to be thirsty', 'to breathe', 'to laugh', 'to cry', would be later words. But such an undertaking would obviously be hopeless. One would come up against levels of language which are no longer accessible. And it is not clear how one would be able to distinguish between primary and secondary words in these deep underlayers of language. If any help is to be expected in this recourse to language, it lies rather in the doubts which one then has about the alleged priority of substantives, doubts therefore about a basic presupposition of Aristotle's philosophy.

Some further considerations may at least aid in clarifying the problem. Descartes distinguishes between the *res cogitans* and the *res extensa*. Following an extreme Aristotelian approach, one would have to consider the *res extensa* as the primary experience and the meaning of *res* and *realitas* would have to be gathered from the *res extensa* and then transferred to the *res cogitans*. This is the way Heidegger interprets the ontological assertions of Descartes.[17] In the brief discussion in Part One of *Being and Time*, Heidegger does not establish the correctness of this interpretation, presumably the detailed discussion of the Cartesian ontology is intended for the second Part. It must remain questionable whether Heidegger would succeed in supporting his interpretation. One could suppose that for Descartes an original self-experience on the part of *res cogitans* is fundamental. And it could also be the case that the meaning of *res* and *realitas* should be reached in this original experience of the self by *res cogitans*.

This discussion also serves to clarify Aristotle's charge of reification directed against the theory of Ideas. Sensible things are pre-eminent being for him, their being is being in the pre-eminent meaning, and only here can being be experienced.

Thus it is self-evident for Aristotle that in the theory of Ideas the being of sensible things is transferred to the being of Ideas. Here too it becomes once again clear that the Aristotelian critique is not exhausted in mere criticism, but that it means to clarify substantive problems and does in fact do so.

But the second step remains problematic. One might even grant that individual things perceived by the senses represent the primary experiences. But how do we get the concept of being from them? Being is evidently a general concept which, according to the present supposition, is first encountered in sensible things. But then the question arises how the concept of being as such is achieved. For the theory of Ideas, as we saw, being can appear as the Idea of being. But Aristotle must begin with his theory of abstraction. For him the concept of being is achieved when whatever exists is grasped in its being. But it cannot be maintained that Aristotle has made this method wholly intelligible. It is not very different for Leibniz. He says: I find being in myself.[18] Now this has to mean: I find being in myself as the being of an individual thing. But how I then arrive at a general concept of being is not satisfactorily explained by Leibniz.

Finally, the third step also remains problematic. If we once assume that the general concept of being is derived from the individual thing, how do we pass from the being of the individual thing to the being of the general? Particularly instructive is the form which the problem takes on in Aquinas. Thomas distinguishes between the being of God and the being of created things and these are for him primarily individual things perceived by the senses. Then he distinguishes priority in being from priority in knowledge.[19] In the order of being, the being of God is primary and the being of created things secondary; in the order of knowledge, the being of created things is primary and the being of God secondary. We are presently concerned with the priority in knowledge. If one takes up the Aristotelian-Thomistic standpoint that the being of individual things represents the first thing experienced and the first thing experienceable, then the question arises how knowledge can ascend from the being of individual things perceived by the senses to the unperceivable being of God. To answer this Thomas develops his thesis of the analogical character of the concept of being.[20] One will have to grant that Thomas has here seen a fundamental ontological fact. But one will hardly find Thomas' presentation wholly convincing, which helps to explain why the thinkers of late Scholasticism, in particular Duns Scotus and Ockham, were not able to accept this doctrine and its presentation by Aquinas. One will have to grant that Thomas opened up the correct path here, but that the methodological difficulties of this path are much greater than Thomas supposed.

If we pass Aristotle's critique of the theory of Ideas in review, it proves to be much more positive than many Platonists have wished to allow. I may perhaps be permitted to repeat that in his debate with his teacher, there are passages in which Aristotle makes use of every legitimate advantage and also of some that are illegitimate. But on the whole his critique lays bare systematic difficulties. It turns on the fundamental questions: What nature does the concept of being have? How is it arrived at? How in particular, should we understand the concept of being associated with the being of Ideas? The weakness of this critique lies in the fact that Aristotle was evidently convinced that he had solved the problematic of the concept of being in his own philosophy. If that were the case, Aristotle's ontological interpretation of the concept of being would have to be both clear and final. We will now raise the question whether this is in fact the case.

56. THE APORIAS OF THE ARISTOTELIAN STANDPOINT

In Aristotle's theory, the general appears primarily as a structure of being. We are thinking in particular of the general involved in the generic concepts of quality, quantity and relation. And with these belong also, as being specially relevant to our reflections, the transcendental properties, which are for Aristotle primarily being and unity. All these general properties are conceived as given in the real world; they are abstracted by thought, that is, highlighted and separated. This theory of Aristotle's grew out of his debate with Plato, but it is by no means so free of aporias or so final, as the members of the Aristotelian-Thomistic tradition are often inclined to suppose.

The ontological interpretation of the general is determined in its basic features by his decisive opposition to any notion of a *chorismos*. This shows the influence of his debate with Plato. Aristotle's basic conviction is that the general does not have a special existence separated from individual things, the general exists in individual things.

This leads to a consequence which, so far as I know, Aristotle does not mention, but one which was later often discussed. If the general exists only in individual things, then it can exist only when there is at least one individual thing to which this general corresponds. This is clearly revealed in the concepts of species. Biological species are of course invariant for Aristotle. Had he considered that biological species might arise and perish, that is to say, die out, then he would have considered that the existence of these concepts is itself changeable. The existence of the species concept 'elephant' is conditioned by the existence of at least one elephant. The species concept is and must be realized in the individual elephant. If the elephants die out—an unreal supposition for Aristotle—then the concept 'elephant' would cease to exist in the true sense. It is just the same with all other general concepts. If there are no more green things, then there is no more green itself. Of course this is an unreal supposition for the Greeks For them there are always green things. If there are no more beautiful things, then beauty as such or, in Plato's terms, the Idea of beauty ceases to exist. But this supposition too the Greeks would hold to be unreal. How could they be supposed to believe that one day everything beautiful would perish? How far Aristotle is removed from Platonist principles becomes clear if one considers justice. According to Aristotle's approach there can be justice only when there are just men, just actions, just judges. Here one begins to doubt his approach. Is it really so that the Idea of justice depends on all these realities? Does not justice rather depend on its distance from actual reality? It is not in fact so, as Plato taught, that there is and will be justice even when there is no just man, and is it not truly doubtful whether there has ever been or ever will be a single, truly just man?

In the case of justice, ethical and ontological questions are fused together. This is seen in a purely theoretical form in the problem of the infinite. Aristotelian realism, taken in its extreme form, encounters great difficulties in the problem of the infinite. We have seen that for Aristotle ontology includes, as it must, an interpretation of arithmetic and geometry. But this raises the problem of the infinite. In the *Physics*, Aristotle at first lays down strict limits. The cosmos is finite,[1] and space is finite.[2] From this it follows immediately that the number of individual things is also finite. Time, on the contrary, is infinite, because the motions of the heavens of fixed stars and the sun, which cause day and night as well as the course of the year, together with all other movements of the heavens are eternal.[3] There have been therefore infinitely many days and nights, and there are infinitely many to come.[4] But this infinity is not a contemporaneous one; the past days and nights no longer exist, the future ones do not yet exist. It is in arithmetic and geometry where the problem of the infinite presents real difficulties for the Aristotelian approach. In Arithmetic it is the infinity of the natural numbers and the resulting infinity of fractions. Following the Greek practice, we can limit ourselves to the infinity of the root fractions, that is, to the sequence 1/2, 1/3, 1/4 ... In geometry it is the infinite extendability and the infinite divisibility of the straight line, in particular the relation between a finite line and the infinitely many points that make it up. One gets the impression that the Greeks were particularly interested in those infinities, which we might call the infinities of the small, that is, the infinity of the root fractions and the infinity of the points in a straight line of length unity, and this is perhaps not a bad choice from the mathematical standpoint.

If one joins a standpoint of extreme realism to a theory of abstraction, there is then simply no possibility for a solution to the problem of the infinite. If one assumes with Leibniz that in every space however small there are infinitely many monads,[5] then one can ground the concept of the infinite in actual reality. But for Aristotle the cosmos in the large is finite in extent and in the small is divided into a finite number of parts. In that case there is in reality no infinite in the strict sense, and it can not then be obtained from reality through abstraction. Aristotle himself saw this quite clearly and he therefore makes a distinction between the actual infinite and the potential infinite.[6] In actual reality there is only a potential,[7] not an actual, infinite.[8] The case of a straight line is particularly clear. Every straight line, and for the Greek interpretation that means every limited straight line, is actually divided into a finite number of parts. It can always be further divided, but this infinite divisibility is always only a potential infinity.[9]

Now this distinction between an actual and a potential infinite may bring many advantages, but it brings no solution to the ontological problem. Everything turns on the question how the potential infinite can be understood. That a limited straight line can be infinitely divided obviously presupposes a thinking and acting being who undertakes the dividing. But this binds the potential infinite to the spontaneity of an acting being, and arithmetic and geometry too, in so far as they depend on the concept of infinity. The potential infinite is thus not a structure of being which could be highlighted through abstraction as, for example, the masculine and the feminine are first given as structures of being and then highlighted through abstraction. From the outset the potential infinite is related to a thinking being.

It is just the same with the ideality which belongs both to arithmetic and geometry. We can limit ourselves to geometry. The straight line, the plane and the circle cannot be found in actual reality. Aristotle understands this very well,[10] but he is not able to provide a satisfactory explanation of it. Perhaps he was given a certain help by his conviction that a perfect sphere did exist in actual reality, for the cosmos is for him a perfect sphere.[11] But here one must consider that the spherical shape of the cosmos is the result of a deduction and, incidentally, a very questionable deduction. Aristotle can certainly not claim that this perfect sphere is reached by an abstraction from reality. The empirical interpretation of arithmetic and geometry will always maintain their importance. It undoubtedly fits something in the facts. But it does not fit the specific structure of arithmetic and geometry: their ideality.

It is therefore doubtful that Aristotle's approach to the ontological interpretation of the general can be carried out consistently and without aporias. General concepts are primarily structures of being, they are highlighted in actual reality by abstraction, this is the thesis. The first question is how these structures are contained in reality. This particular horse has a whole series of structures of being, which all lead to general concepts: it is an animal, it is a horse, it is masculine, it is brown, it is young, it is beautiful. Does each of this properties exist in this horse as a separate reality? That would be the simplest interpretation but it would lead to the old Platonic difficulties. Then there would be a horseness in this horse and another horseness in that horse and Plato would ask: how does it happen that it is the same horseness? But this would bring us right back to the initial point of the question. If, on the other hand, one were to say that the many properties in this horse are not in themselves different, but that only determining thought distinguishes them, one would arrive at a nominalism, which in its extreme form at least is certainly not Aristotle's meaning. One can attempt to introduce here the concept of *fundamentum in re* and say that such a *fundamentum in re* is given for the distinction made in thinking. But it seems that one only postpones the difficulties in the indeterminacy of the new concept '*fundamentum in re*' and that nothing is achieved thereby. One can not get around the question whether the different properties are already different in the thing, and as soon as one answers this one way or the other, one encounters difficulties.

These difficulties pile up in a special way in the case of the transcendental concepts. We already saw that Aristotle essentially recognizes two transcendental properties, being and unity,[12] and he says of them that they differ not in *physis* but in *logos*.[13] Here too the question arises whether the two transcendental properties are already different in the individual thing, or whether they become different only through the spontaneity of thinking. Duns Scotus claims that the transcendental properties are already distinct in particular beings, even though it is only a *distinctio formalis*.[14] But this seems not to be the opinion of Aristotle or of Thomas. Both refer to *logos* for the being of the transcendental properties and both mean thereby, if I am correct, a spontaneous act of *logos*. The transcendental properties, particularly, show with all clarity that the old disjunction will not work. The old disjunction says: something exists either in actual reality or it is mere imagining. Someone is either actually a rich man or he is a poor devil, who is rich only in the imaginings of someone else or perhaps in his own imaginings. This simple disjunction no longer works for the transcendental properties. Instead the existence of *logos* is interwoven with the existence of the transcendental properties and this interweaving cannot be wholly disengaged. Everyone who has studied the transcendental properties has said that the issue turns on *logos*. But as soon as they attempt to say in what way *logos* is involved, unsatisfactory, if not downright contradictory, explanations appear. But the fact that the relation of *logos* to the transcendental properties cannot be fully clarified, does not eliminate the relation itself. The particular importance of the transcendentals for ontology is that they reveal the weakness of the old disjunction between actual reality and mere imagining as well as bringing to light the importance of *logos*.

This significance of *logos* revealed for the transcendental properties applies to the whole realm of the general, for the transcendental properties are general, in fact they are the most general.[15] We can get a closer view of the problem through certain characterizations from the history of philosophy. Aristotle and Thomas are characterized as moderate realists.[16] The concept of moderate realism is obviously conceived as a counterpart to the concept of extreme realism. A moderate realism would then imply the acceptance of certain idealistic or nominalistic aspects into realism. If one characterizes extreme realism in the thesis: being is independent of its being known, then a moderate realism must mean that being is not wholly independent of its being known, and that the spontaneity of *logos* is in some way important for being itself. In order to avoid a premature hardening of views, I speak not of thinking or the subject, but of *logos*. That being in its transcendental properties has a relation to *logos* is explicitly asserted by Aristotle. This assertion may admit of differing interpretations, but that being and unity in their difference are related to *logos*—this is expressly claimed.

It must also be remembered that Aristotle's ontological theory of the being of the general as such relates that being to *logos*. This has always been admitted. But one has to ask, how the general is related to *logos*. That Aristotle did not explain this conclusively strikes me as an important fact for ontology.

The relation of being to *logos* becomes a little clearer under theological aspects. One can see this in Thomas who is, however, here in the genuine tradition of Aristotle. God is *logos*, this assertion of St John's gospel[17] establishes for all Christian philosophical and theological speculation an original connexion between being and *logos*. For Thomas this connexion appears also in a second form, since for him the being of the creature is originally a being thought by God. Every creature is conceived by God from all eternity, at a finite time in creation or in the history of the created world it is translated into actual reality.

This second thesis is of course specifically Christian, for Aristotle the world has not come into being and was not created by God. But when Thomas understands the being of God as a pure *actus*[18] and therewith a pure *logos*, he is none the less developing Aristotle's properties. Aristotle too explicitly characterizes the being of God as pure *Energeia* and to that extent as pure *Nous*.[19] The being of God is so utterly *Energeia* that Aristotle describes this being as νόσις νοήσεως.[20] But if the being of God is pure *Nous*, then being as such cannot differ fundamentally from *logos*. There must then be an original constitutive connexion between being and *logos*. It is thus understandable that Aristotle refers back to the connexion with *logos* both for the being of the transcendentals and also for the being of the general as such.

If one were to leave these connexions out of account in studying Aristotle and if one were to attempt to understand him from the standpoint of a radical realism, one would encounter not a few difficulties. For a radical realism, every general property must exist in every individual being as an independent reality. But then in Socrates his being a man, his being alive, but also his being courageous and educated would each exist as an independent reality. Two questions would then arise. One would be about the unity of the general. If Socrates is brave, and Nicias is brave, and Laches is brave—to recall Plato's dialogue[21]—how does it happen that it is the same bravery which exists so many times. Here would emerge the problem of the multiplication of the general[22] which was such a great problem for Plato. The opposite but in no sense easier question is about the unity of the individual being. If each of these general properties is an independent reality in each individual thing, how does it happen that these many general properties recede to form the unity of the individual thing? If Socrates is a man and a living being, if he is brave and educated, how does it happen that in all these he is still one Socrates?

It becomes apparent that the ontological determination of the general is not free of difficulties in Aristotle either. The difficulties appear whether one assumes—as I understand Aristotle's opinion —a constitutive connexion between being and *logos* or whether one understands being in the sense of an extreme realism as wholly indifferent to its being thought. It may have been these difficulties which caused Aristotle, at the beginning of Book VII of the *Metaphysics*, to describe the question about being as one that is always caught up in aporias.

57. ARISTOTLE AND THE TWO OTHER STANDPOINTS

One can therefore show that for Aristotle the question about being remains aporematic, but one can also show that certain aspects of the Platonic and the Kantian standpoints are contained in the Aristotelian standpoint.

Taking the connexion with Plato first, we have already presented our conviction that Aristotle was a critical Platonist, and that in the sense in which he was a Platonist he remained a Platonist throughout his life. There can also be no doubt that the decisive aspect of Plato's approach, the general normativeness of general concepts, remained important for Aristotle in the same way. It may be that Aristotle's attention was focused especially on the general normativeness of the general concepts in the cosmos. This does not cancel the general normativeness, perhaps it even strengthens it. Aristotle can therefore speak with full right in the plural, when he speaks of the theory of Ideas: we assume Ideas, we say . . .[1] Werner Jaeger's thesis that this use of the plural is a conclusive indication of its time of composition, we regard as unproven.[2] What Aristotle altered in the theory of Ideas is primarily the *chorismos*. If Plato said in many passages and in others seemed to say that the Ideas exist in a unique world of Ideas in a place beyond the heavens, Aristotle indeed will not support this. The Ideas exist, but they exist in sensible things. In this sense Aristotle is attacking not the theory of Ideas as such but rather the manner and mode in which the existence of Ideas is understood.

If Aristotle remained fundamentally an adherent of the theory of Ideas, then one might suppose tht he would also retain the aspect of spontaneity which crops up in Plato's theory of Ideas. And this is in fact the case. One can say further that Aristotle strengthened the meaning of spontaneity. He expresses the meaning of spontaneity in his theory of νοῦς ποιητικός. This is to be sure a difficult and subtle part of the Aristotelian philosophy, but that is to be expected considering the systematic difficulties of the problem of spontaneity.[3]

We can get closer to the problem in Aquinas. One readily sees that Thomas must also take account of the spontaneity of human thinking. For Thomas, God is pure reason, and therefore *actus purus* and pure spontaneity.[4] Now he also understands man as determined fundamentally in the image of God,[5] and it is reason which is copied.[6] But then some reflection of the pure spontaneity of the divine reason must also fall upon the reason of man, and thus Thomas finds himself from the outset required to pay careful attention to the spontaneity of human thinking. Thus it becomes understandable that the theory of *intellectus agens* forms an important part of Thomas' philosophy.[7]

The conception of man as the image of God is of course lacking in Aristotle. None the less several of Aristotle's views make the importance of spontaneity for men quite clear. For Aristotle too God is pure reason[8] and therefore pure *Energeia*.[9] But there is also the notion of a connexion between the being of God and the being of man. If the heavens strive out of love to realize the pure being of God as far as possible,[10] then this striving after the divine model also applies to man himself and to human reason. This explains why the theory of *intellectus agens* is already substantially present in Aristotle.

The spontaneity of *logos* becomes apparent in two problems. The first is the significance of *logos* for the transcendental properties.[11] However one interprets Aristotle's brief hints, already discussed, one thing is clear: the difference between being and unity rests on a distinction made by *logos*.

One might make reference further to a famous passage in the *Physics*, one that is also very difficult to interpret. There Aristotle says that number exists in the numbering soul.[12] Now this is a very broad thesis which one could already understand as nominalism, and even as a very extreme nominalism. But for certain numbers at least this expresses nothing more than an obvious fact. It is the complete arbitrariness of adding which suggests, at least for certain numbers, a recurrence to the act of numbering. If one says: here are three fish, one is always tempted to interpret this number three as an objective reality. We have seen that difficulties appear if one wants to talk here of a real accident. But these difficulties emerge only after a penetrating analysis. When, however, I add together this fish, this man and this stone, and say: these are three, then the connexion of these three things is obviously quite arbitary and produced only by the adding itself. The difference has often been noted. One can furnish drastic examples of it, the Scholastics for example would think of angels as beings which could only be grouped arbitrarily. Some Scholasti philosophers tried to remove the difficulty by distinguishing different modes of number: a number which is a real accident and a number which exists only in numbering. But such a distinction is not easy to carry through. Since the distinction requires us in any case to assume some numbers which exist only in thought, the inclination to interpret all numbers in this way becomes understandable. This would look like nominalism. But two thinkers who can certainly not be regarded as nominalists, namely Duns Scotus and Descartes, have in this sense essentially located number in thought.

The passage in the *Physics* can certainly be interpreted as an expression of the great arbitrariness of addition, and this is in fact a clear case. But whether Aristotle intended to draw decisive consequences from this case for the being of numbers or even for the being of the general as a whole, must remain open. For our consideration it suffices that Aristotle has here seen and expressed the freedom of numbering and thinking which becomes apparent in addition.

To sum up we can say that Aristotle's connexion with Plato is quite obvious. One can add further that Aristotle certainly sees the general first and foremost as a structure of the real world but that he has also expressed in important passages the significance of thinking and, in particular, the significance of the spontaneity of thinking. And these admissions put him into a connexion, even though a very concealed one, with Kant.

CHAPTER XI

THE APORIAS OF THE KANTIAN STANDPOINT

58. THE THINKING SUBJECT

The aporias of the Kantian standpoint culminate in two problems: What is the thinking subject? How are appearance and thing-in-itself distinguished? These aporias reach deeply into the foundations of the Kantian philosophy. Kant is, however, less inclined to aporetic than Plato, and in a certain sense even less inclined than Aristotle. Certainly dialectic constitutes an essential part of the *Critique of Pure Reason*. But Kant also claims to have restricted all antinomies within a definite compass. Here too it is a matter of drawing boundaries, the principal task which the *Critique of Pure Reason* sets itself. All antinomies lie within definite boundaries. If these boundaries are respected, everything outside them is free of contradictions and secure, indeed in its fundamental determinations already given a definitive clarification by Kant himself. Kant makes the explicit claim that the *Critique of Pure Reason* will put an end to previous controversies in philosophy.[1] The *Critique* makes possible the distinction between the soluble and the insoluble problems of reason. The soluble problems are definitively clarified, at least in their basic characteristics, in the *Critique of Pure Reason*.[2]

Kant himself claims that he has reached the goal he set himself.[3] The subsequent course of philosophy gives no evidence that this is actually the case. This situation differs from that of Plato. Plato himself reflected on the aporias which flow from the theory of Ideas. Now Kant did restrict and to a large extent clarify the antinomies. But the aporias we are now considering lie on the boundaries of Kant's thought. They confront Kant but he did not himself reflect on them.

A discussion of the aporias must therefore go considerably beyond Kant's published statements, but it can be grounded on the fact that these aporias have largely come to prominence in the interpretation of the Kantian philosophy.

The difficulties begin with Kant's claim of completeness for his table of the categories.[4] This is a principle and an indispensable claim for the Kantian system. In fact Kant's complaint against Aristotle and against all the philosophical work between Aristotle and himself is precisely that the table of categories was never complete.[5] His table of twelve categories is complete and thereby definitive, that is his fundamental claim. Subsequent development does not confirm him. No matter with what determination individuals have adopted the Kantian philosophy, no matter with what determination men have called themselves Kantians, only a few have regarded the table of categories as complete.

How could the completeness be proved? In the *Critique of Pure Reason*, it is at least clear how Kant himself conceived the proof. The completeness of the table of categories is supposed to be derived from the completeness of the table of judgements.[6] But this only postpones the question of proof. It must remain doubtful whether Kant proved the completeness of his table of judgements, and it must remain doubtful whether one could ever prove the completeness of a table of judgements.

There are of course realms in which one can prove that certain structures are complete and that beyond the assigned number there can be no others. The most famous example is that of the regular solids. In the proof that there are only five regular solids and can be no others, the *Elements* of Euclid finds its highpoint and perfection.

This proof can be checked step by step. Very few would claim that Kant's proof for the completeness of the table of judgements is correct. If one considers wherein the actual driving force for Kant's claim to completeness lies, one will find the optimism of the enlightenment. The optimism of the enlightenment itself knew no bounds. The world is completely knowable, since it is completely known by God. It may well be that we men are not yet able to know everything. Objects of infinitely great complexity cannot be rendered wholly transparent, for them we must be content with approximations. But at least such approximations are largely available to us. This is the optimism which found in Leibniz its most consistent expression, and this is the optimism which at the beginning of modern times encouraged and made possible the rise of modern science. Here it is Kant's great concern to recognize the boundaries. The world in itself is not at all knowable and in the world of appearances the antinomies set the boundaries of knowledge. But for all his setting of boundaries Kant holds fast to one definite realm of the optimism of the enlightenment: reason can understand itself completely. When reason considers itself, its own acts, its own activities, its own capacities, its own abilities, then it can reach a complete knowledge. Reason can only understand what it has itself combined.[7] But this it can understand completely. Kant's adherence to the optimism of the enlightenment is shown in his belief that reason can fully survey its own possibilities. But if one makes these connexions fully clear, one sees how problematical this Kantian optimism is.

The completeness of the tables is, after all, only a preliminary problem. The dominant emphasis of the Kantian theses lies upon the ontological interpretation: the judgements, the categories, the schemata, the principles are acts of thinking. But then the question arises necessarily: what kind of thinking is it we are analysing? Who is thinking? Kant did not himself reflect any further on this question; for that reason it has played an even greater role in the interpretation of Kant.

If one consults the interpreters on this question one finds that three possibilities have crystallized: 1. It is a general reason which thinks. This could be for example a general reason in the sense of the enlightenment, it could also be a world-reason in the sense of a pantheism or, in a more theological form, it could be God's reason. 2. It is the empirical reason of each individual man who thinks. 3. All the expressions used here, such as acting, combining, prescribing laws, and so forth, are intended metaphorically. Instead we are dealing with a network of structures which are in themselves logical structures, made understandable through these images.

The first possibility is essentially the one chosen in German Idealism, and in its theological form particularly by Hegel. Certainly Hegel attacks the rigidity of the Kantian tables. But in the ontological interpretation Hegel holds on to the Kantian principle. For Hegel in particular the categories are movements of thought, acts of thought. The Hegelian logic has assimilated the Kantian judgements, categories, schemata and principles. It is, as Hegel himself says, the representation of God's thoughts before the creation of the world.[8] But then it is primarily God's thoughts, the movements and acts of which we are studying.

Certainly this character of movement is transferred to the thinking of men. But that does not prevent the original pure form from being expressed in the logic, and this form is the divine thinking.

In sharp contrast to this stands the empirical interpretation as represented in particular by Fries,[9] and following Fries, by many neo-Kantians. It is the individual man who thinks and whose necessities constitute the necessities of the Kantian table.

We find the third interpretation in the neo-Kantianism of the Marburg school.[10] Here all assertions about activity and acts are interpreted as images, what lies at the bottom is a purely logical system with immanent logical necessities. All necessities of the tables are fundamental logical necessities or flow from them.

How shall we decide between these alternative interpretations? We should first notice that Kant himself did not explicitly present a solution, otherwise the differing interpretations would not be possible. In order to advance a further step here it may be best to ask about the possible difference between the thinking and the acting subject. Is it the same man who thinks and acts or must we distinguish between them? I do not believe that Kant intended a distinction here or even that a distinction is possible. The thinking and acting man, is that man as noumenon or as phenomenon? We will later discuss this question in detail when we turn to the distinction between phenomenon and noumenon. Here we may assume that the question: who is thinking? may be pursued prior to this distinction. One would then come to the formula which Kant puts at the conclusion of the *Critique of Practical Reason.* The conclusion begins with the famous sentence: 'Two things fill the mind with ever new and increasing admiration and awe, the oftener and more steadily we reflect on them: the starry heavens above me and the moral law within me.'[11] For our consideration the second sentence is also important: 'I do not merely conjecture them and seek them as though obscured in darkness or in the transcendent region beyond my horizon: I see them before me, and I associate them directly with the consciousness of my own existence.'[12] The decisive thing for our consideration is that I as the same person see both before me and that I associate them both with my existence as one self-identical person. Continuing, Kant says expressly that I am associated with two worlds: '. . . and broadens the connexion in which I stand . . .' But I also belong to another world 'which has true infinity . . . with which I recognize myself as existing in a universal and necessary (and not only, as in the first case, contingent) connexion.'[13] It is the same I which is associated with the phenomenal as well as with the noumenal world. But just this shows the significance of the sentence: 'I see them both before me, and I associate them directly with the consciousness of my existence.' Here the two worlds stand in the plural and the I as one and the same sees them both before him and associates them both with the consciousness of his one identical and indivisible existence.

This one and the same I, which is associated with two worlds, must be the I which thinks, acts and prescribes. If that is so then the question about the subject of thinking is connected in the most intimate way with the question about the distinction between the noumenon and the phenomenon, of which we will show in the following that it cannot be answered without aporias. But then the question about the thinking subject must also encounter the same difficulties, which explains why the interpreters cannot reach any agreement. We obtain the result that Kant himself did not decide among the different possible interpretations and that a final decision among them is not possible.

59. APPEARANCE AND THING-IN-ITSELF: THE PROBLEM OF KNOWLEDGE

Already in 1786, five years after the publication of the *Critique of Pure Reason*, Jacobi formulated the problem of the thing-in-itself with astonishing accuracy: '. . . that I cannot get into the system without that presupposition and cannot remain in the system with it.'[1] And in fact Jacobi's two points can be shown to be reasonable.

Without the concept of the thing-in-itself I cannot get into the *Critique of Pure Reason*. Kant himself made this quite clear in working out the *Critique* and, in addition, he specifically asserted it. The Transcendental Aesthetic rests on the distinction between appearance and thing-in-itself. Space and time belong to appearances, they are the forms of appearances. Kant took over this thesis of the phenomenal character of space and time from Leibniz, although he includes a polemic against Leibniz in the Transcendental Aesthetic. Leibniz in turn makes it clear that he stands in the tradition of Plato.[2] Of this distinction Kant says explicitly that it is necessary; 'otherwise we should be landed in absurd conclusion that there can be appearance without anything that appears.'[3]

The concept of appearance proves to be just as fundamental for the Transcendental Analytic. The *a priori* validity of the categories and the principles that flow from them can only be proved if this validity together with space and time are restricted to appearances.[4] An instructive example is afforded by Kant's theory of the *a priori* validity of the causal law. Kant's theory is that the causal law is valid only for appearances and that its *a priori* validity can be proved only for appearances.[5] We can leave out of account whether the causal law has *a priori* validity and whether its *a priori* validity can be proved. If one assumes this Kantian presupposition hypothetically, then one must admit that such a proof could only be achieved on the basis of limited presuppositions, and that the presuppositions Kant has chosen for the purpose, namely limitation to appearances, is thoroughly reasonable.

The distinction between appearance and thing-in-itself also underlies the Transcendental Dialectic. If we limit ourselves to the antinomies, Kant's theory shows that in the first two antinomies it was not observed that the arguments concern appearances and not things-in-themselves: in the first antinomy the dispute about the finite or infinite character of space and time, and in the second antinomy the dispute about finite or infinite divisibility.[6] The third and fourth antinomy are resolved by showing that the thesis and the antithesis each deal with a different realm, one with appearances and one with things-in-themselves.[7] We will discuss the third antinomy in detail below.

Thus it is understandable that Kant introduced at the end of the Transcendental Analytic a separate section bearing the title: 'On the Ground of the Distinction of all Objects in General into Phenomena and Noumena.'[8] Kant here explains that the concept of noumenon is used in two meanings, in a negative and in a positive meaning. Kant says:

'If by "noumenon" we mean a thing so far as it is *not an object of our sensible intuition*, and so abstract from our mode of intuiting it, this is a noumenon in the *negative* sense of the term. But if we understand by it an *object* of a *non-sensible intuition*, we thereby presuppose a special mode of intuition, namely, the intellectual, which is not that which we possess, and of which we cannot comprehend even the possibility. This would be "noumenon" in the *positive* sense of the term.'[9]

The *Critique of Pure Reason* limits itself, at least in the Aesthetic and the Analytic, to the noumenon in the negative sense. By contrast, the noumenon in the positive sense appears in the Dialectic. But it becomes a theme only in the *Critique of Practical Reason*.

On the whole then, and considering Kant's explicit declaration that the concept of appearance presupposes the concept of something which appears, one has to agree with Jacobi's contention that without the concept of the thing-in-itself one cannot get into the *Critique of Pure Reason.*

But Jacobi's other contention is just as reasonable: that with the concept one cannot remain therein. This is best grasped in the modal categories. In his treatment of modalities Kant starts with the traditional method of treatment. Possibility, actuality and necessity were as a rule treated separately. Kant places them under the categories where they constitute the tenth, eleventh and twelfth categories. From this it follows that they must be subject to the general restriction of categories to appearances.

We may limit ourselves to possibility. Agreement with the formal conditions of both intuition and the concepts is required for possibility.[10]

If we limit ourselves to the first presupposition, only that is possible which agrees with the formal conditions of intuition. The forms of intuition, and therefore their formal conditions, are space and time. Only that is possible therefore which can appear in space and time.

Here, quite justifiably, possibility and actuality are determined in relation to experiences in the natural sciences, especially physics. The connexion of the concept of actuality with space and time was already seen by Aristotle, he saw that space and time underlie the simple concept of actuality.[11] For experience in the natural sciences this requirement cannot be doubted. For the natural scientist, in particular for the physicist, only that is possible which can appear in a specific place in space at a specific time. These postulates are basic determinations of possibility and actuality in Newtonian physics, and the determinations are certainly correct in this domain. Because of the strongly concrete character of Newtonian physics its concepts of possibility and necessity must largely coincide with those of simple experience. In this determination of modalities it is clearly shown that the *Critique of Pure Reason* is a theory of experience and largely a theory of Newtonian physics, as Cohen has forcefully demonstrated.[12] Within these limits the restriction of possibility and actuality to spatial and temporal conditions is wholly justified.

But this limitation of possibility and actuality necessarily implies that the modal categories cannot be applied to things-in-themselves. In the meaning of possibility and actuality determined for the Transcendental Analytic, things-in-themselves are neither possible nor actual. This is the second part of Jacobi's comment: with the concept of thing-in-itself one cannot remain in the *Critique of Pure Reason*. Summing up one can say, confirming thereby Jacobi's contention: the result of the Transcendental Analytic, the backbone of the *Critique of Pure Reason*, is that things-in-themselves are neither possible nor actual.

German Idealism and neo-Kantianism largely follow this contention of Jacobi's. German Idealism understands itself as a continuation and completion of the Kantian philosophy, and it considers the critique of Kant's concept of the thing-in-itself as one of its most important tasks. One must free the Kantian philosophy from this relic of an out-dated dogmatic thought, only then can it be completed. In this spirit Hegel says: 'It is this second side to which Kant's attention is exclusively directed. His main idea is to vindicate the categories of self-consciousness as the subjective I. In virtue of this determination his view remains within consciousness and its antithesis and has, after the empirical reports of feeling and intuition, something still left over which is not posited and determined through thinking self-consciousness, a thing-in-itself, something alien to and outside thought—although it is easy to see that such an abstraction as a thing-in-itself is itself only a product of thinking, in fact of abstract thinking.'[13]

In neo-Kantianism also, the confrontation with the concept of thing-in-itself has a great meaning. Here as a rule the thing-in-itself is reinterpreted in such a way as practically to exclude it. Characteristic of this mode of interpretation is Hermann Cohen's view which, with respect to the realm of experience, gave us indispensable insights.

Cohen entitles the thirteenth chapter of his interpretation: 'The Thing-in-Itself and the Ideas'. He begins with a humorous remark: 'Thus the critical philosopher must also lend an ear to the rumours about a "thing-in-itself".'[14] Cohen's talk about a rumour seems to me to be a very extravagant rendering of the fact that the concept of the thing-in-itself stems directly from Kant and that Kant himself explicitly speaks of the thing-in-itself in many passages. Now Cohen interprets the thing-in-itself as the whole of experience:

'We must now realize that this nature which comes to be as a unifying of the totality of principles in one object or by thinking experience as an object, is thereby made into a thing-in-itself. And whether the whole of experience . . . this nature . . . in so far as it is conceived as a thing-in-itself . . .'[15]

Now this reinterpretation applies in a certain way since the concept of the thing-in-itself also appears in the treatment of the transcendental Ideas, that is, in the Transcendental Dialectic. But the reinterpretation does not do justice to the fact that the thing-in-itself is at least as important in the Transcendental Aesthetic and in the Transcendental Analytic. Cohen then says quite summarily: 'The idle talk that Kant has indeed restricted knowledge to that of the appearances, but none the less left the unknowable thing-in-itself standing—this superficial talk must now finally cease after more than a hundred years.'[16] Cohen passes over the fact that what he calls idle talk stands quite plainly in Kant's text. But he at least remarks that his interpretation of the thing-in-itself is not found in this way in Kant: 'confessing from the outset, that Kant did not express the order and disposition of his thoughts, though sharp and definite in their own way, in the manner which I present.'[17]

In this way, starting from the Transcendental Analytic, the thing-in-itself is interpreted away or at least reinterpreted. I do not believe that one must move so far away from Kant's reasoning or from Kant's text. But before we attempt a possible solution we will first consider the problems of the thing-in-itself as they appear essentially in the theory of freedom.

60. THE THING-IN-ITSELF: THE PROBLEM OF BEING

Kant's decision, in the section of the *Critique of Pure Reason* on the distinction between phenomenon and noumenon, to permit the noumenon only in the negative sense correctly describes his procedure in the *Critique* up to that point; in the Transcendental Aesthetic and the Transcendental Analytic the concept of the noumenon is used only in the negative sense. In the *Critique of Practical Reason*, however, he uses it in a positive meaning. In a special study in the *Critique of Practical Reason*, Kant expressly justifies such an extension in its practical use 'which is not possible to it in its speculative use'.[1] Kant is already occupied with this extension in the third part of the *Critique of Pure Reason*, that is, in the Dialectic. We can restrict ourselves to the theory of antinomies and, in particular, to the third antinomy. The thesis states: 'Causality in accordance with laws of nature is not the only causality from which the appearances of the world can one and all be derived. To explain these appearances it is necessary to assume that there is also another causality, that of freedom.'[2] And the antithesis asserts: 'There is no freedom; everything in the world takes place solely in accordance with laws of nature.'[3]

In this antinomy the basic presuppositions of the new natural science collide with the old requirements of religion and ethics. If one takes nature to be Newtonian, one assumes that nature consists solely in a movement of masses according to Newtonian laws, and then the whole course of nature is unalterably given and there is no place left for free acts from religious or ethical reasons. There can be no doubt about the exclusion of free acts in a nature determined by Newtonian laws of motion. One need only reduce nature to a simple case in order to see this clearly. We could suppose that nature consists of two mass-points, whose mechanical data correspond, say, to the data for the sun and the earth. This is certainly an impoverished world but one that is quite possible on the basis of Newtonian physics. Then the two mass-points would describe ellipses, a very large one and a very small one, around the middle point of mass which serves as focal point of the system. If nature consisted only of these two mass-points and if the sole laws of nature were the Newtonian laws of motion, then these revolutions would be unalterably determined for all time. Newton himself had a different opinion. He assumed that God in the creation had arbitrarily laid down the dimensions and the movements of the planets.[4] God hurls the planets, this is the way Kant describes metaphorically Newton's conviction.[5] Newton inferred from this that God could be any time introduce new determinations into the course of nature. In fact he holds that such interventions are necessary in order to restore the balance of energy in the solar system by adding new amounts to replace that lost by friction.[6] Leibniz recognized that such assumptions would contradict the conceptual structure of Newtonian mechanics. The motion of the mass-points must follow the Newtonian laws of motion without exception or it is not lawful.[7] In order to solve the problems which arise here Leibniz distinguishes between two kingdoms, the kingdom of nature and the kingdom of grace.[8] In the kingdom of nature everything happens according to the laws of nature, in particular according to Newton's laws of motion. In the kingdom of grace obtains freedom of acts according to moral laws.[9] The two kingdoms are combined in exact correspondence through the pre-established harmony.[10] And Leibniz likes to use the example of two clocks set at the same time.[11] Whatever difficulties this distinction between the two kingdoms may have, it at least meets the requirements of the natural sciences. It sets apart a closed kingdom, the kingdom of nature, and this closed kingdom is clearly and completely determined by the laws of nature.

In a certain sense Kant takes over Leibniz's solution of the problem of freedom, although he gives up the pre-established harmony. The pre-established harmony was the aspect of the Leibnizian philosophy which was immediately subject to vigorous attack, and it is one of the most unsatisfactory aspects of that philosophy. Kant substitutes for the distinction between the kingdom of nature and the kingdom of grace his own distinction between appearance and thing-in-itself. Here a pre-established harmony is not possible since the noumenal is not in the strict sense accessible to our knowledge. And this constitutes a radical difference from Leibniz.

Kant finds in the distinction between appearance and thing-in-itself the solution of the third antinomy. Thesis and antithesis refer to different realms, the thesis to the noumena and the antithesis to the phenomena. At the end of his exposition Kant discusses thematically the solution of the antinomies. He presents the solution of each antinomy separately and pays by far the most attention to the solution of the third antinomy. Kant first formulates the opposing standpoint: 'If appearances were things-in-themselves ...'[12] For this standpoint the conclusion is inescapable, Kant thinks. '... for if appearances are things-in-themselves then freedom cannot be upheld'.[13] This leads him to the following formulation of his problem: 'Is it a truly disjunctive proposition to say that every effect in the world must arise *either* from nature *or* from freedom; or must we not rather say that in one and the same event, in different relations, both can be found?'[14] Along this line Kant finds his solution: 'Thus the effect may be regarded as free in respect of its intelligible cause, and at the same time in respect of appearances as resulting from them according to the necessity of nature.'[15] Kant then says in conclusion and not without reason: 'This distinction, when stated in this quite general and abstract manner, is bound to appear extremely subtle and obscure.'[16] One sees that the solution rests on the distinction between appearance and thing-in-itself, and that the solution carries the difficulty of how this distinction is to be understood.

Kant gives the solution with the greatest circumspection. He repeatedly presents it as a mere possibility in the sense of a consistent hypothesis.[17] None the less one cannot deny that in this solution he has already begun to use the noumenon in a positive sense. Thus Kant can speak not only of the *causa phaenomenon*,[18] but also of the *causa noumenon*,[19] and similarly of the *substantia phaenomenon*[20] and the *substantia noumenon*,[21] and of the *realitas phaenomenon*[22] and the *realitas noumenon*.[23] The emergence of the positive meaning becomes definite in the *Critique of Practical Reason*. In the section already mentioned above, Kant reflects specifically on this, and in carrying out his *Critique of Practical Reason*, Kant makes repeated use of the distinction between appearance and thing-in-itself, phenomenon and noumenon. The question thus arises, how is this distinction to be understood systematically?

61. THE SYSTEMATIC PROBLEMS OF THE THING-IN-ITSELF

A part of the difficulties in the Kantian problem of the thing-in-itself stems from the fact that, although Kant himself taught the distinction between appearance and thing-in-itself, he did not engage in any further reflections about its meaning. It is true that we here come up against an inevitable boundary. Every philosophy must at some point simply leave the questions it has raised. Thus one could say that Aristotle did not engage in any further reflections on his distinction between the general and the individual. Plato did both; he distinguished between Ideas and sensible things and then went on to reflect on the distinction. His boundary problems lie in other places. It remains a unique bit of luck that Plato reflected so thoroughly on his basic distinction. And it is remarkable that the interpretation of Plato for a long time ignored the problem, although in the last few decades, fortunately, it has begun to receive a thorough discussion. In Kant, however, we find only the distinction between thing-in-itself and appearance, but no reflection on how this distinction is to be understood. It is thus understandable that the problem constitutes one of the great themes of Kant interpretation. We are indebted to Heimsoeth for some fundamental considerations.[1]

If one considers the possibilities of such reflections one will not be able to deny a fundamental justification to the considerations raised by German Idealism and neo-Kantianism and already begun by Jacobi. The Transcendental Analytic led to a determination of possibility and actuality such that on this basis one could not regard things-in-themselves as possible or actual. Certainly it is legitimate to test this basis. The test would show, however, that only one result is possible: in the sense specified by the Transcendental Analytic, things-in-themselves are neither possible nor actual. But perhaps another way is open. The thesis of German Idealism and neo-Kantianism, which we have just mentioned, tend to show that Kant, if one understands him from the standpoint of the Transcendental Analytic, may not speak of the thing-in-itself. But it seems to me that one could turn this reasoning around and begin with the fact that Kant himself does speak of the thing-in-itself. This is a fact and no one will seriously contest it. One can then put the question the other way around: how are we to understand Kant so that he may say what he actually says? How are we to understand Kant so that he may speak about things-in-themselves? If we thus turn the question around, its solution may begin to become visible.

Turning to the modal categories again, this would obviously mean that one could ascribe both possibility and actuality to things-in-themselves. And this in turn means that the meanings of possibility and actuality developed in the Transcendental Analytic cannot be the only ones, and that there must be other meanings of possibility and actuality beyond these, even for Kant. If the question is put in this way, then one quickly sees that the Transcendental Analytic unfolds those meanings of possibility and actuality which the natural sciences use and must use. And in fact in the natural sciences only that is possible and actual which stands or can stand in a space–time connexion. And then one sees quickly that there must be other meanings of possibility and actuality, even in the Transcendental Dialectic, when the questions about the possibility of the concept of freedom and the concept of God are raised.[2]

Freedom is possible, this thesis is one of the essential goals of the Transcendental Dialectic. But the meaning of possibility used here cannot be identical with the one of which the principle of possibility in the Analytic speaks. It is no different with the thesis: freedom is actual. Instead Kant as a rule avoids the term actuality, he prefers to speak of the objective reality of the concept of freedom.[3]

There are however passages in which Kant explicitly speaks of the actuality of freedom.[4] In more recent times the problem has also been seen in the interpretation of Kant, I would draw attention in particular to the studies by Scheeberger on the concept of possibility.[5] Kant speaks of the possibility and actuality of freedom in a remark about the solution of the antinomy of freedom.[6] Perhaps the most pregnant passage is found at the end of the theory of antinomies. Kant says there: 'But once we have allowed ourselves to assume a self-subsistent reality entirely outside the field of sensibility, . . .'[7] The discrepancy with the analytic could hardly be more sharply expressed. The analytic binds actuality to the conditions of sensibility. But here Kant speaks specifically of an actuality which stands entirely outside the field of sensibility.

If one considers the systematic possibilities, one sees that Kant is faced with the same problem as Plato. Plato first ascribed actuality only to the Ideas and was then forced to expand the meaning of actuality and being so that they could also be ascribed to sensible things. In much the same way Kant must now look for an expanded meaning of actuality. It is by no means true that Kant shut his eyes to this problem, instead he tried in different ways to attack it.

The solution which Kant primarily considers is the distinction between a pure and a schematized category. The categories first appear in the table of categories as the pure possibilities of thinking—in the *Critique of Practical Reason* Kant calls them 'mere forms of thought';[8] later in the schematism they become schematized through the modes of time.[9] Kant discusses this primarily for the categories of substance[10] and causality.[11] The categories are first pure concepts, as such they do not yet confer knowledge. If they are to confer knowledge they must be schematized, that is, they must be referred to time and in connexion with time, to space, where relevant. With this schematizing through time and, where relevant, through space, they receive their meaning as knowledge, but they are also restricted thereby to appearances.[12] Therefore the categories not yet schematized are not yet restricted to appearances. Through this reasoning the possibility arises for Kant to apply the categories, i.e., the not yet schematized categories, to noumena.[13] In this way the noumena can be thought but not known, as Kant likes to formulate it.[14] Kant thus arrives at distinctions like *causa noumenon* and *causa phenomenon*, *substantia noumenon* and *substantia phenomenon*, *realitas noumenon* and *realitas phenomenon*, which we have touched upon in the preceeding paragraphs.

This reasoning can then be applied to the modal categories, in particular. Here too there are the pure categories, such as those enumerated in the table of categories,[15] and the schematized categories, as introduced in the chapter on the schematism[16] and applied in the theory of principles.[17] Then the possibility and actuality of freedom would be only conceivable, but not knowable,[18] and the schematized categories of possibility and actuality, on the other hand, would make possible a genuine knowledge. There is in fact a whole series of passages in which Kant says just this in relation to freedom. The possibility and the actuality of freedom one can think, but not know, much less understand.[19] With this careful attitude Kant takes care of many difficulties which appear in the consciousness of freedom.[20] This consciousness of freedom, which is indubitable for Kant, confronts an ontological interpretation with not a few difficulties. In general one cannot say that the difference developed by Kant between thinking and knowing represents a fully satisfactory solution or even that Kant himself regarded it as fully satisfactory.

The second possibility for achieving the required meaning of the modal categories for things-in-themselves would be the concept of analogy. This concept, which was developed by Aristotle and broadly constructed by the Scholastics, retains a certain meaning for Kant. One finds it particularly in theological reflections, for example, when the will of God is being compared to the will of man. In agreement with the tradition Kant holds that this relation can only be an analogy.[21] He also maintains in agreement with the tradition that the concept of creation applied to God and applied to men is used analogously.[22] It might therefore be possible that the concept of analogy plays a role in those places where Kant speaks of the possibility and actuality of the things-in-themselves in relation to the possibility and actuality of appearances.

This problem turns up in all the philosophical concepts in Kant which reach beyond the distinction between appearance and thing-in-itself. There are not a few, and the concept of objective reality and the concept of law seem to be the most important. Both concepts are used in the phenomenal realm as well as in the noumenal, and the question arises therefore whether they are both used with the same meaning. With respect to law the question is whether the moral law is law in the same sense as the law of nature.[23] Since Kant, as we have already noticed, did not himself engage in any further reflection on the problems arising here, a wholly conclusive interpretation can hardly be looked for.

It is no different when we move from the difference of meanings to the difference of modes of being. Here too we find the same difficulties as in Plato. How is the being of things-in-themselves related to the being of appearances? In Kant three solutions are indicated. We find indications of a two-worlds theory, we find the interpretation that appearances are mere representations in us, and finally, we find the interpretation that there is only one and the same being involved, but considered under differing aspects.

With respect to the interpretation as a two-worlds theory, no one will wish to doubt that Kant, as little as Plato or Leibniz, wants to defend a naïve two-worlds theory. None the less one finds formulations in his writings, as in those of Plato or Leibniz, which taken for themselves alone sound like a naïve two-worlds theory. This occurs even in the terminology. When Kant, in the dissertation[24] of 1720 distinguishes between the *mundus sensibilis* and the *mundus intelligibilis* and later between the world of the senses and the world of understanding,[25] such a terminology is not harmless. It is no different when he speaks of 'both worlds'.[26] Perhaps Kant is somewhat more careful than Plato in such expressions. But what already holds for Plato is undoubtedly true for Kant. One cannot charge him with holding a naïve two-worlds theory.

The second interpretation of the relation between appearance and thing-in-itself tends to show that Kant regards the appearances as mere representations. The clearest expression of this is found in the second section of the theory of antinomies which already in its title betrays the meaning: 'Transcendental Idealism as the Key to the Solution of the Cosmological Dialectic.' Here Kant sums up the result of the Transcendental Aesthetic in the following way:

'We have sufficiently proved in the Transcendental Aesthetic that everything intuited in space or time, and therefore all objects of any experience possible to us, are nothing but appearances, that is, mere representations, which, in the manner in which they are represented, as extended beings, or as series of alterations, have no independent existence outside our thoughts. This doctrine I entitle *transcendental idealism*. The realist, in the transcendental meaning of this term, treats these modifications of our sensibility as self-subsistent things, that is, treats *mere representations* as things in themselves.'[27]

In the same vein Kant had said in the Transcendental Aesthetic: 'Time therefore . . . in itself, apart from the subject, is nothing.'[28] And in this sense too he says summarily: 'What we have meant to say is that . . . all the relations of objects in space and time, nay space and time themselves, would vanish. As appearances, they cannot exist in themselves, but only in us.'[29]

This interpretation, that appearances are mere representations in us, is also found in other places. None the less one must doubt whether Kant intended it as the final interpretation. It immediately comes up against the difficulty we have already touched upon. What is the subject, in which appearances are mere representations? We saw already that for Leibniz the phenomena are, in the last analysis, representations *in mente divina* and therefore, in the last analysis, *phenomena Dei*. But this interpretation is no longer possible for Kant. He refers appearances definitely to men. But to which men? That is the question. Furthermore, it is also difficult for this interpretation of the appearances to escape the reproach of subjective idealism.

Thus it is understandable that a third form of interpreting the being of appearances emerges. According to this interpretation it is a matter of one and the same man and one and the same event, viewed from one vantage point as appearance, and from another as thing-in-itself. In the *Critique of Pure Reason* the example used is a lie. Kant says of arbitrary acts, giving lying as an example: 'Before ever they have happened, they are one and all predetermined in the empirical character. In respect of the intelligible character . . . there can be no *before* and *after*; every action . . . is the immediate effect of the intelligible character of

275

pure reason. Reason therefore acts freely . . .'[30] In the *Critique of Practical Reason* Kant used thievery as an example and asks of it: '. . . how can he be called free at this point of time with reference to this action, when in this moment and in this action he stands under inexorable natural necessity?'[31] It is one and the same action which must be ascribed both to the mechanism of nature and to freedom. In so far as it is ascribed to the mechanism of nature it is wholly predictable, even though not wholly so for us.

'It may be admitted that if it were possible for us to have so deep an insight into a man's character as shown both in inner and in outer actions, that every, even the least, incentive to these actions and all external occasions which affect them were so known to us that his future conduct could be predicted with as great a certainty as the occurrence of a solar or lunar eclipse . . .'[32]

The comparison with the solar and lunar eclipse is clear. The lie and the theft stand just as much under the universal determination of the course of nature as do the solar and lunar eclipse. This applies to the lie, however, only in so far as it can be considered an appearance. The same lie must be accorded an intelligible character, and to that extent it is an action which could be done or not done in freedom.

It is therefore one and the same lie which as appearance is completely subject to causal determination, but which is also at the same time the free action of an intelligible being. This reasoning leads more generally to the distinction between an empirical and an intelligible character. It is one and the same man, who has both an empirical and an intelligible character.[33] The further generalization then regards man as both appearance and thing-in-itself—or as Kant likes to say substance-in-itself—and expressed in the other formulations, it regards man as both phenomenon and noumenon. It is also the same man who is both phenomenon and noumenon. Kant therefore solves the antimony of freedom because man as appearance is subject to universal causal determination and man as substance-in-itself is free. The difficulty of uniting freedom with the mechanism of nature[34] is now transferred to the difficulty of uniting phenomenal and noumenal being. It is the same man who is both phenomenon and noumenon. But how are these two distinguished? How are they united? I find no conclusive presentation in the Kantian writings. Kant sometimes speaks of different viewpoints,[35] sometimes of different modes of considering,[36] or similar turns of phrase. Only this much remains clear, that it is the same man who belongs both to phenomena and noumena, both to the world of the senses and to the world of understanding. This is also confirmed by the statement at the end of the *Critique of Practical Reason*, which we have already cited. Kant thus refers the relation of the mechanism of nature and freedom back to the relation of phenomenon and noumenon, but in this basic relation there appear once again new difficulties: 'Man is thus to himself, on the one hand phenomenon, and on the other hand, . . . a purely intelligible object.'[37] Kant says: 'This distinction when stated in this quite general and abstract manner, is bound to appear extremely subtle and obscure, but will become clear in the course of its application.'[38] We cited this once already and we cannot say that Kant has kept his promise of clarifying the obscure distinction by its application. A concluding remark in Kant's *Critique of Practical Reason* will thus remain the final word:

'The solution which is given here to the difficulty will be said to have so much difficulty in it, however, that it is hardly susceptible of a lucid presentation. But is any other solution, which anyone has attempted or may attempt, any easier or more comprehensible?'[39]

This implies that Kant himself had not found a perfect solution and that, in his conviction, every other solution would be likewise burdened with difficulties. And this is exactly what we wish to claim about metaphysics as such.

If this third interpretation of Kant does not achieve a final decision, so do the three interpretations Kant himself considered fail of a decision. We may perhaps repeat that in the first interpretation, phenomena and noumena appear as two worlds. In the second interpretation, phenomena are understood as mere representations. And in the third interpretation, finally, phenomena and noumena are regarded as one and the same thing regarded from different points of view. I do not find in Kant a final decision between these three interpretations, although the third is the one Kant himself strove after. That Kant himself did not reach a final decision rests not only on the fact that he did not engage in a specific reflection on the relations between phenomena and noumena (in spite of the section in the *Critique of Pure Reason* which bears this title), but also, seen from our own standpoint, on the fact that such a final ontological interpretation of a basic distinction is not in itself possible. Kant here runs up against the same boundaries which confronted Plato. Plato also did not succeed in bringing the distinction between Ideas and sensible things into final clarity.

To sum up the problem of the thing-in-itself: one must either restrict possibility and actuality to appearances in the sense of the Transcendental Analytic, or new meanings must be found for possibility and actuality. But this confronts Kant with the same problems as Plato, when the latter wanted to admit being not only in Ideas but also in sensible things. It is therefore not surprising that Kant, no more than Plato, was unable to find a definitive solution to this problem. The task of distinguishing different meanings of being and different modes of being leads rather, necessarily, into aporias.

62. KANT AND THE TWO OTHER STANDPOINTS

For Kant's philosophy too, one can say that it in no way represents an extreme standpoint, instead it contains elements of the approaches of both Plato and Aristotle.

Turning first to his relation to Plato, Kant himself often emphasizes the great significance of Plato. He calls him 'the illustrious philosopher'.[1] In his systematic debate with Plato, agreement and rejection stand closely together. The rejection centres on Plato's failure, as Kant sees it, to reflect on the limits of knowledge.[2] Plato makes a transcendent use of the Ideas and, in his frequent censurings of a transcendent use of the Ideas, Kant is probably thinking of Plato. The positive relation is grounded in the concept of the *a priori*. Arithmetic and geometry are as such *a priori* and in empirical knowledge there are also essentially *a priori* aspects, this is the conviction that binds Kant to Plato. It is especially effective in the ethical *a priori*. The connexion may have come by way of Leibniz; Leibniz always had the historical connexion with Plato in mind and Kant may simply have relied on this connexion as presented to him. Natorp saw the systematic origin of the *a priori* in the *Phaedo*,[3] without intending to claim a direct historical connexion. It is the factor of general normativeness in arithmetic, geometry, the principles of physics, and morality which constituted the beginning point of the theory of Ideas, but also of the Critical Philosophy. This is what binds Plato and Kant together systematically.

Thus it also becomes understandable that the interpretation of Plato from a Kantian perspective, as presented in the Marburg school of neo-Kantianism by Paul Natorp, in spite of all exaggeration none the less makes available a genuine access to Plato. The exaggeration is only increased, however, by the fact that the interpretation of Kant in the Marburg school is also one-sided and extreme. Who today would not be willing to see how important for Plato is the connexion between *logos* and *mythos*? Natorp himself in an epilogue to the second edition of *Plato's Theory of Ideas* has made clear the one-sidedness of the first edition.[4] But on the other hand one should not forget that the philosophy of Plato is not absorbed in *mythos* and that the mood of the *Symposium* does not constitute the whole of his philosophy, although this is so often assumed. Plato's philosophy has a fundamental drive towards *logos* and therewith towards science, in which *logos* comes to expression. By working this out in detail, Natorp made visible a fundamental aspect of the Platonic philosophy, perhaps one should say he made it once again visible. It is certainly an exaggeration when Natorp says that the real prototype of a Platonic Idea is Newton's law of gravity.[5] Still in spite of the exaggeration this conveys something correct. I think

I am justified in making a judgement since I have brought in a quite different connexion, the connexion of the Idea of *hygeia* with the goddess. But it is not difficult to correct Natorp's exaggerations. Once this is done one will be indebted to him for a deeper understanding of Plato. It is the inner connexion between Plato and Kant which this interpretation makes visible, but it is the same connexion which makes the interpretation possible.

The connexion between Kant and Aristotle is not so easy to see. Here too it is a great interpretation that suggests the connexion, this one offered by Maréchal, from the Aristotelian tradition of metaphysics.[6] In a certain sense one could say that Kant inclines to Aristotle at least as much as to Plato. A synthesis of Platonic and Aristotelian aspects was indeed already characteristic of Leibniz. Kant's special interest in Aristotle begins in logic,[7] and here particularly in the theory of judgement and the theory of the categories.[8] Sentroul made this clear in his study of the relation of Kant to Aristotle.[9] It is thus understandable that in Kant's library, so far as we know, Plato was not represented but there was a Greek–Latin edition of Aristotle.[10]

Systematically, the connexion lies in their common conviction about the validity of the general in nature, and by the general they both mean a law of nature. Now it is of course correct that Kant interpreted nature as an appearance, while Aristotle ascribes to logic, mathematics and physics a validity for nature but understands nature, in Kantian terminology, as being-in-itself. Apart from this ontological difference, however, Kant regards logic, mathematics and physics as generally valid for nature, just as much as Aristotle. For Kant this is the meaning of empirical realism and also the reason why he always rightly rejected any attempt to regard his philosophy as absolute idealism.

But even on the basis of Kantian idealism, the connexion can be pursued a step further. Kant characterizes the validity of mathematics and physics as the objective reality of the relevant categories and principles. But this objective reality of the laws of nature by no means depends solely on our spontaneity. Kant emphasizes also our receptivity. Things-in-themselves must also be presupposed, although it is difficult to show how. It could very well be the case that the course of nature should be like a kaleidoscope, that snow should be white today and black tomorrow. Then the lawfulness of nature available in our intuitions and concepts would not bear fruit, since the course of nature would not be receptive to ordering in laws. Certainly, for Kant, all ordering falls on the side of our intuitions and concepts. None the less one must ascribe to thing-in-themselves a capacity to be ordered, without which all our ordering would come to nought. To that extent Kant does not refer the lawfulness of nature solely to our spontaneity. Instead Kant maintains the meaning of receptivity and this means that the connexion with Aristotle is not restricted to the lawfulness of nature but also reaches beyond that.

We arrive, therefore, at the result that Kant has a genuine systematic connexion with Plato as well as with Aristotle, and that Kant himself is well aware of this connexion. About the historical foundation of this connexion we know very little. We do not know whether Kant made use of the original texts. His knowledge of Greek was probably sufficient for him to penetrate into the Greek text with the help of a Greek–Latin edition. But Kant could lean on a rich tradition, particularly on Leibniz, who had gone back to the Greek originals. Certain Latin authors could also be mentioned, particularly Cicero. Christian Wolff presents an abundance of historical material and Kant also had assistance from histories of philosophy, such as the works of Brucker. It is therefore possible to understand the Platonic and Aristotelian aspects in Kant systematically as well as historically.

PART III

METHODOLOGY

CHAPTER XII

METHODOLOGY

63. THE MULTIPLICITY OF PHILOSOPHIES

In this chapter we will attempt to establish conclusively that the method of metaphysics must be an aporematic dialectic. This will require us to discuss the possible forms of dialectic. Above all we will have to come to grips with Hegel's dialectic. We will have to show that Hegel clearly recognized the difference between Platonic dialectic and his own dialectic, for everything turns on this difference. Hegel sets up the requirement of advancing from the Platonic dialectic to the Hegelian dialectic. By contrast, we will require a retreat from the Hegelian dialectic to the Platonic dialectic.

Dialectic recognizes as valid propositions which contradict one another and, in this sense, it recognizes a multiplicity of contradictory propositions. This leads us further to recognize the multiplicity of contradictory philosophies. Plato and Hegel have done this. That there are many philosophies, that these many philosophies are at variance with one another and that, to all appearances, they will always remain at variance with one another—this is a fact. But this fact is not a defect from the dialectial standpoint, it is rather a necessity. It is essential for philosophy that there are many philosophies, philosophy can only exist as a multiplicity of philosophies.

Hegel expresses this in a most convincing way in the introduction to his *History of Philosophy*:

'It is none the less an established fact that different philosophies exist and have existed. . . . But it is necessary to achieve a deeper insight into why the philosophical systems are different. The philosophical understanding of what truth and philosophy are enables one to understand this difference in a sense quite different from that suggested by the abstract antithesis of truth and error . . . We must make this clear, that this multiplicity of philosophies does not harm philosophy itself—the possibility of philosophy; but rather that it is and has always been necessary for the existence of the science of philosophy. That is the essential point.'[1]

This is also Plato's conviction. It is found in a passage which we have already cited. In the *Sophist* Plato reflects on the opposition between Heraclitus and Parmenides. But he does not want to take sides with one or the other, he wishes to allow them both a validity. In this sense he says by way of conclusion, although very cautiously:

'On these grounds, then, it seems that only one course is open to the philosopher who values knowledge and the rest above all else. He must refuse to accept from the champions either of the one or of the many forms the doctrine that all reality is change-less, and he must turn a deaf ear to the other party who represents reality as everywhere changing. Like a child begging for "both", he must declare that reality or the sum of things is both at once—all that is unchangeable and all that is in change.'[2]

An opposing view is found in Aristotle and Leibniz. It is essential to the Aristotelian metaphysics that it should contain a history of Greek philosophy, and the editor of the *Metaphysics* was surely right to place this history of Greek philosophy as the first book, at the beginning of the *Metaphysics*. In this history of Greek philosophy Aristotle goes on the assumption that his predecessors had said much that is true but also much that is false. The task is to separate the true from the false, then to accept and extend the true. Aristotle discerns a process in the history of Greek philosophy, a process that reaches its consummation in the

Aristotelian philosophy.[3] Since then two thousand years have passed and the two thousand years do not tend to justify Aristotle's optimism.

Perhaps even more marked is the optimistic position of Leibniz. Leibniz's relation to other thinkers is that of a great conciliator. He is prepared to come to grips with every other thinker, indeed he regards this as necessary.[4] But this is not mere conciliation, it is the deep conviction that every thinker has said much that is true and also some things that are false. According to Leibniz's well-meaning interpretation, the falsity often lies merely in the expression, which imperfectly renders the correct opinion. To sum up the opinion of Leibniz: we can and must learn from everyone.

The opposition between Hegel and Plato on the one hand and Leibniz and Aristotle on the other is great. Our task will be to make this opposition as clear as possible and then to make a decision between them.

64. THE DIALECTIC OF ZENO

Zeno, the student of Parmenides, wrote sometime around the middle of the fifth century a paper on the antinomies. The essay has been lost,[1] and likewise the presentations of Aristotle[2] and Heraclides Ponticos[3] of Zeno's antinomies. The Platonic dialogue *Parmenides* begins with Zeno reading aloud from this essay.[4] The young Socrates then asks that he repeat the first proposition and this leads into a discussion of the meaning of the essay.[5] Evidently it was not easy even then, when the whole work was available, to say what was Zeno's intention. It is much less easy for us today, since we possess only a few fragments of this essay and some reports about it.

From the surviving fragments we can infer that Zeno had presented at least two groups of antinomies, although we will leave to one side the question of whether and how he himself decided between these two groups. The first group concerns the antinomies of the continuum and continuous motion, the second group concerns antinomies of a purely logical character, for example, those of equality and similarity. Aristotle[6] and Hegel[7] are primarily interested in the antinomies of the continuum, Aristotle in order to resolve them, and Hegel in order to trace in them the beginnings and the foundations of dialectic. Plato is primarily preoccupied with the other antinomies. They had formed the first part of Zeno's essay[8] and can best be designated the logical antinomies.

With respect to the antinomies of the continuum and continuous motion, there can hardly be any doubt that antinomies must result from the meeting of continuous and discrete aspects. Leibniz, who had a strong aversion to dialectic, speaks only of the labyrinth of the continuum.[9] From the discussions of the contemporary search for foundations in mathematics and logic one can draw the conclusion that here we are in fact dealing with genuine antinomies. But we will put the antinomies of the continuum and continuous motion to one side and turn our attention to the logical antinomies.

The first logical antinomy, which is the first one in Zeno's essay, has come down to us on good authority and presumably in the original wording. The aged Parmenides, the vigorous Zeno and the young Socrates have met, Zeno has read aloud his essay, and Socrates has asked him to read once more the first hypothesis of the first argument. Once this has been done Socrates repeats his question in the following form:

'What does this statement mean, Zeno? "If things are many," you say, "they must be both like and unlike. But that is impossible; unlike things cannot be like, nor like things unlike." That is what you say, isn't it?'[10]

In his commentary Proclus reproduces the argument in essentially the same form. We may suppose that the passage in Proclus is a quotation, although Diels locates it not among the fragments, but under the reports.[11]

At the beginning of the Dialectic Kant gives an opinion on this antinomy. He interprets it in the sense of his own theory of antinomies as an antinomy of totality. That which is neither similar nor dissimilar to anything else is, in Kant's interpretation, the universe or perhaps God.[12] But Kant seems to be making use of a report not known to me, he does not seem to have had either the Greek original or a Latin or German translation at hand. The text of the Platonic dialogue and Socrates' discussion developed in it about the meaning of the first antinomy and about Zeno's antinomies as a whole does not give any support for the Kantian interpretation. The text says explicitly: 'If things are many'. It is supported by a citation of Simplicius from another antinomy: 'If there are many things'.[13] But what is it which is many: this is evidently not specifically mentioned in Zeno's essay nor in the didactic poem of Parmenides. It can be inferred, however, from the antinomies of the continuum and from the discussion of Socrates. In the antinomy of the continuum the talk is always about individual things: Achilles, the tortoise,[14] the arrow.[15] One may therefore infer that it is individual things that are meant, and Plato—in the discussion which he puts in the mouth of Socrates—understands it that way. The contradictory members of Zeno's antinomies: one and many, equal and unequal, similar and dissimilar, play an important role in the Platonic antinomies of the second half of the *Parmenides* and one may assume that Plato's antinomies are largely modelled on those of Zeno. If that is so, then one might paraphrase Zeno's first antinomy in the following way: If there are many things, then each of them is both one and many, equal and unequal, similar and dissimilar.

One may suppose that Zeno was not the first or the only one of his time to express such antinomies. One may also suppose that the Sophists often talked of them, though only in a playful way as a kind of game with words. Zeno was probably the first to develop the strict logical form of such antinomies. In our interpretation we follow Plato in assuming that for Zeno it is individual things which are one and many, like and unlike, similar and dissimilar. This is the sense Socrates exemplifies by referring to himself: 'but if someone can show that I am one and many . . .'[16] Socrates repeats this once again by saying: 'Accordingly, if anyone sets out to show about things of this kind—

sticks and stones, and so on—that the same thing is many and one . . .'[17] Zeno's antinomies thus interpreted present no problem, in Plato's opinion. Rather they are easily resolved. In a certain respect Socrates is one in so far as he is one among the seven speakers. But in another respect he is many, for in so far as he has a body, he has a right and a left side. The antinomy can also be resolved ontologically in Plato's conviction. One must imagine that Socrates has a share in differing, mutually contradictory, Ideas; Plato sees no contradiction in this. Contradictions in the true sense and with them also the true dialectic would only appear if the antinomies should reach into the realm of Ideas itself, and that is the goal of the Platonic dialectic, as presented in the second part of the Platonic dialogue *Parmenides*, having been carefully prepared in the first part.

65. THE DIALECTIC OF PLATO

Hegel praises Plato as the great discoverer of the dialectic.[1] This is also our opinion and, furthermore, it is our opinion that Plato's dialectic must be placed much higher than Hegel himself has done. There are, however, formidable difficulties in the way of understanding Plato's dialectic. The principal obstacle is once again the second part of the dialogue *Parmenides*. Many as are the difficulties which Plato's dialogues offer to our understanding, they have been heaped up in a nearly insurmountable way in the *Parmenides*. One can well understand that in the nineteenth century attempts were made to avoid the difficulties by declaring the dialogue inauthentic.[2] This expedient has been dropped today. For systematically it makes no difference who the author is, the question is what systematic claims the dialogue makes. And historically the expedient only adds a new difficulty, for if Plato did not write the dialogue one is left with the question: who did?

Accepting the dialogue as a work of Plato's, the first temptation is to explain away the dialectic. This was the direction taken in the first great interpretation by Plotinus and his students. This interpretation became especially effective in the commentary written by Proclus,[3] and in our own times was emphatically represented by Wundt[4] and Speiser.[5] According to this interpretation the series of hypotheses in the second part are representations of the levels of emanations in Plotinus' sense. One cannot deny that this interpretation finds considerable support in the first and second hypotheses, but in the development of the dialectical hypotheses it becomes steadily weaker and finally appears arbitrary. The commentary of Proclus gets around the problem by restricting itself to the first two hypotheses and for these the interpretation is quite persuasive.

Cornford's interpretation also implies an abandonment of dialectic in the true sense. On his view the different hypotheses imply the development of different meanings of unity.[6] Such a view would see the dialogue *Parmenides* as anticipating Aristotle's later doctrine on the plurality of meaning. In our investigations the connexion between Aristotle and Plato seems so fundamental that we would have no fundamental objections to such a thesis. It must also be admitted that Cornford has succeeded in showing that the plurality of meaning of unity does play a role here. Doubts will be raised only if the interpretation as a whole is narrowed to this point of view. Cornford too gets caught in forced interpretations so that it is difficult to believe this is the only viewpoint for an interpretation.

As soon as one has decided to regard the dialectic as a genuine part of the dialogue, various possibilities present themselves. I will characterize the first possibility as the play-theory. This view interprets the dialectic in the *Parmenides* as play,[7] akin to the thought games and word play of the Sophists. Now it need not be denied that there are arguments in the *Parmenides* which are in fact high-spirited play. But the question is whether the whole of the dialectic of this dialogue can be interpreted as a game, and this strikes me as impossible. The story within a story speaks against this view. One can hardly imagine that Plato would have chosen this momentous inner story of a conversation between Parmenides, Zeno and Socrates for a mere game.

A second possibility is the interpretation which might be called the puzzle-theory. It is represented particularly by Natorp. It is directed primarily at the first part of the dialogue but also has implications for the second. In Natorp's view, the aim of the dialogue is to present the closed system of pure concepts.[8] And the dialogue does do this but, as we will shortly see, for reasons other than those supposed by Natorp. The contradictions presented in both parts of the dialogue are, in Natorp's opinion, only apparent. These are puzzles which Plato has posed to his hearers and readers. If the reader succeeds in solving the puzzles then he has understood Plato by his own intellectual effort and this is the only way he can understand Plato. If he cannot solve the puzzles, then there is no way to help him and he will never understand Plato.[9]

I cannot convince myself that the point of this interpretation, which is to do away with dialectic as a whole or at least to remove the dialectic from this dialogue, is truly grounded in the facts. Here too, it seems to me, one should follow Hegel. Hegel places a high value on the dialogue just because of its dialectic. He says: 'The perfected, genuine dialectic is contained in the *Parmenides*, the most famous masterpiece of Platonic dialectic.'[10] We thoroughly assent to this judgement of Hegel's. We see it as an achievement of the Plato-interpretation of our century that the conviction has once again become lively that it is precisely the interpretation of this dialogue which represents one of the great and decisive tasks in the interpretation of Plato.

For that interpretation one must remember that the term dialectic has both a wide and a narrow meaning for Plato. In the wider meaning, the one preferred in the *Republic*, dialectic simply means philosophy, in so far as it is the theory of Ideas.[11] In the narrower meaning, dialectic means the philosophical standpoint that propositions which contradict each other might both be true, and further, it refers to the assertion and the investigation of such mutually contradictory propositions. In this narrower meaning, which has become the genuine meaning for us, the term occurs in Plato, as far as I know, only in the verb form, not as a substantive or an adjective.[12]

As we saw, the dialogue begins with Zeno reading aloud from his essay on the antinomies, then Socrates discusses Zeno's antinomies using the first one as example. The dialogue then treats the difficulties of the theory of Ideas in the first part. The second part turns to dialectic and the antinomies of unity are systematically presented in the form of eight hypotheses and an intermediate hypothesis, making nine in all. At the end of the section, that is, at the end of the second part, these antinomies are carefully summarized, so that all interpretations which interpret away the dialectic run up against Plato's own summaries. In the first of these summaries Plato says: 'If there is a one such as we have described—a one which is both one and many and neither one nor many . . .'[13] And in the middle of his investigation Plato has this summary: 'Thus, if there is a one, the one is both all things and nothing whatsoever, alike with reference to itself and to the others.'[14] Finally, at the end of the dialogue, Plato gives a summary of the whole second, dialectical part:

'To this we may add the conclusion. It seems that, whether there is or is not a one, both that one and the others alike are and are not, and appear and do not appear to be, all manner of things in all manner of ways, with respect to themselves and to one another.'[15]

In the first part Plato had set himself the task of carrying the dialectic into the Ideas themselves,[16] these summaries show that he himself was convinced that he had succeeded in doing this. Plato himself was convinced that antinomies also exist within the Ideas. This means that every interpretation which wants to interpret away the dialectic runs up against the clear summations of Plato himself.

Once the dialectic of the dialogue is basically recognized, the question then arises what is that unity for which antinomies have here been given. In the second part Plato says nothing about this, he simply speaks of the one. The first part provides some help. There Socrates understands Zeno's antinomies as applying to individual things. When Socrates mentions himself as an example of something that can be both one and many he then, in my opinion, understands Zeno correctly.[17] But then Plato has Socrates continue in such a way as to indicate that this is not yet an upsetting dialectic. But if the Idea of unity itself were both one and many that would be an upsetting dialectic.[18] As an exercise in such a real dialectic the second part is then begun.[19] The unity discussed in the second part is therefore the Idea of unity. This is how we must understand this dialectic and this is how Hegel understood it. He says expressly:

'But these quite general properties Plato understands as Ideas. This dialogue is actually the pure theory of Ideas. Plato shows of the one, that . . . unity as well as all the other Ideas both is and is not, the one is both one and many.'[20]

If the one treated in the second part of the *Parmenides* is the Idea of unity then Plato intends to say: there are antinomies in the pure Ideas. If we confine ourselves to the actual argument of the dialogue we could say: in the pure Ideas of unity and being there are antinomies. I believe I can show in these investigations that this, historically considered, was Plato's aim and that, systematically considered, Plato's aim was correct. Naturally the historical and systematic considerations are closely interwoven even here in this concrete question; Hegel is the best example of that. Whoever is prepared, like Hegel, systematically to espouse dialectic will understand such a dialogue as the historical emergence of dialectic, and whoever succeeds in grasping the Platonic dialogue historically in this sense will, like Hegel, find himself confirmed in his systematic convictions.

It will suffice to investigate the first and second hypotheses. The suppositions runs: If there is a one.[21] In agreement with the first part of the dialogue and in agreement with Hegel we interpret this as follows: If the Idea of unity exists. The first two hypotheses depend essentially on the meaning attached to such a supposition, they depend further on the meaning attached to the proposition in which this supposition is expressed and thereby on the meaning attached to a proposition as such. In the first hypothesis this supposition and every proposition as such are interpreted as strict identities. For an interpretation as strict identity the proposition: the one is, is already too much. On the basis of this interpretation one can only say: one one.[22] One easily sees that on the basis of such a strict theory of identity no assertions of any kind are possible, and on the basis of this interpretation no predicates can be assigned to the one. Plato arrives at this conclusion by deriving the meaning of the proposition solely from the subject, therefore by saying: the one is one and nothing else.[23] For the reader the unfamiliar aspect in all this is that this thesis, which is undoubtedly correct and wholly obvious on the basis of the theory of strict identity, is established by way of the totality of possible predicates. The one is therefore not many,[24] it is not identical with itself and not different from any other.[25]

The second hypothesis takes the supposition: the one is, as asserting: the one has being. If one grants our assumption the supposition can be translated to say: the Idea of unity has the Idea of being or, more strictly in the language of the theory of Ideas, the Idea of unity has a share in the Idea of being. On the basis of this interpretation the one is both one and many. Regarded from the standpoint of its meaning, the one is precisely one.[26] Regarded from the standpoint of its existence, the one is both one and also being,[27] and therefore many.[28] Here too Plato goes about establishing this contradictory thesis by the totality of possible predicates. The one is identical with itself and identical with every other, it is different from itself and different from every other.[29] The thesis is now established by the totality of possible predicates with the result that both the assertion and the negation of every predicate is ascribed to the one. As we saw, Plato carefully summarizes this result of the first two hypotheses by saying: 'if there is a one such as we have described —a one which is both one and many and neither one nor many . . .'[30]

A double dialectic is being constructed here. First of all, every hypothesis is dialectical in itself. Thus the first hypothesis says that the one is neither identical with itself nor different from itself. In this sense the second hypothesis is also dialectical in itself. To give here only a single example, the one is both identical with itself and different from itself. On a second level, the first and second hypotheses stand in dialectical contradiction to each other. According to the first hypothesis no possible determination can be ascribed to the one, according to the second every possible determination can be ascribed to the one. According to the first hypothesis the one is neither identical with itself nor different from itself, according to the second hypothesis the one is both identical with itself as well as different from itself.

The same result, that is, the assertion and negation of all possible predicates is reached in the fourth and fifth hypotheses for the others.[31] And the last four hypotheses are constructed in the same way. Taking the supposition: If the one does not exist,[32] the sixth and seventh hypotheses once again prove the assertion and the negation of all possible predicates for the one, and finally under the supposition that the one does not exist, the eighth and ninth hypotheses once again prove the assertion and the negation of all possible predicates for the others.[33] Thus at the end of the dialogue Plato can summarize the dialectic of the second part in the manner we have already cited:

'To this we may add the conclusion. It seems that, whether there is or is not a one, both that one and the others alike are and are not, and appear and do not appear to be, all manner of things in all manner of ways, with respect to themselves and to one another.'[34]

On the basis of this systematic construction and the careful summaries given for each part, one cannot doubt Plato intended to develop a genuine dialectic. We are not primarily concerned with the question whether Plato's conclusions and proofs are correct in every case. Of course such a question is wholly justified. But one must remember that a mistake in the proof does not permit any conclusion about the truth or falsity of the proposition which has been falsely proved. A proposition may well be correct although there is a mistake in the proof offered for it. If one recalls, for example, the discovery of the infinitesimal calculus, it seems that all the proofs offered at that time, whether by Newton, Leibniz or Euler, are completely insufficient from the standpoint of our contemporary methodological requirements. But the meaning of discovered propositions is not touched by the fact that the proofs presented by the discoverers are as a rule insufficient and not infrequently false. Thus the question of what Plato intended must be separated from the question of what he was actually able to prove about the things he saw and intended. We will now discuss the first question: is the dialectic seen and intended by Plato actually grounded in reality?

Perhaps we can first explain for the reader a not inconsiderable oddity. In each of the hypotheses Plato develops the corresponding claim through the totality of possible predicates. The argument is forced in many passages and manifest fallacies are not wholly lacking. This method of arguing for each claim by the totality of possible predicates includes a table of possible predicates and in effect a table of possible concepts. This affords Natorp a point of entry for his interpretation that it was Plato's purpose in the second part of the *Parmenides* to develop this table of possible concepts.

None the less it remains questionable whether Plato's intention is directed primarily to such a totality of possible concepts. From the construction of the second part it seems rather to follow that Plato wanted to develop the totality of possible contradictions. In this case a definite thesis would underlie the dialogue: if one contradiction exists then all contradictions exist. Odd as this thesis is—and I myself do not believe that the thesis is correct—this is the thesis which seems necessary on the basis of formal logic and also on the basis of Hegel's dialectic. In the two-valued propositional calculus it is a theorem that one contradiction implies every other contradiction. This is apparently what Plato had in mind. Still it must not be overlooked that in this theorem of the propositional calculus we have only an implication and not an inference. In particular, one cannot on the basis of this theorem infer the existence of any particular contradiction. In order to draw any conclusions on the basis of this theorem, the antecedent would have to be proved true; but in two-valued propositional calculus this is impossible. If one were permitted to interpret this theorem of the propositional calculus as a conclusion, it would be an unreal conclusion and would run: If any contradiction occurs then all contradictions will occur. And it would remain unreal since the antecedent can never be true in two-valued propositional calculus. None the less the connexion of this theorem of formal logic with the Platonic view is interesting.

Hegel, whom one may also draw in here, says explicitly that the appearance of dialectical contradictions may not be restricted to one or to a few concepts. Rather it is Hegel's conviction that every concept is contradictory, a contradiction can be demonstrated in every concept.[35] This stands in contrast with the Kantian dialectic and it is also in the debate with Kant that Hegel formulates this view. I cannot see that Hegel's thesis has been proved or even that it is provable; rather I hold the Kantian view to be correct, that one can restrict the antinomies within definite limits. This question will continue to occupy us in the following. Whatever decision one may reach in this question, the connexion between Plato and Hegel on this point remains interesting and will help to clarify Plato's intention. Regardless of the form in which Plato understood this, the argument of the second part rests on the conviction that the existence of one contradiction implies the existence of all contradictions. This must be taken as his intention, Plato may then have developed it well or badly. Still from this point of view Plato's argument proves to be more reasonable and better grounded than has usually been believed. According to the systematic plan of the Platonic dialectic, the question is now narrowed to: did Plato succeed in actually demonstrating at least one contradiction?

Plato must demonstrate at least one contradiction. In my opinion this is systematically possible. I draw support for this both from the results of dialectic historically available and from the problem of the antinomies in the contemporary studies on foundations. I am leaving out of account the question whether Plato presented the contradiction he saw in a truly unobjectionable manner, and I may perhaps recall in this connexion the question of whether Newton, Leibniz and Euler had presented the infinitesimal calculus in an unobjectionable manner. We will confine ourselves to the contradiction of the one and the many, the first one which Plato handled and the one he saw as the systematic source of all other contradictions. In the first hypothesis Plato shows that the one is neither one nor many, in the second hypothesis he shows that the one is both one and many. We may limit ourselves once again to the discussion of the second hypothesis. The one is one, and it is this by definition.[36] But the one is also many, if the supposition: the one exists, is understood in such a way that being is accorded to the one. The one has then two aspects. According to its definition it is unity, according to its existence it is being.[37] But this immediately triggers a *regressus in infinitum*. Unity and being are aspects of the one, and therefore being and unity must be accorded to each of these aspects. The one must have unity and being, and being must also have unity and being.[38] In the systematic difficulties which arise here it is not easy to say whether Plato's presentation is sound in all details; in my opinion, however, everything points toward the view that Plato has here come up against a genuine antinomy.

As far as I can see two different problems confront us, but both lead to the same difficulties. The first problem consists in the fact that being and unity are here placed without qualification in the series of all predicates. In these deduction being and unity stand on the same footing as the other determinations, for example, equality and inequality, similarity and dissimilarity. The fundamental problem of all ontology is the struggle around this question. Are being and unity to be placed on the same footing as all other determinations, in particular, as the categorial determinations, or do they have a special logical and ontological status? After all the discussion of two thousand years it is the second alternative which must be valid. Aristotle and, following him, Thomas and all his followers characterize being and unity as transcendental determinations, thereby distinguishing them from the categorial determinations. We can recall here the thematic discussion of this problem in the first part. Kant explicitly rejects the traditional theory of the transcendentals, but nevertheless says that being is not a real predicate,[39] thereby expressing in another form the same thing Aristotle and Thomas had said in the theory of transcendentals. In the interpretation of

Plato, Ryle was, as far as I know, the first to bring out clearly that the problem confronting us here has to do with the peculiar status of being and unity.[40] If one accepts this presupposition, one receives an important access to the Platonic dialectic although it does not suffice to clarify it completely. If it is the case that being and unity have a special status, how are we to understand the Platonic dialectic? Did Plato himself fully appreciate the peculiar status of being and unity? Does the puzzle theory come into play here? Is the reader supposed to find the peculiar status of being and unity in his own reflections. Or is he supposed to recognize, in Cornford's sense, that unity has many meanings?[41] Are the antinomies resolved if one makes this discovery, or do they persist? On this last question in particular one will hardly find a decision in the Platonic text.

The second problem proves to be no less difficult. It consists in the fact that under Platonic presuppositions being and unity must be referred back to themselves. This holds generally but it becomes especially clear when in the dialogue the one is understood as the Idea of unity and being as the Idea of being. Every Idea is one, this is an ineliminable basic function of every Idea. Every Idea is in its nature a unity. This makes for no difficulties of self-reference for the Ideas of beautiful, good, just, straight, odd and even. But as soon as Plato comes to the Idea of unity, it is clear that the Idea of unity must necessarily also be a unity. It is no different for being. Every Idea is in its nature a being, indeed the true being; in its nature it has being. Once again for the other Ideas this presents no difficulties. But as soon as Plato comes to the Idea of being, it is clear that the Idea of being must be itself a being, the Idea of being is necessarily self-referential.

This consequence cannot be avoided. But what follows from it? Historically considered, what did Plato himself think of as following from it? And what follows from it systematically? First, a *regressus in infinitum*. Plato certainly saw this. He develops this *regressus* explicitly in the first part for likeness[42] and in the second part for being and unity.[43] If one grants this consequence, and one will not be able to avoid it, what then follows? The question would be easy to answer if the *regressus in infinitum* were a proof of impossibility, for instance, a *reductio in absurdum*. Taylor raised the question explicitly and then rightly rejected it.[44] If the infinite *regressus* as such were an impossibility, then the whole infinite series of natural numbers would have to be an impossibility, and this is difficult to contemplate. If an impossibility were present in the Platonic arguments, it could not follow from the infinite regress as such, but must follow from the special kind of regress involved here. This might perhaps be the case but until now it has not been demonstrated.

It is just the same in the problem of self-reference, in our case with the reference of the Ideas of unity and being to themselves. It would be simple if self-reference as such already led to antinomies. Certainly some cases of self-reference do lead to antinomies; but the question remains whether every self-reference as such leads to antinomies. When the first antinomies in the foundations of logic and mathematics were discovered at the beginning of the present century, most researchers assumed that this was the case, and Russell's antinomy which we have discussed is an antinomy of self-reference. But does every self-reference lead to an antinomy? Subsequent developments have indicated that this probably goes too far. For example, 'word' is itself a word and 'substantive' is itself a substantive. One can hardly imagine that we already have an antinomy here; the consequences would be depressing. One may therefore hope that only certain cases of self-reference, even though perhaps the largest part, lead to antinomies, while there are at least a few cases of self-reference which do not do so. To date the question has not yet been decided. Under the assumption that not every self-reference as such leads to antinomies, the problem that arises here cannot be handled according to the usual conditions for self-reference; instead one must investigate the special conditions for the self-reference of being and unity, something which has not yet been done and which probably exceeds the possibilities of formal logic. One may assume, however, in the light of our present knowledge that the self-reference of being and unity leads to antinomies. When the systematic problems are at present so difficult there can be little hope of being able to say what Plato himself thought. The texts are much too brief to permit this. If one considers the problem as a whole one will come to regard it as probable that antinomies are contained in the problems of being and unity. The question whether Plato found a final and conclusive form for such antinomies must be counted a question of the second rank, since a final and conclusive form for them does not yet exist in our own time.

The antinomies of the second part of the dialogue may be regarded as primarily logical antinomies. They contain ontological aspects of course, for their origin lies in the fact that being and unity are understood as Ideas and therefore must themselves be accorded being and unity. But in the construction of the second part Plato has given prominence to the logical aspect. By contrast, the ontological aspect is given prominence in those antinomies which we discussed in Chapter IX. They were the aporias which arose because of the failure to determine the relation of the Ideas to sensible things. It was those aporias which led Plato in the *Sophist* to characterize the question about being as aporematic.[45]

Finally, a third group of antinomies appears in the *Sophist*, which one might call the aporias of the philosophical standpoint. These treat of Plato's relations to Parmenides and to Heraclitus. One gets the impression from the *Sophist* that Plato inclines more strongly to Parmenides, he names him with reverence.[46] The dialogue bearing the name of Parmenides is an impressive testimony to this inclination. This would not quite square with Aristotle's report, however, for he states that Plato was first influenced by the opinions of Heraclitus.[47] However that may be, in the *Sophist* at least Plato does not take sides. He is much more concerned to show—we have discussed this already—that aporias are contained in the positions of both Parmenides and Heraclitus. Whether I say with Heraclitus that everything is flowing or with Parmenides that being is fixed and that every change is alien to it, in both cases, as we have seen, I eliminate the possibility of thought, and in both cases therefore I eliminate the possibility of even thinking the relevant standpoint, whether that of Heraclitus or that of Parmenides. But Plato does not infer from this that we must reject both standpoints. He is much more concerned with bringing these two thinkers, who contradict each other so emphatically, into some kind of synthesis. But Plato says only that he holds this to be necessary; on the question of how such a goal can be reached he leaves us without an answer. On the whole it becomes clear that in the dialectic of the second part Plato comes very close to the Hegelian dialectic, that the dialectic of philosophical standpoints lies very much in the direction of the Hegelian dialectic.

Thus Plato's dialectic is laid out in three areas: the logical dialectic as developed in the second part of the *Parmenides*, the ontological dialectic as presented in the first part of the *Parmenides* and in the *Sophist*, and the dialectic of philosophical standpoints as sketched in the *Sophist*. We will be able to take a further step towards the understanding of Plato's dialectic when we compare it with Hegel's dialectic.

66. THE DIALECTIC OF KANT

Kant's dialectic is broad in scope and it pursues various goals. In the *Critique of Pure Reason* one of its most essential goals is the uncovering of errors.[1] In this sense the Transcendental Psychology, the first part of the Transcendental Dialectic, intends to demonstrate that the traditional proofs for the immortality of the soul are not conclusive. The Transcendental Theology, as the third part, intends in the same sense to show that the traditional proofs for the existence of God lack conclusiveness. For our study the middle section has special significance. It bears the title: On the Antinomies of Pure Reason. And it treats the four antinomies, which Kant describes summarily as follows:

'Whether the world has a beginning [in time] and any limit to its extension in space; whether there is anywhere, and perhaps in my thinking self, an indivisible and indestructible unity, or nothing but what is divisible and transitory; whether I am free in my actions or, like other beings, am led by the hand of nature and of fate; whether finally there is a supreme cause of the world, or whether the things of nature and their order must as the ultimate object terminate thought—an object that even in our speculations can never be transcended.'[2]

The theory of antinomies raises historical questions in the midst of a purely systematic discussion, and their constitutive importance for the *Critique of Pure Reason* has been particularly emphasized by de Vleeschauwer.[3]

To understand the theory one will do best to move from Kant's systematic presentation back to the historical positions. Kant himself gives several hints for such a move. In the third section of the theory of antinomies he presents the antinomy of pure reason as an opposition between dogmatism and empiricism.[4] In developing this section he draws attention to the opposition of Epicureanism against Platonism.[5] If one follows up Kant's indication one will come to see that the opposition between Leibniz and Newton, as expressed in the correspondence between Leibniz and Clarke, must have had a special importance for Kant. Leibniz teaches the spatial[6] and temporal[7] infinity of the world, Newton on the other hand teaches its spatial[8] and temporal[9] finiteness, even though within an infinite space and an infinite time. Leibniz teaches the infinite divisibility, more exactly, the infinite dividedness of matter,[10] Newton defends a theory of atoms,[11] according to which the world is made up of atoms of finite dimensions which are distributed at finite distances throughout empty space. One must bear in mind here that Newtonian mechanics does not contain a decision between an atomic theory and a continuum theory of matter. It can be developed both as a mechanics of discrete mass-points and as a mechanics of the continuum. It seems that the adoption of mass-points stems generally from the followers of Newton. Newton seems to have expressed himself carefully and reservedly on such questions; more exact studies of Newton's own attitude are still lacking.

These general differences between Leibniz and Newton are old aporias. They already appear between Plato and Aristotle. In the *Timaeus* Plato teaches the creation of the world at a finite time,[12] at least the *Timaeus* can be read this way. Aristotle teaches that the world has been in being for an infinite time and will continue in being for an infinite time.[13] This contrast between Plato and Aristotle had great importance for Christian thought, especially in the Middle Ages. As Thomas turned towards the Aristotelian philosophy, he had to come to some understanding of this opposition, and he developed a solution which is systematically close to the Kantian solution.[14]

Kant's great achievement consists in the fact that he does not from the outset take sides with one of the positions, but rather first raises the question whether the problems arising in the antinomies are at all solvable.[15] In the Kantian solution, the first and second, the mathematical, antinomies are distinguished from the third and fourth, the dynamic, antinomies. In the mathematical antinomies the contradicting claims are both false,[16] in the dynamic antinomies they can both be true.[17]

For the question of decidability Kant first investigates the structure of the claims which appear here, and he recognizes that they make assertions about the totality of the world. But this raises the question whether assertions which are meaningful and decidable about parts of the world are still meaningful and decidable when they are asserted of the world as a whole. It could thus be the case that assertions which are meaningful and decidable about parts of the world lose this character when they are referred to the totality of the world. Thus every observable part of the world has a beginning and an end, both with respect to space and with respect to time. The question is whether the world as a whole must have a beginning and an end. Kant recognizes this structure of the antinomies. He shows that assertions taken from parts of the world essentially lose their meaning when referred to the totality of the world.

If the antinomies are recognized in this sense as an illusion,[18] and a fallacy,[19] this by no means ends the problem for Kant. He is convinced that one must also recognize that we have here a necessary illusion and a necessary fallacy. This rests on the fact that an interplay appears here. Kant says for example of the first antinomy:

'For suppose: *First*, that *the world has no beginning*: it is then too *large* for our concept . . . Or suppose that *the world has a beginning*, it will then, in the necessary empirical regress, be too small for the concept of the understanding.'[20]

On the one hand, we must think a totality. But whatever totality we may think, it proves to be too small, it must be superseded by a larger. This interplay, first to posit a whole, then to surpass every posited whole by a larger, is the basis for the antinomies. This is revealed in a very concrete way by Archytas: 'If I go to the end of the world and there stretch out my arm . . .'[21] Wherever I posit the end of the world, I can always go there and once more stretch out my arm, thereby exceeding the limits which have just been set.

In the contemporary research into questions of foundations it has been shown that a whole series of antinomies in logic and mathematics are connected with these Kantian reflections. The antinomy of the set of all sets corresponds so exactly to them that one might think it had been discovered as an example of the Kantian reflections, although that is certainly not true. Hessenberg[22] was the first, so far as I know, to point out this connexion of certain antinomies of logic and mathematics. Zermelo[23] and Weizsäcker[24] have also drawn attention to the connexion. We can see today that the solution of these antinomies would depend upon breaking off this interplay between ending and new beginning at some point. There must be a whole which cannot be further interpreted as the beginning element of a new process. Whether such a cut-off point is at all possible and where it is to be located—on these questions there are today various opinions, of which however no one has yet received general acceptance. If one compares Kant's theory of antinomies with the concrete considerations of the Greeks and with the abstract considerations of modern foundations-studies, one will have to recognize that Kant's insight into the interplay between an ending regarded as final and the breaking out none the less of a new beginning represents a penetrating insight into the nature of thinking and into the origin of the antinomies.

The situation is somewhat different for the two last antinomies, and indeed Kant himself distinguished between the mathematical and the dynamic antinomies. We can concentrate our reflections again on the third antinomy, the antinomy of freedom. The thesis says:

'Causality in accordance with laws of nature is not the only causality from which the appearances of the world can one and all be derived. To explain these appearances it is necessary to assume that there is also another causality, that of freedom.'

And the antithesis says:

'There is no freedom; everything in the world takes place solely in accordance with laws of nature.'[25]

This antinomy is rooted in the causal concept of modern times. The Greeks saw the lawfulness of nature only in the heavens. Here below, they thought, much can happen by accident and thus they retained here below enough room for the free activity of men. This was changed when Newton brought down the laws of nature from heaven to earth, when he assigned the laws of nature not only to the movements up there in the heavens but also to the movements here below on the earth. One sees the scope of the Newtonian determinations best by placing oneself within the viewpoint of the theory of discrete mass-points and then assuming the simplest case, namely, that the world consists of only two mass-points. Then the movement of these two mass-points is wholly determined, they run their unchanging course throughout all time. In this world no free actions are possible, not because no free beings could exist in such a pathetically simplified world, but because an initiative of free beings would remove all lawfulness from these movements. The problem is not changed if we increase the number of mass-points. It is also not changed if we assume a number so large that it is for us practically infinite. It still remains a closed system of discrete mass-points and the course of its movements is fully determined on the basis of classical physics by the Newtonian laws. We would have an exhaustive knowledge of the course of these movements if we possessed the faculties of a Laplacean demon.

There is no place in this system for the old requirements of religion and ethics. Newton seems to have considered the problem and to have taken a different view. His opinion apparently was that God by a free choice had created the laws and the conditions of the system and therefore that He by free choice can impose new laws and new conditions at any time.[26] In any event, this is the way his students understood him. Leibniz saw the issue more clearly. A divine initiative into the course of a mechanical nature would eliminate its lawfulness. Also God's action is subject to the principle of sufficient reason. It follows from this that God would not arbitrarily alter the laws and conditions of motion. In an absolute sense, of course, God could give new laws and new conditions.[27] But the laws and conditions of motion actually given by God are contained in the structure of the best of all possible worlds. To change them would imply that God had not created or could not sustain the best of all possible worlds; this then God would not do. The free action of men is also subject to the principle of sufficient reason, but in Leibniz's opinion this principle does not eliminate freedom. The course of motion in nature remains strictly determined. If the freedom of action is to be consistent with the strict determination of the course of nature, then, in Leibniz's view, a distinction of kinds of being must be made. He therefore distinguishes the kingdom of grace from the kingdom of nature,[28] and he is clearly aware that he is continuing the old Platonic distinction between the world of Ideas and the world of phenomena.[29]

It is this distinction of Leibniz's that Kant, for his part, is carrying further. The distinction between the phenomenal and noumenal world makes possible for Kant the solution of the antinomy of freedom. The phenomenal world is subject to strict causal determination,[30] man as a noumenal being can none the less act freely.[31] We have already discussed, in the second Part, the difficulties of this Kantian distinction. We can at the moment put these difficulties to one side; our question now is not what Kant has achieved, but what he intended.

The upshot of the Kantian theory of antinomies is that in the first two antinomies both claims are false, while in the last two antinomies both claims are correct, but must be referred to different modes of being. In the systematic evaluation of this principle one can say that the basic concepts which figure in this solution: the causally determined nature and the freely acting man, can and must be more clearly defined. But one may assume that the necessary and possible refinement of these basic concepts will not lead us out of the antinomical and therefore not out of the dialectical character of these problems. On the basis of the discussions of foundations in logic, mathematics and physics, one could say instead with great probability that Kant has here hit off a genuine truth and that he has already succeeded in giving it a very clear form.

To sum up: the Kantian theory of antinomies can be characterized by two aspects. The first aspect derives from Kant's recognition that the antinomies he is studying all concern the problems of a totality. This is the positive and enduring significance of Kant's theory of antinomies. The second aspect is more difficult. Kant is convinced that his treatment includes all antinomies. In the sphere of the *Critique of Pure Reason* there are four and only four antinomies. There are no others beyond these.[32] From the outset one will find it difficult to suppress doubts about the number, and this number which fits so well in the Kantian systematic was arrived at only because Kant associated two problems with each of the first two antinomies, quite justifiably in the first antinomy and quite artificially in the second. But we can bracket the question of the number, and concentrate on the principle. Kant claims that one can restrict all antinomies within a definite sphere. Only within this limited and systematically explorable sphere do antinomy and dialectic occur. What lies outside this sphere, in particular, logic, mathematics and physics, is free of antinomies.

It is just this point that Hegel most sharply criticizes. To him, the limitation of the antinomies to the cosmological concept of totality is a basic mistake. He praises Kant's great achievement of rediscovering the antinomies,[33] but he is convinced that not only the cosmological concept of totality but every concept as such is antinomical.[34] It is characteristic that Hegel formulates his conviction in the course of a reflection on Kant. We have seen that Plato held the same conviction. One can only understand the second half of the *Parmenides* to mean that every concept is dialectical, for Plato. And in the modern research into foundations one also comes to the conclusion that the antinomies extend much further than Kant had thought, that they extend into logic and mathematics.

It is not easy to achieve a systematic decision. Let us first formulate once again the two opposing claims. Hegel and Plato say: If a single concept is antinomical then all concepts are antinomical. Kant says: There is only a limited number of antinomies. Now this is certainly not a disjunction such that one of the claims must be true and the other false. It would also not be a disjunction if one expanded the formulas: All concepts are antinomical, and as counterclaim: All antinomies can be restricted to a definite sphere. One can object again both claims that they have not been proved and that the question must remain open whether they are at all provable. With respect to Hegel's claim, Hegel himself certainly did not prove that every concept is antinomical. His allusion to the attempts of the Sophists can hardly count as a proof. With our contemporary resources one might formulate the task of such a proof very concretely. One can imagine a naïve theory of sets in which the antinomy of the set of all sets has not yet been removed. Then, according to Hegel's principle: where there is one contradiction, all other contradictions follow, we should be able to show from the contradictory character of the set of all sets that every set of this theory is contradictory. In the same theory there are sets representing one and two. Therefore one must show that in this theory one and two are contradictory. Such a proof has to date not been given, and it does not appear that such a proof could ever be given. To do this, one would have to be able to show that what belongs to a particular set— the set of all sets is contradictory—belongs also to every element of this set, and such a proof is hardly to be expected. But one does not need to conclude from this that the totality of all contradictions can be included within a limited sphere. It could rather be the case that the totality of all contradictions is an open domain, and this seems extremely probable. If this were the case, we would have been brought back to Kant's conviction: not all concepts are contradictory.

67. THE DIALECTIC OF HEGEL

For our investigations of the Hegelian dialectic, the *Logic* will be regarded as the centre of the Hegelian philosophy and all assertions about the Hegelian dialectic must in the last analysis be supported from the *Logic*. Nevertheless Hegel's *History of Philosophy* has great importance both pedagogically and systematically for the understanding of his dialectic. Of course this *History of Philosophy* is available to us only in the form which Hegel's students prepared for the *Gesamtausgabe*. Nevertheless the editors had Hegel's lectures in manuscript[1] and a series of presumably very good lecture notes.[2] And the editors themselves had certainly heard Hegel's lectures. Hegel presented the series of lectures nine times. He had just begun them a tenth time,[3] when death suddenly overtook him. For our study it is of great value that Greek philosophy was treated in detail and that within the treatment Plato's dialectic was assigned a large space. Moreover the problems of our study were again thoroughly discussed in the introduction to the lectures. Hegel had intended to publish this *History of Philosophy* himself,[4] and in view of this intention, the introduction and the section on Greek philosophy had already been largely worked through. This *History of Philosophy* is important for us because, as we will see shortly, for Hegel the systematic development of dialectic, as presented in the *Logic*, and the historical course of philosophy, as presented in the *History of Philosophy*, run on parallel tracks.

The introduction culminates in a reflection on the plurality of philosophies. It is true that an evaluation of this plurality has been attempted by many philosophers, perhaps by all philosophers worthy of the name. But no one has expressed this so clearly as Hegel, and we therefore believe that we will do well to let ourselves be guided in this question by Hegel.

The plurality of philosophies is a fact. Philosophers quarrel with one another, that is certain. In other sciences too, there are often temperamental debates. But philosophers have always quarrelled and they always will quarrel. This is the first thing one notices when one considers philosophy. But how are we to understand this plurality of philosophies, this quarrelling among the philosophers. Is it a defect in philosophy? Do the philosophers lack the good will to understand one another or do they lack the capacity to do so?

Hegel affirms the plurality of philosophies and, in a certain sense, also the quarrelling of philosophers. He says:

'We must make this clear, that this multiplicity of philosophies does not harm philosophy itself—the possibility of philosophy; but rather that it is and has always been necessary for the existence of the science of philosophy. That is the essential point.'[5]

If this affirmation of the multiplicity of philosophies is correct, two further questions are then posed: How are we to understand this multiplicity? In what is this multiplicity grounded? Hegel answered, I believe correctly: It is a mark of the task, the problem and the theme of philosophy that it cannot be exhausted in a single philosophy, and thus philosophy becomes dialectical according to its historical reality[6] and its systematic nature.[7] Here too we will follow Hegel's lead. We will only diverge from Hegel—and then emphatically—on the question of how to understand this multiplicity. Hegel answers with the concept of development. The dialectical multiplicity of philosophies represents a development.[8] This development appears in two guises as the development of the historical forms[9] and as the systematic development of pure thought.

Hegel says: 'According to this idea I claim that the sequence of systems of philosophy in history is the same as the sequence in the logical derivation of the conceptual determinations of the idea.'[10]

The historical development is presented in the *History of Philosophy*, the systematic development in the *Logic*.

This development is both necessary[11] and intelligible.[12] The two aspects of the development, necessity and rationality, are actually only two aspects of the same basic phenomenon. The development's necessity can be made intelligible, both in its historical as well as in its systematic course. But Hegel by no means claims that the form in which he has himself presented this development is already perfect. This applies to the *History of Philisophy* certainly, since Hegel did not live to give that book its final form. But it applies also to the *Logic*, even in its corrected form in the second edition.[13] But these factual defects of the Hegelian *Logic* and the Hegelian *History of Philosophy* do not hinder the objective necessity and rationality. And the fact that the development is dialectical also does not eliminate its necessity and rationality. On the contrary, it is Hegel's conviction that dialectic is the sole possibility by which the inner connexion of pure thought in the *Logic* and the corresponding inner connexion of historical forms of thought in the *History of Philosophy* can be understood.[14] This gives rise to our final task, which is to make clear that one must grant Hegel's contention about the necessity for a multiplicity of philosophies, but that one cannot follow him in his conviction about a necessary and rational development. I am not able to see in the historical course of philosophy a development in Hegel's sense. The contrast which appears here is, at bottom, the contrast between the Hegelian and the Platonic dialectic. Hegel himself saw this contrast clearly and we can therefore begin by following his presentations of this contrast.

68. HEGEL'S DEBATE WITH THE PLATONIC DIALECTIC

If the historical course of philosophy represents a development, then the relation of the Hegelian dialectic to the Platonic dialectic must also represent a development. The specific character of the Hegelian dialectic must become clearer if one contrasts it with the Platonic dialectic, and Hegel himself did this deliberately.

As he begins the discussion of Plato's dialectic in the *History of Philosophy* he says in this vein:

'Formal philosophy cannot look at dialectic in any other way than as being the art of confusing ordinary conceptions or even the concepts, in order to show their nullity and make their result wholly negative. This dialectic is found frequently in Plato, sometimes in the more Socratic and moralizing dialogues, sometimes also in the many dialogues which refer to the conceptions held by the Sophists about science. But the concept of the true dialectic is that it indicates the necessary movement of the pure concepts, not as if they were themselves thereby dissolved into nothingness, the result is rather that they are just these movements . . . and . . . the general is precisely the unity of these opposed concepts. We do not find a perfect awareness of the nature of dialectic in Plato, but we do find the reality: namely the absolute being known in this way in pure concepts and the movement of these concepts.'[1]

Dialectic as we find it among the Greeks has, in Hegel's view, only 'the purpose of confusing and dissolving the finite conceptions of men.'[2] It is in general not the true dialectic.[3] The speculative dialectic, which we find in Plato's approaches, is the most interesting and also the most difficult thing in his works.[4] Such a negative judgement of the Platonic dialectic is found also in the *Logic*. There Hegel says: 'The dialectic which Plato uses in the *Parmenides* to discuss being, must also be regarded as a dialectic of external reflection.'[5]

Hegel therefore distinguishes two forms of dialectic. The first form, which is found in Greek thought, by the Sophists generally, but in a certain sense also by Zeno and Plato, is a dialectic of external reflection,[6] a negative dialectic.[7] Hegel's dialectic, on the other hand, is a true dialectic,[8] a speculative[9] dialectic, an absolute[10] dialectic.

These two forms of dialectic are distinguished by the fact that the negative dialectic is satisfied to exhibit contradictions. Once the contradictions are exhibited the goal of this dialectic is reached. Concepts in which there are contradictions do not exist. But the absolute dialectic has recognized that contradictions are necessary. Only in them is the movement of thought and the movement of history completed. Contradictions do not simply refute something; in the complex expressiveness of Hegel's term *Aufheben*, they annul, transcend and retain.

This difference between the absolute and the negative dialectic represents at the same time a systematic and a historical development. The negative dialectic of the Greeks is only an imperfect form. It is the absolute dialectic of Hegel which leads dialectic as such to its completion, thereby annulling and retaining the dialectic of the Greeks as the imperfect form.

Now this also holds fundamentally for the relation of the Hegelian to the Platonic dialectic. The negative dialectic constitutes a large part of the Platonic dialectic.[11] Thus Hegel's absolute dialectic is the completion of the Platonic dialectic.[12] But also to the extent that indications of a speculative dialectic are found in Plato,[13] these are only the first indications and Plato himself was not aware of the absolute character of certain aspects of his dialectic, in so far as they are there at all. Only when the speculative dialectic is completely developed and only—which is the same thing—when the dialectic is aware of its absolute and speculative character, only then has dialectic reached its completion, in Hegel's conviction.

The decision on the possibilities of dialectic depends on this opposition between Hegel and Plato. Of course Hegel, as was his right, chose the terminology which favoured his own standpoint. In order to make an objective reflection possible, it is therefore appropriate to break away from the Hegelian terminology. The term 'negative dialectic' contains from the outset a prejudicial judgement. If one looks for a term which would be fairer to the Platonic dialectic, the term 'aporematic' seems very appropriate since it plays such a large role in the Platonic dialogues. One would then distinguish an aporematic dialectic in Plato's sense from an absolute dialectic in Hegel's sense. In this terminology one could then test the possibility that the aporematic dialectic of Plato represents only an early and therefore imperfect level of the absolute dialectic, and that Hegel's absolute dialectic thus constitutes the perfection of Plato's aporematic dialectic. But one must also consider the possibility that Hegel's dialectic is an exaggeration, even a form of *hubris*.

It could therefore be that the Platonic dialectic, just because of its aporematic character, remains within the limits of a possible dialectic. It could also be that the possibilities of dialectic as such exclude an absolute dialectic and permit only an aporematic dialectic. If one puts the question historically, it then runs: Does the transition from the Platonic dialectic to the Hegelian dialectic lead to a development on a higher level, to completion? Is the Platonic form the imperfect and the Hegelian form the perfect? Must we, with Hegel, venture the step from Plato to Hegel, or must we on the contrary return from Hegel back to Plato? In our conviction this question demands a decisive answer. Hegel's dialectic exceeds the possibilities of dialectic as such. Plato's, on the other hand, remains within its limits. We must go back from the absolute dialectic of Hegel to the aporematic dialectic of Plato.

69. ON THE POSSIBILITIES OF DIALECTIC

In considering the possibilities of dialectic the first requirement obviously is that contradictions exist or can be constructed. Evidently such a contradiction can exist. This is for example the case when one adds to an established determination of a concept the opposite determination. Many paradoxes introduced by the Greek Sophists are of this type. But a contradiction need not be so patent. It is thus for instance with the concept of the highest natural number. Every finite set of natural numbers has a highest and it seems obvious to interpret this as a property which can be asserted of every set of natural numbers. And at the beginning of the modern era this was often done. One quickly encounters antinomies, however, if one raises the question whether this highest number is odd or even.[1] A little reflection is needed in order to recognize that the set of all natural numbers and every infinite set of natural numbers cannot have a highest number.

Things are rather more difficult with the concept of the highest velocity. On the basis of classical mechanics this concept is contradictory and Leibniz showed this by a thought experiment.[2] Today we realize that the contradiction does not lie in the concept of velocity as such but rather depends on the special conditions of classical mechanics, and insight into the nature of the contradiction presupposes a long reflection.

From this point of view there are obviously two extreme possibilities initially available in the sphere of the general. The first possibility is that every concept is contradictory so that in the extreme case, for any given property of any given concept the opposite property could be proved, and therefore that the contradictory of every proposition could be proved. We have seen that this is Hegel's conviction.[3] We have already remarked that one could hardly assert that Hegel had proved this extreme claim. If one considers for example elementary arithmetic, to date it has not been shown by Hegel or his followers that it contains contradictions, let alone that every concept in it is contradictory. One can simplify still further and consider an arithmetic of finite number. One could go to the two-valued propositional calculus, which can be interpreted as an arithmetic of two numbers. To date there exists no ground for the supposition that the two-valued propositional calculus contains contradictions. Thus Hegel's thesis must be either incorrect as such or subject to restrictions which have still to be supplied.

With respect to that theorem of two-valued propositional calculus that we mentioned above: any particular contradiction implies every other contradiction, it is obviously closely connected with the Hegelian thesis and it seems to support it. But it should not be overlooked that this theorem follows from the general definition of implication and that it therefore only claims an implication. In no sense does it claim that from one particular contradiction all others could be deduced, and therefore could not be considered a general proof of the Hegelian claim.

The extreme thesis opposed to Hegel's is that there are no contradictions at all, and that in particular logic and mathematics are entirely free of contradictions. This is the great thesis of

Leibniz. And in the present century we may ascribe the same thesis to Hilbert, Husserl and Scholz. On this view one assumption is laid down: If a contradiction appears, somewhere there has been a mistake. The mistake has either been made in the chain of deductions or it lies already in the underlying definitions or axioms. The mistake can and must be laid bare; once discovered, the contradictions which have arisen with it will fall away.

This reasoning contains a thesis of existence which, so far as I can see, underlies the thought of all these philosophers and is especially marked in Leibniz: a contradictory concept, a *terminus falsus* is not a concept at all, it does not exist as a concept.[4] This holds in the same sense for Hilbert, Husserl and Scholz. Consistency is a condition for existence, a necessary condition, but also a sufficient condition for existence. Of course this standpoint presupposes that the consistency can be proved. Leibniz and Hilbert in particular have seen this. The proof of consistency is then at the same time a proof of existence. Leibniz makes this very clear. For him no contradictory concept can exist, but every concept which is consistent at the same time exists. But then an existence proof as proof of consistency must be supplied for every concept, even though for many concepts it is by no means easy to see at the outset whether or not they are contradictory. Such a proof is of course necessary for Leibniz as he himself recognized, but on the basis of his logic and his theory of concepts the proof cannot be carried out in general.[5]

In the same way Hilbert recognized that it is necessary for his position to prove the consistency of mathematics. He struggled for this proof with all the presuppositions available to him as a great mathematician and several times believed that he had the proof already in hand. Hilbert's struggle for the proof of consistency of mathematics as a whole yielded important results. That this proof did not succeed and that no general proof for the consistency of mathematics as a whole can succeed, as we learn from Gödel's studies, these are for philosophy the most important results of the foundations research of our time, and we hope that the discussion of Gödel's theorem in a general metaphysics will be regarded as justified.

Between these two extreme positions there obviously exists a middle position: some concepts are contradictory, others are not. This position suggests the hope of being able to include the contradictions within a definite sphere, so that everything outside that sphere would be free of contradictions. This is Kant's position. For him, as we have seen, dialectic is restricted to a determinate and wholly explorable sphere. If we limit ourselves to speculative reason as it is treated by Kant in the *Critique of Pure Reason*, then the possibilities of dialectic are completely encompassed by the Transcendental Psychology, the Transcendental Cosmology and the Transcendental Theology. Among them, Transcendental Cosmology, in particular, leads to four antinomies, no more and no less. The theoretical disciplines which do not belong to this sphere, in particular logic and mathematics, are consistent. This was the general conviction of mathematicians, logicians and philosophers throughout two thousand years down to the beginning of the present century, and we have noted how Husserl gave the clearest expression to this conviction with his theory of the definite manifold. Today this general thesis can no longer be maintained, at least not in its optimistic form. The emergence of antinomies was taken by logicians and mathematicians as an invitation for a complete revision of the basic concepts of their sciences. Whether such a revision can be carried so far that all difficulties are resolved, this is a question to which we cannot today give a safe answer, and which one can perhaps never answer in a wholly safe way. It is quite unlikely that anyone today would write the bold sentence which Wittgenstein placed in the foreword to his *Tractatus*.

'On the other hand the *truth* of the thoughts communicated here seems to me unassailable and definitive. I am, therefore, of the opinion that the problems have in essentials been finally solved.'[6]

This claim corresponds to similar claims made in the *Critique of Pure Reason*.[7] One cannot say that the claims to finality made in the *Critique of Pure Reason* have been granted, and with respect to the claims of finality in the *Tractatus*, the later Wittgenstein was probably their most severe critic.

Although it would be difficult to regard Kant's ideas as the final solution, his fundamental conception could still be correct, namely, that only some concepts are contradictory, not all. The appearances support this in a certain sense. The antinomies of the foundations lie somehow on the periphery. Thus it becomes understandable that many mathematicians are satisfied with the pragmatic interpretation that the antinomies are peripheral, and that in the inner realms of mathematics, so to speak, everything is in good order. And one can continue to work further on the actual tasks of mathematics as if the antinomies of the foundations had never appeared. In so far as this interpretation claims to be only a practical, not a fundamental, solution, a certain justification cannot be denied it.

There are two possibilities for separating off the antinomies. Either one determines the realm in which antinomies appear or one determines the realm in which no antinomies appear. Kant followed the first way. It was his conviction that one could systematically derive the totality of antinomies. Once they are systematically and therefore completely derived, it is obvious that the realm in which antinomies can appear has been exactly defined. Kant did not do justice to development. The antinomies of logic and set-theory are outside the realm marked off by Kant, although they are related to it. Within this new, larger realm no one has yet attempted a systematic derivation of the totality of possible antinomies.

On the other hand, one can attempt to mark off the realm of the consistent. This was attempted first by Leibniz and then by Hilbert. But the task is much more difficult than one could suppose. On the basis of the Leibnizian theory of judgement it is not soluble. It would presuppose that one had the totality of basic concepts and that one could derive from it the totality of consistent compound concepts. But on the standpoint of Leibniz the totality of basic concepts cannot be given and he himself, as we saw already, was not able to provide a single instance of a concept ultimately interpreted as a basic concept. Hilbert took a different path. He assumed that a proof is a finite structure and it seemed to him possible to prove the consistency of mathematics as a whole. Oskar Becker very early raised objections to this and we know today that Hilbert did not succeed because success was impossible.

Another possibility would be to attempt a revision of the basic concepts. This is the approach followed by most experts today. One considers, for example, that the concept of set in use today is not precise enough, and one hopes that after a precise rendering of the basic concepts, in particular therefore of the concept of set, the antinomies will disappear. But none of the many proffered solutions has won general acceptance and little hope is held out for a general solution. Most studies of these questions are doomed to failure because they are framed in two general terms.

If one were to attempt, in the style of Husserl, a definition of the concept of theory in general such that it would encompass the totality of consistent theories, one would—as far as we can see—come into an open domain. In such an open domain there is little prospect of achieving results of any significance. There remains then only the approach of starting from concrete theories and gradually rising to more abstract ones. One might begin, say, with the two-valued propositional calculus or perhaps with a carefully delimited theory of natural numbers. From this beginning one could ascend step by step to more complicated theories. This is the approach adopted today by many experts and it has led to the achievement of noteworthy results.

Even so, an objection can also be raised here. A decisive result can be achieved only if one restricts oneself to a finite domain in the strict sense of the word. One may consider only a finite set, n, of formulae, such that this n does not exceed a given upper limit. But theories which are definite in this strict sense are obviously uninteresting. Two-valued propositional calculus and elementary arithmetic only become interesting if one has available an infinite number of formulae. But then one must introduce, either openly or in covert fashion, an axiom of infinity. One can for example introduce an operation which is indefinitely repeatable, such as the constructing of sets, addition, or substitution. But one must then assume that the indefinite repetition of such an operation is consistent. What is at stake is not whether the operation in its repetition is as such consistent, which with a sufficiently careful definition we all hope, but whether that consistency is provable. But if every proof is essentially a proof from something, among the presuppositions of the consistency proof for an infinite domain must be an axiom of infinity. The proof of the consistency of logic and mathematics must therefore presuppose the consistency of some axiom of infinity, and these considerations too lead back to Gödel's results.

On the whole, it seems that a satisfactory determination of the possible scope of contradictions is not to be looked for. Hegel's claim that all concepts are contradictory, a claim that also seems to underly the structure of the Platonic dialectic in the *Parmenides*, has not yet been proven. The opposite claim of Leibniz that all existing concepts are consistent is not provable, if it is meant to be more than a mere tautology. Kant's idea of deriving systematically the totality of possible contradictions does not stand the test. Finally, it does not seem possible to delimit a consistent domain of sufficiently large scope. Thus the contradictions will remain what they have basically always been, a pragmatic problem. One must wait and see what contradictions appear within sufficiently large domains and then attempt to render the contradictions innocuous in each particular case. This result is by no means so unsatisfactory as it might at first appear. For why should logic and mathematics be islands of bliss, in which an absolute security is guaranteed by some special patent, a security which is nowhere else granted to men? Why should not logic and mathematics also share in the insecurity and frailty of human existence?

70. THE FORMS OF DIALECTIC

We have granted a considerable space to the problem of dialectic. If we now look back on this discussion we see that different forms of dialectic can be distinguished. Of course these forms cannot be strictly separated, they are related and as a rule appear in a mixed form. Nevertheless much can be clarified if we make such distinctions as are possible. Firstly, it will be good to keep the meaning of the term 'dialectic' as narrow as possible. Plato knows, as we saw, a narrower and a broader meaning. In the broader meaning dialectic means for him simply the theory of Ideas. In this broader meaning he uses the term 'dialectic' interchangeably with the theory of Ideas, for example in the *Republic*, and it seems as if he uses it only in this broader meaning. But in fact he makes use of the other, narrower meaning, although apparently only in the verb form, as an investigation of contradictions. We will restrict the term to this narrower meaning. This will also be a narrower usage than the Kantian one. Kant understands by dialectic quite generally the theory of the unfounded use of certain concepts, particularly the transcendental Ideas, and this allows him to include under dialectic transcendental psychology, transcendental cosmology, and transcendental theology. In Kant's terms, we are restricting dialectic to transcendental cosmology, therefore to the theory of antinomies in the true sense, although we will drop Kant's limitation of only four antinomies. In this sense we will use 'dialectic' to refer to a standpoint and a discipline. Dialectic is a standpoint when it represents the conviction that propositions which contradict one another can both be true and further, that they can both be proved true. Dialectic is a discipline when it is pursued as the study of possible contradictions. It is a discipline which seeks out and exhibits contradictions. It will prove the contradictory propositions, investigate the meaning of the contradictions and the grounds for their appearance. It will, finally, not avoid the task of safeguarding the practical work of the sciences so far as possible from the threats presented by contradictions. In this sense one can distinguish four forms of dialectic: a logical, a dynamic, a cosmological and an ontological dialectic.

By a logical dialectic we understand the theory of contradictions as they can appear in logic and in certain problems of mathematics. The antinomy of the set of all sets is a classical example of this type. Also the first antinomies of Zeno, for example those about likeness and unlikeness, if they are truly antinomies, belong here. Finally, many of the antinomies from the dialectical part of the *Parmenides* belong here too.

As the second form, we will consider the dynamic antinomies. They are those antinomies which emerge in the conceptual interpretation of becoming and change. Here belong most of Zeno's antinomies, for example, the flying arrow or Achilles and the tortoise. In the second part of the *Parmenides* Plato often makes use of dynamic antinomies. Hegel's dialectic essentially has its origin and true meaning here. Here too belong the antinomies of the continuum which preoccupied Leibniz. These are antinomies which develop in the encounter of discrete structures with continuous structures. In particular the dynamic antinomies spring from the attempt to grasp a continuous process by means of a discrete schema, this was already made clear by Aristotle.

The cosmological antinomies in their purest form are represented by the Kantian theory of antinomies, their source is the concept of the totality of the world, and the attempt to apply determinations to this totality which could only be valid for restricted parts of it. The cosmological antinomies also reach far back into Greek thought, as we saw in the antinomy of spatial finitude and the infinity of the cosmos.

As ontological antinomies I will understand those antinomies which appear in assertions about being. One finds them when one distinguishes between being and unity, one finds them when different modes of being are to be distinguished, and one finds them if from these different modes of being one is singled out as the pre-eminent mode. There are ontological antinomies in Kant in his distinction between appearance and thing-in-itself. We have seen that Kant does not subsequently make this distinction an explicit theme. But the formulation with which Jacobi discovered these difficulties leads directly to an ontological dialectic. In Plato we find an ontological dialectic when, in the *Sophist* and in the first part of the *Parmenides*, he discusses the distinction between the Ideas and sensible things and the being of Ideas as such. In the *Sophist* Plato refers specifically to the aporematic character of assertions about being. In the first part of the *Parmenides* it is the problems of determining the being of the Idea which lead to an ontological dialectic. He did not there formulate the ontological dialectic of the theory of Ideas in the strict antinomic form which he developed in the second part of the *Parmenides*. But Plato developed this ontological dialectic of the theory of Ideas much further than Kant developed the dialectic for the relation between appearance and thing-in-itself. Thus, in substance, the ontological dialectic of the theory of Ideas is recognizably present in Plato.

Finally, one can also speak of a dialectic of standpoints. In this dialectic of standpoints the systematic possibilities of dialectic which we have just distinguished come together in different ways. The historical possibility of dialectic arises from the systematic possibility of dialectic. For Plato, it was presented as a dialectic between Parmenides and Heraclitus. In this theory of antinomies Kant referred the historical dialectic of standpoints back into the purely systematic, only a few fragments of that historical dialectic of philosophical standpoints remain in his theory of antinomies. It was Hegel who recognized with decisive clarity the connexion between the systematic dialectic and the historical dialectic of standpoints.

In these studies we are primarily concerned with the ontological dialectic. Although we have made extensive references to the logical and cosmological dialectic, these forms of the dialectic were not our true goal. Their treatment was intended only to prepare for the study of ontological dialectic; the more easily recognized logical, dynamic and cosmological dialectic were intended to make our access to ontological dialectic easier. But our real concern in this general metaphysics is with ontological dialectic.

This is the place to ask about the possible form of a presentation of dialectic as such. Bolzano reflected on the possible form of a presentation of a science and the *Elements* of Euclid are perhaps the best example of a systematically progressive presentation. This raises the question whether dialectic can be presented in such a systematically progressive form. As Kant begins the presentation of the antinomies he remarks that this is not possible. Even the external form of the book as a continuous text must be given up here; Kant places thesis and antithesis in right and left columns side by side. In the dialectic of the *Parmenides* Plato places eight parallel theses one after the other, to which an auxillary hypothesis is added, making nine hypotheses in all.

The dialectic of Zeno seems also to have had a similar construction in parallel theses. Here too it is Hegel who has most clearly seen the issue. Between the *Logic* and the *History of Philosophy* there is no systematic sequence. One can begin with the *Logic*, although that is not easy, but one can also begin with the *History of Philosophy*, and here the access is easier. But from the systematic standpoint neither of the two presentations takes priority. This is made wholly clear in the *Encyclopedia*. Hegel's dialectic contains parts which are equivalent and interchangeable.

From all this one may draw the conclusion that a dialectic cannot be represented in a systematic sequence, but only in a reticular connexion. The author of these studies required a long time to realize that many things in these studies which seem to be repetition and constantly repeated repetition arise necessarily out of this inner reticular connexion of a dialectic.

71. THE METHOD OF METAPHYSICS AS APOREMATIC DIALECTIC

Following Plato and Hegel, metaphysics must recognize the plurality of metaphysical standpoints. This plurality is not a defect, it constitutes the essence of metaphysics and of philosophy as such. Every metaphysics must recognize this as Plato intended it and as Hegel has clearly expressed it. When Hegel attempts to build this plurality into an absolute dialectic, however, metaphysics must take up its stand against him. Metaphysics may not understand itself as an absolute dialectic in the sense of Hegel, it may only understand itself as a negative dialectic in Hegel's sense. If one adopts the term we have suggested then metaphysics may only understand itself as an aporematic dialectic.

The history of philosophy testifies unmistakeably for the plurality. Whatever be the significance of Plato, of Aristotle, and of Kant, after the subsequent course of philosophy it is not to be expected that one of these three great standpoints will be recognized as the only correct one and that this will permit the other two standpoints to be proved false. The assertions of philosophy evidently cannot be clearly separated into the true and the false. At least Plato never expected this. In the *Seventh Letter* he expressed this point clearly. He there denies that he has ever set down his philosophy in a book and he evidently is thinking of a text-book.

In not a few passages Aristotle expresses himself in such a way as if he were claiming finality for his philosophy. And with respect to logic at least one must allow that he has laid a foundation which has endured and will continue to endure. But so marked a follower of the Aristotelian philosophy as Thomas Aquinas has clearly recognized that it cannot be the task of philosophy to swear by Aristotle; he contemplated instead a synthesis between Aristotle and Plato as his task. Perhaps the claim of finality in the Aristotelian philosophy refers primarily to special regions, to logic, to physics, to ethics. Otherwise one would not be able to understand why Aristotle says in the *Metaphysics* that the question about being has always been aporematic in the past, is so now in the present and will always continue to be aporematic in the future.

In certain respects, Kant holds a similar view. The claim to have provided a final and therefore a strictly binding solution is certainly great. If one considers this claim more closely, however, one sees that it is essentially referred to special domains, in particular to the table of judgements and the table of categories. In other problems Kant knows very well that we may not hope for a definitive solution. The inner connexion of our capacities for knowledge remains problematic. Intuitions and concepts spring from one root, but our gaze cannot penetrate into these depths of the mind. And for Kant the self-consciousness of freedom and the self-consciousness of the noumenal self remain inexplicable. For Kant this self-consciousness stands beyond all doubt but he does not believe that we can even understand its possibility in the true sense. A third aporematic problem in Kant is the relation between appearance and thing-in-itself. The fact that these fundamental questions are open-ended makes it quite understandable that Hegel's dialectical philosophy has grown out of Kant's philosophy, and Hegel himself has drawn attention to their inner connexion.

One cannot therefore understand the quarrel of the philosophers in such a way that one day one of the philosophies will prove itself to be the sole correct one; one must rather recognize that this quarrel represents a genuine dialectic. In this fundamental approach we must follow Hegel. Such an interpretation is also suggested by certain developments in contemporary studies of foundations. In the first decades of the present century three directions were set down: the logicism of Russell, the formalism of Hilbert, and the intuitionism of Brouwer. These directions were caught up in controversy and their respective advocates, perhaps even their founders, expected that their own direction would win the day. It turned out otherwise. First, it was soon recognized that the three great positions on foundations were intimately connected with the old philosophical standpoints, Hilbert was intimately connected with Plato, Russell with Aristotle, and Brouwer with Kant. It is thus understandable that the debate between the three great positions in no sense ended with a victory of one of them over the others. Instead the problem has shifted and we now attempt to understand what each of the three positions on foundations actually claims and what it achieves, what it achieves for the understanding of logic and mathematics and what it achieves in the understanding of thinking in general. This makes intelligible the modern attitude as represented, say, by Quine. Quine himself is an avowed nominalist. But this by no means leads him to a flat rejection of Plato; it leads instead to the opposite claim, that one must learn to understand Plato. The author of these studies proceeds on the same fundamental conviction both in relation to the three great directions of research into foundations and in relation to the three great philosophical standpoints. He knows that he is attached in a special way to the philosophy of Kant. But he is also convinced that one cannot understand Kant's philosophy, and that one cannot understand philosophy of any kind, if one will not attempt to understand Plato and Aristotle.

If we may now summarize in this sense our methodological investigations and therewith the drift of the whole book, it appears necessary first to acknowledge the plurality of philosophies and the plurality of standpoints. That we have tied this plurality to three standpoints is a methodological decision which was none the less suggested by systematic considerations. Acknowledgement of the plurality of standpoints is the insight which philosophy owes to Hegel. If one concentrates this plurality in three standpoints, one is enabled to formulate it both historically and systematically. Considered historically, it is the plurality of Plato, Aristotle and Kant; considered systematically it is the determination of the being of the general as Idea, as law of nature and as activity of thought.

If one grants fundamentally the fact of this plurality, then the further task arises of understanding it. What are the causes of this plurality? Is there a unity which pulls together this plurality, and what kind of unity would this be?

Where lie the causes of this plurality? Aristotle and Leibniz orient themselves essentially on the concrete sciences. There one proposition after another is admitted and the propositions thus admitted are fitted together into a whole, the whole of logic, the whole of arithmetic. On this view philosophy too admits one truth after another. In the utterances of the philosophers there is much that is false but also something that is true. If then the falsity is excluded and only the true retained, then on this view philosophy too puts together items of knowledge step by step into a whole. We noted that a particularly instructive example of this is Aristotle's theory of the principles. According to Aristotle's interpretation many of the thinkers who preceded him had seen the problem of the principles. If one excludes the false and develops the true further, one will bring the theory of principles to its final form and completion. But the subsequent course of philosophy did not confirm Aristotle in his conviction about the finality of his theory of principles. We have ourselves attempted to present another interpretation of the theory of principles, according to which that theory is a never-ending task.

Much more subtle than Aristotle's interpretation is the interpretation given by Hegel, and we should follow Hegel a good part of the way. Hegel sees the cause of the plurality of philosophies in this, that it is impossible for philosophy to say what it wants to say in one proposition and that it is wholly impossible for philosophy to say what it wants to say in an apodictic proposition. What philosophy wants to say can only be said in many propositions and only in propositions which are dialectically opposed to one another. Here Hegel is undoubtedly right. The difficulties appear when Hegel summarizes the totality of dialectical assertions of philosophy into one system, even into a dialectical system. This is the point on which, in my opinion, we can no longer follow Hegel.

Perhaps the problem becomes completely clear in the very first philosophical opposition, that between Parmenides and Heraclitus.

It is certain that the philosophical principles of Parmenides and Heraclitus contradict each other. In the interpretation of Hegel there is between them a systematic and a historical development. But I cannot see that Hegel has proved this. It has not been proved that a philosophy of continually changing becoming represents a higher level, systematically and historically, than a philosophy of unmoving being. Parmenides held the opposite conviction. For him, there is only a philosophy of unmoved being, a philosophy of becoming is for him a philosophy of dunces.

That may be strongly put, but Plato also gives no indication that he regards the philosophy of Heraclitus as a higher form. The general impression yields the opposite conclusion that Plato placed Parmenides above Heraclitus. We therefore follow Hegel in his conviction of the necessity for many philosophies, but we do not follow him in his notion of a development. At the same time we reject any tendency toward an overestimation of historical development in so far as it represents an extreme interpretation of historical events. We oppose to this the conviction that the differences we have developed systematically and historically must be seen as lying on the same level. We do not believe that Hegel has proved that the Aristotelian philosophy represents a higher form than the Platonic, and the Kantian philosophy a higher form than the Platonic or the Aristotelian; at least this does not hold on the basis of the principles developed here.

We are thus convinced that the determination of the being of the general cannot be expressed in a single proposition and that it cannot be expressed in an apodictic proposition. The determination of the being of the general must be presented from many points of view and it is only from considerations of method that we have concentrated this plurality into three standpoints.

This plurality of standpoints can be called dialectical in a broader sense. The theses do not stand opposed to one another in the strict sense of the dialectic, as do the thesis and antithesis of the Platonic and Kantian dialectic. But in a broader sense one can say that the different ontological standpoints contradict one another and this is the way their diversity has always been interpreted. In such an extended sense this is also a dialectic.

Two reasons can now be established to show that this dialectic must be understood as an aporematic dialectic. The first reason consists in this, that the individual standpoints, taken singly, cannot be made free of aporias. The self-consciousness of the great thinkers and the history of philosophy agree in testifying that each of these three standpoints in some passages encounters aporias. The second reason for the aporematic character of this dialectic lies in this, that the plurality of possible standpoints cannot be systematically deduced and therefore cannot be exhaustively presented. One can never be sure that an investigation, like the present one, has grasped the essential features of those standpoints which have actually appeared to date. Perhaps the standpoint of Descartes, for example, should have been regarded as a fourth. Much less can it be proved that the totality of possible standpoints is represented in those standpoints which have actually appeared to date. The possibility cannot be excluded that a new principle will be discovered in the future. On the basis of our studies there seems little likelihood of such a possibility. But it is another question whether new possibilities can be excluded with certainty and for all time. Perhaps we do not yet know well enough the general, the being of which we are trying to determine. Perhaps thought contains wholly new possibilities of the general, possibilities which will have an influence on the determination of the being of the general. From this it would follow that the determination of the being of the general is a task which is never complete, which can never finally and conclusively be brought to an end. But if we have today once again achieved the insight that the path of science never comes to its end, why should the task of philosophy be one that can be completed? It is the task of ontology to undo every newly achieved insight, to find new aporias for every newly achieved insight. The basic description of metaphysics is the one Plato gave of it at its very beginning: ἡμεῖς δὲ πρὸ τοῦ μὲν ᾠόμεθα, νῦν δ' ἠπορήκαμεν.

BIBLIOGRAPHY

(A list of the editions used and of the more frequently cited books)

Aristotelis Opera. Ed. Academia Regia Borussica, Berlin, 1831 ff.

Ast (Fridericus Astius), *Lexicon Platonicum sive Vocum Platonicarum,* Index Darmstadt, 1956.

Augustinus, *Opera Omnia. Patrologia Latina,* ed. Migne, Vol. 32–47, Paris 1845 ff. (Abbreviated as *ML*).

Bolzano, B., *Wissenschaftslehre.* 4 Volumes. Sulzbach, 1837, New Impression of Vols. 1–4. Leipzig, 1929–31, Ed. by W. Schultz (Abbreviated as *WL*).

Bonitz, H., *Index Aristotelicus.* Berlin, 1870.

Dedekind, R., *Gesammelte Mathematische Werke.* Ed. by R. Fricke, E. Noether and O. Ore. Brauschweig, 1930 ff.

Descartes, *Oeuvres.* Ed. by Ch. Adam and P. Tannery. Paris, 1897 ff.

Diels (Ed.). *Die Fragmente der Vorsokratiker,* 4 Volumns. Berlin, 1922.

Duns Scotus, J., *Opera Omnia*—Paris, 1891 ff. (Vives); Ed. Romana, 1950. (The *Opus Oxoniensa* abbreviated as *Op. ox.* the *Reportata Parisiensia* as *Re. Par.*).

Euklidis Opera Omnia. Ed. by J. L. Heiberg and H. Menge. Leipzig, 1883 ff.

Gauss, C. F., *Werke.* Ed. by the Königlichen Gesellschaft der Wissenschaften at Göttingen, 1870 ff.

Gredt, J., *Elementa Philosophiae Aristotelico-Thomisticae,* Barcelona, 1960–61.

Hegel, G. W. F., *Sämtliche Werke,* Ed. Glockner, Stuttgart, 1927.

Heidegger, M., *Sein und Zeit. Erste Hälfte,* in *Jahrbuch für Philosophie und Phänomenologische Forschung,* Vol. VIII, Halle, Niemeyer, 1927 (Abbreviated as *SuZ*).

Husserl, E., *Ideen zu einer reinen Phänomenologie und Phanomenologische Philosophie.* Halle, 1913 (Abbreviated as *Ideen*).

Jacobi, F. H., *Werke.* Leipzig, 1812.

Kant, I., *Gesammelte Schriften,* Ed. of the Königlich-Preussischen Akademie der Wissenschaften. Berlin, 1910 (*The Critique of Pure Reason* is cited by the A and B editions only).

Kronecker, L., *Werke.* Ed. K. Hensel. Leipzig, 1895 ff.

Leibniz, G. W., Ed. Erdmann: *Opera philosophica quae extant latina, gallica, germanica omnia.* Scientia Aalen, 1959 (Abbreviated as *E*).

Die philosophischen Schriften. Ed. by C. I. Gerhardt, Vols I–VII, Berlin, 1875 ff. (Abbreviated as *GP*).

Leibnizens mathematische Schriften, Ed. by C. I. Gerhardt, Vol. I–VII, Berlin, 1849 ff. (Abbreviated as *GM*).

Sämtliche Schriften und Briefe. Ed by the Preussischen Akademie der Wissenschaften. Darmstadt, 1923 ff. (Abbreviated as *Ak*).

(The *Nouveaux Essais sur l'entendement humain* are abbreviated as *NE*; the other smaller works of Leibniz are cited by name).

Locke, J., *An Essay concerning Human Understanding.* London, 1801.

Martin, G., *Wilhelm von Ockham, Untersuchungen zur Ontologie der Ordnungen.* Berlin, 1949.

Immanuel Kant, Ontologie und Wissenschaftstheorie, Köln, 1951.

333

Klassische Ontologie der Zahl, Kant-Studien Erg.-Heft 70, Köln, 1956.
Leibniz, Logik und Metaphysik, Köln, 1960.
Mendelssohn, M., *Gesammelte Schriften,* 7 Volumes. Leipzig, 1843–45.
Newton, I., *Philosophiae naturalis principia mathematica.* Editio Ultima, Amsterdam, 1714 (Abbreviated as *Principia*).
Nietzsche, F., *Werke.* Leipzig, 1923.
Ockham, W. v., *Quaestiones in quattour libros Sent.* Lugduni, 1495. Argentinae, 1483 (Only the first book).
Quodlibeta septem. Paris, 1487. Argentinae, 1491.
Summa totius logicae. Venice, 1508.
Platonis Opera. Ed. J. Burnet. Oxford, 1900 ff.
Werke, trans. by F. Schleiermacher. Berlin, 1856 and Rowohlt.
Plotin, *Enneades,* Ed. E. Brehier. Paris, 1924 ff.
Russell, B., see Whitehead.
Suarez, *Opera Omnia.* Ed. D. M. Andre. Paris, 1856.
Thomas Aquinas, *Opera Omnia, Editio Leonina.* Rome, 1882 ff.
Whitehead, A. N., *Process and Reality, An Essay in Cosmology.* New York, 1941 (Abbreviated as *PR*).
Whitehead-Russell, *Principia Mathematica,* 3 Volumes. Oxford, 1910 ff. (Abbreviated as *PM*).
Wittgenstein, L., *Schriften von L. Wittenstein,* Frankfurt, 1960.
Tractatus Logico-Philosophicus, London, 1922.
Philosophical Investigations.

TRANSLATOR'S NOTE

In rendering quotations I have used the following standard editions: Aristotle, *Works,* Ed. by Smith and Ross, Oxford University Press; Kant, *The Critique of Pure Reason,* trans. by Norman Kemp-Smith, Macmillan, 1929; *The Critique of Practical Reason,* trans. by L. W. Beck, Liberal Arts Press, 1956; Plato, *Collected Dialogues,* Ed. Hamilton & Cairns, Bollingen, 1961; Husserl, *Ideas,* trans. by W. Gibson, Allen & Unwin, 1931; Heidegger, *Being and Time,* trans. by J. Macquarrie, Harper & Bros, 1961.

NOTES

1

1. A. Comte, *Cours de philosophie positiviste*, 6 vols., Paris, 1830–42, VI, 645 ff. and I, 6.
2. J. S. Mill, *A System of Logic, Rationative and Inductive*, 2 vols., London, 1843.
3. *Tractatus* 4.21.
4. *Tractatus* 4.46.
5. *Tractatus* 6.53.
6. *Tractatus* 4.0031.
7. *Philosophical Investigations* I, 23.
8. Nietzsche, *Werke*, II, 40.
9. Nietzsche, *Werke*, II, 38.
10. Heidegger: *Platons Lehre von der Wahrheit*, Bern, 1947, p. 49.

2

1. *Sophist* 244 A.
2. *Met.* VII, 1; 1028 b 4.
3. Kant, *Schriften* XVII, 495.
4. Mendelssohn II, 235; see also Kant, *Schriften* XIII, 115.
5. Preface A ix.
6. A 23, B 38.
7. A 235 ff., B 294 ff.
8. Kant, *Schriften* V, 50 ff.

3

1. *Sophist* 243 D.
2. *Sophist* 242 C f., and especially 243 D–E.
3. *Sophist* 243 E.
4. *Sophist* 243 D.
5. *Met.* III, 4; 1001 a 3.
6. *Met.* VII, 1; 1028 b 2.
7. *Sophist*, Infinitive 243 E, Participle 244 B.
8. Heidegger, *Vom Wesen des Grundes*, 4th Ed., Frankfurt, 1955, p. 15.
9. *Tractatus* 4.0031.
10. *Sophist* 244 A.
11. H. Reiner, 'Die Entstehung und ursprüngliche Bedeutung des Namens Metaphysik' in *Zeitschrift für philosophische Forschung*, 8 (1954) p. 210 ff., 9 (1955) p. 77 ff.
12. Chr. Wolff, *Philosophia sive Ontologia*, Frankfurt-Leipzig, 1729.
13. The earlier work is still called: *Grundzüge einer Metaphysik der Erkenntnis*, 1st Ed., Berlin, 1921; the later work is then called: *Zur Grundlegung der Ontologie*, Berlin, 1935.

4

1. *Cat.* I; 1 a 1–13.
2. J. and W. Grimm, *Deutsches Wörterbuch*, Leipzig, 1854 ff.; Vol. IV, Leipzig, 1877, IV, 2; 2083 a.
3. *SuZ*, par. 12, p. 53 f.
4. *Met* IV, 2; 1003 a 34.
5. *Met* V, 7; 1017 a 7 ff.
6. *Met.* VI, 2, 1026 a 33 f; IX, 10, 1051 a 34; XIV, 2, 1089 a 26.
7. *Met.* V, 6, 1015 b 16; X, 1, 1052 a 15 ff.; *Phys.* I, 2, 185 b 7.

8. Thomas, *Sum. theol.* I, 13, 5; *Comm. in met.* 885 f.
9. Duns Scotus, *Op. ox.* 3, 3, 2, 6; *Op.* IX, 102. E. Gilson: *Johannes Duns Scotus*, I, III, p. 89 (German Ed. Düsseldorf, 1959) C. Balic: 'Circa positionis fundamentales J. Duns Scoti,' *Antonianum*, 28 (1953), pp. 261–306, esp. p. 278 ff. Ockham, *Quodlibeta* V, q. 14; *I Sent* d. 2 q. 9 P; *I Sent* d. 3 q. 8 E.

5

1. *Phaedo* 79 A.
2. *Met.* I, 5; 985 b 25.
3. *Met.* I, 5; 986 a 17.
4. Democritus B 125, Diels II, 168.

6

1. *Phaedo* 78 DE.
2. *Ibid.*, 74 AC.
3. *Ibid.*, 78 D and 100 D.
4. *Ibid.*, 80 B.
5. *Ibid.*, 79 A.
6. *Ibid.*, 78 DE.
7. *Republic* 505 A and 509 B.
8. J. Burnet, *Greek Philosophy*, London, 1950, Par. 119, p. 154 f.
9. A. E. Taylor, *Plato*, London, 1960, p. 176.
10. *Met.* I, 6; 987 b 30 f.
11. *Phaedo* 100 D.
12. *Ibid.*, 100 C.
13. *Ibid.*, 100 D.
14. *Ibid.*, 101 CE.
15. It must remain open whether one can here have Eudoxus in mind. Cf. P. Natorp, *Platons Ideenlehre*, 2. Ed., Leipzig, 1921, p. 211.
16. A. E. Taylor, *Plato*, p. 201 f.
17. *Phaedo*, 101 BC.
18. P. Natorp, *op. cit.*, esp. p. 154 ff. and Index, p. 550.
19. B. Liebrucks, *Platons Entwicklung zur Dialectik*, Frankfurt, 1949, p. 10.
20. *Parmenides* B 6, 1–2, Diels I, 232 f.
21. *Sophist* 246 BC.
22. Hegel, *Werke* XVIII, 201.

7

1. *Sophist* 249 C.
2. *Ibid.*, 249 D.
3. *Ibid.*, 249 B.
4. *Ibid.*, 249 B.
5. *Ibid.*, 249 D.
6. *Ibid.*, 248 A.
7. D. Ross, *Plato's Theory of Ideas*, Oxford, 1951, p. 107.
8. F. M. Cornford, *Plato's Theory of Knowledge*, London, 1957, p. 243.
9. D. Ross, *op. cit.*, p. 106, note 1.
10. *Sophist* 248 E f.
11. *Ibid.*, 248 CE.
12. *Ibid.*, 243 D, 244 A, and 244 B.
13. R. Robinson, *Plato's Earlier Dialectic*, Oxford, 1953.
14. *Laches* 190 B, 190 D and others.

15. *Euthyphro* 5 D.
16. *Republic* 331 C ff.
17. *Theatetus* 145 E and 146 E.
18. *Parmenides* 137 C ff.
19. *Soph. El.* 34; 183 b 7.
20. *Met.* XIII, 4; 1078 b 24.
21. Simplicius, *Comm. in Arist. Phys.*, 23.21, in Diels I, 77—Thales A 13.
22. *Met.* I, 5; 986 a 15–17.
23. Hegel, *Werke*, XVII, 253.
24. Parmenides, B 4, 3, Diels I, 232.
25. Parmenides, B 8, 6, Diels I, 235 f.
26. Parmenides, B 8, 34, Diels I, 238.
27. *Sophist* 244 A.
28. Cf. Heidegger, *SuZ*, Introduction, p. 1 ff., and par. 6, p. 19 ff.

8

1. J. Burnet, *Greek Philosophy*, Par. 72, p. 90.
2. Ast, *Lexikon Platonicum* II, 492 f. and Bonitz, *Index Aristolelicus* 544 a 6–25.
3. *Laws* III, 697 B.
4. Cf., for example, *Phaedo* 76 D, 78 D, 101 C.
5. *Philebus* 26 D, 27 B.
6. D. Peipers, *Ontologia Platonica*, Leipzig, 1883, p. 28 f., and R. Hirzel, 'Ousia' in *Philologus* 72 (1913), p. 42 ff.
7. Cf. P. Natorp, *Platons Ideenlehre*, Index article 'Sein', p. 563.

9

1. W. Jaeger, *Aristoteles*, Berlin, 1923, p. 172.
2. *ontologia generalis*, *Met.* VII, 1; 1028 b 4.
3. *theologia naturalis*, *Met.* VI, 1; 1026 a 18.
4. *scientia universalis*, *Met.* I, 3; 983 a 24; I, 2; 982 b 2.
5. *Met.* III, 1; 996 a 4.
6. *Met.* III, 4; 1001 a 3.
7. *Met.* III, 4; 1001 a 3.
8. *Met.* I, 9; 992 b 18.
9. Cf. the citations of *Met.* Book V in *De gen. et corr.*, 336 b 29; *Phys.* 191 b 29; *Met.* X, 1; 1052 a 15.
10. W. Jaeger, *Aristoteles*, p. 174.
11. *Met.* V, 7; 1017 a 8–a 22.
12. *Met.* V, 7; 1017 a 22–30.
13. *Met.* IV, 2; 1003 a 33 and also see: Fr. Brentano, *Von den mannigfachen Bedeutungen des Seins nach Aristoteles*, Freiburg, 1862, Chap. 5, Par. 3, pp. 85–98.
14. *Met.* V, 7; 1017 a 31–35.
15. *Met.* V, 7; 1017 a 35–b 9.
16. *Met.* VII, 1; 1028 a 10 f.
17. Thomas, *Summa Theologica*, I, 13, 5.
18. *Met.* IV, 1; 1003 a 11.
19. *Met.* IV, 1; 1003 a 33.
20. *Met.* VII, 1; 1028 a 10.
21. *Met.* VII, 1; 1028 b 2.

10

1. *Met.* V, 8; 1017 b 10–26.
2. *Phys.* II, 1; 192 b.

3. *Phys.* II, 1; 192 b 33.
4. *Phys.* II, 1; 192 b 22.
5. *Cat.* V; 2 a 11–18; *Cat.* V; 2 b 7.

11

1. Heidegger, *SuZ*, p. 324 and 362.
2. *Phaedo* 79 A.
3. Nietzsche, *Werke*, II, 38.

12

1. E.g., *Met.* III, 4; 999 b 2.
2. *Cat.* V; 2 a 11 f and 2 b 7.
3. *Cat.* V; 3 a 8.
4. *Cat.* V; 2 a 14 and 2 b 7.
5. R. Demos, 'The Structure of Substance according to Aristotle' in *Phil. Phen. Res.*, 5 (1945), pp. 255–68; D. Sachs, 'Does Aristotle have a Doctrine of Secondary Substances?' in *Mind*, 25 (1948), pp. 221–25; Chang-Hwan Chen, 'Aristotle's Concept of Primary Substance in Books Z and H of the Metaphysics' in *Phronesis*, 2 (1957), pp. 46–59.
6. *Met.* X, 1; 1053 b 16.
7. *Met.* V, 8; 1017 b 21 and *Cat.* V; 2 a 14; *Cat* .VII; 8 a 13–15.
8. Cf. Gredt, 180, 2, I, p. 162 and the passage from Thomas cited there: *De pot.* 9, 2 ad 6.

13

1. *Principia*, I, 48, *Oeuvres* VIII, 22.
2. *Meditationes* IV; *Oeuvres* VII, 53, 19–22.
3. *Principia* I, 51; *Oeuvres* VIII, 24.
4. *Ibid.*, I, 52; *Oeuvres* VIII, 24 f.
5. *Ibid.*, I, 51; *Oeuvres* VIII, 24.
6. *Ibid.*, I, 52–54; *Oeuvres* VIII, 24–26.
7. *Ibid.*
8. Leibniz, *De primae phil. emendatione*; *E* 122 a, *GP* IV, p. 468 f.
9. Whitehead, *PR*, p. 9 f.
10. Heidegger, *SuZ*, 19–21.

14

1. *NE Introduction; E* 194 a; *GP* V, 41; *Ak.* VI, 6, 47.
2. *Theodizee* I, 20; *E* 510 a; *GP* VI, 115; *Monadologie* 43; *E* 708 b; *GP* VI, 615; *NE* IV, 14; *E* 379 b; *GP* V, 429; *Ak* VI, 6, 447; *Letter to Des Bosses*; *GP* II, 438.
3. *Letter to Thomasius; E* 51 b; *GP* I, 21.
4. *De stylo phil. Nizolii; E* 63 b; *GP* IV, 147.
5. *NE* I, 3, 18; *E* 221 a; *GP* V, 96; *Ak* VI, 6, 105.
6. *Letter to Bierling; E* 678 b; *GP* VII, 502.
7. *Theodizee*, Causa Dei . . ., 58; *E* 657 a; *GP* VI, 447.
8. *Monadalogie* 25; *E* 707 a; *GP* VI, 611; *NE* II, 9, 11; *E* 235 b; *GP* V, 126; *Ak* VI, 6, 139.
9. *Monadologie* 29; *E* 707 b; *GP* VI, 611.
10. *Ibid.*, 14–15; *E* 706 a; *GP* VI, 608 f.
11. Hegel, *Werke* XIX, p. 461, note.
12. *Letter to Dangicourt; E* 745 b.
13. *De modo distinguendi . . .; E* 445 a/b; *GP* VII, 322.

14. *Letter to Clarke*, III, 4; *E* 752 a; *GP* VII, 363; cf. also *E* 756 a/b; *GP* VII, 372 f.; *E* 760; *GP* VII, 384 f.; *E* 766, *GP* VII, 395 f.
15. *Letter to Des Bosses; E* 713 a/b; *GP* II, 486.
16. *NE* II, 12, 3; *E* 238 b; *GP* V, 132; *Ak* VI, 6, 145.
17. *Considérations sur le principe de vie* . . .*; E* 430 a; *GP* VI, 540 f., and *Monadologie* 79; *E* 711 b; *GP* VI, 620.
18. *Letter to Remond; E* 702 a; *GP* III, 606, and *Letter to Foucher; GP* I, 391 f.
19. Cf. G. Martin, *Leibniz*, 36.
20. *De ipsa natura* . . .*; E* 156 b; *GP* IV, 508, and *Specimen dynamicum* . . ., *GM* VI, 236 ff.

15

1. B 307.
2. *Schriften*, V, 50.
3. *Schriften*, V, 54.
4. *Schriften*, V, 55.
5. *Schriften*, V, 56.
6. *Schriften*, V, 46.
7. *Schriften*, V, 53.
8. A 566, B 594.
9. Jacobi, *Werke*, II, 304.

16

1. *Grundzüge einer Metaphysik der Erkenntnis*, 1. Ed., Berlin, 1921.
2. *Zur Grundlegung der Ontologie*, Ontologie 1. Bd., Berlin, 1936
3. *Möglichkeit und Wirklichkeit*, Ontologie 2. Bd., Berlin, 1938.
4. *Der Aufbau der realen Welt*, Ontologie 3. Bd., Berlin, 1940.
5. *Zur Grundlegung der Ontologie*, p. 151 and p. 241.
6. *Ibid.*, pp. 242–322.
7. *Grundlegung*, p. 65.
8. *Ibid.*, p. 66.
9. *Ibid.*, p. 312.
10. *Möglichkeit und Wirklichkeit*, p. 422 ff.; *Grundlegung*, p. 312 f.
11. 'Ziele und Wege der Kategorialanalyse', in *Kleine Schriften*, Berlin, 1955, p. 94, note 1.
12. *Grundlegung*, p. 280, p. 282, p. 314.
13. *Ibid.*, p. 314.
14. *Ibid.*, p. 282.
15. 'Being is independent of being known.' *Grundlegung*, p. 161.
16. Cf. G. Martin, 'Aporetik als phil. Methode' in *Ges. Abhandlungen*, Bd. I. Köln, 1961, p. 195; and in N. Hartmann, *Der Denker und sein Werk*, Ed. by H. Heimsoeth and R. Heiss, Göttingen, 1952, pp. 249–55.

17

1. *SuZ*, p. 39 ff.
2. *SuZ*, pp. 19–21.
3. *SuZ*, p. 27.
4. *SuZ*, p. 324.
5. *SuZ*, p. 27, Macquarrie translation p. 49 f.
6. This holds in spite of the formulation: 'The following investigations have become possible only on the foundation laid by E. Husserl . . .' and note 1 on p. 38.
7. *SuZ*, p. 27, Macquarrie translation p. 50.
8. *SuZ*, 7, pp. 28–39.

9. *SuZ*, p. 28.
10. *SuZ*, p. 227, Macquarrie translation p. 269 f.
11. *SuZ*, p. 226, Macquarrie translation, p. 269.
12. *SuZ*, p. 41.
13. *SuZ*, p. 193.
14. *SuZ*, p. 193, 'Care, as a primordial structural totality, lies "before" every factical "attitude" and "situation" of Dasein, and it does so existentially *a priori*; this means that it always lies *in* them.' Macquarrie translation, p. 238.
15. *SuZ*, p. 19.
16. *SuZ*, p. 21.
17. *SuZ*, p. 47.
18. *SuZ*, p. 47, note 1.
19. *SuZ*, p. 48, note 1.
20. *SuZ*, p. 4, 6, 38.
21. *SuZ*, p. 94.
22. *Met.* X, 2; 1053 b 16–21.

18

1. *Principia Mathematica*, Oxford, 1910 f.
2. H. Scholz, *Mathesis Universalis*, Basel, 1961, p. 388 ff.
3. *PR*, p. 32 ff.
4. *Ibid.*, p. 64.
5. *Ibid.*, p. 124.
6. *Ibid.*, p. 223 ff.
7. *Ibid.*, p. 317 ff.
8. *Ibid.*, p. 321 f.
9. *Ibid.*, p. 65.
10. Whitehead, *Science and the Modern World*, Cambridge, 1953, p. 98 f.
11. *Ibid.*, p. 174 f.
12. *PR*, p. 447.
13. Whitehead, *Science and the Modern World*, p. 196 f. and I. Leclerc, *The Relevance of Whitehead*, London, 1961, p. 175.
14. *PR*, p. 54 and I. Leclerc, *op. cit.*, p. 176 f.
15. Whitehead, *Modes of Thought*, Cambridge, 1938, p. 96 and I. Leclerc, *op. cit.*, p. 176.
16. Cf. I. Leclerc, 'Form and Actuality' in *The Relevance of Whitehead*, pp. 69–89.

19

1. Locke, *Essay*, II, 12, 6 and II, 13, 17.
2. Leibniz, *NE* II, 12, 6; *E* 238 b, *GP* V, 133, *Ak.* VI, 6, 145. *NE* II, 13, 19; *E* 240 b f., *GP* V, 137, *Ak.* VI, 6, 650.
3. Gredt I, 161 ff., and 179 f.
4. Descartes, *Principia* I, 51; *Oeuvres* VIII, 24.
5. A 147, B 186.
6. A 146, B 186.
7. A 80, B 106.
8. B 131.
9. B 132.
10. *Schriften* XIV, 213.
11. *Met.* V, 8; 1017 b 10 ff.
12. *Cat.* V; 2 a 11–19.
13. Cf. 10 above. Aristotle gives enumerations in several passages: *Met.* V, 8; 1017 b 10–13 and *Met.* VIII, 2; 1028 b 8–13 and *Phys.* II, 1; 192 b 8–11.

14. *Met.* V, 8; 1017 b 23/4.
15. *Met.* I, 3; 983 b 9/10.
16. *Phys.* II, 1; 192 b 14.
17. *Phys.* II, 1; 192 b 14–16.
18. *De generatione* II, 3; 330 a 30 ff.
19. *Sophist* 247 E.
20. Leibniz, *De primae philosophiae emendatione* . . .; *E* 121 b, *GP* IV, 468.
21. *Ibid.*, *E* 122 a, *GP* IV, 468 9.
22. Leibniz, *NE* II, 12, 6; *E* 238 b; and *NE*, II, 13, 19 (See note 2).
23. Leibniz, *Letter to Des Bosses*; *E* 686 a, *GP* II, 457 and *Discours de Metaphysique*, S 8; *E* 819 b, *GP* IV, 432.
24. Leibniz, *Rémarques sur la lettre de M. Arnauld*; *GP* II, 43.
25. Leibniz, *De primae philosophiae emendatione* . . .; *E* 121 f., *GP* IV, 468 f.
26. Leibniz, *Dd ipsa natura*; *E* 156 b, *GP* IV, 508.
27' Leibniz, *Theodizee* 393; *E* 617 b, *GP* VI, 530.
28. Leibniz, *Monadologie* 1; *E* 705 a, *GP* VI, 607.
29. *Ibid.*, 63; *E* 710 a, *GP* VI, 617.
30. Leibniz, *Examen* . . .; *E* 693 b, *GP* VI, 586 and *Letter to Hanschium*, *E* 445 a ff.; *Letter to Foucher*, *GP* I, 391 2.
31. *Sophist* 247 E.
32. *Ibid.*, 248 E/249 A.
33. Leibniz, *De primae philosophiae emendatione* . . .; *E* 122 a, *GP* IV, 469.
34. Heidegger, *SuZ*, p. 96.
35. *Ibid.*, p. 95.
36. *Ibid.*, p. 41.
37. *Ibid.*, p. 11 (4).
38. Whitehead, *PR*, p. 443.

20

1. Homer, *Odyssy*, 18, 192.
2. Passow, *Griechisches Wörterbuch*, 5. ed., Leipzig, 1851 ff., p. 1565 b.
3. *Cat.* IV; 1 b 27 and *Cat.* XV; 15 b 17 ff.
4. *Cat.* XV; 15 b 22.
5. *Cat.* IV; 2 a 3.
6. *Cat.* IV; 2 a 3.
7. G. Martin, *Ockham* 48, p. 211 ff.
8. Thomas, *Sum. theol.* I, 11, 1 ad primum.
9. *Ibid.*, III, 77, 1, c. and *Sum. C. Gent.* IV, 63.
10. Thomas, *I. Sent* 12, 1; cf. also Gredt II, 20, p. 155 and F. Brentano, *Von den mannigfachen Bedeutung des Seienden nach Aristoteles*, Freiburg, 1862, Cap. V, 10.
11. Thomas, *I. Sent.* 26, 2, 1; *De Pot.* 7, 11, c.; *Sum. theol.* I, 28, 1, c.
12. Ockham, *Sum. tot. log.* I, 55.
13. *Met.* V, 14; 1020 b 9 and *De generatione* . . . II, 1–8; 328 b 26 to 335 a 23.
14. *Met.* V, 14; 1020 b 10.
15. Democritus A 45, Diels II, 95 and according to Aristotle, *Phys.* 1, 5; 188 a 22.
16. Democritus B 125, Diels II, 168.
17. Descartes *Principia* I, 53; *Oeuvres* VIII, 25, 14 f.
18. *Ibid.*, IV, 29; *Oeuvres* VIII, 218.
19. *Ibid.*, I, 69; *Oeuvres* VIII, 33/4.
20. E.g. H. Herz, *Prinzipien der Mechanik*, 2. ed., Leipzig, 1910, Vol. III, p. 54.
21. *Ibid.*, Vol. III, p. 13.
22. Locke, *Essay* I, 8, 9/10.

23. Leibniz, *Monadologie* 14/15; *E* 706 a, *GP* VI, 608 f.
24. A 166, B 207.
25. Whitehead, *PR*, p. 447.

21

1. Leibniz, *De modo distinguendi*; *E* 444 a, *GP* VII, 320.
2. A 265, B 321 and A 285, B 341.
3. *Sophist* 255 B ff.
4. *Cat.* IV; 1 b 27 and *Met.* V, 15; 1020 b 25 to 1021 b 12.
5. *Met.* XIV, 1; 1088 a 23.
6. B. Russell, *A Critical Exposition of the Philosophy of Leibniz*, 2. ed., London, 1951, p. 9 and p. 12.
7. L. Couturat, *La Logique de Leibniz*, Hildesheim, 1961, p. 210 and Russell, *op. cit.*, p. 17.
8. Leibniz, *Letter to Wagner*; *E* 420 a, *GP* VIII 516 and cf. Couturat, *loc. cit.*, and G. Martin, *Leibniz*, 7.
9. N. Hartmann, *Möglichkeit und Wirklichkeit*, Vorwort, p. iii f.
10. *Met.* XIII, 2; 1077 a 9.
11. G. Martin, *Ockham*, 29.
12. G. Martin, *Leibniz* 8 and 30.
13. *Phaedo* 74 A.
14. *Sophist* 255 D.
15. B. Russell, *The Principles of Mathematics*, 2. ed., London, 1937, p. 7 f.
16. Plotinus, *Enn.* VI, 1; 1053, 15.
17. Cajetan, according to Gredt II, 164.
18. Suarez, *Disp. Met.*, d. 47, p. 11, *Opera* II; 2, 500. 1, CD and cf. F. Brentano, *op. cit.*, Chap. V, 10; A. Horvath, *Metaphysik der Relationen*, Graz, 1914, p. 49 and A. D. Sertillanges, *Der Hl. Thomas von Aquin*, Köln, 1954, p. 116.
19. Ockham, *I. Sent.* I, 30, 1 ff.
20. Thomas, *Sum. theol.* I, 13, 7.
21. Thomas, *I. Sent.*, d. 31 q.1. and *Comm. in met.* (to *Met.* X, 3).
22. Duns Scotus, *Op. ex.* II, d. 1 q. 4; *Opera* XI, 101 b and 173 b; *Op. ex.* I, d. 19 q. 1; *Opera* X, 170 a, Rome, V, p. 286 f.
23. Duns Scotus, *Op. ox.* II, d. 1 q. 4; *Opera* XI, 101 ff.
24. *Ibid.*, I, d. 31 q. unica; *Opera* X, 489 a ff., Rome, VI, 203 ff.
25. Ockham, in *I. Sent.* d. 30 q.1.
26. G. Martin, *Ockham* 46.
27. Leibniz, *Letter to Clarke*, V, 47; *E* 769 a, *GP* VII, 401; in the translation of Cassirer (Ed.): *Leibniz' Hauptschriften*, Leipzig, 1903, Vol. 1, p. 184 f.
28. B. Russell, *Principles* . . ., p. 7 f.
29. Whitehead, *PR*, p. 35.
30. Heidegger, *SuZ*, p. 87 ff.
31. Leibniz, *NE* II, 25; *E* 276 a, *GP* V, 210, *Ak.* VI, 6, 227 and *NE* II, 12, 3; *E* 238 b, *GP* V, 132, *Ak.* VI, 6, 145.
32. Leibniz, *Letter to Clarke* V, 47; *E* 769 a, *GP* VII, 401.
33. Leibniz, *Principes de la nature* . . . 3; *E* 713 a, *GP* VI, 498 f.
34. Leibniz, *Letter to Des Bosses*; *E* 436 a, *GP* II, 305.
35. Leibniz, *Dialogus de connexione inter res et verba*; *E* 77 a.

22

1. B 133 f.
2. G. Ryle, 'Plato and Parmenides' in *Mind*, 48 (1939) p. 146 f.
3. *Met.* III, 4; 1001 a 4.

4. Thomas, *De veritate*, I, 1, c.
5. Duns Scotus, *Rep. par.* II, 1, 6; *Opera* 23, 555 b.
6. G. Martin, *Ockham*, 7, 16, 29, 46.
7. *Parmenides* 129 CD.
8. Thomas, *Sum. Theol.* I, 11, 1, ad primum.
9. *Ibid.*
10. *Ibid.*
11. Leibniz, *De Principio Individui*; *E* 5 a; *GP* IV, 25; *Ak.* VI, 1, 18.
12. Duns Scotus, *Op. ox.* II, 1, 4; *Opera* XI, 122 a. cf. also P. Minges, 'Die distinctio formalis des Duns Scotus' in Theol. *Quartalsschrift* 90 (1908) abd *J. Duns Scoti doctrina phil. et theol.*, Quaracchi, 1908.
13. Duns Scotus, *Rep. par.* I, 19, 3; *Opera* XXII, 236 a.
14. Ockham, *Sum. tot. log.*, I, 55.
15. Ockham, *I. Sent.* 30, 1.
16. Ockham, *I. Sent.* 30, 5, 1.
17. G. Martin, *Ockham*, p. 217 and the same 'Ist Ockhams Relationstheorie Nominalismus?' in *Franzisk. Studien* 32 (1950), *Ges. Abhandlungen*, 1961, p. 19 ff.
18. *Met.* X, 2; 1053 b 20.
19. *Met.* X, 2; 1054 a 13.
20. *Met.* X, 2; 1054 a 16.
21. Thomas, *Sum. Theol.* I, 11, 1 ad primum.
22. *Met.* IV, 2; 1003 b 22.
23. In many places, e.g., *Phaedo* 80 B.

23

1. *Met.* XIII, 1; 1076 a 36.
2. *Laches* 192 B.
3. Whitehead, *Science and the Modern World*, Cambridge, 1953, p. 26.
4. Bolzano, *WL* 19; I, 78.
5. R. Carnap, 'Uberwindung der Metaphysik durch logische Analyse der Sprache' in *Erkenntnis* 2 (1931) p. 233 f.
6. W. Stegmüller, *Das Wahrheitsproblem und die Idee der Semantik*, Vienna, 1957, p. 263.
7. R. Carnap, *op. cit.*, 227 ff.
8. W. Stegmüller, *op. cit.*, 262 ff.
9. R. Carnap, *op. cit.*, 235.

24

1. K. Bühler, *Sprachtheorie*, Jena, 1934, p. 256 ff.
2. *Ibid.*, p. 74.
3. *Ibid.*, p. 73 ff. and p. 398 ff.
4. *De interpretatione* 4; 16 a 26 ff.
5. W. Porzig, *Das Wunder der Sprache*, Bern, 1957, p. 109 ff.
6. Leibniz, *Letter to Vagetius*; *Ak.* II, 1, 497 and *Monadologie* 33/34; *E* 707 b, *GP* VI, 612.
7. Leibniz, *NE* I, 1, 4; *E* 207, *GP* V, 68, *Ak.* VI, 6, 75 and *NE* I, 1, 18; *E* 210 b, *GP* V, 78, *Ak.* VI, 6, 82.
8. Leibniz, *Theodizee* 44; *E* 515 b, *GP* VI, 127 and *Letter to Clarke* II, 1; *E* 748 b, *GP* VII, 356.
9. Leibniz, *NE* II, 21, 3; *E* 250 a, *GP* V, 156, *Ak.* VI, 6, 170 and *Euclidis Prota*, *GM* V, 183.
10. Leibniz, *Letter to Clarke* II, 1; *E* 748 a, *GP* VII, 355.
11. *Met.* IV, 3–8; 1005 a 19 ff.

12. *Republic* 510.
13. *Ibid.*, 526.
14. *Ibid.*, 527 D ff.
15. *Met.* I, 2; 982 a 28, *Met.* I, 8; 989 b 33, *Met.* I, 9; 991 a 28, *Met.* VII, 1; 1046 a 8, *Met.* XIII, 3; 1077 b 22, *Met.* XIII, 3; 1077 b 29 and *Phys.* II, 2; 193 b 26.
16. A 80, B 106.
17. A 142 f., B 181 f.
18. A 70, B 95.
19. A 161, B 200.
20. B 150 f.
21. B 19.
22. H. Cohen, *Kants Theorie der Erfahrung*, 3. ed., Berlin, 1918, Chap. VII.
23. For a more exact determination of logic see 41.
24. For a more exact determination of arithmetic see 28.

25

1. F. M. Cornford, *Plato and Parmenides*, London, 1951, p. 154.
2. *Met.* V, 6; 1015 b 16–34 and *Met.* X, 1; 1052 a 18/19.
3. *Met.* V, 6; 1015 b 34–1016 a 3 and *Met.* X, 1; 1052 a 20.
4. *Met.* VII, 17; 1041 b 12.
5. *Met.* V, 6; 1016 a 1 and X, 1; 1052 a 24.
6. *Ibid.*
7. *Met.* X, 1; 1052 a 24.
8. *Met.* V, 6; 1016 a 1.
9. *Met.* V, 6; 1016 a 3 and X, 1; 1052 a 20 f.
10. *Met.* V, 6; 1016 a 8.
11. *Met.* V, 6; 1016 a 17–32 and X, 1; 1052 a 22/23.
12. *De coelo* II, 4; 285 b 4.
13. *Met.* V, 6; 1016 b 3 and X, 1; 1052 a 27.
14. *Met.* X, 1; 1052 a 28.
15. *Met.* V, 6; 1016 a 32–b 1 and X, 1; 1052 a 29–34.
16. Leibniz, *Letter to Des Bosses*; E 685 b; GP II, 457.
17. Leibniz, *Monadologie* 1; E 705 a; GP VI, 607.
18. Leibniz, *NE* II, 12, 7; E 238 b; *GP* V, 133; *Ak.* VI, 6, 146 and *Eclaircissement* . . . E 131 a; *GP* IV, 494.
19. Leibniz, *Letter to Des Bosses*; E 685 b; GP II, 457.
20. Leibniz, *De rerum originatione radicali*; E 147 a; *GP* VII, 302 and *NE* II, 13, 21; E 241 a; *GP* V, 138; *Ak.* VI, 6, 151.
21. Leibniz, *Letter to Des Bosses*; E 439 a; GP II, 314.
22. B 130 f.
23. A 80, B 106.
24. H. Cohen, *Kants Theorie der Erfahrung*, p. 674 f.

26

1. *Republic* 505 A, 509 B, 517 B C.
2. *Sophist* 218 ff.
3. H. Leisegang, *Die Platondeutung der Gegenwart*, Karlsruhe, 1929.
4. *Sophist* 257 A.
5. *Ibid.*, 254 D, 255 A/C.
6. *Ibid.*, 254 D, 255 C/E.
7. Leibniz, *Meditationes*; E 80 b, GP IV, 424.
8. *Ibid.*

9. Leibniz; cf. *Theodizee* 99; *E* 660 a; *GP* VI, 453 and *NE* II, 2, 1; *E* 227 a, *GP* V, 109, *Ak.* VI, 6, 120 and *NE* II, 21, 3; *E* 250 a, *GP* V, 156, *Ak.* VI, 6, 170 as well as *NE* II, 30, 3; *E* 292 a, *GP* V, 245, *Ak.* VI, 6, 264.
10. Leibniz, *Discours de Métaphysique* 8; *E* 819 b, *GP* IV, 433.
11. Leibniz, *Meditationes*; *E* 80 a, *GP* IV, 424.
12. Leibniz, *De synthesi et analysi universalis* . . .; *GP* VII, 294.
13. Augustine, *De diversis quaestionibus*, LXXXIII, q. 46, n. 2; *ML* 40, 30.
14. Leibniz, *Monadology* 43; *E* 708 b, *GP* VI, 614.
15. Leibniz, *Theodizee* I, 20; *E* 510 a, *GP* VI, 115.
16. A 80 f., 5 106 f.
17. A 81 f., B 107 f.
18. A 137 ff., B 176 ff.
19. A 334, B 391.
20. A 408, B 435 ff.
21. A 462 ff., B 490 ff.
22. A 476, B 504.
23. A 528, B 556.
24. Hegel, *Werke*, IV, 227 and IV, 545 ff.
25. Hegel, *Werke*, XVII, 290 and 344 and IV, 32.
26. Hegel, *Werke*, IV, 17.
27. Hegel, *Werke*, IV, 227 and IV, 545 ff.
28. Hegel, *Werke*, IV, 46.
29. Hegel, *Werke*, IV, 52.
30. *Ibid.*
31. Hegel, *Werke*, XVIII, 225.
32. Bolzano, *WL* 54; I, 237 and 48; I, 215.
33. Bolzano, *WL* 19; I, 77.
34. *Ibid.*, I, 78.
35. *Ibid.*
36. *Ibid.*, I, 76.
37. *Ibid.*, 55; I, 239.
38. Husserl, *LU* I, 63; I, 231.
39. Husserl, *Ideen*, p. 135/6.
40. Husserl, *LU*, 70; I, 250.
41. *Ibid.*, I, 251.
42. *Ibid.*
43. *Ibid.*, I, 250.
44. *Ibid.*, 69; I, 247.
45. *Ibid.*, 60; I, 219.
46. Husserl, *Ideen*, p. 134.
47. Husserl, *LU* 69; I, 247.
48. *Ibid.*, I, 247 f.

27

1. *PM* II, 83; Theorem 110, 643.
2. G. Frege, *Grundgesetze der Arithmetik*, 2. ed., Darmstadt, 1962, p. 253 f.
3. Whitehead, 'Mathematics and the Good' in *Science and Philosophy*, New York, 1948, p. 111.
4. B. Russell, *Principles*, 100, p. 101.
5. *PM* I, 60.
6. *Ibid.*, I, 77.
7. *Ibid.*, I, 60.
8. G. Ryle, 'Plato and Parmenides' in *Mind*, 48 (1939) p. 135, 147.

9. Vlastos, 'The Third Man Argument in the Parmenides' in *Philosophical Review*, 63 (1954) p. 319 ff.
10. G. Hessenberg, 'Grundbegriffe der Mengenlehre', in *Abh. der Frieschen Schule*, *NF* I, 1904, p. 633.
11. Fraenkel and Bar-Hillel, *Foundations of Set Theory*, Amsterdam, 1958, p. 3.
12. Leibniz, *Theodizee* 44; *E* 515 b, *GP* VI, 27.
13. Husserl, *Ideen* 72, p. 133 f.
14. D. Hilbert, *Grundlagen der Geometrie*, Leipzig-Berlin, 1913, pp. 238–48.
15. cf. H. Scholz, *Mathesis Universalis*, p. 406.
16. Leibniz, *De cognitione, veritate et ideis*; *E* 80 b, *GP* IV, 425.
17. G. Martin, *Leibniz*, 17.
18. D. Hilbert, *Grundlagen der Geometrie*, p. 250 and p. 258.
19. B. Russell, *Principles*, p. 104 f.
20. *PM* Introduction, Chap. 2; I, 37 ff.
21. *PM* I, 48.
22. *PM* I, 127 f.
23. W. v. Quine, 'Whitehead' in *Great Philosophers*, p. 152.
24. B. Russell, *Principles*, p. 692.
25. cf. Quine, *op. cit.*, p. 153.
26. Whitehead, 'Mathematics and the Good', p. 111.
27. L. Brouwer, *Over de grondlagen der wiskunde*, Amsterdam and Leipzig, 1907, p. 8
28. cf. Kronecker, *Werke*, III, 1, p. 274.
29. cf. P. Lorenzen, *Einführung in die operative Logik und Mathematik*, Berlin, Göttingen, Heidelberg, 1955.
30. cf. G. Hessenberg, *op. cit.*
31. Leibniz, *Letter to Des Bosses*; *E* 439 a, *GP* II, 316 ff.
32. A 506, B 534.
33. Fraenkel, Bar-Hillel, *Foundations*, Cap. V, 6, p. 303 ff.

28

1. K. Gödel, 'Über formal unentscheidbare Sätze' in *Monatsheft für Mathematik und Physik*, 38 (1931), pp. 173–98.
2. B. Rosser, 'An Informal Exposition of Proofs of Gödel's Theorem and Church's Theorem' in *Journal of Symbolic Logic*, 4 (1938), pp. 53–60.
3. A. Mostovsky, *Sentences Undecidable in Formalized Arithmetic, An Exposition of the Theory of Kurt Gödel*, Amsterdam, 1952.
4. W. Stegmuller, *Unvollständigkeit und Unentscheidbarkeit*, Vienna, 1959.
5. Fraenkel and Bar–Hillel, *Foundations*, Chap. V, 6, p. 303 ff.
6. K. Gödel, *op. cit.*, p. 174.
7. *Ibid.*, p. 186.
8. *Ibid.*, p. 175 and 190.
9. *Ibid.*, p. 187.
10. *Ibid.*, p. 175.
11. Fraenkel and Bar–Hillel, *Foundations*. p. 10.
12. K. Gödel, *op. cit.*, p. 193.
13. Husserl, *LU* I, p. 251.
14. K. Gödel, *op. cit.*, p. 176 and p. 196.
15. K. Gödel, *op. cit.*, p. 196.

29

1. Leibniz, *Letter to Clarke* II, 1; *E* 748 a; *GP* VII, 355.
2. Leibniz, *Letter to Varignon*; *GM* IV, 92 f. *Leibnitiana, Elementa Philosophiae arcanae de summa rerum*, ed. J. Jagodinsky, Kasan, 1914, Fragment 120.

NOTES

3. G. Saccheri, *Euclides ab omni naevo vindicatus*, Milan, 1733, Theorem XXXIII.
4. R. Bonola, *Die nicht-euklidische Geometrie*, trans. by H. Libmann, Leipzig–Berlin, 1908, p. 45.
5. J. H. Lambert, *Theorie der Parallelinien*, cited in the new edition of F. Engel and P. Stäckel, *Theorie der Parallelinien von Euklid bis auf Gauss*, Leipzig, 1895, 82, p. 202 f.; cf. also W. S. Peters: *J. H. Lamberts* . . . Diss., Bonn, 1961, p. 60.
6. Kant, *Schriften* I, 23/24.
7. W. Bolyai, *Theoria Parallelorum*, Math. Annalen 49 (1897).
8. cf. N. J. Lobaschevsky, *Geometrische Untersuchungen zur Theorie der Parallelinien*, Berlin, 1840.
9. Gauss, *Werke*, VIII, 159 ff.
10. B. Riemann, *Ges. math. Werke*, 1. ed., Leipzig, 1892, Vol. 1, p. 254 ff.
11. H. Poincaré, *Wissenschaft und Hypothese*, Leipzig, 1906, p. 42 f.
12. A. Einstein, 'Auf die Riemann–Metrik u. dem Fernparallelismus gegründete einheitliche Feldtheorie, *Math. Annalen*, 102, p. 685 f. Cf. also K. Menger, 'Die Relativitätstheorie und die Geometrie', in *Living Philosophers: Einstein*, ed. by Schilpp, p. 328 ff. (German Edition).
13. B. Riemann, *Werke*, I, p. 283 f. and note 10.
14. H. Poincaré, *op. cit.*, p. 49.
15. Husserl, *LU* I, 232 and I, 250 f.
16. D. Hilbert, *Grundlagen*, 12.
17. F. Gonseth, *Determinisme et libre arbitre*, Neuchâtel, 1944, p. 150.
18. P. Bernays, 'Grundsätzliches zur "philosophie ouverte",' in *Dialectica* 2 (1948), p. 273 ff.
19. G. Hasenjäger, *Einführung in die Grundbegriffe* . . ., Munich, 1962, p. 127.
20. Fraenkel and Bar-Hillel, *Foundations*.
21. N. Bohr, *Kausalität and Komplementarität in Erkenntnis*, 6 (1936), p. 293 f.
22. W. Heisenberg, *Wandlungen in den Grundlagen der Nat.-wiss.*, 6 ed., Leipzig, 1945, p. 46.
23. Cf. M. Planck, *Wege zur physikal. Erkenntnis*, 4. ed., Leipzig, 1944, p. 135.
24. E. Schrödinger, *Anmerkungen zum Kausalproblem*, Erkenntnis, 3 (1932/33), p. 65 ff.
25. L. de Broglie, *Die Elementarteilchen*, Hamburg, 1946, p. 68 f.
26. D'Alembert, Discours préliminaire de l'Encyclopédie in *Oeuvres philosophiques, historiques et littéraires*, Paris, An XIII (1805), I, p. 232–33.
27. H. Hankel, *Die Entwicklung der Mathematik in den letzten Jahrhunderten*, Akadem. Antrittsrede, Tübingen, 1869, p. 34.

30

1. Husserl, *LU* I, pp. 251–2.
2. H. Hankel, *Vorlesungen über die complexen Zahlen und ihre Functionen*, I, Teil, *Theorie der complexen Zahlsysteme*, Leipzig, 1867, I, p. 11.
3. Gauss, *Werke*, II, 178.
4. Dedekind, *Werke*, III, 315.
5. M. Cantor, *Vorlesungen über die Gesch. der Math.*, 4. ed., Leipzig–Berlin, 1922, I, p. 128; and cf. Aristotle, *Met.* V, 15; 1021 a 13.
6. Kronecker, *Werke*, III, I, p. 274.
7. G. Martin, *Arithmetik und Kombinatorik bei Kant*, Itzehoe, 1938.
8. G. Peano, *Arithmetices Principia*, Turin, 1889.
9. Bar-Hillel, *op. cit.*, p. 165–6.
10. D. Hilbert, *Grundlagen*, 12.
11. Bar–Hillel, *op. cit.*, p. 165–6.
12. B VIII.

13. Leibniz, *Letter to Wagner*, E 420 a, *GP* VII, 516; *E* 421 b, *GP* VII, 519; *E* 423 b, *GP* VII, 522.
14. Scholz, *Mathesis*, p. 400.
15. *PM* I, 1, A1, p. 90 ff.
16. Wittgenstein, *Tractatus* 5. 1 ff.
17. J. Lukasiewicz and A. Tarski, *Untersuchungen über den Aussagenkalkül*, Comptes rendues des Séances de la Société des Sciences et des Lettres de Varsovie, Warsaw C1. III, Vol. 23 (1930), p. 38 ff.
18. *Ibid.*, p. 41.
19. J. Lukasiewicz, *Philosophische Bemerkungen zu mehrwertigen Systemen des Aussagenkalküls, loc. cit.*, p. 75.
20. H. Reichenbach, *Philosophical Foundations of Quantum Mechanics*, Berkeley, Los Angeles, 1948.
21. G. Günther, *Idee und Grundriss einer nicht-aristotelischen Logik*, Hamburg, 1959.
22. P. Linke, 'Die mehrwertigen Logiken', *ZphF* 3 (1948), p. 539 f.
23. Lewis and Langford, *Symbolic Logic*, New York, 1932.
24. O. Becker, *Einführung in die Logistik, vorzüglich in den Modalkalkül*, Meisenheim, 1951.
25. N. Hartmann, *Möglichkeit und Wirklichkeit*, p. 95 ff.
26. L. E. J. Brouwer, 'Mathematik, Wissenschaft und Sprache' in *Monatshefte f. Math. u. Phys.* 36 (1929), p. 153 to 164; and Fraenkel, *Foundations*, p. 227 ff.
27. A. Heyting, *Les Fondements des mathématiques, Intuitionisme, Théorie de la demonstration*, Paris, 1955, Collection de Logique math., Série A IX.
28. Euclid, *Elementa* IX, 20.
29. P. Lorenzen, *Operative Logik*, p. 3.

31

1. *Parmenides* 135 c f.
2. Kant, *Schriften* V, 53.
3. A 321, B 378.
4. Kant, *Schriften* V, 49.
5. Leibniz, *Letter to Clarke* II, 1, *E* 748 a/b, *GP* VII, pp. 355–6.
6. Cf. G. Martin, *Leibniz* 7.
7. Husserl, *LU* I, pp. 250–51.
8. Husserl, *LU* I, p. 251.
9. Husserl, *LU* I, p. 232.
10. Husserl, *LU* I, p. 249.
11. Husserl, *LU* I, p. 251 f.
12. P. Natorp, *Die logischen Grundlagen der exakten Wissenschaften*, Leipzig–Berlin, 1921, p. 253.

32

1. H. Leisegang, *Platondeutung der Gegenwart*, Karlsruhe, 1929.
2. H. W. B. Joseph, *An Introduction to Logic*, Oxford, 1961, p. 130 and Gredt I, p. 143.
3. *Sophist* 218 ff.
4. *Anal. Post.* II, 13 ff.; 77 b 21 ff.
5. Gredt, 33, I, 39.
6. Leibniz, *Meditationes*; *E* 79 b, *GP* IV, 423.
7. *Met.* V, 3; 1014 b 9 f.
8. Leibniz, *Discours de Mét.* 8, *E* 819 b, *GP* IV, 433.
9. Leibniz, *Meditationes E* 79 b, *GP* IV, 423.
10. *Met.* V, 3; 1014 b 9 f., and *Anal. Post.* I, 19–23; 81 a 10 ff.
11. Euclid, *Elementa* I, def. 1.

Notes

12. *Ibid.*, def. 4.
13. *Ibid.*, def. 7.
14. Leibniz, *Letter to Giordano*, 1689. *GM* I, 196 and Couturat, *Logique*, Chap. VI, 14, p. 201.
15. O. Becker, *Grundlagen*, p. 203.
16. Euclid, *Elementa* VII, 2.
17. *Met.* X, 1; 1053 a 30.
18. *Parmenides* 143 C–144 A.
19. Duns Scotus, *Op. ox.* I, 24, q. un.; *Opera* X, 268 b f.; Rome V, 366 f.
20. Leibniz, *NE* IV, 7, 10; *E* 363 b, *GP* V, 394, *Ak.* VI, 6, 413 f.
21. *Met.* V, 6; 1016 b 23.
22. Thomas, *Comm. in met.* 866–7, 874–5.
23. G. Cantor, *Ges. Abhandlungen*, p. 289.
24. *Ibid.*, p. 290.
25. Frege, *Grundgesetze*, 41, I, 57.
26. *Ibid.*, 42, I, 58.
27. *PM* I, 216 f.
28. *PM* I, 347.
29. *PM* I, 340.
30. *PM* I, 168.
31. *PM* I, 360.
32. *PM* I, 369.
33. *Met.* XIII, 7; 1081 a 15.

33

1. *Anal. Post.* I, 19–23, in particular 84 a 30.
2. Leibniz, *NE* IV, 7, 1; *E* 360 a, *GP* V, 388, *Ak.* VI, 6, 407.
3. Leibniz, *Letter to Clarke* II, 1; *E* 748 a, *GP* VII, 355.
4. Husserl, *Ideen*, p. 135.
5. A. Tarski, *Über einige fundamentale Begriffe der Metamathematik*, C. R. Warsaw CL. III, 23 (1930), p. 28.
6. R. Bonola, *Die nicht-euklidische Geometrie*, Leipzig, 1919, p. 124 ff.
7. *PM* I, 96 ff.
8. Lukasiewicz and Tarski, *Untersuchungen*, p. 37.
9. Archimedes, *Ausg*, übersetzt von E. Nizze, Stralsund, 1824, p. 12.
10. *Ibid.*, p. 44.
11. Euclid, *Elementa*, V, def. 4.
12. *Phys.* VIII, 10; 266 b 12.
13. D. Hilbert, *Grundlagen* 12 and 33.
14. M. Pasch, *Vorlesung über ebene Geometrie*, 2. ed., Leipzig, 1912, p. 21.
15. G. Peano, *Arithmetices Principia*, Turin, 1889.
16. *PM* II, 200.
17. *PM* II, 203.
18. *PM* II, 200, 203.
19. *PM* II, 125.
20. *PM* II, 203.
21. *PM* II, 263.
22. B. Russell, *Principles of Mathematics* I, 10, p. 8 ff.
23. E. Zermelo, 'Beweis dass jede Menge wohlgeordnet werden kann,' *Math. Annalen* 59 (1904), p. 514.
24. B. Russell, 'On some difficulties in the theory of transfinite numbers and other types' in *Proceedings of the London Math. Society* II, 4 (1907), p. 47 f.

25. *PM* II, 70.
26. T. Skolem, 'Über die Unmöglichkeit einer vollständigen Charakterisierung der Zahlenreihe vermittels eines endlichen Axiomensystems.' *Norsk. Math. Forenings Skrifter* 2, 10 (1933), p. 73 ff.
27. A. Tarski, *op. cit.*, p. 28.

34

1. Husserl, *Ideen*, p. 135.
2. Husserl, *Die Krisis der europäischen Wissenschaft und die transzendentale Phänomenologie*, Den Haag, 1954, Beilage XXVIII to 73 (1935), p. 508. Another interpretion is given in H. G. Gadamer, *Die phänomenologische Bewegung in Philosophische Rundschau* 11 (1963), p. 25 f.; cf. also: H. Scholz, *Mathesis Universalis*, p. 334: 'freed from the dogma of two-valued logic'.

35

1. Euclid, *Elementa* I, Postulata I, 1.
2. *Met.* IV, 3; 1005 a 20 and *Anal. Post.* I, 10; 76 b 23–34.
3. *Republic* 511 B/C.
4. *Met.* II, 3; 998 a 21 and *Met.* V, 1; 1012 b 34; *Anal. Post.* III, 9; 76 a 14.
5. *Republic* 533 D.
6. O. Becker, *Grundlagen der Math. in geschichtlicher Entwicklung*, Freiburg–München, 1954, p. 27.

36

1. Hegel, *Werke*, XVII, 47.

37

1. *Phaedo* 101 C and 104 E.
2. *Ibid.*, 104 D.
3. *Ibid.*, 101 B.
4. *Ibid.*, 101 B.
5. *Republic* 524 E and *Sophist* 244 B.
6. *Phys.* III, 6; 206 b 32; and *Met.* XII, 8; 1037 a 20; *Met.* XIII, 8; 1084 a 12; *Met.* XIII, 8; 1084 a 31.
7. *Met.* I, 6; 987 b 20; *Met.* XIII, 6; 1080 b 7.
8. *Parmenides* 143 C ff.
9. J. Stenzel, *Zahl und Gestalt bei Platon und Aristoteles*, Leipzig–Berlin, 1924.
10. O. Becker, *Zwei Untersuchungen zur antiken Logik*, Wiesbaden, 1957, in particular: Zum Problem der platonischen Idealzahlen, pp. 1–22.
11. *Met.* XIII, Chap. 7 ff.
12. A. E. Taylor, *Plato*, p. 503.
13. Whitehead, 'Mathematics and the Good', p. 69.
14. *Phaedo* 74 A ff.
15. *Met.* I, 9; 990 b 8/9.
16. *Met.* I, 9; 990 b 10/11.
17. *Met.* XIII, 1; 1076 a 36.
18. Philolaus B 11, Diels I, 411 f.

38

1. *Letters* 342 A ff.
2. *Republic* 510 D.

NOTES

3. *Met.* IX, 992 a 15–21.
4. Leibniz, *Dialogus de connexione; E* 77 a; *GP* VII, 191.
5. *Republic* 526 D/E.

39

1. *Republic* 529 CD.
2. *Ibid.*, 530 A.
3. *Timaeus* 39 D.
4. *Republic* 529 CD.
5. *Met.* I, 5; 986 a 8 f.
6. Newton, *Principia* III, Prop. XXIV, Theorema XIX.
7. H. Hertz, *Die Prinzipien der Mechanik*, Leipzig, 1910, Vol. III, p. 53 and H. Hermes, *Eine Axiomatisierung der allgemeinen Mechanik; Forschungen zur Logik*, Neue Folge Heft 3, Leipzig, 1938.
8. Cl. Schäfer, *Die Prinzipe der Dynamik*, Berlin, 1919.
9. M. Planck, *Einführung in die allgemeine Mechanik*, Leipzig, 1938, p. 44.
10. E. Mach, *Erkenntnis und Irrtum*, Leipzig, 1906, p. 192.
11. N. Bohr, 'Diskussion mit Einstein über erkenntnistheoretische Probleme in der Atomphysik' in: *Albert Einstein als Philosoph und Naturforscher*, ed. Schilpp, Stuttgart, 1951, p. 115.
12. Whitehead, *PR*, p. 331 ff.
13. Newton, *Optice*, Lausannae et Genevae, 4. ed., 1740, t. III, q. 31.
14. Leibniz, *Letter to Clarke* I, 4; *E* 746 b, 747 b f.; *GP* VII, 352–3.
15. Leibniz, *Letter to Hanschium*; *E* 748 a/b.
16. Leibniz, *Letter to Clarke* II, 1; *E* 748 a/b. *GP* VII, 355.
17. Leibniz, *Réponse aux Objections contre le Système de l'harmonie Préétablie*; *E* 460 a, *GP* IV, 594.

40

1. *PM* I, pp. 90–126.
2. W. v. O. Quine, *Mathematical Logic*, 2. ed. Cambridge, Mass., 1951.
3. Scholz–Hasenjäger, *Grundzüge der math. Logik*, Berlin, 1961, pp. 13–124.
4. *Ibid.*, p. 120 ff.
5. *Ibid.*, p. 84.
6. Hilbert–Bernays, *Grundlagen* I, 66.
7. H. Scholz, *Mathesis Universalis*, p. 431 ff.
8. Hilbert–Bernays, *op. cit.*, p. 10 f.
9. Bolzano, *WL*, Einleitung 25, p. 112.

41

1. Chr. Wolff, *Cosmologia generalis*, Frankfurt–Leipzig, 1731.
2. *De coelo* II, 4; 287 b 15.
3. *Ibid.*, I, c. 5; 271 b 1 ff.
4. *Ibid.*, II, c. 13; 293 a 15 ff.
5. *Ibid.*, I, 3; 270 b 22.
6. *Ibid.*, II, 12; 292 b 27.
7. *Ibid.*, I, 2; 268 b 11 ff.
8. In many places, e.g., *Met.* XII, 7; 1072 a 18 ff.
9. *Met.* XII, 8; 1073 b 17.
10. *Met.* XII, 8; 1073 b 18 ff.
11. *Met.* XII, 8; cf. *Commentary* of David Ross, Oxford, 1924, p. 393.
12. *Met.* XII, 8; 1074 a 14.

13. *De coelo*, III, 2; 301 a 20 ff.
14. *De generatione et corruptione* II.
15. E.g. *Met.* III, 2; 997 b 20 and *Met.* XIII, 3; 1078 a 14.
16. *Met.* XIII, 3; 1078 a 14.
17. Philolaus B 6, Diels I, 408 ff.
18. *Met.* I, 9; 990 b 11.
19. *Met.* III, 2; 997 b 35.
20. *Met.* III, 2; 998 a 3 ff.
21. *Met.* XIII, 2; 1077 a 1 ff.
22. A 854, B 882.

42

1. W. Jäger, *Aristoteles*, Berlin, 1923, p. 18 ff.
2. *Met.* XIII, 1; 1076 a 8.
3. *Met.* XIII, Chap. 1–3.
4. *Met.* XIII, Chap. 4–5.
5. *Met.* XIII, Chap. 6–9.
6. *Met.* XIII, 1; 1076 a 36.
7. *Met.* XIII, 3; 1077 b 25 and XII, 8; 1073 b 17 ff.
8. *Met.* XIII, 3; 1077 b 20 f.
9. *Met.* XIII, 3; 1077 b 25.
10. *Met.* XIII, 3; 1077 b 26.
11. *Met.* XIII, 3; 1077 b 28.
12. *Met.* XIII, 3; 1078 a 22.
13. *Physics* II, 2; 1094 a 10.
14. Newton, *Principia*, Auctoris Praefatio ad lectorem.
15. M. Pasch, *Voerlesungen über neuere Geometrie*, 2. ed., Leipzig, 1912, p. 3.
16. H. Helmholtz, *Über den Ursprung und die Bedeutung der geometrischen Axiome*, *Vorträge und Reden*, Vol. II, Braunschweig, 1884, p. 28 ff.
17. H. Poincaré, *Wissenschaft und Hypothese*, p. 49 f.
18. A. Einstein, 'Auf die Riemann–Metrik und den Fernparallelismus gegründete einheitliche Feldtheorie', *Math.–Anallen*, 102, p. 685 f. and cf. K. Menger, 'Die Relativitätstheorie und die Geometrie', *Living Philosophers*, *A. Einstein*, ed. by Schilpp, p. 328 ff. (German edition).

43

1. *Met.* XIV, 1; 1090 a 13 and XIII, 3; 1078 a 12.
2. M. Cantor, *Vorlesungen*, 4. ed., p. 181 ff.
3. O. Becker, *Grundlagen*, p. 41.
4. Bolzano, *WL* I, 25, p. 112.
5. Whitehead, 'Mathematics and the Good', p. 79.
6. Ockham, *Sum. tot. log.* I, 44.
7. Cf. G. Martin, *Ockham*, 14.
8. Cf. *Ibid.*, 55.
9. Leibniz, *NE* I, 1, 5; *E* 208 a, *GP* V, 73, *Ak.* VI, 6, 77.
10. Leibniz, *Letter to Clarke* V, 47; *E* 768 a, ff., *GP* VII, 400 ff.
11. Leibniz, *Letter to Des Bosses*; *GP* II, 438.
12. Leibniz, *Textes inédits*, ed. Grua, Paris, 1948, I, p. 396.
13. Leibniz, *Letter to Des Bosses*, *E* 436 a, *GP* II, 305.
14. Gauss, *Werke*, II, 175 ff.
15. Leibniz, *Monadologie* 65; *E* 710 b, *GP* VI, 618.
16. Leibniz, *Letter to Des Bosses*; *E* 434 b, *GP* II, 300.

17. Cf. G. Martin, *Leibniz*, 17.
18. *PM* I, p. 225 f.
19. *PM* I, 381.

44

1. *Met.* IV, 1; 1003 a 21 ff.
2. *Met.* IV, 2; 1003 a 33 ff.
3. *Met.* IV, Chap. 3 f.; 1005 a 19 ff.
4. *Met.* IV, 3; 1005 a 19 ff., particularly 1005 b 18 f.
5. *Met.* IV, 3; 1005 b 23.
6. D. Ross, *Met. Comm.*, Oxford, 1924, I, 264.
7. Augustinus, *De div.*, q. 83, 46, 2; *ML* 40, 30 f.
8. Leibniz, *Letter to Hanschium*; *E* 446 a.
9. Wittgenstein, *Tractatus* 4.21.
10. *Ibid.*, 4.26.

45

1. B 129/130.
2. H. Cohen, *Kants Theorie der Erfahrung, op. cit.*, p. 326.
3. M. Heidegger, *Kant und das Problem der Metaphysik*, Bonn, 1929, p. 68.
4. I. Heidemann, *Spontaneität und Zeitlichkeit*, Köln, 1958.
5. B 41.
6. A 142, B 182.
7. A 146, B 186.
8. P. Natorp, *Logische Grundlagen, op. cit.*, p. 98 ff.
9. A 142, B 182.
10. B 129/130.
11. *Phys.* IV, 14; 223 a 21.
12. Petrus Aureolus, *In IV.* 11. *sent.*, Rome, 1594. I, 549, I, *E*.
13. *Ibid.*, I, 552, 1, F.
14. Cf. G. Martin, *Ockham* 15–17.
15. Thomas, *Sum. theol.* I, 30, 3.
16. Ockham, *Sum. tot. log.* I, 44.
17. Ehrle, 'Kard. Peter von Kandia', *Franziskaner-Studien*, Beiheft 9, Münster, 1925.
18. G. Martin, *Ockham*, p. 216 ff.
19. Leibniz, *De stylo philosophico Nizolii*; *E* 63 b, *GP* IV, 147.
20. Leibniz, *Monadologie* 43; *E* 708 a/b, *GP* IV, 614.
21. *Sap.* XI, 21.
22. *Matth.* X, 30.
23. Leibniz, *NE* I, 1, 5; *E* 208 a, *GP* V, 73, *Ak.* VI, 6, 77.
24. Dedekind, *Werke*, III, 317.
25. *Ibid.*, p. 335.
26. Euclid, *Elementa* IX, 20.
27. A 717, B 745.
28. *Met.* I, 6; 987 b 22 f.

46

1. B 137/138.
2. Cf. H. G. Zeuthen, *Gesch. der Math. im 16. and 17. Jhrdt.*, Leipzig, 1903; cf. O. Becker, Grundlagen, p. 90 f.; cf. E. Niebel, 'Untersuchungen über die Bedeutung der geometrischen Konstruktion in der Antike', *Kant–Studien–Ergänzungsheft*, 76, Köln, 1959.

3. Euclid, *Elementa* I, 10.
4. *Ibid.*, IV, 9.
5. *Ibid.*, I, 9.
6. *Ibid.*, Postulata 2 and 3, Book I.
7. *Ibid.*, I, Postulata 2, 3, def. 23.
8. A 713, B 741.
9. A 717, B 745.
10. *Schriften* VIII, 190 ff.
11. B 14.
12. Leibniz, *NE* IV, 7, 1; *E* 360 a, *GP* V, 387, *Ak.* VI, 6, 406 ff.
13. G. Martin, *Kant*, p. 28 f.
14. Husserl, *LU* I, 250.
15. M. Geiger, *Systematische Axiomatik der euklidischen Geometrie*, Augsburg, 1924.
16. D. Hilbert, *Grundlagen*, p. 30.
17. *Ibid.*, p. 1.

47

1. A 127.
2. H. Cohen, *Kants Theorie der Erfahrung*, 3. ed., 1918, p. 518 ff.
3. Cf. G. Martin, *Kant* 11.
4. B 165.
5. Kant, Logik, Einleitung III, *Schriften* IX, 25.
6. M. Heidegger, *Kant und das Problem der Metaphysik*, p. 187.
7. *Met.* I, 1; 980 a 20 ff.
8. Kant, *Schriften* V, 119 ff.
9. M. Heidegger, *Holzwege*, Frankfurt, 1950, p. 70 ff.
10. J. Schultz, *Prüfung der Kantischen Kritik der reinen Vernunft*, Königsberg, 1789–92.
11. Kant, *Letter to Schultz*, *Schriften* X, 554 ff. (2 ed.).
12. B XIII
13. P. W. Bridgman, *The Logic of Modern Physics*, Macmillan, New York, 1960, p. 31 ff.
14. H. Hertz, *Die Prinzipien der Mechanik*, Ges. Werke Vol. III, 2, 1910, p. 53.
15. A. Einstein in *Great Philosophers*, 1955, p. 505 (German Ed.) 'A. Einstein als Philosoph und Naturforscher', ed. Schilpp, Stuttgart, 1951, in the same volume see also 'Einsteins Nachwort: Bemerkungen zu den in diesem Bande vereinigten Arbeiten'.

48

1. A 57, B 81 f.
2. *Schriften* IX, 11 ff.
3. *Ibid.*, 114 f.
4. *Ibid.*, 101 ff. (A 70, B 95).
5. A 80, B 106.
6. B 106 f.
7. K. Reich, *Die Vollständigkeit der Kantischen Urteilstafel*, Berlin, 1932, 2. ed., 1948.
8. B 16 f.
9. A 6, B 10.
10. Leibniz, *Letter to Clarke* II, 1; *E* 748 a, *GP* VII, 355; and *Letter to G. Wagner*; *E* 422 a, *GP* VII, 519.
11. N. Goodman, *The problem of Universals*, Notre Dame, Indiana, 1956 and N. Goodman and W. Quine, 'Steps toward a Constructive Nominalism', in *Journal of Symbolic Logic*, 12 (1947), p. 105 ff.
12. W. b. O. Quine, *Word and Object*, New York and London, 1960, p. 233 ff.

13. R. M. Martin, 'The Principle of Nominalism' in *Philos. Studies*, Vol. XIV (1963), pp. 33–37.
14. Wittgenstein, *Tractatus*, 2 and 2.01.
15. *Ibid.*, 4.21 ff.
16. *Ibid.*, 4.25 ff.
17. *Ibid.*, 6.126.
18. *Ibid.*, 5.43.
19. *Parmenides* 129 A.
20. *Met.* I, 9; 990 b 13.
21. Bolzano, *WL* I, 19, p. 77.
22. A. Heyting, *Die formalen Regeln der intuitionistischen Logik*, Sitzungsbericht der Preussischen Akademie der Wissenschaften, Phys. und Math. Klasse, Berlin, 1930.
23. P. Lorenzen, *Einführung in die operative Logik und Math.*, Berlin, 1955.

49

1. *Sophist*, 249 B f.
2. *Met.* I, 3; 983 b 6 ff.
3. *Met.* I, 5 and 6; 988 a 2 f.
4. *Met.* I, 3; 984 a 16 ff.
5. *Met.* I, 3; 983 a 26 ff.
6. Leibniz, *Letter to Wagner*; *E* 425 b, *GP* VII, 526.
7. Hegel, *Werke*, XVII, 47.

50

1. *Phaedo*, 79 A.
2. *Ibid.*
3. Descartes, *Principia* I, 48; I, 49, *Oeuvres*, VIII, 22 ff.
4. Chr. Wolff, *Ontologia*, 2 ed., 1736, 148, p. 123.
5. *Phaedo*, 100 B and *Republic*, 479 A and *Symposium*, 211 E.
6. *Phaedo*, 100 B and *Republic*, 505 A ff.
7. *Phaedo*, 65 D.
8. *Ibid.*, 101 BC.
9. *Ibid.*, 104 D.
10. *Ibid.*, 101 B.
11. *Ibid.*, 105 A and 101 B.
12. *Ibid.*, 104 D.
13. *Ibid.*, 103 E.
14. *Ibid.*, 74 A.
15. *Ibid.*, 83 B and *Timaeus*, 51 A.
16. *Ibid.*, 79 A.
17. *Ibid.*, 79 A and 80 B.
18. *Ibid.*
19. *Ibid.*, 78 DE.
20. *Ibid.*, 74 A.
21. *Ibid.*, 78 D.
22. *Ibid.*, 78 D.
23. *Phaedrus*, 247 CD and 249 C.
24. Hegel, *Werke*, XVIII, 201 and 224.
25. Nietzsche, *Werke*, II, 38.
26. E. Lask, *Ges. Schriften*, ed. E. Herrigel, Tübingen, 1923 f., I, 32; III, 4.
27. *Phaedo*, 62 B.
28. *Ibid.*

29. *Ibid.*, 61 D.
30. *Phaedrus*, 247 C.
31. *Ibid.*, 247 E.
32. *Met.* I, 9; 990 a 34–990 b 8.
33. P. Natorp, *Platons Ideenlehre*, p. 384 ff.
34. *Ibid.*, p. 410, and see Index, p. 550 b.
35. G. Martin, 'Die Hygieia und die Ideen' in the *Festschrift für Carl Diem*, Frankfurt and Vienna, 1962, pp. 11–16.
36. *Symposium*, 210 E–211 E.
37. *Phaedo*, 75 D.

51

1. *Phaedo*, 76 D and *Phaedrus*, 247 CD.
2. Hegel, *Werke*, XVIII, 201.
3. *Sophist* 244 A.
4. *Republic*, 486 D.
5. *Met.* I, 6; 987 a 30.

52

1. *Phaedo*, 78 DE.
2. *Ibid.*, 74 A.
3. *Ibid.*, cf. 79 A.
4. *Timaeus*, 28 A.
5. *Phaedo*, 97 CF.
6. *Ibid.*, 100 D.
7. *Parmenides*, 127 BC.
8. A. E. Taylor, 'Parmenides, Zeno and Socrates' in *Philos. Studies*, London, 1934, p. 40.
9. *Parmenides*, 132 B.
10. *Ibid.*, 132 BC.
11. *Ibid.*, 130 D ff.
12. *Ibid.*, 131 B.
13. *Ibid.*, 131 C.
14. *Ibid.*, 131 B.
15. *Republic*, 508 ff.
16. *Ibid.*, 508 ff. and 515 E ff.
17. *Parmenides*, 131 C.
18. *Ibid.*, 131 D.
19. *Ibid.*, 132 DE.
20. *Ibid.*, 133 B.
21. Cornford translation, p. 927.
22. *Parmenides*, 134 BC.
23. *Ibid.*, 135 A–C.
24. Fr. Uberweg, *Untersuchungen über die Echtheit und die Reihenfolge der platonischen Schriften*, Vienna, 1861, p. 180 ff.
25. P. Natorp, *Platons Ideenlehre*, p. 224.
26. *Ibid.*, p. 384 ff. and esp. p. 399.
27. cf. H. Cherniss, *Aristotle's Criticism of Plato and the Academy*, Baltimore, 1940.
28. *Met.* I, 6; 987 b 12.
29. *Parmenides*, 130 E f.
30. *Met.* I, 9; 990 b 22–991 a 8.
31. *Met.* XIII, 4; 1078 b 30.

32. *Met.* I, 9; 990 b 34 f.
33. *Parmenides*, 130 B f.
34. *Phaedrus*, 247 C.
35. *Met.* I, 9; 990 b 17.
36. *Ibid.*
37. G. Ryle, *op. cit.*, *Mind*, 48 (1939), p. 147.
38. *Parmenides*, 132 A.
39. *Republic*, 597 C and *Timaeus* 31 A.
40. *Parmenides*, 132 A.
41. *Soph. El.* 22; 179 a 3.

53

1. *Republic* 525 D f.
2. *Met.* I, 6; 987 b 14.
3. *Timaeus* 39 D.
4. *Republic* 529 CD.
5. *Timaeus* 29 A.
6. *Ibid.*, 29 B.
7. *Ibid.*, 51 CD.
8. *Ibid.*, 49 C.
9. P. Natorp, *Platons Indeenlehre*, p. 162 and p. 410.
10. *Goethe*, *Jub.–Ausg.*, ed. E. V. D. Hellen, Stuttgart and Berlin, 1902–12, Vol. 40, pp. 72 and 27.
11. B. Liebrucks, *Platons Entwicklung zur Dialektik*, Frankfurt, 1949, p. 35.
12. *Phaedo*, 75 D.
13. Augustine, *De div.*, q. 83, 46, 2, *ML* 40, 30 f.
14. Cf. Leibniz, *Monadologie* 48; *E* 708 b, *GP* VI, 615; *Theodizee* 20; *E* 510 a, *GP* VI, 115; *an Hanschium*; *E* 445 b.

54

1. W. Jaeger, *Aristoteles*, *op. cit.*, p. 9.
2. Bonitz, *Index Aristotelicus* 598/9.
3. *Zu Platons Altersvorlesung 'Uber das Gute'*, cf. passages in Zeller, *Phil. der Griechen*, 4–7 ed., Leipzig, 1920–23, II. Bd., 1, p. 712, Note 3 and Aristoxenos, *Harm. Elementa*, ed. Rome, 1954, II, Bd., p. 30; and also Aristotle, *Met.* XIV, 4; 109 1b 13 and Theophrastes in Simplicius, *Comm. in Phys.* 26, 23.
4. W. Jaeger, *Aristoteles*, *op. cit.*, p. 2.
5. *Ibid.*, p. 42 ff.
6. Especially clear for example in Kant, *De igne*, *Schriften*, I, 369 ff.
7. Cf. Kant, 'The Amphiboly of Concepts of Reflection' (A 260, M 316 ff.
8. Kant, *Schriften* VIII, 247 ff.
9. Cf. P. Wilpert, 'Ein Quellwerk zur Gesch. des Platonismus' in *ZfphF* VII (1953), pp. 585–91 and *Zwei Aristotelische Frühschriften über die Ideenlehre*, Regensburg, 1949.
10. W. Jaeger, *op. cit.*, p. 9.
11. *Anal. Post.* I, 22; 83 a 33.

55

1. *Met.* I, 6; 987 b 13.
2. *Met.* I, 9; 991 b 3.
3. *Met.* I, 9; 990 b 17.
4. *Met.* III, 2; 997 b.

5. *Met.* I, 9; 991 b 3.
6. *Parmenides,* 132 AB.
7. *Soph. El.* 179 a 3.
8. *Met.* I, 9; 990 b 15.
9. *Phaedo* 74 AB.
10. *Sophist* 255 CD.
11. *Parmenides* 131 D.
12. *Ibid.,* 130 A/E.
13. *Met.* I, 9; 992 b 18.
14. *Met.* I, 9; 990 b 34/5.
15. *Met.* IV, 2; 1003 a 33 ff.
16. *Sophist* 244 A.
17. Heidegger, *SuZ* 19–21, p. 89 ff.
18. Leibniz, *NE* I, 3, 18; *E* 221 a, *GP* V, 96, *Ak.* VI, 6, 105.
19. *Met.* V, 11; 1018 b 9 ff. and Thomas, *comm. in met.* 936 ff.; *S. Th.* I, 13, 6.
20. Thomas, *Sum. Th.* I, 13, 5; *comm. in met.* 536, 539, 1344, 2197.

56

1. *De coelo* I, 5; 271 b 1 ff.
2. *Met.* XI, 10; 1067 a 13 f.; *Phys.* III, 5; 205 a 31; *De coelo* I, 6; 273 a 14.
3. *Met.* XII, 7; 1072 a 21.
4. *Phys.* VIII, 1; 251 b 19 ff.
5. Leibniz, *Letter to Des Bosses*; *E* 436 a, *GP* II, 305 and *Theodizee* 195; *E* 564 a, *GP* VI, 232.
6. *Phys.* III, 6; 206 a 16 f.
7. *Ibid.,* III, 5; 206 a 7.
8. *Ibid.,* III, 5; 204 a 8 ff.
9. *Ibid.,* III, 7; 207 a 32 ff.
10. *Ibid.,* II, 2; 194 a 10.
11. *De coelo* II, 4; 287 b 15.
12. *Met.* IV, 2; 1003 b 22 and VII, 4; 1030 b 10 and X, 2; 1054 a 13.
13. *Met.* IV, 2; 1003 b 22 and X, 2; 1053 b 20.
14. Duns Scotus, *Op. ox.* II, q. 1, d. 4; *Opera* XI, 122 a.
15. Duns Scotus, *Rep. par.* II, q. 1, d. 6; *Opera* XXII, 555 b.
16. Gredt, I, 109.
17. *Joh.* 1, 1.
18. Thomas, *Sum. theol.* I, 2, 3 and I, 3 ,2 and I, 25, 1.
19. *Met.* XII, 7; 1072 a 25.
20. *Ibid.,* XII, 9; 1074 b 34.
21. *Laches* 192 B.
22. *Parmenides* 132 A f.

57

1. *Met.* I, 9; 990 b 9; and I, 9; 990 b 16.
2. W. Jaeger, *Aristotle,* p. 191 ff.
3. The phrase νοῦσ ποιητικόσ itself does not appear in Aristotle cf. Bonitz, *Index Aristotelicus* 491 b 3; but on the other hand the phrase ἕν ποιοῦν occurs in *De Anima* III, 6; 430 b 6.
4. Thomas, *Sum. theol.* I, 25, 1 c.
5. *Ibid.,* I, 3, 1, 2.
6. *Ibid.,* I, 3, 1, 2 and I, 93, 1.
7. *Ibid.,* I, 79, 3.

8. *Met.* XII, 9; 1074 b 34.
9. *Met.* XII, 7; 1072 a 26.
10. *Met.* XII, 7; 1072 b 3 ff.
11. *Met.* IV, 2; 1003 b 23.
12. *Phys.* IV, 14; 223 a 22 f.

58

1. A xii.
2. A xiv, B xxiv.
3. A xv, A xx, B xliv.
4. A 80, B 106.
5. A 81, B 107.
6. A 69, B 94.
7. B 130.
8. Hegel, *Werke*, IV, 46.
9. J. F. Fries, *Neue Kritik der Vernunft*, Heidelberg, 1807, I, p. xxxvi.
10. Cf. H. Cohen, *Kants Theorie der Erfahrung*, 3. ed., Berlin, 1918, cap. 8 c, p. 404 ff.
11. Kant, *Schriften* V, 161 ff.
12. *Ibid.*, p. 161 f.
13. *Ibid.*, p. 162.

59

1. Jacobi, *Werke*, II, 304.
2. Leibniz, *Letter to Hanschium*; E 445 b.
3. B xxvi–xxvii.
4. A 130.
5. A 216/7, B 263/5.
6. A 504 f., B 532 f.
7. A 535 ff., B 563 ff.; A 540 f., B 568 f.
8. A 235, B 294 ff.
9. B 307.
10. A 218, B 265/6.
11. *Phys.* IV, 1; 208 a 29.
12. H. Cohen, *Kants Theorie der Erfahrung.*
13. Hegel, *Werke* IV, 13.
14. H. Cohen, *op. cit.*, p. 640.
15. *Ibid.*, p. 642.
16. *Ibid.*, pp. 659–60.
17. *Ibid.*, p. 658.

60

1. Kant, *Schriften* V, 50 ff.
2. A 444, B 472.
3. A 445, B 473.
4. Newton, *Optice* III, *op. cit.*, q. 31.
5. Kant, *Schriften* XIV, 279 and II, 144.
6. Newton, *Optice* III, *op. cit.*, q. 31.
7. Leibniz, *Letter to Clarke* I, 4; E 746 b/747 a, GP VII, 352.
8. Leibniz, *Theodizee* 118 and 340; E 535 a, GP VI, 168 and E 602 b, GP VI, 316.
9. Leibniz, *Monadologie* 79; E 711 b, GP VI, 620.
10. *Ibid.*, 86; E 712 a, GP VI, 622.
11. Leibniz, *Système nouveau . . .*; E 128 a, GP IV, 485 f.
12. A 535, B 563.

13. A 536, B 564.
14. *Ibid.*
15. *Ibid.*
16. A 537, B 565.
17. A 537 f., B 585 f., and *Schriften* V, 47.
18. A 545, B 573.
19. Kant, *Schriften* V, 55.
20. A 146, B 186 and A 561, B 589.
21. A 276, B 332.
22. A 146, B 186.
23. Kant, Refl. 6286, *Schriften* XVIII, 554.

61

1. H. Heimsoeth, *Studien zur Philosophie I, Kants metaphysische Ursprünge und onto-logische Grundlagen; Kant-Studien-Ergänzungsheft* 71, Köln, 1956.
2. Kant, *Schriften* V, 47 and A 535, B 563; A 558, B 586, Schriften V, 134.
3. Kant, *Schriften* V, 4 and V, 42.
4. A 557, B 585 and *Schriften* V, 4 and V, 47.
5. G. Schneeberger, *Kants Konzeption der Modalbegriffe*, Basel, 1952.
6. A 557 f., B 585 f.
7. A 566, B 594.
8. Kant, *Schriften*, V, 136.
9. A 137 ff., B 176 ff.
10. A 143, B 183 and A 147, B 187.
11. A 144, B 183.
12. A 147, B 187.
13. Kant, *Schriften* V, 5 f.
14. Kant, *Schriften* V, 141.
15. A 80, B 106.
16. A 144, B 184.
17. A 218, B 265.
18. B xxvi.
19. Kant, *Schriften* V, 49.
20. Kant, *Schriften* V, 42 and V, 160.
21. Kant, *Schriften* V, 484 and *Schriften* IV, 357 ff.
22. Kant, *Schriften* V, 465 and V, 464.
23. H. Hermann, *Das Problem der objektiven Realität bei Kant*, Diss., Mainz, 1961.
24. Kant, *Schriften* II, 385.
25. *Schriften* V, 50.
26. *Schriften* V, 87.
27. A 490 f., B 518 f.
28. A 35, B 51.
29. A 42, B 59.
30. A 553, B 581.
31. Kant, *Schriften* V, 95.
32. Kant, *Schriften* V, 99.
33. A 549, B 577 ff.
34. Kant, *Schriften* V, 100.
35. Kant, *Schriften* V, 102.
36. Kant, *Schriften* V, 99 and A 543, B 571.
37. A 546, B 574.
38. A 537, B 565.
39. Kant, *Schriften* V, 103.

62

1. A 313, B 370.
2. A 314, B 371, note.
3. P. Natorp, *Platons Ideenlehre*, p. 143.
4. *Ibid.*, p. 459 ff.
5. *Ibid.*, p. 410.
6. J. Maréchal, *Le point de départ de la métaphysique*, 4 vols., Paris, 1923.
7. B viii.
8. A 81, B 107.
9. C. Sentroul, *L'objet de la métaphysique selon Kant et selon Aristote*, Louvain, 1905.
10. A. Warda, *Kants Bücherei*, Berlin, 1920, p. 45.

63

1. Hegel, *Werke*, XVII, 46, 47.
2. *Sophist* 249 CD.
3. *Met.* I, 7; 988 a 17.
4. Leibniz, *Letter to Wagner*; *E* 425 b, *GP* VII, 526.

64

1. Zenon B 1–4; Diels I, 173.
2. Aristoteles' Schrift über Zenon, Diels Zenon I, p. 170.
3. Herakleides Pontikos über Zenon; lost fragment Diels I, p. 170.
4. *Parmenides* 127 C.
5. *Parmenides* 127 C f.
6. *Phys.* VI, 9; 239 b 9.
7. Hegel, *Werke*, XVII, 329.
8. *Parmenides*, 127 C.
9. Leibniz, *Letter to De Volde*; *GP* II, 282.
10. *Parmenides*, 127 E f.
11. Zenon A 15; Diels I, 169.
12. A 502, B 530.
13. Zenon B 1, B 3; Diels I, 173 and 175.
14. *Phys.* VI, 9; 239 b 14.
15. *Phys.* VI, 9; 239 b 30.
16. *Parmenides* 129 C.
17. *Ibid.*

65

1. Hegel, *Werke*, XVIII, 226.
2. Fr. Überweg, *Untersuchungen über die Echtheit*, Vienna, 1861, p. 180 ff.
3. Proclus, *Comm. in Platonis Parmenidem, Opera Inedita*, Vol. 3, Paris, 1864, new edition Hildesheim, 1961.
4. M. Wundt, *Studien zur platonischen Dialektik*, 2. ed., Stuttgart, 1959.
5. A. Speiser, *Ein Parmenides-Kommentar*, 2. ed., Stuttgart, 1959.
6. F. M. Cornford, *Plato and Parmenides*, London, 4. ed., 1958, p. 154.
7. Cf. J. Burnet, *Greek Philosophy*, London, 1950, p. 263; A. E. Taylor, *Plato—the Man and his Work*, 6. ed., London, 1949, p. 351; G. Ryle, 'Plato's Parmenides' in *Mind*, 48 (1939), p. 129.
8. Cf. P. Natorp, *Platos Ideenlehre*, p. 245.
9. *Ibid.*, p. 224.
10. Hegel, *Werke*, XVIII, 240.
11. *Republic*, 536 D and 534 E.

12. *Philebus*, 17 A.
13. *Parmenides*, 155 E.
14. *Ibid.*, 160 AB.
15. *Ibid.*, 166 C.
16. *Ibid.*, 129 C f.
17. *Ibid.*, 129 C.
18. *Ibid.*, 129 B/129 E.
19. *Ibid.*, 135 C ff.
20. Hegel, *Werke*, XVIII, 243.
21. *Parmenides* 137 C.
22. *Ibid.*, 142 C.
23. *Ibid.*, 143 D.
24. *Ibid.*, 137 C.
25. *Ibid.*, 139 B.
26. *Ibid.*, 137 D.
27. *Ibid.*, 142 D.
28. *Ibid.*, 143 A.
29. *Ibid.*, 145 C.
30. *Ibid.*, 155 E.
31. *Ibid.*, 157 A.
32. *Ibid.*, 160 B.
33. *Ibid.*, 165 E.
34. *Ibid.*, 166 C.
35. Hegel, *Werke*, IV, 237 and 545 ff.
36. *Parmenides*, 142 C.
37. *Ibid.*, 142 CD.
38. *Ibid.*, 142 DE.
39. Kant, A 598, B 626.
40. G. Ryle, *art. cit.*, *Mind*, 48 (1939), p. 324 f.
41. F. M. Cornford, *Plato and Parmenides*, p. 154.
42. *Parmenides*, 132 AB.
43. *Ibid.*, 143 A.
44. A. E. Taylor, 'Parmenides, Zeno and Socrates' in *Philos. Studies*, London, 1934, p. 47.
45. *Sophist* 244 A.
46. *Sophist* 237 A and *Theatetus*, 183 E.
47. *Met.* I, 6; 987 a 32.

66

1. A 297, B 354.
2. A 463, B 491.
3. A 529, B 557 and cf. H. J. Vleeschauwer, 'Wie ich jetzt die Kritik der reinen Vernunft entwicklungsgeschichtlich lese' in *Kantstudien*, Bd. 54/5 (1963), pp. 351–68.
4. A 466, B 494.
5. A 471, B 499.
6. Leibniz, *Letter to Clarke* III, 5 and IV, 13; *E* 752 a, *GP* VII, 363/4 and *E* 756 a, *GP* VII, 373.
7. *Ibid.*, III, 6 and IV, 15; *E* 752, *GP* VII, 364 and *E* 756 b, *GP* VII, 373/4.
8. *Ibid.*, IV, 13; *E* 756 a, *GP* VII, 373.
9. *Ibid.*, IV, 15; *E* 756 b, *GP* VII, 373/374.
10. *Ibid.*, Apostille zu IV; *E* 758 b, *GP* VII, 377/8.
11. Newton, *Optice* III, q. 31.
12. *Timaeus* 73 C ff.

13. *Phys.* IV, Cap. 6–9.
14. Thomas, *comm. in Arist. phys.* VIII, 2; *Opera* II, 367 ff.
15. A 501, B 529.
16. A 528, B 556.
17. A 532, B 560.
18. A 506, B 534.
19. A 500, B 528.
20. A 486, B 515.
21. Archytas, A 24; Diels I, 330.
22. G. Hessenberg, *Grundbegriffe der Mengenlehre*, Abhandlungen der Frieschen Schule, NF I, 1904, p. 633.
23. E. Zermelo, Cantor, *Ges. Abhandlungen*, ed. by Zermelo, p. 377, note 2.
24. C. F. v. Weizsäcker, 'Das Verhältnis der Quantenmechanik zur Philosophie Kants' in *Zum Weltbild der Physik*, Leipzig, 1947.
25. A 444, B 472.
26. Newton, *Optice* III, q. 31 and *Letter to Bentley* in *Newtoni Opera quae extant omnia*, 1782, IV, p. 431 f. (according to Kant, *Schriften* XIV, 280).
27. Leibniz, *Letter to Clarke*, III, 13 and *E* 757 b and *GP* VII, 366.
28. Leibniz, *Monadologie* 79, *Theodizee* 318, 340; *E* 711 b, *GP* VI, 620; *E* 597 b, *GP* VI, 305; *E* 602 b, *GP* VI, 316.
29. Leibniz, *Letter to Foucher* (1687), *GP* I, 391 f.
30. A 540, B 568.
31. A 541, B 569.
32. A 415, B 442; A 462, B 490.
33. Hegel, *Werke*, IV, 54.
34. Hegel, *Werke*, IV, 227 and 545 ff.

67

1. Hegel, *Werke*, XVII, 2 ff.
2. *Ibid.*, 3 (preface by Michelet).
3. *Ibid.*, 1.
4. *Ibid.*, 3.
5. *Ibid.*, 47.
6. Hegel, *Werke*, I, 59.
7. Hegel, *Werke*, IV, 51.
8. Hegel, *Werke*, XVII, 48 ff.
9. Hegel, *Werke*, I, 59.
10. *Ibid.*, 59.
11. *Ibid.*, 57 and I, 66.
12. *Ibid.*, 48 and I, 60 and I, 66.
13. Hegel, *Werke*, IV, 34/35/36.
14. *Ibid.*, 36.

68

1. Hegel, *Werke*, XVIII, 222 f.
2. *Ibid.*, 225.
3. *Ibid.*
4. *Ibid.*, 226.
5. Hegel, *Werke*, IV, 112.
6. *Ibid.*
7. Hegel, *Werke*, XVIII, 230.
8. *Ibid.*, 225 and 227.

9. *Ibid.*, 226.
10. Hegel, *Werke*, V, 349.
11. Hegel, *Werke*, IV, 53.
12. Hegel, *Werke*, XVIII, 246.
13. *Ibid.*, 225.

69

1. Leibniz, *Letter to Jean Gallois und Joh. Bernoulli*; *Ak.* II, 1, 226 and *GM* III, 535
2. Leibniz, *Meditationes*; *E* 80 a, *GP* IV, 424.
3. Hegel, *Werke* IV, 227 and 545 ff.
4. L. Couturat, *Opuscules et fragments inédits de Leibniz*, Paris, 1903, *passim* and p. 397.
5. G. Martin, *Leibniz*, 17, p. 97 ff.
6. Wittgenstein, *Tractatus*, p. 28 (Preface).
7. A xx.

INDEX